THE CONCEPTUAL ROOTS OF MATHEMATICS

The Conceptual Roots of Mathematics is a comprehensive study of the philosophy of mathematics, which is – as the book shows – central to epistemology and metaphysics.

J.R. Lucas argues for a 'chastened Logicism'. He claims that though mathematical arguments are a priori, they are not all always deductive. Our mathematical concepts are grounded in logic, although often developed to something essentially new.

Mathematical argument is viewed in a new way, as a two-person dialogue rather than a formal proof-sequence. Peano's Fifth Postulate and the Axiom of Choice can be justified if we construe them not as would-be truths, but as principles of argument between two rational seekers after truth. Geometers will be relieved to learn that geometry is neither a branch of physics nor a purely formal exercise, and will be intrigued by a 'consumers' guide' to geometry that recommends Euclid's as the Best Buy.

J.R. Lucas is a Fellow of the British Academy. He was Fellow and Tutor of Merton College, Oxford, and is the author of several books, including *A Treatise on Time and Space*, *Space, Time and Causality* and (jointly) *Spacetime and Electromagnetism*. He has written extensively on the implications of Gödel's theorem, and his article 'Minds, Machines and Gödel' has been much attacked and much defended.

INTERNATIONAL LIBRARY
OF PHILOSOPHY
Edited by Tim Crane and
Jonathan Wolff
University College London

The history of the International Library of Philosophy can be traced back to the 1920s, when C.K. Ogden launched the series with G.E. Moore's *Philosophical Papers* and soon after published Ludwig Wittgenstein's *Tractatus Logico-Philosophicus*. Since its auspicious start, it has published the finest work in philosophy under the successive editorships of A.J. Ayer, Bernard Williams and Ted Honderich. Now jointly edited by Tim Crane and Jonathan Wolff, the ILP will continue to publish works at the forefront of philosophical research.

Other titles in the ILP include:

PERSONAL IDENTITY AND SELF-CONSCIOUSNESS
Brian Garrett

THE SCEPTICAL CHALLENGE
Ruth Weintraub

DISPOSITIONS: A DEBATE
D.M. Armstrong, C.B. Martin, and U.T. Place
Edited by Tim Crane

PSYCHOLOGY FROM AN EMPIRICAL STANDPOINT
Franz Brentano
Edited by Oskar Kraus, English Edition edited by Linda L. McAlister
With a new introduction by Peter Simons
Translated by Antos C. Rancurello, D.B. Terrell, Linda L. McAlister

G.E. MOORE: SELECTED WRITINGS
G.E. Moore
Edited by Thomas Baldwin

THE FACTS OF CAUSATION
D.H. Mellor

REAL TIME II
D.H. Mellor

THE CONCEPTUAL ROOTS OF MATHEMATICS

An essay on the philosophy of mathematics

J.R. Lucas

London and New York

First published 2000
by Routledge
11 New Fetter Lane, London EC4P 4EE

Simultaneously published in the USA and Canada
by Routledge
29 West 35th Street, New York, NY 10001

Routledge is an imprint of the Taylor & Francis Group

Typeset in Times by the author using TEX
Printed and bound in Great Britain by
TJ International Ltd, Padstow, Cornwall

British Library Cataloguing in Publication Data
A catalogue record for this book is available from the British Library

Library of Congress Cataloging in Publication Data
Lucas, J.R. (John Randolph), 1929–
The conceptual roots of mathematics / J.R. Lucas.
       p.   cm.
Includes bibliographical references and index.
1. Mathematics–Philosophy.   I. Title.
QA8.4.L833   1999   99–20193
      510′.1–dc21   CIP

ISBN 0–415–20738–X

Introduction

The *Roots*? For many years I lectured in Oxford on the Conceptual Foundations of Mathematics; but, as I did so, I became increasingly uncomfortable with Descartes' metaphor of an edifice for which foundations were the appropriate basis. Pedagogically it was bad: it meant spending a lot of time on recondite logic-chopping, the point of which could not be understood until much later in the course, when we were on to proper mathematical topics. Metaphysically it was dubious, too. If I had been as clever as Archimedes, I might have been able to move minds, given a firm starting point, but no firm starting point was, or, as I came to believe, could, be given. To start from the absolutely incontestable was to start from nowhere. Here was where we were, and there was where we might be, but any journey of exploration or justification had to start from some point or other, and any actual starting point could be put in question by a skilful sceptic.

I worked through these difficulties in my British Academy Lecture, "Philosophy and Philosophy Of", and there suggested that another of Descartes' metaphors was more appropriate: we should think of mathematics not as a building based on foundations, but as a tree grounded in the soil of our general conceptual structure, and growing both up and down.[1] This metaphor, too, is inadequate, but less so than the building one, and so I adopt it in the title for this work.

I start and end with Plato. He was right to distinguish mathematical arguments from empirical ones, but failed in his various attempts to characterize them positively. He was his own severest critic, and outlined, as alternatives to Platonism, approaches we can recognise as proto-formalist and proto-logicist.

The paradigm mathematical discipline was geometry, and in Chapter Two I argue that its axioms cannot be taken as being

---

[1] *Descartes: the Philosophical Works*, tr. E.S.Haldane, and G.T.R.Ross, i, 2nd edn., Cambridge, 1934, p.211; cited by Bernard Williams, *Descartes*, Penguin, 1978, p.34.

simply self-evident, and cannot be merely postulated either. Geometry is not just a formal discipline, but is subject to conceptual constraints arising from its place in our conceptual structure, and the accompanying operational needs. Various geometries are possible, but a *Which?* guide to geometry recommends Euclid's as the Best Buy.

Formalism is considered more fully in Chapter Three. It has its uses, not only for checking arguments, and revealing fallacies, but for revealing similarities between different branches of mathematics, and as a topic of study in itself. Nevertheless, Formalism offers an inadequate account of mathematical knowledge. It secures validity at the price of vacuity, and does not at all conform to the actual practice of mathematicians.

A logicist approach to the natural numbers is developed in Chapters Four, Five and Six. Frege's account of the cardinal numbers as answers to the question "How many?" reveals the similarity between the number nought and the negative existential "quotifier" (negative existential quantifier, as it is generally called). Dedekind's ordinal approach lights up the systematic structure of the natural numbers, which can be grounded uniquely if we take nought as the first number, the number than which there can be no fewer, so that counting down is always a finite procedure. Peano's abstract approach raises the converse problem of counting forwards. I suggest that Peano's Fifth Postulate (and the Axiom of Choice) should be construed as principles of argument between two rational seekers after truth, rather than assertions of arcane truth. Once the principle of recursive reasoning, as I call it, is accepted, we can think of all the natural numbers, of which, as the Schoolmen often observed, there are an infinite number. Different concepts of infinity, with their associated difficulties, are discussed in Chapter Seven. The Intuitionists, like Aristotle, reject actual infinites, allowing only the potential infinite. But their "selective scepticism" is unstable, being vulnerable to more extreme scepticism on the part of finitists and ultra finitists; and any arguments they can adduce against these can in turn be used by classical logicians against Intuitionist scruples.

Infinite sets can be mapped into proper subsets of themselves, and hence a formal system that includes the natural numbers can be so coded that statements about it can be represented within it. Gödel was thus able to construct a well-formed formula somewhat analogous to the Liar Paradox, and in Chapter Eight Gödel's theorem is explained, and its implications, which greatly alter our understanding of logic and logical argument, discussed.

Traditional Logicism has had too narrow a view of logic, and has sought to base the whole of mathematics on the natural numbers and set theory. In Chapter Nine I seek to show how much of mathematics is, instead, grounded in the logic of transitive relations. Equivalence relations give us group theory and category theory; ordering relations give rise to discrete, dense and continuous orderings, as well as to lattices and trees. Some interconnexions between equivalence and ordering relations are sketched, and two paradigms exhibited, set theory, seen as a structure rather than ontologically, and mereology, the logic of the part-whole relation, to which mathematicians have not given the attention it deserves.

Whitehead hoped to base geometry and topology on a mereological foundation, and though his project failed, it is illuminating to see how far we can go in developing "Prototopology", in order to have available the concept of extensive magnitude, which we need for a proper theory of measurement, discussed in Chapter Eleven.

Chapter Twelve is called, provocatively, "Down with Set Theory". Not that I have anything against sets—indeed some of them I have made use of myself. But sets have been accorded undue significance in the philosophy of mathematics, and I want to cut them down to size. In part it is merely a matter of nomenclature: what passes for set theory is really transfinite arithmetic, a fascinating subject of great interest, but beyond the horizon of most mathematicians. If we view it as a relational structure, we can compare the Axiom of Extensionality with the Identity of Indiscernibles, and see the Axiom of Foundation as a paradigmatic stipulation rather than a fundamental ontological fact. Not all the problems of set theory are thus easily dissolved, and much mystery remains. But less.

Philosophers of mathematics often pose their questions as between stark alternatives: Either Platonism or Intuitionism; Platonism is more than we can be expected to stomach; so Intuitionism is our only hope. It is a natural method of argument in metaphysics, but has the disadvantage of concentrating effort on pointing out the defects in rival doctrines, rather than accommodating their strong points within a more inclusive account. In the course of the first twelve chapters the starkness of the alternatives has been much softened. Logic is no longer confined to first-order logic, logical truths are no longer invariably analytic, logical argument is no longer confined to argument that must, on pain of self-contradiction, be conceded. Gödel's theorem shows that however fully we formalise a system, there will still be some arguments evidently valid, but not in virtue of conforming to the canons of formal validity laid down. Instead of taking formally valid deduction as the one and only paradigm, we should see it as an extreme case, where we are having to argue with a recalcitrant fool. In the standard case, however, the argument is with a like-minded seeker after truth, and much of mathematical argument is shaped by an underlying dialectical structure. Our Logicism is less sharp also in that our mathematical concepts are not held to be definable in purely logical terms, but only *grounded* in logic, often developed by extrapolation to something essentially new.

Logicism thus watered down no longer excludes all elements of Platonism. Although epistemological platonism is, as Plato himself realised, too *simpliste* to be wholly satisfactory, there is an element of pattern-recognition in our achieving mathematical knowledge. Often the identification of the correct pattern is achieved only after a long and complicated dialectic, in which the "eye of the mind" is guided much more by argument than by any extra visual acuity. The visual metaphor, though sometimes natural, is apt to mislead.

Ontological platonism is often expressed in misleading terms too. The arguments we use are ineluctable, their conclusions objectively true, the patterns we discern are not mere figments of our imagining, but really there, out there. But however strongly we maintain that e and π are part of the furniture of the universe, there is nowhere out there that we can locate them, and unlocatable furniture is not an attractive bargain. But it is an effect of language rather than of thought. We can seek objectivity, without thinking it must be embodied in material objects. Chemists have no difficulty in believing in the Periodic Table, and would not change their mind if astronauts could not find it anywhere in space. A platonist ontology is objectionable, only if we take it for granted that to exist is to exist as a material thing. Many modern philosophers make that assumption, and much philosophy of mathematics is massaged so as to conform to a prevailing materialism. It is an important question, and one to which the philosophy of mathematics is relevant, but it is not the concern of this book, which is concerned only with mathematics, and how it should be correctly understood.

I have apologies to make. I idiosyncratically abandon the standard usage, and describe terms such as 'all', 'some' and 'none' as "quotifiers". I hope thereby to bring home the great difference between the question "How many?", in Latin *Quot?*, to which a natural number is a natural answer, and the question "How much?", in Latin *Quantum?*, to which a numerical answer can be given only with considerable artifice, ultimately depending on the logic of transitive relations, the topic of Chapter Nine. Quantifying is what quantity surveyors should do, not logicians. In a similar spirit, I abandon the traditional symbols, $(\forall x)$ and $(\exists x)$. They are difficult to type. Worse, they obscure their relation to other Boolean symbols. By writing the existential quotifer as (Vx), following the example of Geoffrey Hunter (*Metalogic*, London and Basingstoke, 1971, p.139), I bring out the analogies with $\lor$, and the set-theoretical $\cup$ and $\bigcup$. For the universal quotifier I desert the purity of an inverted V for the convenience of a simple (Ax), with a capital A the right way up because not only is it easier for typing, but it is easier for the beginner, since A suggests All. A does resemble an inverted V, and to that extent the analogies with $\land$, $\cap$, and $\bigcap$.

Perhaps I should apologize to rigorist readers for my lack of rigour. There is a trade-off between full formal rigour and intelligibility. I have tried to be intelligible, and have left out many trees in the hope of showing the outline of the wood. In part, no doubt, it betrays my natural sloppiness of mind. In part it is a reaction against the needless obfuscation of many articles in mathematics and logic. But I hope I shall succeed in conveying my argument to more readers than those put off by the informality of the exposition, and that those who are sharp enough to spot holes are clever enough also to see how they could be blocked.

I should also apologize to many North American thinkers for not discussing their work in the detail it deserves. I have learnt much from their writings, but very often have found that they are addressing a different question from the one I am seeking to answer. Very often they are starting with some wide-ranging metaphysical view—nominalism, physicalism, naturalism—and are trying to show how mathematics can be fitted into that scheme. It is a perfectly proper exercise—metaphysics on the grand scale—and one I hope some day to attempt myself. But my present objective is more limited. Although the philosophy of mathematics anyone adopts *is* influenced by his general metaphysical presuppositions, as also the philosophy of history, he adopts, or philosophy of art, I want, so far as possible, to concentrate on considerations arising within the discipline. It is a philosophy of mathematics arising from mathematics rather than a philosophy of mathematics stemming from elsewhere.

I have many debts to acknowledge: I have been fortunate in my position, my colleagues and my pupils. It was good for me that Oxford set up a joint school in Mathematics and Philosophy, thus bringing me in touch with colleagues who shared my interests, enabling me to try out ideas on pupils, and giving me the stimulus to focus my thoughts in communicable form. It was good for me also that in David Bostock I had a colleague who shared my interest in the philosophy of mathematics, and, while often disagreeing with what I said, was ready to think about it and respond to it; and who, by shouldering burdens which otherwise would have fallen on me, gave me the time to crystallize my thoughts in writing. It is for this reason that I dedicate the book to him, and to all my colleagues.

East Lambrook

Christmas 1998

Note on Logical Symbolism

Older text books express the universal quantifier by brackets surrounding the variable alone, (x). Modern text books usually have an inverted A, $(\forall x)$. It is better to have $(\mathbf{A}x)$, with a capital A the right way up because not only is it easier for typing, but it is easier for the beginner, since A suggests All, and also resembles an inverted V, with useful analogies with $\land$, the sign for conjunction, with $\cap$, the cap of set theory, and $\bigcap$, the inverted U, for intersection. For the same reason it is desirable to symbolize the existential quotifier not by the usual $(\exists x)$, but by $(\mathbf{V}x)$, to bring out the analogies with $\lor$, and the set-theoretical $\cup$ and $\bigcup$. Likewise the null set (or empty set) is represented by Λ. (See fn. 44 in §9.11.)

Material implication, which is rendered, sometimes inaccurately, in English by 'if ....,then:....', is represented by $\rightarrow$. In older text books it was often rendered by a horseshoe $\supset$; $\supseteq$ would have been better, as it is an antisymmetric relation (see §9.1), but is inconveniently cumbersome.

For ease of reading, brackets are often omitted, the convention being that $\neg$ binds most tightly of all, and $\land$ binds more tightly than $\lor$, which in turn binds more tightly than $\leftrightarrow$, which in its turn binds more tightly than $\rightarrow$. Sometimes, however, brackets are retained, where they seem to make the outline of the formula easier to grasp. Many authors abbreviate 'if and only if' to 'iff', which is convenient, particularly in macaronic prose, where it is desirable to have mathematics and English all on one line.

Logical Symbols

English	Standard	Old	Here
and	$\land$	$\cdot$	$\land$
and/or	$\lor$	$\lor$	$\lor$
not	$\neg$	$-$	$\neg$
if...then	$\rightarrow$	$\supset$	$\rightarrow$
if and only if	$\leftrightarrow$	$\equiv$	$\leftrightarrow$
all x	$(\forall x)$	(x)	$(\mathbf{A}x)$
some x	$(\exists x)$	$(\exists x)$	$(\mathbf{V}x)$
null set x	$\emptyset$	$\emptyset$	Λ

Contents

to

David Bostock

and

all my colleagues

Chapter 1
Plato's Philosophies of Mathematics

1.1   *Meno*

The philosophy of mathematics begins with Pythagoras, who believed that mathematics gave us the key to understanding reality, but it is Plato who first gave it articulate form. In the *Meno* he proves that mathematics is known *a priori*— that is, without appeal to sense experience.[1] He starts talking to a slave boy, and by a series of questions elicits from him a method of constructing a line $\sqrt{2}$ as long as a given one, using a special case of Pythagoras' theorem. The general proof of Pythagoras' theorem is difficult: for two thousand years it was the *Pons Asinorum* for school boys. In the *Meno*, however, Plato considers the special case of an isosceles right-angled triangle, where even someone who has never done geometry in his life can be brought to see how to construct a square with area twice that of a given square.

Readers often complain that Plato's argument is unfair, because Socrates uses leading questions. But, although he does use leading questions, he is careful not to tell the slave boy any particular empirical facts. This is borne out by the boy's making several mistakes along the way. He first suggests that, to get a square twice the area of the given one, we should take one with side twice as long. But, Socrates objects, that will not work, and draws a diagram on the sand, like Figure 1.1.1, and shows, very obviously,

---

[1] *Meno*, Stephanus pages 82-85. (All references to Plato's dialogues are to the pages in the Stephanus edition.)

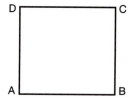

Figure 1.1.1 How can we draw a square with twice the area of the given square *ABCD*?

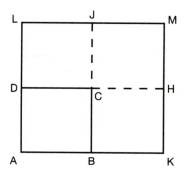

Figure 1.1.2 The Boy's First Suggestion: the square on *AK* is twice that on *AB*.

that if we have AK twice AB, then the square AKML will be not twice but four times the area of ABCD (Figure 1.1.2). So, says the boy, let us try with a side one-and-a-half times the length of the original side. That suggestion is gone over too, and we reach the conclusion that $(1.5)^2$ is not equal to 2 (Figure 1.1.3).

So, after these two false starts we arrive at the real solution, which is to construct a square on the diagonal of the original square, and Socrates shows why such a square must have an area that is half that of the big square, AKML, itself four times that of the original, ABCD. The slave boy finds this argument convincing, and—what is more important—so does everyone who attends to it. The argument is given in Figure 1.1.4.

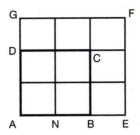

Figure 1.1.3 The Boy's Second Suggestion: $\sqrt{2} = 1.5$. But, argues Socrates, the square on AE is nine times that on AN, whereas the square which has twice the area of $ABCD$ should be eight times that on AN.

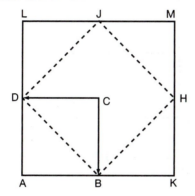

Figure 1.1.4 The Real Solution: the square on DB *is* twice that on AB. For the square $DBHJ$ is the sum of the four triangles DBC, CBH, HJC, and CJD, and each of these is half the corresponding square, $ABCD$, $BKHC$, $CHMJ$ and $JLDC$, and half four is two.

1.2   *A Priori*

> ### Question
> 1. *How* do we know mathematics?

Plato's conclusion is that mathematical knowledge is *a priori*, that is, that it is not based on the evidence of the senses, either our own, or other people's transmitted to us by some form of communication. In this mathematics differs from most other subjects. With the exception of logic, and possibly philosophy, most subjects depend one way or another on empirical evidence which is at some stage or other based on people seeing, hearing, or feeling things. In scientific laboratories there are balances and spectrometers, and complicated instruments to detect fundamental particles, such as muons. We could not detect a muon unless either we had seen something—a flash on a screen, a track on a photographic plate, a trail in a bubble chamber—or had heard something—a click on a Geiger counter, or had had some other sensory experience. Equally, those studying the humanities, although they do not go to laboratories, do go to libraries, where they can read reports of what men did in time past. We cannot know that the Battle of Hastings took place in 1066, unless we can find a report from someone who was there, or from someone who was told by someone who was there, or something that was done in consequence of the battle, or some other word or deed which we can take as evidence of there having been a battle. We may base our knowledge on the *Anglo-Saxon Chronicle*, or on the Bayeux Tapestry; but we reckon that they are reliable sources of information only because they are, immediately or ultimately, based on what men actually witnessed with their eyes, their ears, or their other sense organs. Even in literary criticism, which is much more a matter of imagination, insight and flair, if we want to propound a serious interpretation of, say *King Lear*, we must actually have read the text. Mathematics is different. Although later I shall have to qualify what I am now saying and admit that mathematics, too, is quite often known second-hand,[2] it is true, nevertheless, that one can do mathematics on one's own. It is potentially a solipsistic, or, as we might even say, autistic, discipline. Autistic children cannot relate to other people, and are characteristically bad at the humanities, but can be good at mathematics. One does not have to know, one does not have to like, other people, in order to be a mathematician, whereas it is very difficult to study the humanities without some liking, or at least some disliking, for people. So mathematics is something which can be done, although with difficulty, by someone who is blind, deaf and deprived of all tactile sensation, and who, moreover is in solitary confinement. If I had had the misfortune to fall into the hands of the Communists, and had been sent to Siberia for

---

[2] See below, §7.4, and §14.9.

thirty years, I should be unable to while away the time by studying chemistry or ancient history, but I could still in my cell do prime number theory. And that puts mathematics in a class apart.

If not Empiricism, then What?

1.3 Relevance

But there is a difficulty. What is the relation between mathematics, which is pure, and reality, which is relevant? If mathematical truths apply to empirical reality, as they surely do, they must be vulnerable to empirical refutation. Protagoras, one of the leading Greek sophists and a precursor of modern empiricism, argued that geometry was not true *a priori* but empirical in content and false. For geometry teaches that a tangent touches a circle in just one point, whereas casual observation reveals that they are coincident over a short length. If we observe a wheel on a road, or a hoop on a pavement, or a top lying on a table, we see that they do not touch at just one point, but are evidently touching over some small, but finite, distance.[3] This is a matter of simple observation. Look at any bicycle. The propositions of mathematics, Protagoras concluded, are not true *a priori*, but are simple synthetic propositions, and, in the case of those actually asserted by mathematicians, in fact false. Plato is worried by this argument: his answer is "So much the worse for wheels and hoops and tops, and all particular exemplifications of circles".[4] He distinguishes the ideal circles of our thought from their imperfect exemplifications in the world around us. If I turn a top on a lathe, although it is more or less a circle, it is not a perfect circle. Similarly, no bicycle wheel is a perfect circle. But that is not telling us anything about geometry, but only about bicycling. Geometry expresses *a priori* truths about ideal shapes which material objects only imperfectly approximate to. Protagoras has not produced a counter-example to geometrical truth, but simply an example of material imperfection.

---

[3] Aristotle, *Metaphysics*, II, 2, 997b34-998a4. (All references to Aristotle are to the pages in the Bekker edition.)

[4] Plato, *Seventh Letter*, 343a.

Two Questions

1. *How* do we know mathematics?
2. What is mathematics *about*?

The distinction between our concepts and the material objects to which they are applied is important and often lost sight of. Plato gives another example in the *Phaedo*.[5] We have the concept of two things being equal, for example two sticks being equal in length. If we were to examine them closely, it is a fair guess that we should find that they were not exactly equal. Indeed, until the advent of quantum mechanics, it was a fair guess that no two material objects were exactly equal in length. Nevertheless, we have the concept of being exactly equal in length. We know that if A is exactly equal to B and B is exactly equal to C, then A is exactly equal to C. We might be faced with a series of objects, each apparently exactly equal to the next, but the first visibly smaller than the last. We do not then suppose that we have refuted by experimental test the claim that exact equality is a transitive relation; we do not say that even if A is exactly equal to B and B is exactly to C, A may not be exactly equal to C. Instead, we blame our application of the concept, and say that although we could not see it, some of the objects cannot have been exactly equal to the others. Rather than amend our clear and distinct idea of exact equality, we cast doubt on our use of it in the individual case.

As a first move it is fair enough to try blaming the application rather than the concept itself for any discrepancy with empirical observation, but we cannot be sure that the attempt to shift the blame will always be successful. In the two cases cited the discrepancy is not great, and the explanation plausible—the hoop touches the road for only a short distance, the first and last members of the series are only a little different in length, and it is quite likely that the hoop should have deformed a little, as a rubber tyre visibly does, and that very small inequalities should have been invisible, although their sum was visible. In other cases, however, the discrepancy might be great and no plausible explanation available. If the angles of a triangle added

---

[5] *Phaedo*, 74-76.

up to much less or much more than two right angles, it would be
implausible to impute gross experimental error, and a few checks
could eliminate that possibility altogether. On any one occasion
Agamemnon might have miscounted if he reckoned that there were
seven heroes in one ship, five in another, and yet not twelve in
the two together, but if repeated checking by a chartered accoun-
tant still failed to conform to our simple arithmetical equation

$$7 + 5 = 12$$

we should be at a loss to know what to say.

Protagoras would have known what to say. An empirical generalisation, though hitherto well confirmed, had at long last been
falsified. It is an attractive answer. It was put forward in the last
century by Mill, and in recent years by Kitcher and Gillies.[6] Mill's
arguments, in spite of Frege's scathing criticisms,[7] are not bad. He
argues, as does Hume, against all forms of *a priori* and necessary
knowledge; it is by long experience that I learn that seven plus
five equals twelve. It is a synthetic truth; not, as Kant had made
out, synthetic *a priori*, but synthetic *a posteriori*. It is a position that has found favour with many modern philosophers, but
it has never found favour with the majority of mathematicians.[8]
Mathematicians, who have experienced the force of mathematical
argument, do not believe that it is just the result of a Humean con-
ditioning process, that they have so often discovered by experiment
or been told by a teacher, that Pythagoras' theorem is true, that
now they have got into the habit of believing it and cannot break
themselves of the habit. They follow Plato, and maintain that
mathematical truth is, indeed, *a priori*, and then seek to reconcile
the Pythagorean intimation that it does give us some knowledge
of reality with the objection put forward by Protagoras that any
statements about reality are vulnerable to empirical falsification.

What Plato himself does is to disconnect mathematical truth
from too close a contact with empirical reality. It is not something

---

[6] J.S.Mill, *A System of Logic*, London, 1843, Book II, chs. 5 & 6, Book
III, ch.24; Philip Kitcher, *The Nature of Mathematical Knowledge*, New
York, 1983; D.A. Gillies, *Frege, Dedekind, and Peano on the Foundations
of Arithmetic*, Assen, 1982, chs. 3 & 4.

[7] G.Frege, *The Foundations of Arithmetic*, 1884, tr. J.L.Austin, Oxford,
1950, §7.

[8] But see below, §2.4.

Schools of Mathematical Philosophy

	Empiricism	Platonism
Leading Exponents	Protagoras Mill Gillies Kitcher	Early Plato Hardy Gödel
How Do We Know?	By Observation	By Thinking *A Priori*

Table 1.3.1

peculiar to Plato to insulate cherished truths against unfavourable counter-instances; it is the argument of experimental error, often used by scientists when their theories come into collision with the evidence. But Plato pushes it very much further than modern scientists do. Modern scientists are prepared in the end to abandon even their most cherished theories in the face of adverse empirical evidence, whereas Plato dismisses empirical evidence from the outset as completely irrelevant. He takes a very low view of empirical truths about material objects. Material objects, because of their imperfect and transitory natures, cannot be the subject of genuine knowledge. If there is a conflict between them of mere empirical observation, it is the latter that must be rejected. In Book VII of the *Republic* he ridicules astronomers who spend their nights looking up at the sky instead of doing mathematical calculations. "Don't be so silly", he says, "as to waste your time lying on your back, looking up at the night sky: just think."[9] Such a move is effective, but costly. It offers mathematical propositions absolute security against empirical refutation, but at the cost of complete disconnexion between mathematics and empirical reality. Plato means by ἀστρονομία, *astronomia*, not astronomy, but "rational mechanics", something in the same sort of line as the classical Newtonian mechanics taught in schools, in which one makes no observations but simply performs calculations and solves problems; or like the General Relativity studied by theoretical physicists or pure mathe-

---

[9] *Republic*, 529-530.

maticians, who are solely concerned with the solutions to differential equations, the determination of boundary conditions, and the discovery of elegant derivations, and hardly at all with empirical observation. But rational mechanics, although eminently rational and often highly elegant, may not be true of the external world. As we now know, Newtonian mechanics is not completely true under all conditions. It does not detract from the intellectual interest of Newtonian mechanics as a formal mathematical system, or its value as an educational exercise. But its claim to complete truth is compromised in our eyes by its failure to conform completely with empirical fact. Not so for Plato. In his eyes, if rational mechanics does not agree with the external world, so much the worse for the external world. Faced with the possibility of disagreement between mathematical rationality and empirical reality, he saves the relevance of mathematics by down-grading empirical reality so as to be less real than some other sort of reality, capable of being known *a priori*, of which mathematical truth is a paradigm example. Real reality for Plato is that possessed by the "forms", as the word εἴδη (*eide*) is usually translated, and any other sort of reality is only of lower degree. The relevance of mathematics is saved by denying the ultimate relevance of any other sort of reality that could impugn the truth of mathematical theorems. For Plato, therefore, mathematics is both true *a priori* and relevant, just because only the sort of reality that mathematical truth reveals is accounted fundamentally real and relevant.

1.4   What Are We Talking About?

Plato avoided refutation at the hands of Protagoras by claiming that the objects of mathematical discourse are not simple material objects, which manifestly fail to conform to mathematical expectations, but something else, more real and definitely different. But what exactly are the objects of mathematical discourse? Plato uses two words to describe them: εἴδη (*eide*), which in Latin was translated as *species*, and ἰδέαι (*ideai*), from which comes our word 'idea'; but in modern English the word 'idea' is too psychological to express what Plato meant. In technical philosophy the word 'universal' is the best equivalent, but fails to express the strong visual connotations of the Greek words, which was partly expressed in the standard translation 'forms', but might be better rendered by 'aspects' or 'features', or better, 'shapes' or 'patterns', since

Plato's whole theory is very much influenced by his thinking about geometry. He develops it in books VI and VII of the *Republic*, and says that what we are talking about in geometry and mathematics generally are abstract entities which are timeless, spaceless, and impersonal. When I talk about the diagonal of the square, or the nine-point circle, or the Euler line, I am not talking about the often rather sketchy and highly imperfect drawing on the blackboard, but about something which underlies all particular exemplifications of squares and diagonals, nine-point circles, or Euler lines, and is independent of each of them. The very fact that we use the definite article, and talk of *the* square, *the* nine-point circle, *etc.*, bears witness to this; and by the same token, it would be absurd to ask *where* the square was, or to ask *when* the nine-point centre came to be on the Euler line, or to suggest that Pythagoras' theorem might hold for you but not for me. So Plato's answer to the question "What is mathematics about?" is that it is about something timeless, spaceless and objective.

Plato has been much criticized, but also much imitated: chemists learn the Periodic Table; in the Periodic Table are arranged many abstract entities—Hydrogen, Deuterium, Lithium, Chlorine, and they have places in the Periodic Table, just as Plato said they should. These places in the Periodic Table are not spatial ones, they are not temporal ones, they are not a matter of personal predilection: they are relations of a quasi-spatial kind between entities that are spaceless, timeless and impersonal. Equally on a syllabus, there may be listed various topics to be covered—group theory, Lebesgue measure theory, geometry—which again are not located in space, nor in time, nor are a matter of personal predilection. Such entities can both be referred to and be meaningfully talked about. Unless we are prepared to make out that the whole of modern scientific discourse is meaningless, and to forswear all talk of the Periodic Table and of biological species, it is unreasonable to object to Plato's talk of mathematical objects on metaphysical grounds. It is difficult to deny that mathematics is in some sense objective, accessible to every ratiocinating thinker, and independent of time and space. And Plato's language expresses that.

But it also expresses more. Plato himself held that great consequences followed from the existence of forms, and many philosophers since have agreed, some holding with Plato that if the forms exist, then things are not the only things to exist, and that

There are more things in heaven and earth, Horatio,
than are dreamt of in your philosophy.[10]

and, in particular, that materialism is therefore proved false, and
that souls can exist as independent entities and survive the dis-
solution of our mortal bodies. Others have concluded that since
these consequences may well follow from the existence of abstract
entities, abstract entities cannot really exist, and we must recon-
strue our ways of talking about mathematics and natural science
so as not to seem to presuppose the existence of anything with
embarrassing metaphysical consequences. Since the time of Plato
there have been strong and sustained objections to his account of
a non-spatial, non-temporal, impersonal world of invisible, intangi-
ble and immaterial entities. It is partly a matter of taste, a dislike
of ontological extravagance. But also there is an element of fear.
If, besides all the ordinary things in the external world, there are
a whole lot of other things that exist, the realm of being seems
overcrowded; the over-population problem is particularly acute if
we venture into Cantor's paradise of transfinite numbers, and find
ourselves piling infinity upon infinity in endless, and incomprehensible profusion. They fear that if they once allow that there are
more things than can be touched or seen, they are on a slippery
path which may lead to their having to acknowledge the existence
of values or even of God, than which nothing could, in their conception, be worse.

These endeavours are not perverse: any serious thinker will try
to form as good a picture as he can of what the world is really
like, and will need to consider the evidence of our mathematical
experience and our mathematical knowledge, and whether they can
be accommodated in the view he is being led to adopt. But these
extraneous concerns make it difficult to formulate a philosophy
of mathematics *per se*, and difficult to do justice to the accounts
being offered. Since a full resolution of these issues lies outside
the philosophy of mathematics, it will not be attempted in this
book. So far as we can, we shall concern ourselves only with those
considerations that arise within mathematics, and only in the final
chapter take account of extraneous considerations.

Within mathematics, the existence of abstract mathematical

---

[10] *Hamlet*, I, v, 166.

objects has been generally reckoned to commit us to more than the bare legitimacy of using ordinary mathematical discourse. Platonic Realism, as it may be termed, lays claim to there being objective truth. We discover mathematics rather than invent it. Mathematical truth does not depend on our say-so. If Beethoven had been aborted, there would have been no Eroica: but if Pythagoras had never been born, Pythagoras' theorem would still have been true. It follows from the objectivity of mathematical truth that mathematical entities have properties independently of our knowing what they are, and so are subject to the Law of the Excluded Middle and the Principle of Bivalence. Platonic Realism is on this score opposed to Intuitionism.[11] The third claim is similar, and is to do with reference. If numbers and other mathematical entities exist independently of us, they can be referred to successfully without precise specification, whereas if they were only artefacts of our own devising, it would be incumbent on us to say exactly what it was we had in mind before we could expect someone else to know what it was we were talking about. This has become important with regard to the "vicious circle principle". In analysis and elsewhere we sometimes have occasion to define a number as a Dedekind cut of numbers satisfying some particular condition. There is no problem about this if numbers exist independently of us. In that case all we are doing is to give a pointer towards the number we are talking about in terms of a readily understood general specification. But if numbers do not exist independently of us, and are simply called into being as mental constructs of our own devising, then a critic can complain that in constructing a particular number by reference to all the numbers satisfying a certain condition, we have constructed it in terms of itself. On this score Platonic Realism is opposed to Constructivism. The real existence of mathematical entities entitles us to refer to them without completely characterizing them, and therefore can quantify (or as we shall later term it, "quotify") over them "impredicatively" in process of defining them.[12]

Platonic Realism thus has many attractions. It not only legit-

---

[11] See further below, §§7.4, 7.5.

[12] See Kurt Gödel, "Russell's Mathematical Logic", reprinted in Paul Benacerraf and Hilary Putnam, eds., *Philosophy of Mathematics*, 2nd ed., Cambridge, 1983, p.456. See further below, §16.3.

---

1. Mathematical entities are talkable about
2. Mathematical truth is objective
3. Principle of Bivalence holds (and LEM and DN)
4. Impredicative sets are admissible

Table 1.4.1

imises mathematical discourse generally, but licenses certain forms of inference which mathematicians often have occasion to use. Although philosophers have qualms about platonism, most working mathematicians are platonists, in so far as they articulate any philosophy of mathematics. Platonism is not to be dismissed simply on the score that many philosophers are alarmed at the ontological extravagance of Platonic Realism. But the objections are not to be dismissed either. No less telling than the ontological doubts about the existence of mathematical entities are epistemological problems, which turn on the question "How do we come to know mathematical truth?". "Platonism seems obvious when you are thinking about mathematical truth", said W.D.Hart, "but impossible when you are thinking about mathematical knowledge."[13]

1.5   How Do We Know?

Philosophers find *a priori* knowledge difficult. Many are empiricists, and hold that all knowledge must be founded on sense-experience, even though it is evident that much of our knowledge is not founded on sense-experience—I know where I shall have lunch tomorrow not because I have made a prediction founded on sense-experience, but because I have made a decision. But even non-empiricists find it hard to free themselves from perceptual metaphors with dangerously misleading connotations. Plato, in his first thinking about mathematics, says we come to know mathematical truth with the "eye of the mind". It is an intelligible answer in view of the *Meno* experience. Later Whewell, the

---

[13] Reviewing Mark Steiner, *Mathematical Knowledge*, in *Journal of Philosophy*, **74**, 1977, pp.118-119.

Schools of Mathematical Philosophy

	Empiricism	Platonism
Leading Exponents	Protagoras Mill Gillies Kitcher	Early Plato Hardy Gödel
How Do We Know?	By Observation	By Thinking *A Priori*
What Are We Talking About?	Empirical Phenomena	εἴδη Forms (or Patterns)

Table 1.4.2

Master of Trinity, Cambridge, spoke of "imaginary looking".[14] It accords with our experience. When one is trying to master a proof, one concentrates very much, and one's whole body becomes tense, much as when one is trying to see something at a distance. One feels one is trying to focus one's mind in much the same way as one focuses one's gaze, even though one may have one's eyes shut. The perceptual metaphor is a very natural one. Admittedly, it is a metaphor; but it is one that commends itself to mathematicians, as characterizing how it seems when they are trying to do mathematics. To give a more modern example, G.A. Hardy, in an article in *Mind* wrote:

> I have myself always thought of a mathematician as in the first instance an *observer*, a man who gazes at a distant range of mountains and notes down his observations. His object is simply to distinguish clearly and notify to others as many different peaks as he can. There are some peaks

---

[14] W.Whewell, *Philosophy of the Inductive Sciences*, London, 1840, vol.i, Book II, ch.8, §5, p.130, (in 1847 edn. vol.i, ch.9, §5, p.135), *History of Scientific Ideas*, London, 1858, i, 140.

which he can distinguish easily, while others are less clear. He sees A sharply, while of B he can obtain only transitory glimpses. At last he makes out a ridge which leads from A, and following it to its end he discovers that it culminates in B. B is now fixed in his vision, and from this point he can proceed to further discoveries. In other cases perhaps he can distinguish a ridge which vanishes in the distance, and conjectures that it leads to a peak in the clouds or below the horizon. But when he sees a peak he believes that it is there simply because he sees it. If he wishes someone else to see it, *he points to it*, either directly or through the chain of summits which led him to recognize it himself. When his pupil also sees it, the research, the argument, the *proof*, is finished. The analogy is a rough one, but I am sure that it is not altogether misleading. If we were to push it to its extreme we should be led to a rather paradoxical conclusion; that there is, strictly, no such thing as mathematical proof; that we can, in the last analysis, do nothing but *point*; that proofs are what Littlewood and I call *gas*, rhetorical flourishes designed to affect psychology, pictures on the board in the lecture, devices to stimulate the imagination of pupils. This is plainly not the whole truth, but there is a good deal in it.[15]

Hardy is one of the few mathematicians to express for the benefit of philosophers his own thinking about the nature of mathematical truth and mathematical discovery. He is an uncompromising Platonist. To the question *What are we talking about?*, he answers that we are talking about things that are there; they are real objects, although not visible objects. And to the question *How do we know?*, he answers that we know by seeing with the eye of the mind, by actually looking. It is a form of realism in which independently existing objects are seen with the mind's eye, and objective truths discovered about them.

[15] *Mind*, 1929, p.18; but see S.F.Barker, "Realism as a Philosophy of Mathematics", in J.J.Buloff, ed., *Foundations of Mathematics*, Berlin, 1969, pp.1-9, and P.Bernays, "Sur la Platonisme dans les mathématiques", *L'Enseignment Mathématique*, **34**, 1935, pp.52-69; tr. in Paul Benacerraf and Hilary Putnam, eds., *The Philosophy of Mathematics*, 2nd ed., Cambridge, 1983, pp.258-271.

Besides the virtues already noted of making mathematics independent of empirical evidence, not limited by space or time, and of securing the objectivity of mathematical truth, Hardy's account has the further virtue of expressing its accessibility to every mind. Although the abstract entities talked about by mathematicians— call them forms, or universals, or sets, or shapes, or patterns, or concepts, or what you will—are a bit hard to swallow, once swallowed they give a simple and satisfying answer to the question of what mathematicians talk about and also the question of what makes mathematical propositions true. Mathematicians talk about numbers in much the same way as artists talk about colours and to say that six comes between five and seven is to ascribe a certain relation to five, six and seven, in much the same way as to say that yellow comes between green and orange or purple between red and blue ascribes a similar relation to colours. In each case the proposition is reporting facts, not superficial contingent facts but deep necessary facts, and it is in virtue of those facts that what is said is true. In order to ascertain them it is necessary to focus attention on them, but not to be in any particular place at any particular time, or to use any particular sense organ. With history or astronomy, I can tell you that you were not at the right place at the right time to make the relevant observation, whereas it is clean contrary to the *ethos* of mathematics that any aspiring mathematician should be disqualified on such grounds. Mathematics is, in principle, accessible to all who wish to study it. It may be difficult in practice, but in its ideology it is totally non-esoteric.

Although few mathematicians have been as articulate as Hardy, most have had Platonist leanings. Of course, we need to be careful. To ascribe explicit views to someone who has not explicitly espoused them is always hazardous. And there is much ambiguity in exactly what Platonism in mathematics is. In due course we shall have to refine the term. But it is useful to give general guidance, even though it may need to be modified in detail. Besides Hardy, Frege (in a manner of speaking), Gödel, and Bernays, are mathematicians who have expressed doctrines which are generally in line with those I have ascribed to Plato. And most working mathematicians, although reluctant to express any very definite views on the philosophy of mathematics, when they do say what they think they are doing, incline towards Plato's views rather than to any of his rivals'. Gödel draws a specific parallel between the apprehension of mathematical truth and sense perception:

> But, despite their remoteness from sense experience, we do
> have something like a perception also of the objects of set
> theory, as is seen from the fact that the axioms force them-
> selves upon us as being true. I don't see any reason why we
> should have less confidence in this kind of perception, *i.e.*,
> in mathematical intuition, than in sense perception, which
> induces us to build up physical theories and to expect that
> future sense perceptions will agree with them and, more-
> over, to believe that a question not decidable now has mean-
> ing and may be decided in the future. The set-theoretical
> paradoxes are hardly any more troublesome for mathematics
> than deceptions of the senses are for physics.[16]

Many other mathematicians have spoken similarly.[17] Their tes-
timony, like that of Hardy and Gödel, should be taken seriously,
but is not conclusive. There are objections. Whereas the objections to Plato's ontology were on account of its being too lush, the
objections to his mathematical epistemology are on account of its
being too *simpliste*. The perceptual analogy does not carry any
weight. No coherent account is offered of how we come to know
mathematical truths. What relation can a finite and time-bound
mortal like myself have with the timeless and immaterial entities
of Plato's imagining? Particularly in recent years, when causal
theories of knowledge and reference have been in vogue, the epistemological consequences of Plato's theory of forms have been taken
as a powerful argument against it.

Both the ontological and the epistemological objections have

---

[16] Kurt Gödel, "What Is Cantor's Continuum Problem?" (Supplement to
Second Edition), reprinted in Paul Benacerraf and Hilary Putnam, eds.,
Philosophy of Mathematics, 2nd ed., Cambridge, 1983, pp.483-484; and in
The Collected works of Kurt Gödel, ii, ed.S.Feferman, Oxford, 1990, p.268.
For further discussion, see below, §14.9.

[17] Mark Steiner, *Mathematical Knowledge*, Ithaca, NY, 1975, ch.4, §VI,
pp.134-137; C. Parsons, "Frege's Theory of Number", in Max Black, ed.,
Philosophy in America, London, 1965, pp.180-203; L.H.Tharp, "Ontological Reduction", *Journal of Philosophy*, 68, 1971, p.162; P.Cohen, *Set Theory and the Continuum Hypothesis,* New York, 1966, pp.150-151; Penelope
Maddy, "Perception and Intuition", *The Philosophical Review,*, LXXXIX,
1980, pp.163-196.

been put forward in a very different context by J.L. Mackie. In his book, *Ethics: Inventing Right and Wrong*, he argues for moral subjectivism on the grounds that the only alternative is Platonism, and that values, if they existed, would be extremely queer sorts of things, and that there is no intelligible account available of how we could come to know them.[18] Exactly the same points can be made against mathematical Platonism. And the same rebuttals can be used to counter them. Values may be queer sorts of object, as also imaginary numbers, the nine-point centre, and the alternating group of order twelve: but so are quarks, electrons, alpha-particles and pions. The world is full of strange objects. Queerness is no bar to existing. Unless we adopt a know-nothing policy, and refuse to acknowledge that anything could exist unless it be of a familiar sort, we must allow that many unusual objects have been shown to exist, and that we should not lay down antecedent stipulations on what we may be led to posit. A hard-line common-sense philosopher can maintain that neither mathematics nor ethics nor metaphysics nor science can compel us to acknowledge the existence of anything we were not familiar with at the age of ten, but he does so at the cost of cutting himself off from most modern science and many traditional realms of discourse. Although we may legitimately be wary of multiplying entities needlessly, we cannot rule out Plato's abstract entities on those grounds alone.

A more specific difficulty with mathematical entities assails those modern philosophers who believe in a causal theory of knowledge: they do not see how it is possible to account for knowledge of immaterial objects within the confines of the causal theory of knowledge.[19] But the causal theory of knowledge is barely a theory at all. In part it is an attempt to block a loophole in the account of knowledge as justified true belief: it is not enough that

---

[18] J.L.Mackie, *Ethics: Inventing Right and Wrong*, Penguin, 1977, ch.1, §9, pp.38-42.

[19] Paul Benacerraf, "Mathematical Truth", *Journal of Philosophy*, **70**, 1973, pp.661-680; reprinted in Paul Benacerraf and Hilary Putnam, eds., *The Philosophy of Mathematics*, 2nd ed., Cambridge, 1983, pp.403-420. See also W.Hart, "The Epistemology of Abstract Objects", *Proceedings of the Aristotelian Society, Supplementary Volume*, **53**, 1979, pp.153-164; and P.Kitcher, "Introduction", *Revue Internationale de Philosophie*, **42**, issue 4, 1988, p.397.

a true belief is justified—it must be justified in the right way, and the causal theory claims that the right way is a causal way. But a justified true belief could be caused in the wrong way: a brain in a vat may be induced by suitable stimulation to hold a belief which is true, and for which it has adequate justification. The causal theory does not succeed in blocking the hole in traditional accounts of knowledge. Only if we take 'cause' in a wide, and elastic, sense can the causal theory serve its purpose, and then there is no difficulty in having abstract entities explaining observable phenomena. I can explain the distribution of bagatelle balls rolling down a pinboard by the Gaussian curve $y = e^{-x^2}$, the distribution of spots on a leopard's skin by the solution to a differential equation, and the shape of crystals, and the properties of fundamental particles, by the theory of groups. The reason why we all agree that 257 is a prime number is not that we have mysterious commerce with an abstract entity, but that, being rational truth-seekers, we believe what is true, and it is true that 257 is a prime number. Only if we are wedded to an extremely *simpliste* account of knowledge should knowledge of abstract entities seem problematic, and then the trouble lies in the account of knowledge, not in mathematics. A modern philosopher who does not see how he can enter into cognitive causal relations with π, should have comparable difficulty in getting into cognitive contact with the halogen group in the periodic table, the colour aquamarine, or the Alleluia Chorus, for these too are abstract entities, not located in time or space.

Objections based on the causal theory of reference are equally unpersuasive. The theory is based on a paradigm of reference to material objects, and has been over-extrapolated from too narrow a base. It may be that Fido obtains his name by baptism: it does not follow that π and e and $\sqrt{-1}$ needed similarly to be immersed in terrestrial water in order to acquire their names, or to be intelligibly talked about. We should be cautious in accepting the deliverances of modern theories. Modern theories may be wrong. It is their function to account for what we actually know and can talk about, not to be a strait-jacket preventing us from knowing things we do know, or talking about things we do talk about. Philosophers may be unable to understand how we can know mathematical truths, but they have a bad track record at being able to understand anything. In the middle of the twentieth century, philosophers aired their inability to see how we could know anything about the past, but it did not lead historians to go out of business; nor did the inability to solve the problem of "other minds" lead to actual autism. The contemporary inability to see how mathematical knowledge is possible should be seen in context of the mid-century inability to have knowledge of the past, or to see how one person could know whether another person had feelings. It is a difficulty to which anyone studying the philosophy of mathematics should address himself, but not a doubt that should debar him from adopting that account which seems to do most justice to the phenomena.

1.6 Modality

The severest critic of platonism was Plato. Although he never abandoned the Theory of Forms completely, he was acutely aware of the difficulties it gave rise to, and kept on criticizing it and revising his thought not only about the Forms but about the nature of mathematical thinking generally. Mathematical thinking is coercive. Mathematical truth not only can be known *a priori*, but is necessary. There is something compelling about it. We see it in the *Meno* proof. It is not only valid, but irresistible. It leaps out of the page at us. Once we have seen it, we are compelled to accept it. That feature guided Plato, and has guided the majority of other mathematicians and mathematical philosophers, in their thinking about the nature of mathematics. Mathematical truth has some sort of necessity about it, which contrasts with the merely contingent beliefs we have about the world of sense experience. There is a hardness about mathematical truth which makes it not only ineluctably true, but profoundly true, because it is immune to the changes and chances of this fleeting world of transient phenomena, and tells us about not what just is, but what must be, the case. It is difficult to give a visual exegesis of necessity. As Hume pointed out, we cannot see necessity. The logical geography of the world of forms may show how different forms are connected, but cannot show that they have to be the way they are. The metaphors we use—cogent, coercive, compelling—are muscular, rather than visual, and call for a different sort of exegesis. Typically we come to feel its force by trial and failure.[20] The boy tried $(1.5)^2$, and found that it did not equal 2. If mathematical proofs are alleged to be

[20] See J.R.Lucas, *Space, Time and Causality*, Oxford, 1985, ch.3, pp.35-36.

irresistible, we naturally ask what will happen if we try to resist them. We ask not simply "How do we come to know mathematics?" and "What is mathematics about?", but the further question "What happens if we refuse to concede the conclusion of a proof?".

Three Questions

1. *How* do we know mathematics?
2. What is mathematics *about*?
3. *What happens* if we do not accept a mathematical proof?

According to the Theory of Forms, if we do not see, it simply shows that we lack mathematical vision. It is a little like being colour-blind. But this is implausible. If someone does not concede the truth of Gödel's theorem, we *argue* with him, not take him to an oculist. More importantly, although to be colour-blind is to lack a certain perceptual capacity, which is a disqualification for a career in the navy or driving trains, it is relatively disconnected from other intellectual powers. Mathematics is more intimately connected with them. To assimilate mathematical incompetence to colour-blindness is like assimilating moral insensitivity to colour-blindness. In each case the failure is wrongly characterized as mere perceptual failure; too much else is involved. Although Plato would have been happy to acknowledge that great mathematical ability is a natural gift, which a few people have and most people lack, he cannot continue to hold that it is *just* a form of seeing without losing a sense of its integral connexion with the rest of thought and of its necessity.[21]

Plato rejects "platonism", because it gives no account of modal force of *Meno* argument.

One cannot "see" necessity.

Once we grasp the proof of a mathematical theorem, we feel the force, the irresistible force, of the argument. We are compelled

---

[21] See further, §16.6.

to acknowledge that it must be so. The cogency of mathematical argument is quite different from the cogency of empirical fact.
With the latter we are compelled to acknowledge that it is so; with
the former we are compelled to acknowledge that it *must* be so.
Mathematics has modal subtleties that geography lacks. Plato's
analogy, between the world of mathematical objects and the world
of everyday experience, is to that extent defective. And Plato himself began to develop a theory of mathematical argument to take
account of its compelling force and the necessity of its conclusions.

If not Platonic realism, then What?

1.7 Cogency

Plato sought to give an account of why mathematical truth was
necessarily true. The necessity arose from the nature of argument.
As he developed his theory of argument, he was impelled to view
good arguments as inherently incontrovertible, and to accept as
valid only those that could not be coherently gainsaid.

Most arguments are not like that. We often argue with the
intent of getting those we argue with to accept our views, and
sometimes we succeed—else we should have abandoned the activity altogether. But although arguments can carry conviction, in
most cases they are not *maximally* coercive. The force of reason
is, to a greater or lesser extent, resistible. Often we do not resist it: we may not want to, or we may be unwilling to pay the
price of resistance: but we could, and whether we do or not depends on us, our attitudes and purposes. For argument in general
is two-sided. We can distinguish a *proponent* and a *respondent*,
the former putting forward a claim, the latter responding, perhaps
accepting it, perhaps disputing it, sometimes asking for justification, sometimes putting forward objections and counter-claims or
counter-arguments. Arguments are variable and complex, and it is
not at all easy to schematize them. But for our present purpose it
is enough to remark that typically the development of an argument
depends on both the proponent and the respondent. Arguments
are arguments *between*.

Arguments are for the most part holistic and cumulative. In
history, in literature, in the law courts, in morals, the proponent

is trying to convey a complete over-all judgement as to what happened, what the interpretation of a play really is, whether the accused committed the crime, what ought in the circumstances to be done. Sometimes he succeeds in conveying his way of seeing them, and we come to see things as he sees them, much as a mathematician does on Hardy's account.[22] Sometimes, indeed, his account may be compelling. But it does not have to be. Some small detail may entirely alter the aspect of the case, and we may be unconvinced that no such detail will emerge. A holistic cumulative case may convince, but there is always logical room for some further consideration, some further 'but', and so the argument, even if weighty, even if decisive, is not conclusive, not *maximally* coercive.

If mathematical arguments are to be maximally coercive, there must be no room for a further 'but', and so they cannot be effectively two-sided. We need to know with whom the mathematician is arguing, and be sure that he does not let any weak contention pass. Often the mathematician is arguing with other mathematicians, who are very ready to follow the wave of his hand, and see whatever it is that his proofs are intended to indicate. But Plato had occasion to argue with sophists, who would not concede anything willingly, and he had to use arguments that would have to be accepted by the most stubborn of them, even by Thrasymachus, who appears in the first book of the *Republic* and is not going to give an inch unless he has to. Valid arguments, Plato came to think, must be ones that would compel assent from anyone, even the most recalcitrant, even the fool with whom Anselm argued. Ironically, mathematics, one of the most difficult of disciplines, aims to address its arguments to the most moronic, and to articulate them so that even a computer is compelled to concede. Many difficulties have ensued for our proper understanding of the nature of mathematics. But the connexion that Plato sensed between universal validity and maximun coerciveness none the less remains.

Equally, if mathematical arguments are to be maximally coercive, they cannot be cumulative and holistic: a cumulative case could always be improved by some further consideration which finally clinched the argument; and with a holistic argument, someone may fail to appreciate the whole picture, or point out some detail, which, he maintains, flaws the whole case. Plato rejected

---

[22] See above, §1.5, pp.11-12.

the holistic approach of poetry, drama and rhetoric, and laid it down as a mark of rationality that a serious argument could stand up to the most searching and detailed scrutiny by question and answer. Although he himself, in his myths and elsewhere, was well able to mount a concerted artistic appeal, and although in the *Protagoras* he showed himself aware of the fact that a face could not be regarded simply as a sum of its parts,[23] the main thrust of his thought was against the holistic approach, and in favour of the analytic, because only thus could he force assent from the Thrasymachus-ly disinclined. If we had merely a platonist vision of mathematical truth, it would be indistinguishable from our apprehension of insights in, say, literary criticism. I might see a pattern, and point it out to a friend, but he might see it quite differently, and press his differing interpretation on me. One of us might be right, and might be successful in convincing the other of the rightness of his views; but wise men do not always think alike, and their judgements, though weighty, are not maximally coercive.

In order to be coercive, a proof must not rest simply on a wide-ranging ability to discern patterns. If you fail to see it when I point it out to you, we must be able to locate the area of disagreement, and pin it down to something definite. A mathematical proof is not an assessment of the case as a whole, where the whole is wide open to different specifications, and contrary interpretations, but a finite list of definite items which can be checked over for the elimination of all dispute. If I put forward what claims to be a mathematical argument, and you do not accept the conclusion, I am entitled to ask you where it breaks down, and you are obliged to point out what you regard as the flaw in my reasoning. We can then concentrate on that, and you must show that this is a weak link in the argument, and my purported proof is invalid, or I must show that it is a valid step, and your objection, on this point at least, fails. We reduce the disagreement from a general debate about the argument as a whole to a particular dispute about the individual steps.

1.8 Deduction

A proof breaks an argument down into a finite number of separate steps, and will be valid as a whole, provided all the steps are. And these, Plato saw, would be incontrovertible if they were deductive

---

[23] *Protagoras* 329d.

inferences.

Plato discovered deduction. In his disputes with sophists he found that there was almost no position so unreasonable that some would not take it. The only way to oust them was to show that their position was completely self-contradictory. In the first book of the *Republic* we see him manoeuvring Thrasymachus into a formal self-contradiction,[24] and this is exactly in accord with the prescription he gives in the *Phaedo*. There he gives as one test of the tenability of a philosophical thesis "to see whether its consequences agree or disagree among themselves".[25] It is clear that this must be a negative test. If the consequences of a thesis disagree among themselves, that is, if they are, when taken together, self-contradictory, or, as logicians say, mutually inconsistent, then the thesis must be rejected: but if the consequences are consistent, that does not show that the thesis is true—many consistent positions are nonetheless false. Plato also proposes a positive test.[26] A thesis is to be accepted if it can be derived from another which is itself acceptable to both the parties. And this must be true, even for Thrasymachus, if the derivations are deductive, that is, if it would be self-contradictory to concede the premises and to deny the conclusion. We often define deductive arguments by saying that a deductively valid argument is one where the conjunction of the premises with the negation of the conclusion is inconsistent; just as we can define an analytic proposition as one whose negation is itself inconsistent.

One might ask why Thrasymachus should be all that worried about avoiding inconsistency: many people get away with inconsistency, and Thrasymachus and his friends were only concerned with what they could get away with. Athens, like Britain, was a free country, and there was no law against contradicting oneself. If I am minded to stand up at Hyde Park Corner, and proclaim that the square on the hypotenuse of a right-angled triangle is not equal to the sum of the squares on the other two sides, nothing very terrible will happen to me. So what is the sanction? Where is the necessity? Plato found an answer. He discovered the Law of Non-Contradiction. He formulates it in the fourth book of the *Re-*

---

[24] *Republic* I, 339.

[25] *Phaedo* 101 de.

[26] *Phaedo* 100a.

public, and makes considerable use of it in his own arguing. Even
the most recalcitrant sophist, even Thrasymachus, cannot afford to
be caught out in self-contradiction—because those who contradict
themselves thereby render themselves unintelligible, and cease to
be talking comprehensible Greek, and are merely exercising their
vocal chords in meaningless babble. There is thus some constraint
on what can be meaningfully said, and some sanction even against
the most determined sceptic. From this necessity of avoiding inconsistency there follows a canon of coercive argument.

Schools of Mathematical Philosophy

	Empiricism	Platonism	Formal Logicism
Leading Exponents	Protagoras Mill Gillies Kitcher	Early Plato Hardy Gödel	Late Plato Frege Russell
How Do We Know?	By Observation	By Thinking *A Priori*	Deducing
What Are We Talking About?	Empirical Phenomena	εἴδη Forms (or Patterns)	Propositions
What Happens If You Do Not See?	Abandon Thesis	Change Your Subject	You Can't Be Understood

Table 1.8.1

If I cannot maintain, with any hope of being understood, an
inconsistent set of propositions, then if I allow all except one of that
set of propositions to be true, I cannot myself deny the negation of
the remaining proposition in my own mouth or gainsay its negation
in anyone else's. That is, I cannot, on pain of inconsistency, refuse
to concede the negation of that proposition, having acknowledged
the others to be true. And this is what it is to be a *deductive*

argument. In symbols, if

$$P,\ Q,\ R\ \vdash$$

then

$$P,\ Q\ \vdash\ \neg R$$

that is,

> if $P,\ Q,\ R$ together are inconsistent,
>
> then $P,\ Q$ together entail $\neg R$).

Plato was immensely taken with deductive argument. Many simple mathematical arguments can be put in deductive form, and then possess the sense of necessity that simple seeing is unable to convey. Later we shall argue that inconsistency is not the only sanction a reasonable man is sensitive to, and that Plato has in consequence construed mathematical argument too narrowly.[27] But almost all philosophers have followed Plato in taking deductive argument as the paradigm of valid argument, and seeking to explicate all mathematical reasoning in terms of it alone.

1.9　Whence the Premises?

In the sixth and seventh books of the *Republic*[28] Plato continued the theory of argument he began in the *Phaedo*. Although it is easy to formulate and apply a negative criterion for rejecting a thesis—a thesis is to be rejected if it is inconsistent—it is more difficult to apply the positive criterion. The positive criterion—that a thesis is to be accepted if it deductively follows from premises acknowledged to be true—is applicable *provided* some premises are acknowledged to be true. But the same question then arises about them. Whenever we try to justify mathematics in terms of deductive logic alone, we are faced with the problem of where we are going to get our initial premises from.

There are three possibilities: the premises may be self-evident, and should be granted without demur; they may be established as following from other already established premises; or they some may be simply postulated—granted for the sake of argument perhaps —but with no justification offered for their truth. Each of

---

[27]　§6.6, §7.5, and §14.6.

[28]　*Republic*, 509-535.

Status of Axioms

The Axiomatic approach can be developed in three ways:

1. The axioms are self-evident; epistemological Platonism and traditional geometry
2. The axioms are truths of logic, and can be proved; Logicism
3. The axioms are neither true nor false; Formalism

---

these possibilities has been adopted by some thinkers, and gives rise to a different philosophy of mathematics.

That some propositions should be self-evident is not evidently absurd—the American Declaration of Independence is not to be laughed out of court. Although it is not clear how we come to know self-evident truths, many truths have seemed self-evident to many thinkers down the ages. In particular, Euclid's postulates were generally taken to express self-evident truths. In the next chapter we shall explore that approach in seeking to understand geometry in the light of principles we can reasonably regard as self-evident.

If not self-evident, then What?

perhaps justified?

But Plato is uneasy. He feels impelled to try and give an account, λόγον διδόναι (*logon didonai*), of the suppositions, ὑπο-θέσεις (*hupotheseis*), to free them from their hypothetical status and show that they are really to be believed, not just supposed. These are axioms, ἀξιώματα, things worthy to be believed. For Plato they are truths yet to be established, but in due course to be vindicated. That can be done. We can justify the axioms of one system by showing them to be theorems of another, seemingly less open to question. Plato here shows himself to be proto-Logicist. The Logicists hope to derive the whole of mathematics from pure logic, which can plausibly be regarded as a starting point that does not need to be supposed, but can be taken for granted without further question. The Logicist programme, which will be further discussed in Chapters Four, Five and Six, has been very influential, even if not completely successful on the terms originally set. But

Plato is still uneasy. However far we go back, there will always be some fundamental system whose axioms are in need of justification without there being any more fundamental system within which they can be established as theorems. At the end of the sixth book of the *Republic*, he embarks on the search for the ἀρχή ἀνυπόθετος (*arche anupothetos*), the unpostulated starting point for all mathematical argument, but does not really find it,[29] although he thinks it has something to do with the Form of the Good, ἡ ἰδέα τοῦ ἀγαθοῦ (*he idea tou agathou*). There is an impression of his trying to perform a logical version of the Indian rope trick. The ἀρχή ἀνυπόθετος (*arche anupothetos*) will always elude us, if the only method of establishing truth is a deductive proof from premises.

If the premises are not self-evident and cannot be justified, the only recourse is to postulate them. It is indisputable, once postulates have been granted, that they have been granted, and since the whole argument depends on their being granted, no further argument can arise on that score. The Formalist, by lowering his sights from what is alleged to be true to what has actually been conceded, achieves a correspondingly greater degree of certainty. Plato himself felt this, and the geometers who carried through his programme of axiomatization bear witness to the same tendency in not attempting to justify the hypotheses, but simply demanding that certain assumptions be granted, and going on from there. The Greek word αἴτημα, *aitema*, like the English word 'postulate' carries the sense of the imperative (or optative) rather than the indicative mood, much better than the word ἀξίωμα, *axioma*, does. The axiomatic approach is, as far as the axioms are concerned, "*fiat*ory" rather than justificatory. And it is reasonable then to enquire whether in view of the difficulties in finding an ultimate justification for first principles, we should not adopt a Formalist philosophy of mathematics.

If not justified, then What?

perhaps postulated?

The Greeks were not driven far along the *fiat*ory track, and never sought to formalise mathematics completely, but the fact that

---

[29] But see further below, §3.7.

Plato's successors were driven to postulate axioms and stipulate some definitions, raises the question why Plato did not himself adopt an explicitly Formalist approach. An answer can be read out of two dark passages in the *Republic*, in which Plato is criticizing the methodology of geometers in his own day, and in which he almost anticipates the criticisms we might have made of Hilbert's programme for mathematics in the 1920s and 1930s. He says[30]

> You know of course how students of subjects like geometry and arithmetic begin by positing odd and even numbers, or the various figures and the three kinds of angle, and other such data in each subject. These data they take as known; and, having adopted them as assumptions, they do no feel called upon to give an account of them to themselves or to anyone else, but treat them as self-evident. Then, starting from these assumptions, they go on until they arrive, by a series of consistent steps, at all the conclusions they set out to investigate.

> Geometry and allied studies do to some extent apprehend reality; but cannot yield anything clearer than a dream-like vision of reality, so long as they leave the postulates they use unshaken and cannot give any rationale of them. If your premise is something you do not know, and your conclusion and the intermediate steps are a tissue of things you do not know, and your conclusion and the intermediate steps are a tissue of things you do not know, by what mechanism can this mere formal consistency become a real science.

Plato is not exactly right. It is not a tissue of consistency, but of validity, itself based on *in*consistency, that is characteristic of a Formalist approach. Nevertheless his criticism is astonishingly prescient, and might well have been written in the twentieth century AD rather than the fourth century BC.[31] It recognises a trade-off between validity and vacuity. If we insist on more and more cogent canons of validity, we can have them, and ensure that what we

---

[30] *Republic* VI, 510c2-d3, VII, 533b6-c5; tr. F.M.Cornford, pp.220, 248.

[31] Compare Bertrand Russell, "Mathematics and the Metaphysicians", reprinted in *Mysticism and Logic*, p.75 of Penguin edition, and quoted by Robin Gandy, "Thus mathematics may be defined as the subject in which we never know what we are talking about nor whether what we are saying is true."

assert cannot be gainsaid by anyone, no matter how unreasonable. But we achieve this by evacuating what we say of all content. Instead of saying that a 3-4-5 triangle is a right-angled triangle, I say merely that *if* you grant me Euclid's axioms, then you cannot on pain of inconsistency deny me Pythagoras' theorem, and so must in particular allow that a 3-4-5 triangle is a right-angled triangle. But why should you grant me Euclid's axioms? Plato feels that he must give a reason, even though he cannot do so satisfactorily. A Formalist, by contrast, reckons that no reason can be given or even asked for; Euclid's axioms are just the way he wants to proceed. They are constitutive of Euclidean geometry. There is no reason why you should do Euclidean geometry, but if you are going to, then you must accept Euclid's axioms. It is like cricket: there is no reason why you must leave the wicket if you are bowled; it is a free country, and if you choose to stay at the wicket after your mid-stump has been sent flying by the bowler, there is no law against it. Only, you are not playing cricket then. To play cricket is simply to abide by the rules of cricket, and to do Euclidean geometry is similarly constituted by our abiding by Euclidean axioms. There is nothing wrong, either legally or morally, in doing non-Euclidean geometry, any more than there is in playing rounders or American baseball. All the Formalist says is that non-Euclidean geometry is not Euclidean geometry, and if you do not accept the axioms of Euclidean geometry you are not playing the Euclidean game.

But mathematics does not seem to be just a game. Mathematical propositions present themselves as being meaningful and as being true. Both the meaningfulness and the truth of mathematical propositions are lost on a strict formalist account of mathematics. Although the postulates can be construed as constituting an *implicit* definition of the terms employed, they fail to characterize them uniquely and so do not succeed in defining them properly.[32] And much more obviously, deductive arguments can establish the truth of the conclusion only if the truth of the premises can be satisfactorily shown, and not merely assumed.

This is why Plato, although impelled towards the Formalist approach, does not go the whole way with it. He wants to give his mathematics content, and therefore cannot be content merely to postulate his axioms, but must seek to establish them on a firm log-

---

[32] See below, §2.4, §6.3.

ical basis, which will make them both meaningful and true. Plato, although much attracted by the rigour of the Formalist approach, and the satisfactory answer it gives to the third of our questions— *what happens if you don't see a mathematical argument?*—is repelled by the concomitant vacuity of mathematical propositions, and the unsatisfactory answer given to the first of our questions— what are we talking about?. That still is the most obvious and telling objection to Formalism.

Plato's axiomatic approach cannot be altogether adopted for reasons that he himself was dimly aware of. But we can pursue each option further than he did. In the next chapter we shall consider the discipline where the first alternative, namely that the axioms really are neither postulated nor derived but in some other way incontrovertibly worthy to be believed, has seemed plausible— geometry. Under modern scrutiny the appearance of self-evident truth has diminished, and many geometers espouse a form of Formalism intended to escape Plato's charge of meaninglessness. It will be discussed in chapter three. In chapters four, five and six we shall pursue a "soft logicist" programme, in which we press back the assumptions, τὰς ὑποθέσεις ἀναιροῦσα (*tas hupotheseis anairousa*), no longer taking axioms for granted or simply postulating them, but seeking to justify them, if not by deduction, then in other ways, which will make it reasonable to accept them, though not actually inconsistent to deny them.

Chapter 2
Geometry

2.1 Euclid

> **If not Logicism, then What?**

Holes have been picked in Euclid's arguments in the last hundred years. Hilbert uncovered a number of assumptions Euclid failed to make explicit.[1] A full formulation of the axioms necessary for the rigorous development of Euclidean geometry is now available. It is much more complicated, and much less intelligible, than Euclid's presentation, and we should ask ourselves what exactly the point of axiomatization is. Euclid high-lighted certain assumptions he needed in order to prove geometrical theorems, but took others— assumptions of order and of continuity—for granted. They are not assumptions we normally question, although undoubtedly they can be questioned. If we want absolute formal rigour, as Hilbert did, then we should make all our assumptions absolutely explicit, as Hilbert did, and produce a formally valid proof-sequence. But we achieve formal rigour at a price. Whereas Euclid's presentation is intelligible and has immense intellectual appeal, Hilbert's is unintelligible, except to those who already know their geometry

---

[1] David Hilbert, *Foundations of Geometry*, originally published as *Grundlagen der Geometrie*, Leipzig, 1899.

backwards, and has no appeal for the wider public. Contemporary opinion among philosophers of mathematics discounts this, and regards Hilbert as having done a proper job which Euclid did only imperfectly. But this is to assume a formalist standpoint which is itself open to question. Without decrying the value of Hilbert's work from the formalist point of view, we may wonder whether this was what Euclid was, or should have been, trying to do. Outside formal logic, the axiomatic approach remains much more in the spirit of Euclid than of Hilbert. Physicists often present Newtonian mechanics, the Special Theory of Relativity, the General Theory of Relativity, or quantum mechanics, in terms of axioms, which high-light the peculiar assumptions of the theory in question, but take a lot else for granted. It is a perfectly reasonable procedure, not only for introducing the subject to schoolboys, but for identifying it concisely for professionals. For the most part, in identifying or expounding Euclidean geometry our need is to distinguish the peculiar features of that geometry from others which might reasonably be put forward instead. That each line defines an order and is continuous is not normally in question, and it only clutters up communication to anticipate questions that are not going to be asked. Brevity is not only the soul of wit, but the condition of communication. Total explicitness is not only often uncalled for, but obfuscatory. Euclid should not be criticized for his lack of rigour, but praised for his sense of relevance.

2.2 The Fifth Postulate

Plato's programme was premature. But geometry was axiomatized, the programme being carried out by Eudoxus and Euclid, who succeeded in deriving it all from five special axioms or postulates, in Greek αἰτήματα (*aitemata*), together with some general notions, κοιναὶ ἔννοια (*koinai ennoiai*), of a purely logical character, *e.g.* that if a is equal to b and c is equal to b, then a is equal to c.

The five postulates Euclid wanted us to grant were:
1. To draw a straight line from any point to any point.
2. To produce a finite straight line continuously in a straight line.
3. To describe a circle with any centre and diameter.
4. All right angles are equal to one another.
5. If a straight line falling on two straight lines makes the interior angles on the same side less than two right angles, the two straight lines, if produced indefinitely, meet on that side on which are the

angles less than two right angles.

These were generally taken to express self-evident truths. This is somewhat surprising, in that the first three are not really propositions at all, but instructions expressed in the infinitive, and the last too complex to be self-evident—no finite man can see it to be true, because no finite man can see indefinitely far to make sure that the two lines actually do meet in every case. Many other formulations of the fifth postulate have been offered, both in the ancient and in the modern world, in the hope of their being more self-evidently true. Among them we should note:

a) From a point not on a given line one and only one line can be drawn parallel to the given line. (Playfair)

b) The sum of the angles of a triangle equals two right angles.

c) Given a figure, another figure is possible which is similar to the given figure and of any size whatever. (Wallis)

d) There exist two unequal triangles with equal angles. (Saccheri—and perhaps also Plato)

e) In a right-angled triangle, the square on the hypotenuse equals the sum of the squares on the other two sides. (Pythagoras)

It is far from obvious that these propositions are equivalent. Playfair's is the closest to Euclid's, and can be regarded as a modern version of it, explicitly mentioning parallel lines, and alone deserving the name "parallel postulate". The triangle property, that the sum of the angles of a triangle equals two right angles, is fairly easily shown to be equivalent. Much more significant are the axioms about similar triangles, put forward in a stronger form by John Wallis, an Oxford don of the Seventeenth Century, and in a weaker by Geralamo Saccheri, a Jesuit priest in the Eighteenth Century. Granted Wallis' axiom (c), we can prove that the sum of the angles of a triangle equals two right angles, as in Figure 2.2.1.

Another argument, displayed in Figure 2.2.2, shows that Pythagoras' theorem is easily proved by means of similar triangles.

We may ask, on behalf of generations of schoolboys who have struggled with Euclid's "windmill" proof of his proposition 1.47, why Euclid preferred his much more cumbersome proof. The answer lies in the last assumption in the proof given in Figure 2.2.2, and the difficulties due to the existence of incommensurable magnitudes, itself established as a consequence of Pythagoras' theorem. The *Meno* argument shows that the diagonal of a square has length $\sqrt{2}$ times that of the sides. But $\sqrt{2}$, as Pythagoras or one of his

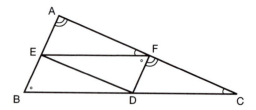

Figure 2.2.1 Proof of $\triangle$ from Wallis: let ABC be a triangle. Let $\triangle AFE \approx \triangle ABC$ and half the linear size. Then

$$\frac{AF}{AB} = \frac{AE}{AC} = \frac{FE}{BC} = \frac{1}{2}$$

So $AF = FB$ and $AE = EC$.
Let $BD = DC$, and hence $FE = BD = DC$.
Then (some argument left out here) $\triangle CED \approx \triangle CAB$, whence $ED = (1/2)AB = FB$.
So in $\triangle EFD$ and $\triangle BDF$ $EF = BD$, $DE = FB$, and FD is common.
So $\triangle EFD \equiv \triangle BDF$, and $\angle DEF = \angle FBD$.
But $\angle BCA = \angle FEA$ and $\angle CAB = \angle CED$
[and $\angle ABC = \angle FBD$].
So $\angle ABC + \angle BCA + \angle CAB = 180°$.

followers discovered, cannot be expressed as the ratio of two whole numbers, and the similar triangles approach, which says that the ratios of the sides in similar triangles is equal is therefore suspect. Euclid later, in his theory of proportion, almost anticipated Dedekind's definition of a real number, but in his geometrical exposition preferred the technically more complicated but conceptually less suspect approach which did not invoke similar triangles at all.

A chance remark in the *Gorgias* suggests that Plato was thinking about similar triangles at about the time he was seeking to establish the foundations of geometry. In *Gorgias* 508a5-7 he distinguishes "geometrical" from "arithmetical" equality, the former being only proportionate, whereas the latter is a strict equality. Aristotle takes up the distinction in his *Nicomachean Ethics*, and again in his *Politics*, and makes it the basis of his exegesis of dis-

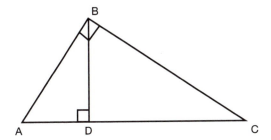

Figure 2.2.2 Proof of Pythagoras by Similar Triangles: let $\triangle ABC$ have B a right angle. Drop perpendicular from B to AC at D. Then $\triangle ADB \approx \triangle ABC$ and $\triangle BDC \approx \triangle ABC$.

$$\text{So } \frac{AD}{AB} = \frac{AB}{AC}$$

$$AD.AC = BC^2$$

$$\text{and } \frac{DC}{BC} = \frac{BC}{AC}$$

$$DC.AC = BC^2$$

So $(AD + DC).AC = AB^2 + BC^2$. So $AC^2 = AB^2 + BC^2$. [We have assumed that angles of $\triangle$ add up to $180°$, and that AD/AB *etc.* are well behaved.]

tributive justice. Plato and Aristotle saw that there was some universality about the concept of justice, and that justice require that we treat like alike, but wanted to avoid the implication that what was sauce for the goose was necessarily and always sauce for the gander; justice, Plato argued, required that we treat like cases alike, but also that we treat unlike cases differently. "Geometrical equality" enabled Plato and Aristotle to reconcile the underlying principle that there should be some similarity of treatment for all with there being differences of actual treatment in different circumstances. Each person should be given their fair share, said Aristotle, but their fair share was proportional to their ἀξία (*axia*), their merit, and this depended on circumstances. This distinction blunted the edge of the egalitarian arguments of fifth-century Athens, and had important consequences for political thought in the ancient world.

The proof of Pythagoras' theorem is the culmination of Euclid's first book, and we have indicated how it can be proved not merely from Euclid's own fifth postulate but from Wallis' proposition about similar triangles. It is natural to ask whether it can in turn be proved from Pythagoras' theorem taken as an axiom. In fact it can. It is easiest to show Saccheri's axiom (d), that, granted the Pythagorean proposition, there must be two triangles of the same shape but different sizes.

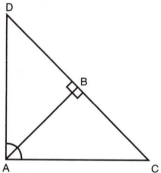

Figure 2.2.3 Proof of Saccheri from Pythagoras: let $\angle ABC$ be a right angle; let $BA = CB$. Extend CB to D so that $BD = CB$. Then $\triangle ABC \equiv \triangle ABD$; so $AD = AC$ and $\angle BDA = \angle BCA$, and, since $\triangle ABC \equiv \triangle DBA$, $\angle BAC = \angle ADB$.

$$\text{By Pythagoras} \quad AC^2 = BA^2 + CB^2$$
$$= 2CB^2$$
$$AD^2 = BA^2 + BD^2$$
$$= 2BD^2 = 2CB^2$$
$$AC^2 + AD^2 = 4CB^2$$
$$= CD^2.$$

So $\angle CAD$ is a right angle, and $\triangle ABC \approx \triangle CAD$ QED.

It is only slightly more complicated—and left to the reader—to give a procedure for constructing a triangle of arbitrary size similar to a given triangle. The fact that the Pythagorean proposition, instead of being taken as a theorem to be proved from Euclid's axioms, could be taken as itself being the characteristic axiom of that geometry suggests that we might rename Euclidean geometry "Pythagorean geometry". Although Euclid, along with Plato and Eudoxus, was responsible for its being systematized as an axiomatic theory, we shall be led to regard the Pythagorean proposition as being from some points of view its most characteristic and fundamental feature.[2]

The alternative formulations of the fifth postulate are less cumbersome and may be more acceptable than Euclid's own version, but they are none of them so self-evident that they cannot be questioned. Certainly Pythagoras' theorem is far from being obviously true, something that should be granted without more ado. In fact, none of the alternative formulations was felt to be completely obvious, and they all seemed in need of some further justification. Both Wallis and Saccheri were seeking a better justification,[3] and Saccheri devoted years to trying to prove the fifth postulate by a *reductio ad absurdum*, assuming it to be false and trying to derive a contradiction. The attempt failed, but in the course of it he unwittingly discovered non-Euclidean geometry. The theorems of this non-Euclidean geometry were so strange that Saccheri took them to be absurd, even though he could not derive a formal inconsistency; but, though strange, they were really quite consistent, and were later recognised to be theorems of a certain sort of non-Euclidean geometry, "hyperbolic" geometry as it came to be called.

2.3 Non-Euclidean Geometries

Hyperbolic geometry was first discovered as such by Bolyai, a Hungarian, and independently by Lobachevsky, a Russian, at the beginning of the Nineteenth Century. Instead of Playfair's postulate that from a point not on a given line one and only one line can be drawn parallel to the given line, they postulated that from a point

---

[2] See further below, §2.8.

[3] John Wallis, *"De Postulato Quinto"*, *Opera Mathematica*, Oxford, 1693, vol ii, pp.665-678; Gerolamo Saccheri, *Euclides ab omni naevo vindicatus*, Milan, 1733, tr. George Bruce Holland, Chicago, 1920.

not on a given line more than one, indeed infinitely many, lines could be drawn parallel to the given line. Later in the Nineteenth Century Riemann modified the parallel postulate the other way, so that not even one parallel line could be drawn; this required some other modification of the other axioms, but with such a modification produced another consistent non-Euclidean geometry, which was called "Elliptical" geometry.

Non-Euclidean geometries are strange, but seem less so now that we are familiar with them than when Saccheri first encountered them. It is easiest to visualise non-Euclidean elliptic geometry by considering the surface of some sphere, such as that of the earth or of an orange. It is easy then to see that if great circles are taken to be "lines", there are no parallel lines in elliptic geometry. Any two great circles meet; indeed, they meet not once but twice, as the meridians of longitude meet at both the North Pole and at the South Pole. (The so-called "parallels of latitude" are not parallels at all, because they are not, under this interpretation, straight lines, but, rather, circles.) If we consider an octant of an orange, or the spherical triangle on the earth's surface marked off by the meridian of Greenwich, the Equator, and longitude 90° West, we see that it has a right angle at each vertex, so that the sum of its angles adds up to three right angles, 270°, instead of only two right angles, 180°. A smaller triangle will have the sum of its angles nearer to 180°, to which it will tend as the triangle gets smaller and smaller. Indeed, if we know how big the angles are, we can tell what the sides must be; the only spherical triangles with each of their angles 90° are those whose sides are one quarter of the circumference of a great circle. This illustrates the Wallis–Saccheri thesis that there are no similar triangles of different size in this non-Euclidean geometry. It is easily seen in the case of the octant that the Pythagorean proposition is far from true, for in that case $\mathbf{h} = \mathbf{a} = \mathbf{b}$. In the same way the circumference of a circle drawn on the surface of a sphere is less than $2\pi r$. If we take the North Pole as centre and have a radius of one quarter of a great circle, we should draw the Equator, whose length is not $2\pi \times ((1/4)\times$ (a great circle)) but just (a great circle): that is to say, the ratio of the circumference to the radius of this circle is not 2π but 4. The surface of a sphere has positive curvature: if we consider two mutually orthogonal planes intersecting along a line which is itself perpendicular to the surface, each plane intersects the surface in a curve whose concave side lies in the same direction as the other's; their product, therefore, which defines the curvature of the surface, is positive, whichever way the concave sides face.

Elliptic Geometry
Riemann
No parallel (symbolically E_0)
$\triangle$ more than 180° (symbolically $\triangle_>$)
$h^2 < a^2 + b^2$ (symbolically $P_<$)
circumference $< 2\pi r$ (symbolically $O_<$)
surface of sphere
positive curvature (symbolically C_+)

Table 2.3.1

It is much more difficult to envisage a surface with negative curvature. The surface of a saddle, or a mountain pass, is an example. On such a surface the circumference of a circle is more than 2π times the radius, and correspondingly the square on the hypotenuse is greater than the sum of the squares on the other two sides. It is less easy to see that the sum of the angles of a triangle is less than $180°$, but if we consider how a very small divergence in one's path on a mountain pass can lead to widely separated destinations, we can accept that a triangle could have its angles adding up to less than $180°$. If we take this triangle feature to the limit, it follows that there is a minimum area of a triangle. This once again shows how the Wallis–Saccheri postulate fails for non-Euclidean geometry. It also draws attention to another feature of non-Euclidean geometries. Both hyperbolic and elliptic geometry have "natural units"; in hyperbolic geometry there is a minimum area a triangle can have, and in elliptic geometry there is a maximum length a line can have. (This is why for elliptic geometry we need to modify

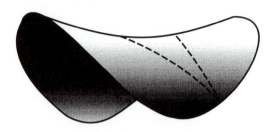

Figure 2.3.1 A saddle showing a triangle with angles all nearly zero, but still encompassing a substantial area

not only Euclid's fifth postulate but his second, which takes it for granted that a straight line can be extended indefinitely far.)

Non-Euclidean geometries remain strange. We can bring ourselves to have some understanding of them and to visualise them to some extent, but they have features that are unfamiliar and may remain unwelcome even after prolonged acquaintance, but that is not to say that they are inconsistent. And in fact non-Euclidean geometries *are* consistent.

It is easy to say that a geometry is consistent, difficult to show it. Saccheri had concluded that the system he was investigating was so absurd as to be inconsistent, and who was to prove him wrong? In the end Felix Klein did prove him wrong, by means of a "relative consistency proof" of a type that has come to be of great importance in the foundations of mathematics. Klein produced a model of hyperbolic geometry in Euclidean geometry. He considered part of the Euclidean plane—the interior of a given circle—and by redescribing the interior of that circle in a particular way showed that under the new description the axioms of hyperbolic geometry were satisfied. He then argued that if they were after all inconsistent, then there would be a corresponding inconsistency in the Euclidean plane, and Euclidean geometry would be inconsistent too. So, contrapositively, hyperbolic geometry was consistent provided Euclidean was; hyperbolic geometry was consistent relative to Euclidean geometry.

Klein's own proof is complicated. We can appreciate the thrust of his argument if we consider instead a relative consistency proof

Hyperbolic Geometry
Bolyai, Lobachevsky
More than one parallel (symbolically E_+)
$\triangle$ less than 180° (symbolically $\triangle_<$)
$h^2 > a^2 + b^2$ (symbolically $P_>$)
circumference $> 2\pi r$ (symbolically $O_>$)
surface of saddle or mountain pass
negative curvature (symbolically C_-)

Table 2.3.2

by means of the models just given. The axioms of two-dimensional elliptic geometry are satisfied on the surface of a sphere, with points in elliptic geometry being represented by points on the surface of the sphere, and lines in elliptic geometry being represented by great circles on the surface of the sphere. If the axioms of elliptic geometry were inconsistent, then we could produce a proof-sequence, as shown in Table 2.3.3, in which every line (represented on the left-hand side of the table) was a well-formed formula of elliptic geometry, and either was an axiom or followed from one or more previous lines by some rule of inference, and the last line was of the form $A \wedge \neg A$. But now consider this proof-sequence not as a sequence of well-formed formulae about points and lines in elliptic geometry, but as well-formed formulae about points and great circles in a two-dimensional subspace of three-dimensional Euclidean geometry (represented on the right-hand side of the table). What were axioms under the elliptic interpretation are now true propositions and can be proved from the axioms of three-dimensional Euclidean geometry represented by additional lines at the top of the proof-sequence on the right-hand side). We could therefore fill out our proof-sequence to prove these from the axioms of three-dimensional Euclidean geometry. If the proof in elliptic geometry ended in a well-formed formula of the form $A \wedge \neg A$, the proof in three-dimensional Euclidean geometry would end in a well-formed formula of the form $A' \wedge \neg A'$, which essentially is of the form $A \wedge \neg A$ too, and three-dimensional Euclidean geometry would be inconsistent also. So granted that three-dimensional Euclidean geometry is not inconsistent, elliptic geometry is not inconsistent either; that is to say, granted that three-dimensional Euclidean geometry is consistent, then elliptic geometry is too.

Elliptic Plane Geometry		3-dimensional Euclidean Geometry
		· · · · · · extra
		· · · · · · extra
		· · · · · · extra
———	translates into · · · · · ·	
———	translates into · · · · · ·	
———	translates into · · · · · ·	
———	translates into · · · · · ·	
$A \wedge \neg A$	translates into $A' \wedge \neg A'$	

Table 2.3.3

Non-Euclidean geometries are thus vindicated on the score of consistency. And in the absence of downright inconsistency mathematicians have been hard put to it to justify excluding them on any other grounds.

2.4 Formal and Physical Geometry

Euclidean geometry was dethroned. It was a great upset. It was thought that the foundations of truth had been entirely shaken, and that God was no longer in His heaven, because Euclidean geometry was no longer true. Established ways of thinking were unsettled in much the same way as they were by Einstein's theory of relativity at the beginning of the twentieth century. Philosophers were forced to rethink the status of geometry. They concluded that geometry could be regarded in two ways. It could be regarded formally; in that case it was simply a consistent formal system in which certain conclusions followed from given axioms; or it could be regarded substantially, as making substantial assertions about the external world of space and matter, in which case it was open to falsification in the same way as any other scientific theory, much as Protagoras had held. We shall consider these two alternatives in turn.

If not Self-evidence, then What?

perhaps Formalism after all

If we take geometry to be simply a formal system in which conclusions follow from premises or axioms, we are not concerned with semantics or interpretations of geometrical terms, but only the syntactical properties they are given by the formation rules, rules of inference and axioms. Thus all we can say is that *given* Euclid's axioms Pythagoras' theorem follows; or, formally,

Euclid ⊢ Pythagoras

This is simply a formal derivation in first-order logic, and can be equivalently expressed by the deduction theorem

⊢ Euclid → Pythagoras

which would be a theorem of first-order logic in a system to which had been adjoined some additional symbols but no extra axioms. On the formal analysis there is nothing special about the axioms. We have complete freedom to choose any axioms we like. This is good news for graduates doing research: instead of being confined to just Euclidean geometry, they have a whole range of other geometries which may be investigated and written about; at the very least, we have increased the supply of topics by a factor of three, and if we start altering other Euclidean postulates, besides the fifth, the supply is increased very much more. But there is a cost. Formal freedom is purchased at the cost of substantial vacuity. As we depart further from the Euclidean prototype, the geometries become more weird and less real, and we seem more to be doodling with meaningless marks on bits of paper and less to be discovering anything significant or true. An example is given by the rules of a certain lunch club.[4]

---

[4] Quoted from C.W.O'Hara and D.R.Ward, *An Introduction to Projective Geometry*, Oxford, 1937, pp.17-18; and Morris R. Cohen and Ernest Nagel, *An Introduction to Logic and Scientific Method*, London, 1961, Ch.VII, 3,

(1) Periodical lunches were to be given by the club, and they were to be attended only by members of the club.

(2) Every member of the club was to meet every other member at least once, but not more than once, at one of the club's lunches.

(3) The lists of members selected by the Secretary to attend any two lunches were never to be entirely different; at least one member was to be present at both.

(4) The President, the Treasurer, and the Secretary were to be the only members present at the first lunch, and at all subsequent lunches there were to be at least three members present.

These rules are, on the face of it, perfectly straightforward, but on further examination, especially in the context of a discussion of geometry, may seem fishy. And, indeed, they are. They are the axioms of incidence of a finite projective geometry, with 'member' doing duty for a point, and 'lunch' for a line, and 'attending' for being on. Formally, if we concentrate on the syntactical structure of the system implicitly defined by these axioms and take no account of their interpretation or substantial content, there is no difference between the axioms of a finite projective geometry and the rules of a lunch club. We can, if we like, call the study of such a formal system "geometry", but we could equally well call it "lunchology", and, remembering Plato's criticisms,[5] wonder whether lunchology was a study worthy of a grown man. The purely formal characterization of geometry fails to capture what is specifically geometrical about it. Lunch clubs have nothing to do with γεωμετρεῖν (*geometrein*), measuring the earth.

If not Formalism, then What?
                    perhaps Formal Empiricism
                    (or Protagoreanism) after all

The standard modern view has been to distinguish the purely formal syntactic approach from a semantic one which is more in the tradition of Protagoras. We consider not just the axioms of geometry, say those of Euclid, but those axioms in conjunction with a physical interpretation. The standard physical interpretation is that under which light rays are taken to be straight lines.

pp.137-138.

[5] *Republic* VII, 533b6-c5; quoted above, in §1.9.

Instead then of postulating the axioms of Euclidean geometry, we should consider the conjunction of those axioms with a physical interpretation, and ask whether they were in point of fact really true. Riemann asked this question, and considered not the Pythagorean proposition, which we may abbreviate **Pyth**, but △, whether the angles of a triangle added up to 180°, and measured the angles at the tops of three distant mountains, and found that within the limits of observational accuracy they did. In this way geometry could be regarded as an empirical science, and verified in the same way as any physical theory might be, and thus far found true. Protagoras has been re-instated.

Poincaré develops this argument to reach the opposite conclusion. Since the thesis that is subjected to empirical check is not just the set of Euclid's axioms but the conjunction of Euclid's axioms with a certain physical interpretation, we can always hold on to Euclid's axioms, provided we make suitable adjustments to the interpretation. Provided light rays are allowed not to define straight lines, then even if the measured angles of a triangle do not add up to 180° the truth of Euclidean geometry is not impugned.[6]

Although Poincaré is making an important point, which needs serious consideration, his use of the word 'convention' is unfortunate. Real conventions are ones where there is absolutely nothing to choose between two courses of action—*e.g.* whether to drive on the right side or the left side of the road, or whether to regard multiplications as more or less binding, so far as omitted brackets go, than addition—and we need to have a rule in order to be able to understand one another and concert our actions. The choice of a geometry is not like this. There may be good grounds, perhaps empirical, perhaps not, for choosing between one geometry and another. Hempel claims that there are.[7] He argues that we should consider not just the simplicity of the geometry but also that of the geometry *together with* the physical interpretation. If there are two

---

[6] H.Poincaré, *Science and Hypothesis*, tr., pbk., New York, 1952, chs. III, IV and V; excerpted as "Non-Euclidean Geometries and the Non-Euclidean World", in H.Feigl and M.Brodbeck, *Readings in the Philosophy of Science*, New York, 1953, pp.171-180.

[7] C.G.Hempel, "Geometry and Physical Science", *American Mathematical Monthly*, **52**, 1945; reprinted in H.Feigl and Wilfrid Sellars, *Readings in Philosophical Analysis*, New York, 1949, pp.238-249.

physical interpretations, $PhysInt_1$ and $PhysInt_2$, then sometimes Euclid + $PhysInt_1$ may be more complicated than Riemann + $PhysInt_2$, and so we have rational grounds for preferring the latter, even though the former may be consistent with the observed facts. Hempel suggests that we should choose the best, that is, the simplest, combination of geometrical axioms and physical interpretation taken together. If we think of different physical interpretations $PhysInt_1$, $PhysInt_2$, $PhysInt_3$, we shall have different semantic interpretations of the axioms and theorems of geometry, which we can represent by $\models$.

So we might have $PhysInt_1 \models$ **Pyth**

where **Pyth** is the Pythagorean proposition,

but $PhysInt_2 \models \neg$**Pyth**

and $PhysInt_3 \models \neg$**Pyth**,

so that although there was an interpretation, say $PhysInt_1$, under which **Pyth** was true, nevertheless we were more concerned with another interpretation, say $PhysInt_2$, under which **Pyth** was false. If, for example, $PhysInt_2$ is one in which straight lines are taken to be light rays, then although Riemann's experiment confirmed the thesis $\triangle_=$, that the angles of a triangle add up to 180° to within the limits of accuracy available terrestrially in his day, we now have theories, adequately confirmed by observation, according to which triangles defined by light rays have angles adding up to more than 180°.

So $PhysInt_2 \models \neg\triangle_=$,

and, correspondingly, $PhysInt_2 \models \neg$**Pyth**.

Although we could stick to Euclidean geometry *coûte que coûte*, it would be unreasonable to do so; the combination of an elliptic geometry with Einstein's General Theory is a better buy than Euclidean geometry together with some enormously complicated physics, which interpreted lines in such a way—$PhysInt_1$—that $PhysInt_1 \models$ **Pyth**, but at the cost of a whole lot of *ad hoc* hypotheses and a number of implausible assumptions.

2.5 Conceptual Constraints

Hempel's exposition is beautifully clear, his arguments have much cogency, and his conclusions have been widely accepted, so much so that they constitute the current orthodoxy. Nevertheless they are open to criticism. Although he is entirely right in insisting, as against Poincaré, that we need to consider not just a geometry by itself but the combination of a geometry with an interpretation, he concentrates too exclusively on physical interpretations, and does not consider the other constraints that operate. In the first place the very distinction between geometry and physics gives rise to some conceptual pressures that ought to be recognised: and secondly, there are links between some basic concepts of geometry and other concepts outside geometry which greatly limit the range of possible interpretations.

The argument from the General Theory of Relativity is one-sided. We do not have just one unified physical theory which presupposes a particular geometry and can be put to empirical test as a whole, but a number of different theories and many untheoretical views of the natural world. Geometry is not part of one such theory of the physical world, but rather a back-cloth against which many theories, as well as untheoretical views, can operate. There is a division of labour between geometry and physics. Physics is concerned with cause and effect, and seeks to give explanations of phenomena in terms of laws of nature. It is no part of geometry's function to do any of these, but to provide a schema of reference and description which enables propositions about the world to be formulated and discussed, and to discover the relations between different propositions of this sort. Granted such a function, geometry is subject to various requirements. Thus the causal inefficacy of space and time follows from geometry's being not itself involved in giving causal explanations, and in turn imposes conditions of homogeneity and isotropy which are of geometrical consequence.

The separation between geometry and physics may, however, be denied. The programme of geometrodynamics is to bring together physics and geometry, and to reduce physical explanations to geometrical ones. In Einstein's General Theory forces are replaced by a complicated curvature of space. If the programme is successful, then there will be no distinction between geometry and physics, and the objection will fail. So much may be granted. But a programme is not a fact. And if geometrodynamics is successful, what we shall have is not geometry, but geometrodynamics. The possibility of a monistic account of the whole of nature was put forward by Spinoza, and has been vigorously pursued by contemporary physicists. If it is realised in fact, it will engender considerable alterations in our conceptual structure, and the old distinction between geometry and physics will be subverted. But as long as we are talking about geometry and not geometrodynamics, there is a contrast between geometry and physics, and this contrast imposes conceptual constraints on the sort of geometry it is reasonable to adopt.

According to the orthodox account, a point and a straight line are only implicitly defined by the axioms of geometry, and we are entirely free to choose any interpretation which conforms to the axioms. In particular, in plane projective geometry 'point' and 'line' are dual, and we can interchange them without any alteration of meaning or truth: thus in the Lunch Club it makes no difference whether we take a 'member' to be a point, and a 'lunch' to be a line, or *vice versa*. But this is not true. Points and lines are not merely implicitly defined by the axioms: other definitions have been given or attempted which show their other conceptual links. Let us survey them systematically.

We have first some mereological and categorial differences:
1. (i) A point has no parts (Pythagoras)
   (ii) A point has position but no magnitude, whereas
   (i′) A straight line has parts
   (ii′)(a) A straight line has position *and* direction
   (ii′)(b) A straight line has length but no breadth

We have secondly topological differences between a point and a line (not necessarily straight):
2. (i)(a) A point cannot have a boundary, but
      (b) can be a boundary
   (ii)(a) A line can have a point as a boundary, and
      (b) can be a boundary of a surface
   (iii)(a) A surface can have a line as a boundary, and
      (b) can be a boundary of a volume

More generally, we have a number of possible definitions of a straight line. A straight line:
3. (i)   is the shortest distance between two points
   (ii)   is a breadthless length
   (iii) is the path of a light ray

(iv)   looks straight

(v)   has no kinks

(vi)   lies evenly on itself

(vii)   is the axis of a 3-dimensional rotation

(viii) is the intersection of two planes

(ix)   is that of which the middle covers the ends.[8]

Pythagoras' characterization of a point as something that has no parts connects the concept of a point with "mereology" (from the Greek word μέρος (*meros*), part), the study of the *part of* relation.[9] The *part of* relation is an ordering relation, and under that ordering points are the minimal elements. This is also why they are said to have no magnitude: which may be understood either as saying that their size is zero or as saying that the question "How much?" cannot be asked of points at all. Points are being defined in a counter-Anselmian way. Anselm defined God as *id quo maius nequeat cogitari esse*, that than which nothing can be imagined to be greater: if we define a point as that which has no parts, or as that whose magnitude is zero, we are saying in effect that it is *id quo minus nequeat cogitari esse*, that than which nothing can be imagined to be smaller. Points are thus not just entities that satisfy the axioms of some formal geometrical theory but are linked to mereology and Aristotle's category of Quantity, "How much?".

Even if we construe 'having no magnitude' in the definition of a point as meaning that the category of Quantity is inapplicable, the category of Place, "Where?" is applicable. Points have position. We can always ask of a point where it is. There is at least this categorial connexion, and it is one that differentiates points from lines, for of lines we can ask not only where they are, πού (*pou*), but in what direction they go, πόθεν/ποî (*pothen/poi*), whence/whither. As regards mereology, lines are clearly distinct from points, for we can ask of a line one type of "How much?" question, namely "How long?", although we cannot ask "How wide?", or if we do we shall get only a null answer. Hence the definition of a line as a breadthless length. It is minimal in one sort of way, but not in every way, as a point is.

---

[8] Plato, *Parmenides*, 137e3-4.

[9] See below, §9.12, ch.10, and §11.5; but note that the *part of* relation considered there is serial, and has no minimal elements, whereas the Pythagorean definition assumes a *part of* relation that is non-serial.

The distinction implicit in the way in which a line can and cannot have parts is made more explicit in topology. Topology gives an inductive definition of dimension in terms of boundaries. The null set has dimension -1; points, which have no boundaries, have dimension 0; lines, whose boundaries are points, have dimension 1; surfaces, whose boundaries are lines, have dimension 2; and so on. Plato was on the track of this. In the *Meno* he defines a plane figure as the boundary of a solid: στερεοῦ πέρας σχῆμα εἶναι (*stereou peras schema einai*).[10] There is much proto-topology in Plato and Aristotle. Although we think of Kant as the founder of topology, and rightly, we should recognise more than we do the first efforts in that direction made by the Greeks.

Topological characterizations of lines do not imply straightness. A straight line is a particular sort of line, and one way of picking out a straight line from others is, as Hempel correctly remarks, that light travels in straight lines unless reflected or refracted. But this is not the only way; nor is it merely a contingent fact which could just as well have been otherwise. Often, admittedly we rely on the physics of the light ray, as when we look down a ruler's edge to see if it is straight. But this not an arbitrary choice on our part. We can *see* that light goes in straight lines (to within the range of observational exactitude) by looking at the beams cast by the sun through holes in a shutter in a dusty room or through the clerestory windows in a cathedral in winter. From the fact that we can see the light going in straight lines it follows that we must have some other criterion of straightness than simply that it is the path of a light ray. So it cannot be an arbitrary choice of definition on our part. And indeed, if they looked crooked, we should no more look down the edge of a ruler to judge its straightness than we actually judge the straightness of a stick by seeing how it looks when partially immersed in water.

Nor is light our only recourse for determining straightness. If light were not available, or thought to be not reliable, we could test a ruler with a taut string. A straight line is the shortest distance between two points. It is a "geodesic" characterization of straightness, and one much favoured in the General Theory of Relativity. It involves further concepts, such as that of 'distance' and 'being between' points, but they can be at least partly defined without

[10] *Meno*, 76a7.

presupposing that of straight line. A different approach again is to check two straight edges against each other by running them along each other. If they really are straight they will fit snugly together all the time: if both are kinked together, they will fit in one position but not in others. In extreme cases we can see or feel the kinks and reject the line as not being straight out of hand. Straightness excludes kinks, which are points of singularity. In this we are following Euclid's definition of a straight line as one which lies "evenly on itself". In modern parlance a straight line has perfect translational symmetry along itself. It also has perfect rotational symmetry around itself. An axis of rotation is a straight line, and I could test a thin rod for straightness by turning it slowly on a lathe.

It is worth also noting the sophisticated way in which an "optical plane" is made. Optical planes need to be very flat indeed, and lens grinders would first grind two planes together, then each against a third, and then against each other, and so on. Clearly, when two planes are ground against each other we cannot be sure that they are flat: one might be slightly convex and the other correspondingly concave. If the second is then ground against a third, any high point of the second will score a corresponding low point on the third. But when this is ground against the first, low point will be opposite low point, and high opposite high, and so the highs will grind each other down. More mathematically, if any point of the first is x above the plane, the corresponding point on the second will be x below, *i.e.* $-x$ above, and on the third will be x above, which will tend to grind the original high down to $-x$. Each grinding operation tends to convert x into $-x$, *i.e.* multiply by -1. So with three planes being ground against one another, the total effect is to multiply x by $(-1)^3$. The only stable situation is that in which $x = (-1)^3 x$, *i.e.* $x = -x$, which is possible only when $x = 0$. Given a way of producing an optical plane, we can then produce a very straight line as the intersection of two optical planes.

We thus have many different ways of producing, or checking, straight lines. In our normal experience these different ways cohere, although it is possible to conceive worlds—for example with continually varying refractive media—in which they do not all cohere. This is not to say that they are all independent. As with some other basic concepts which are linked with several others, some of the linkages are secured by deeper connexions. Those between straight lines and light rays seem relatively contingent. That between straight lines and the geodesic property of being the shortest distance between two points is not a *physically* contingent matter, but we could perhaps conceive things being arranged differently—it much depends on our concept of distance, and the curvature of space. The symmetry properties of straight lines seem more fundamental, together with what we have taken for granted thus far, its continuity and one-dimensionality, which characterize not only straight lines, but lines and curves of any sort. It seems reasonable, therefore to make no mention of light rays or geodesic properties in defining a straight line, but to characterize it conceptually as a one-dimensional continuous curve unbounded and infinite in extent which is symmetric under translation along itself and rotation around itself.

2.6 Which Geometry?

> ### If not Formal Empiricism, then What?

If purely formalist and empiricist accounts of geometry are rejected, we are faced once again with the question "Which geometry should we choose?". We cannot say, as the Formalists do, that they are all on a par, so long as they are all consistent, and there is nothing for it but to make a purely arbitrary choice—although we should concede to the Formalists that we are free to make an arbitrary choice if we so please, and that much may be learned from the study of a geometry considered solely as a formal system: and we cannot, as the Empiricists do, leave it entirely to sense-experience to decide between different formal systems—although the verdict sense-experience gives to a geometry **plus** an interpretation is weighty, and we cannot go on maintaining, without some modification or gloss, a geometry together with an interpretation which flies in the face of the empirical evidence. We therefore have to ask ourselves how we should choose a geometry, granted that there are many consistent ones to choose from.

Let us tabulate them with their special features in order to make an informed choice between them as in a consumers' magazine:

The *Which?* Guide to Geometries

Hyperbolic	Euclidean	Elliptic
Bolyai, Lobachevsky	Pythagoras, Euclid	Riemann
More than one parallel (symbolically E_+	Exactly one parallel E_1	No parallel E_0)
$\triangle$ less than 180° (symbolically $\triangle_<$	$\triangle = 180°$ $\triangle_=$	$\triangle$ more than 180° $\triangle_>$)
$h^2 > a^2 + b^2$ (symbolically $P_>$	$h^2 = a^2 + b^2$ $P_=$	$h^2 < a^2 + b^2$ $P_<$)
circumference $> 2\pi r$ (symbolically $O_>$	$c = 2\pi r$ $O_=$	$c < 2\pi r$ $O_<$)
surface of saddle or mountain pass	flat plane surface	surface of sphere
negative curvature (symbolically C_-	zero curvature C_0	positive curvature C_+)
minimum area	no natural unit	maximum length maximum area

Table 2.6.1

None of these geometries is conclusively ruled out: none of them is inconsistent. We cannot say of any of them Not Recommended, and must allow that any one of them may be the most suitable for some particular purpose. Nevertheless, we can give rational guidance for the general user on the strength of some of the features listed in the table, and conclude that Euclidean Geometry is the Best Buy and this for several reasons.

In the first place Euclidean geometry is both more specific and more flexible than either of its competitors. It is more specific in respect of the first six of the features listed in the table after the makers' name, for instance when it specifies an equality instead of merely a *greater than* or *less than*. On each of these counts, it is given a star. It is also given further points for its greater flexibility, manifested in the bottom row. With an elliptical geometry we have to ask what its unit of length is—the length of its great circles, so to speak. Such a geometry would not be available for lengths greater than the maximum one. In choosing it we are foreclosing our subsequent freedom of conceiving. Although if the length is very large, we are unlikely to come up against empirical evidence against it, we may always want to consider, if only hypothetically, some length that is greater, and it is a restriction on our freedom of thought to rule it out in advance. Similarly, though less embarrassingly, it is a pity to be cumbered with either a maximum area of the whole space—the area of the surface of the earth—in elliptic geometry, or a minimum area any triangle can have in hyperbolic geometry. It is better to be able to triangulate our space as closely as we please without any geometrical restriction.

The flexibility of Euclidean geometry is shown more clearly in the Saccheri–Wallis formulation, which in effect assigns to Euclidean geometry alone the possibility of having two figures the same shape but different sizes. In elliptic geometry, as we saw with the octant of a sphere, the shape determines the size, and the same holds good of hyperbolic geometry. There is no possibility in those geometries of a scale model, and instead of being able to characterize objects and other figures by reference to their shape and their size independently, we should have only one, linked way of characterizing them. Euclidean geometry has more degrees of freedom, and is therefore better suited to its function of being a descriptive back-cloth against which physical phenomena can be described and physical theories formulated and tested. Whereas for a scientific theory, such as physics, flexibility may be a fault, and prevent the theory being put to the test and made liable to falsification, for geometry, with its different aims, flexibility is not a weakness but a strength. It increases the descriptive potentiality of geometry, which is what we want, and the fact that it is at the cost of falsifiability is no criticism, since it is not the function of geometry to offer falsifiable predictions or explanations.

It may seem paradoxical that we claim on behalf of Euclidean geometry both that it is more specific and that it is more flexible and generally available. But there is no paradox. In saying that a geometry is Euclidean, we are saying all we need to say in order to characterize it completely: in saying that it is hyperbolic or elliptic, we are not characterizing it completely: we need to say further what its curvature is—it has to be some particular negative or positive number, not just negative or positive; we need likewise to say what the minimum area of a triangle or the maximum length of a straight line is, by how much the angles of a triangle fall short of or exceed two right angles, by how much the circumference of a circle exceeds or falls short of π times its diameter. There is just one Euclidean geometry, whereas there are whole families of hyperbolic and elliptic geometries, each different from the others, and each having its own peculiarities, of curvature, of the sum of the angles of a triangle, and of the ratio of the circumference of a circle to its diameter, which preclude its easy application to some conceivable cases. Euclidean geometry, by contrast, is exact: in every Euclidean geometry triangles add up to the same, the ratio of circumference to diameter is always the same, the curvature is always the same—*viz.* 0; but the one and only Euclidean geometry, once specified, is available in a wide variety of cases, and is thus more multi-purpose.

The same considerations apply with the number of parallels. Euclidean geometry, having exactly one, is more specific than hyperbolic geometry, which has infinitely many, though in this case not more specific than elliptic, which has none. But the latter is a defect when it comes to establishing a system of reference. On the surface of the globe, lines of longitude intersect at the poles: 10°E and 90°N is the same as 10°W and 90°N. This is a defect in a system of reference. We want there to be a one–one correspondence between points in the space and sets of coordinates. If this is to be so, we need "topological parallelism", that is that lines (not necessarily straight) defined by all the coordinate(s) except one being constant should always exist and never intersect. These do not have to be, so far as this argument goes, straight lines—we can have curvilinear coordinates—and do not demand geometrical parallelism. But the use of straight lines in elliptic geometry is ruled out, and the use of Euclidean parallel straight lines is strongly suggested.

2.7 The Theory of Groups

Plato had argued against all forms of operationalism and constructivism in mathematics, because mathematics ought to turn the mind towards the abstract contemplation of timeless reality. He admitted that the actual linguistic practice of geometers would suggest the opposite, but he, and Aristotle after him, saw it as a weakness, not a clue to an understanding of what was really going on: "they talk ridiculously τε καὶ ἀναγκαῖον (*te kai anankaion*),

<for want of better terms> or <yet this is how they have to>[11] as
though they were doing things and using the language of action—
'squaring', 'applying', 'adding'—whereas the point of study is
knowledge, not action".[12]

It was unfortunate that Plato's and Aristotle's influence was so
great that although the language of operations remained part of the
standard vocabulary of geometers—as we noted in §2.2, Euclid's
first three postulates are instructions, couched in the infinitive,
rather than primitive propositions couched in the indicative—it
was not taken seriously until Felix Klein propounded his *Erlangen Program*, in which he suggested that geometry be approached
not axiomatically but through the groups of operations which left
geometrical features invariant.[13] Topology was to be seen as the
study of what was left unaltered under the group of all continuous
transformations. Hyperbolic geometry, and with somewhat more
difficulty elliptic geometry, could also be given a group-theoretical
characterization. Euclidean geometry turned out to be the geometry which was unaffected by the group of translations, rotations
and reflections, which was therefore called the Euclidean group.
The Euclidean group leads us to Euclidean geometry in much the
same was as, on one presentation, the Lorentz group leads us to
the Special Theory of Relativity.[14]

A sceptic about the pre-eminence of Euclidean geometry might
allow the propriety of the group-theoretical approach, but query
the importance of the Euclidean group, and ask:

What is so good about the Euclidean Group?

[11] The former version is that of F.M.Cornford *The Republic of Plato*, Oxford, 1941, p.238; the latter is my tendentious rendering to bring out the
nuance of Plato's recognition that operational terms were, however much
he disliked them, a necessary part of the mathematician's vocabulary.

[12] *Republic* VII 527a6-b1; *Metaphysics* K, 1064a30, cf. A, 989b32.

[13] Felix Klein, "*Vergleichende Betrachtungen über neuere geometrische For-
schungen*", Erlangen, 1872; revised version in *Mathematische Annalen*,
43, 1893, pp. 63-100. See also H.Helmholtz, "The origin and meaning of
geometrical axioms", *Mind*, **1**, 1876, pp.301-321.

[14] See P.E.Hodgson and J.R.Lucas, *Spacetime and Electromagnetism*, Oxford, 1990.

One partial answer is the purely abstract one that the group generated by the operation of reflection is the simplest non-trivial group, while the group of rotations is the paradigm continuous cyclic group and the group of translations is the paradigm serial continuous group. The Euclidean group is thus a group of peculiar simplicity, and corresponding importance.

Another partial answer is due to Helmholtz.[15] The Euclidean group preserves rigid motions, and rigid motions are presupposed by our philosophy of measurement,[16] and are obviously of importance if we are to manipulate material objects in the world around us. This is a practical consideration. There is also a "communication argument". Granted that you and I are different corporeal beings, differently located in space, but talking about the same things, what we shall be best able to talk to each other about will be those aspects that are the same from either of our points of view. That is, the pressures of communication between observers who necessarily, when communicating, are doing so at approximately the same time, and therefore while occupying different positions in space, will lead them to pick out those features that are invariant under translation and rotation—which together form the "proper Euclidean group", (thus differing from the full Euclidean group in not containing reflection)—and so the geometry defined by that group naturally assumes importance in the eyes of limited communicators who cannot be in the same place at the same time.[17]

This argument has been countered by T.G. McGonigle, who points out that rigid motions are possible in any space of constant curvature.[18] At first sight there seems to be an inconsistency between the claim that Euclidean geometry is characterized by the Euclidean group and the claim that rigid motions are possible in spaces in which geometrical features are not invariant under the

[15] "The Origin and Meaning of Geometrical Axioms (ii)", *Mind* **3**, 1878, pp. 212-225.

[16] See below, §2.8 and §12.3; and J.R.Lucas, *Space, Time and Causality*, Oxford, 1985, pp. 85-86.

[17] See further, J.R.Lucas, *"Euclides ab omni naevo vindicatus"*, British Journal for the Philosophy of Science, **20**, 1969, pp. 185-191; and J.R.Lucas, *Space, Time and Causality*, Oxford, 1985, pp.111-113.

[18] T.G.McGonigle, *British Journal for the Philosophy of Science*, **21**, 1970, pp.185-191.

Euclidean group. If we consider the surface of an orange, it is evident that spherical triangles and other shapes can be slid around on the surface without distortion, and it would seem, therefore, that they are being translated and rotated. But when we consider it more deeply, we see that the apparent translations are not real translations, because when iterated enough they come back to where they began. They are in fact not translations, but rotations around a somewhat distant centre of rotation. Instead of having a group of simple rotations together with translations, we have a group of more complicated rotations with different radii of rotation. Such a group would indeed preserve rigid motions, and in the limit would be indistinguishable from the Euclidean group. But it is in a sense more complicated. Although there is only one sort of operator—rotation around some centre of rotation—it is one with a variable parameter—the radius of rotation—whereas the Euclidean group, though having two sorts of continuous operator, has no further parameters to specify. There is a trade-off between one type of simplicity and another, but we can argue both abstractly that the Euclidean group is the simplest group that preserves rigid motions, and as a matter of practice that it is in terms of translations and simple rotations that we construe the motions of material objects around us. We could be wrong. It could be that what we regard as translations are really rotations around a very distant centre of rotation. But we regard them, naturally enough, as translations, and once we distinguish translations from rotations, we are committed to the Euclidean group, and so to Euclidean geometry.

2.8 Pythagorean Geometry Has a Better Metric

The Pythagorean proposition, we saw,[19] can be taken as an axiom instead of a theorem to be proved, and in many ways is a more characteristic feature of the resulting geometry than Euclid's complicated parallel postulate. And we can argue for Pythagorean geometry on the score of its characteristic proposition, $P_=$, being better than the characteristic propositions, $P_<$ and $P_>$, of hyperbolic and elliptic geometries respectively. For $P_=$ **is the simplest sensible rule for assigning an overall measure to separations spanning more than one dimension.**

[19] In §2.2.

We need first to explain why geometry should be concerned with assigning measures, and secondly to justify the claim that the Pythagorean rule is the simplest sensible one to adopt. As regards the first question, we may be content to make the etymological point that geo*metry* should be concerned with assigning a *metric*. Although geometry has developed since the Egyptians used it to measure the plots of earth along the Nile, and has been more concerned with shapes than with absolute size, it is only in Pythagorean geometry that the two are distinct, and in them relative size remains important. Some geometries—projective geometry, for example—take no account of size, but most do; and in so far as geometry is to be applied, as in laying out a tennis court, it is important that numbers should be assignable to segments of straight lines and curves.

Mathematicians often define a metric on a space as a function d from the cartesian product of the space with itself into the non-negative real numbers.

$$S \times S \xrightarrow{\;d\;} \Re^{0,+},$$

subject to four conditions:

(i) $d(x,y) = 0$ iff $x = y$
(ii) $d(x,y) > 0$
(iii) $d(x,y) = d(y,x)$
(iv) $d(x,z) \geq d(x,y) + d(y,z).$

We may naturally ask why these conditions should be imposed on any metric function. (i) expresses the thought that a point has no length (magnitude)[20] and that any two distinct points define a straight line and a segment of it having length. (ii) expresses the thought that a point is a minimal limit of a line.[21] (iii) expresses the thought that length is isotropic. (iv) is the so-called triangle inequality, and lays down that the distance between any two points cannot be more than the sum of the distances between each and some third point, but may be less. It establishes an upper bound for composite magnitudes, and expresses the ancient principle that the whole may not be more than the sum of its parts.[22]

---

[20] See above, §2.5, 1.(i) and (ii).

[21] See above, §2.5, 2.(ii)a) and below, §12.5.

[22] See below, §12.4.

If we accept these conditions as partly constituting what it is to be a measure of distance, we are led to look to certain functions as plausible measure functions. (i) suggests that $d(x, y)$ should be a function of $x - y$; (ii) and (iii) suggest that it should be a function of $(x - y)^2$ or $(x - y)^4$, or $(x - y)^6$, ...*etc.*; and if we are to take the n-dimensional case, then the most natural additive, always non-negative, symmetrical function is

$$d = \sqrt{(x_1 - y_1)^2 + (x_2 - y_2)^2 + ... + (x_n - y_n)^2}.$$

Of the three geometries on offer, we should therefore choose the one which has $P_=$, that is to say Euclidean geometry, in which alone Pythagoras' theorem holds true, and yields an exact equality between the square on the hypotenuse and the sum of the squares on the other two sides of a right-angled triangle.

The right angle is not just a particular angle, but expresses the independence of the different dimensions. The Greek for 'rectangular' is ὀρθογώνιος (*orthogonios*), from which the word 'orthogonal' comes. Orthogonality often expresses independence, especially in Fourier analysis, where different periodic components of a function are represented by different dimensions, and Parseval's theorem expresses in Hilbert space a close analogue of Pythagoras' theorem. In quantum mechanics, as we move from Schrödinger's wave mechanics to Heisenberg's matrix representation, we set great store by diagonal matrices in which the product of two vectors comes out as a sum of squares, thus again paying tribute to the pre-eminence of the Pythagorean rule. (But we should note that the analogy is not exact. In quantum mechanics we deal with Hermitian matrices, operating on complex vectors and their conjugates; nevertheless the analogy is close enough to be suggestive.)

In a slightly different way, Euclidean geometry facilitates the use of the parallelogram rule for compounding displacements in different directions, and hence velocities, accelerations and forces also. If, however, in elliptic geometry I start as it were at the North Pole, go $1/4 \times$(a great circle) South, turn 90° and go $1/4 \times$(a great circle) East, turn 90° and go $1/4 \times$(a great circle) North, turn 90° and go $1/4 \times$(a great circle) South, I shall not end up where I started. The order in which I carry out the displacements is not commutative; so that the parallelogram rule is no longer natural for compounding displacements, and not available at all for compounding velocities, accelerations, or forces.

It is clear that these arguments, like those of the two previous sections, are not deductive. There is no inconsistency in supposing that the distance function is given by

$$d(x,y) = \Sigma|x_i - y_i|$$

or by

$$d(x,y) = \left(\Sigma(x_i - y_i)^4\right)^{1/4}$$

or . . . , nor in having shape dependent on size, nor in having no topological parallels. It is clear also that these arguments are not inductive. Equally, they are not just promulgating an arbitrary convention. They are rational arguments, though neither deductive not inductive ones. It is rational to seek greater simplicity, greater generality and greater unification, and these arguments appeal to those considerations.

2.9 Desargues

We have found a number of different ways in which the axioms of a geometry may be justified. There is one further one which cannot be called in aid of Euclid's axioms, but is available for plane projective geometry, and is of importance elsewhere in mathematics. In plane, that is two-dimensional, projective geometry "Desargues' Theorem" is *not* a theorem but has to be postulated as an extra axiom. Desargues' theorem states that if two triangles are centrally perspective, they are axially perspective, that is, if AA', BB', CC' are concurrent (at O), then if D is on BC and $B'C'$, and E is on CA and $C'A'$, and F is on BA and $B'A'$, D, E and F are collinear.

Desargues' theorem is *not* a theorem in two dimensions. There are non-Desarguian two-dimensional geometries, although they are fairly unlovely. In standard two-dimensional projective geometry it is necessary to postulate Desargues' theorem as an axiom. But in three, or more, dimensions it is a theorem, and can be proved quite easily. For we can prove that DEF is a straight line in three-dimensional geometry if it is the intersection of two planes. And that is easily proved by considering the various different planes the relevant lines must be in.

Desargues' theorem thus offers a further criterion of mathematical truth. If we suppose that the other axioms of plane projective geometry are P_1, P_2, P_3, P_4, and Desargues' theorem is D_5,

$$\text{then} \quad P_1, P_2, P_3, P_4 \neg \vdash D_5$$

$$\text{but}\quad P_1, P_2, P_3, P_4, P_6, P_7, P_8 \vdash D_5$$

where P_1, P_2, P_3, P_4, P_6, P_7, P_8 is a natural generalisation of P_1, P_2, P_3, P_4.

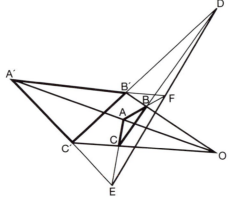

Figure 2.9.1 Desargues' "Theorem": if AA', BB', CC' are concurrent (at O), then if D is on BC and $B'C'$, and E is on CA and $C'A'$, and F is on BA and $B'A'$, D, E and F are collinear.

Not all generalisations are natural generalisations, but obviously 3-dimensional projective geometry is a natural generalisation of 2-dimensional projective geometry, and the fact that Desargues' theorem *is* a theorem in a two-dimensional subspace of a three-dimensional projective geometry is a weighty reason for holding it to be true even if it cannot be deduced from the other axioms of two-dimensional projective geometry alone.

2.10 Conclusions

Our *Which?* survey of geometry yields a more complex picture than either the Formalist or the Empiricist had supposed. Our choice of geometries and of interpretations of geometrical terms is not arbitrary, but is guided by six different sorts of consideration:

1. There are conceptual links between geometrical and other concepts which limit the application of terms such as 'point', 'line', or 'plane', and lead us to adopt some propositions as true and to reject others as false.

2. As between one geometry and another, it is rational to choose the one which is more specific. Euclidean geometry is more specific than either hyperbolic or elliptical geometry because

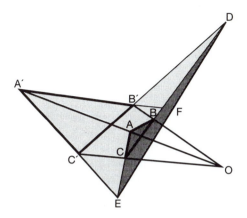

Figure 2.9.2 Desargues' Theorem in three dimensions turns entirely on the intersections of the various planes: since BB' and CC' intersect at O, the lines $BB'O$ and $CC'O$ are co-planar, and so the points B, B', O, C, C' are all co-planar, and so BB' and CC' must intersect, at D. Then D is co-planar with B, B', C, C', and so is in every plane that includes BC, and so in ABC, and is in every plane that includes $B'C'$, and so in $A'B'C'$. By exactly similar reasoning, since CC' and AA' intersect at O, the lines $CC'O$ and $AA'O$ are co-planar, and so the points C, C', O, A, A' are all co-planar, and so CC' and AA' must intersect, at E, say. Then E is co-planar with C, C', A, A' and so is in every plane that includes CA, and so in ABC, and is in every plane that includes $C'A'$, and so in $A'B'C'$. Again, by exactly similar reasoning, since AA' and BB' intersect at O, the lines $AA'O$ and $BB'O$ are co-planar, and so the points A, A', O, B, B' are all co-planar, and so AA' and BB' must intersect, at F, say. Then F is co-planar with A, A', B, B' and so is in every plane that includes BA, and so in ABC, and is in every plane that includes $A'B'$, and so in $A'B'C'$. So D, E and F are all in both ABC and $A'B'C'$ and thus in the line common to these two planes.

(a) its curvature is exactly zero, whereas theirs is either any constant negative number (hyperbolic) or any constant positive number (elliptical);

(b) the angles of a triangle in Euclidean geometry add up to exactly 180° whereas in hyperbolic geometry it is merely less than, and in elliptical geometry it is merely more than, 180°;

(c) the square on the hypotenuse is exactly equal to the sum of
the squares on the other two sides of a right-angled triangle, whereas in the other geometries, again, there is only an
inequality, not an equality;

(d) the ratio of the circumference of a circle is exactly 2π in
Euclidean geometry, but only $> 2\pi$ in hyperbolic, and $< 2\pi$
in elliptic, geometry.

3. Conversely, Euclidean geometry is more flexible than hyperbolic and elliptic geometry, in that the size of figures is not determined by their shape, and there is no fixed unit of length or of
area in Euclidean geometry. Euclidean geometry is scale-invariant
and metrically amorphous. In choosing Euclidean geometry, we
are not committing ourselves to other choices, which are therefore
left open. Euclidean geometry thus provides a suitable back-cloth
to physics or any other explanatory scheme, in that it does not
pre-empt the answers they may give to further questions. If we
want geometry to have a low profile, being able to accommodate a
variety of other explanatory schemata, then Euclidean geometry is
the least obtrusive one we can have. But to accept this option is
to choose a particular role for geometry, and not that proposed in
geometrodynamics, where a single integrated explanatory scheme
is sought.[23]

4. We can look at geometry not axiomatically but group-theor-
etically; in that case the Euclidean group is singled out as the most
basic, in as much as it is generated by the simplest non-trivial discrete group, the simplest continuous cyclic group and the simplest
continuous serial group. There are good epistemological and practical reasons why communicating agents who occupy different loca-
tions in space at any one time should attach significance to features
that are invariant under the Euclidean group of transformations.

5. A metric needs to satisfy some conditions if it is to be coherent. If there is more than one dimension, some symmetric function is needed to add distances in independent directions. The
Pythagorean rule is the simplest one that satisfies the conditions.

6. A geometry, or indeed any mathematical theory, may be

---

[23] How do considerations 3 and 4 relate? 3 says that if something is relevant
its bearing should be spelled out precisely: 4 says that often it is good to
have one feature irrelevant to another. So either deem one feature totally
irrelevant, or else say exactly what its relevance is.

embedded in another theory which is a natural generalisation of it, and the axioms of the smaller theory may then emerge as theorems of the larger. In particular, an n-dimensional geometry may be embedded in an $(n + 1)$-dimensional one, or an n-dimensional one in one with an infinite number of dimensions (a Hilbert space, for example). The more general theory, just because it is a more general theory, justifies the axioms of the more specific theory, which are seen as being just a special case of a more fundamental truth.

These considerations are not, of course, deductive proofs. They are, rather, what Mill described as "considerations...capable of determining the intellect either to give or withhold its consent".[24] They could be denied without inconsistency. But often the consequences of denying them would be awkward, and would need some explanation themselves, which we might find hard to give. There is a *prima facie*, though not conclusive, argument in their favour.

They apply not only to geometry, but to other axiomatic systems too, such as set theory and Peano Arithmetic.[25] Set theory is not just a formal system in which we can choose any axioms we like, but is, also, constrained by conceptual links with other ranges of discourse. $\in$ could not be a reflexive relation; the axiom of foundation asserts an anti-Anselmian doctrine of ultimate *ur*-elements that are utterly minimal. A set theory with the Generalised Continuum Hypothesis is more exact than one without, in as much as it specifies that there is no cardinal between any transfinite cardinal and the cardinal of its power set, whereas without such an axiom there is an indeterminate range of possible situations. It is better to come down definitely in favour of discreteness (or, for that matter, density) than to leave the question open. In a rather different way the Axiom of Choice may be defended as a natural generalisation of a principle of finite choice that is unquestionably true. The group-theoretical approach to geometry may be paralleled by an entirely fresh approach to set theory from the stand-point of category theory or the theory of games, which may yield entirely new insights into it, and may make some axioms seem obviously true (or obviously false).

[24] J.S.Mill, *Utilitarianism,* ch.1, p.4 in Everyman ed.

[25] See below, §6.5.

Chapter 3
Formalism

3.1 *More Geometrico*

For two thousand years geometry was the paradigm of rigorous reasoning. To argue *more geometrico* was an ideal many philosophers set themselves. Spinoza set out his philosophy as a series of propositions, each following from its predecessors. Locke, in spite of his criticisms of Descartes, thought he could establish morality as a sequence of deductions from self-evident truths. But, attractive though the ideal of rigorous reasoning undoubtedly is, when we come to reflect on it, we find ourselves impelled towards Formalism. It is not only that axioms are easier to postulate than to justify,[1] but the principles of inference themselves, under scrutiny, require a formal exegesis. Some formalist tendency is implicit in Plato's Theory of Forms, but often Formalists define their position in opposition to straightforward Platonism. Formalists see themselves as radicals—though often, like other radicals, they turn out to be extremely conservative.[2] They reject the Platonic Establishment, and are not prepared to swallow guff, or bow down before the great tradition of classical mathematics. They will not make a great act of faith, and believe in a world of Forms, or any other abstract or supersensible entities. Everything must be re-authenticated to their own satisfaction at the bar of reason. And they will be difficult to satisfy. Only the most rigorous proofs will

---

[1] See above, §1.9.

[2] Hilbert, in particular, sought to preserve Cantorian set theory by making it an entirely formal discipline. See below, §14.7.

do. No handwaving, no appeals to intuition will be countenanced. Every assumption must be stated clearly, every rule of inference made quite explicit. Only the most rigorous arguments are worthy of mathematics. Mathematics is not just Plato playing pleasantly with yesful youths by the banks of the Ilyssus, and getting them to say that they see lovely patterns laid up in heaven, but a tough game played against a tough opponent who is as sceptical as it is possible to be and will not let anything pass unless he absolutely has to. It is much harder playing that way, but at least we can be sure that anything we succeed in proving is a real achievement and is something we can be absolutely sure of; having eliminated the sloppy, we can be proud of what remains.

The radical spirit is easy to empathize with, and has much to commend it. But dissatisfaction by itself does not constitute a clear specification of an alternative position. In fact there are many, and we need to distinguish various types of ontological, epistemological and methodological Formalism. Much of the mathematical drive towards Formalism, however, stems from its proven value as a method of doing mathematics, which is indeed great, but does not constitute an adequate account of mathematical knowledge, although it does lead to one particular field of insightful research.

Varieties of Formalism

We need to distinguish:
1. ontological formalism
2. method of formalisation
3. epistemological formalism
4. study of formal systems

3.2 Formalising

The great merit of arguing *more geometrico* was, in the eyes of the
philosophers, its cogency; but for mathematicians it has been val-
ued equally much for revealing hidden assumptions and eliminating
errors and loop-holes in seemingly plausible arguments. Only when
Hilbert set about formalising geometry, were hidden assumptions,
overlooked by Euclid, finally brought to light. When naive set
theory was found to be inconsistent, the natural response was to
formalise it, so that dubious assumptions could be identified, and
safer axioms adopted.[3]

Formalising an axiomatic system may enable us to prove its
consistency, either relative to another axiomatic system,[4] or, occasionally, in some more fundamental way.[5] It enables us to abstract
the fundamental shape of a system, and see the bones unencumbered by superficial flesh. Much as the theory of groups enables us
to discern a common pattern in the permutations of change-ringing
and the SU_3 groups of particle physics, so the Formalist can point
out the structural similarity of topology and the modal logic **S4**.[6]

3.3 Maximum Cogency

All mathematicians formalise. Formalists go further, and claim
that Formalism gives the best account of what mathematics really
is, and how we come to know it. Ontological Formalism draws
much of its support from metaphysical principles that lie outside
mathematics, and it will be discussed in Chapter Fifteen. Epistemological Formalism arises naturally from the cogency of formal
argument. If our argument is absolutely cogent, its conclusions are
certain, and can be known for sure; and they alone can be properly
said to be known.

The pursuit of maximum cogency determines the structure of
formal argument. In order to have the muscle of compulsion, it
is broken up into smaller proofs, λήμματα (*lemmata*), which in
turn are composed of single steps, each one of which is undeniable.
If the slave-boy maintains that the square root of 2 is 1.5, he is

---

[3] See below, §12.4.

[4] See above, §2.3.

[5] See below, §3.4.

[6] See below, §10.2.

led step by step to the conclusion that the square of 1.5 is 2.25, not 2. Provided each step is recognised as cogent, the whole finite sequence of steps is recognised too. Unless the critic can fault one of the steps, he must allow that the whole sequence constitutes a proof of the last conclusion. Whereas in other disciplines there are arguments on either side, and we have to weigh arguments for and arguments against, in a mathematical proof there are no arguments against, and once the proof is given, we do not have to consider anything else, but can end with a QED, or as they say in America, "period".

Moreover, if an argument is to be maximally cogent, each step must be one that even the most recalcitrant opponent will have to concede. Instead of the intelligent and cooperative young men of Plato's preference, opponents must be assumed to be stupid and obstinate. An argument is not really cogent unless it works even on morons and sceptics. Plato thought that the one sanction which could compel assent from even the minimum conceder was that communication would break down unless we used words according to established patterns of use.[7] But there are border-line cases. Meanings are not entirely fixed, nor always clear-cut. Often we change the meaning of a word as conditions change or knowledge increases. Bachelors are no longer unmarried men, but can be married, although relatively junior—"Bachelors of Arts"—and can be female—"bachelor girls". At one time it was analytic that every atom of an element had the same atomic weight, and then, with the discovery of isotopes, it became non-analytic and false. Lawyers often dispute about the exact meaning of some crucial term. Is a flying boat a boat or an aeroplane? Are roller-skates a vehicle? Not only is it often unclear what the rules are that govern the meaning of particular words, but sometimes the rules for the use of words incorporate non-deductive inference patterns. What is a gentleman? We may quote Newman's definition or the Fifteenth Psalm, but still it will be unclear how the term is to be applied in many cases, unless we can assess what a man does, and decide whether it is the sort of behaviour we should expect of a gentleman. And to decide that, we have to make moral and social judgements of an inherently disputable kind. Arguments from meaning are not always quite as incontrovertible as had been thought, nor are they

---

[7] See above, §1.8.

always within the compass of a moron.

Faced with these difficulties about the validity of inference, philosophers have three possible responses, similar to those open to them when the truth of the premises of deductive arguments came into question.[8] Occasionally it may be possible to establish the validity of the inference in question by appeal to other more basic ones that are not in question; thus derived rules of inference can be established in a formal system on the basis of more fundamental rules of inference. Or we may restrict deductive inferences to those involving a few key terms—the sentential connectives, such as 'and', 'or', 'not', 'if'—about which there is general agreement. Or we may simply stipulate how terms are to be understood by giving a formal definition of them. Often at first definitions are in terms of ordinary words, and we are still using ordinary language, though a "regimented" version of it; but if we want to be free of misleading associations, it is better to constitute an entirely formal system, the rules of which are all explicitly laid down, with no appeal to ordinary usage.

Axiomatic Approach

Premises	Inferences
Self-evident truths	Meaning rules in natural language
Theorems of more basic theory	Derived rules of inference
Postulates	Stipulated transformation rules

Formal systems minimise the demands made on both the intelligence and the cooperativeness of the opponent. The stock of symbols is small and the rules for manipulating them explicit. I do not have to be a man of culture to be able to recognise the symbol 'p' and to follow the rules for its manipulation, as I—arguably—do if I am to use the words 'gentleman' or 'civilisation' correctly. If Hardy can discern some distant truth and I cannot, we can resolve the matter. Instead of his just saying "It is obvious" he puts

---

[8] See above, §1.9.

forward what purports to be a proof, and I scrutinise it, needing only to recognise a limited number of symbols and a limited
number of inference patterns. Formalisation reduces the scope of
dispute. Instead of juicy substantial issues, which we might well
disagree about, as each tries to make his own holistic assessment,
we have to agree on only a few formal questions—whether the
symbol is a p or a q, whether a formula has a certain specified
shape, whether a sequence of formulae conforms to some specified
pattern or not. The ability required for doing formal logic is minimal pattern-recognition, well within the compass of morons and as
sceptic-proof as anything can be.[9]

Once the opponent is capable of minimal pattern-recognition,
the Rule of Substitution must be allowed. The pattern of[10]

$$(((p \vee q) \vee r) \vee ((p \vee q) \vee r)) \rightarrow ((p \vee q) \vee r)$$

is evidently the same as that of

$$(p \vee p) \rightarrow p$$

so much so that even *l'homme moyen sensuel* can recognise it,
and a refusal to acknowledge the similarity would be proof positive that the opponent was simply not playing the game. So, too,
some principle of generalisation must be allowed. If I can prove for
any arbitrary instance that a certain property holds, then it holds
for every instance. More care is needed in specifying this general
principle as a precise rule, because of the difficulty in laying down
exactly what is arbitrary and what is typical in the instance under
consideration. But difficult though it is to formulate general rules,
particular instances often admit of no doubt. Complicated verbiage
may be needed to lay down exactly under what conditions a rule of
generalisation holds, but in very many cases it is undeniable that
if for any x we have

$$(Fx \vee Fx) \rightarrow Fx,$$

then it is true for all x; or in symbols

---

[9] See §14.9.

[10] For logical symbols, and in particular the "quotifiers" (A) and (V) (normally written ($\forall$) and ($\exists$)), see note on logical symbols on p.xi.

$$(\mathbf{A}x)((Fx \vee Fx) \to Fx).$$

If the demands on the opponent's intellectual capacities are to be minimised, the number of types of pattern that need to be recognised must be few. But the types of question to be addressed are many. If formal arguments are to be widely applicable, it must be because the few permitted types of inference are used again and again and again in various combinations so as to resolve a wide variety of different problems. There must be much repetition of standard inferences. And if repeated application of standard inferences is not to result in unmanageable complication, there must be some rule of detachment whereby some simple lemma can result from preceding argument and be itself the premise for the next steps. The Rule of *Modus Ponens* is such a rule. It entitles us from the premises $p \to q$

and p

to infer q

The pressures which lead us to regard argument *more geometrico* as the paradigm of rigorous argument lead us on to the proof-sequences of §2.3. Maximum cogency on our part is brought forth by minimum intelligence and cooperativeness on the part of our opponent, which in turn requires that the rules of inference be few, and hence a sequence of steps, some of which result in formulae simpler, or at least no more complicated, than those that preceded them.

The pressure to minimise the types of inference the opponent has to recognise is great, and thanks to the Deduction Theorem it is usually possible in formalising a system to replace a rule of inference by a premise. Such a move is often convenient, and in some cases unobjectionable, but it can distort our understanding of mathematics.[11] In any case we cannot go the whole way in replacing rules of inference by additional postulates. Lewis Carroll had Achilles try this at the behest of the tortoise, only to be involved in an infinite regress. No matter how many extra premises we are granted, we need at some stage to make an inferential move from premise to conclusion. Total explicitness will always elude us. We need not only to know *that* the premises are true, but to know *how*

---

[11] See below, §6.5-§6.8, and §12.6.

to argue from them. However blind we suppose our opponent to be, he cannot be altogether inferentially opaque.

3.4 The Theory of Formal Systems

The study of formal systems, whether or not Formalism gives an adequate account of mathematics, is an interesting topic in its own right, like group theory, and one that illuminates questions arising in the foundations of mathematics.

Formalism yields consistency proofs. If we can map a non-Euclidean geometry into Euclidean geometry, then proof on the inconsistency of non-Euclidean geometry could be turned into a proof of the inconsistency of Euclidean geometry. So, contraposing, the non-Euclidean geometry is consistent, provided Euclidean geometry is.[12]

A somewhat different, but equally effective, consistency proof is the "proof by erasure" which can be used to prove the consistency of predicate calculus and first-order logic. We do it by a species of "shut-eye" somewhat akin to that used to establish the consistency of the Axiom of Choice or the Continuum Hypothesis. In predicate calculus we shut our eyes to all the individual variables and quotifiers,[13] and view the predicate variables as propositional variables. Predicate calculus consists of propositional calculus together with some extra axioms and one further rule of inference, the Rule of Generalisation. The Rule of Generalisation lays down that if $\Gamma(x)$ is a theorem, where x is a free individual variable in $\Gamma(x)$, then $(Ax)\Gamma(x)$ is a theorem too:

$$\text{If } \vdash \Gamma(x) \text{ then } \vdash (Ax)\Gamma(x).$$

If we erase the individual variables and quotifier from this, we have

$$\text{If } \vdash \Gamma \text{ then } \vdash \Gamma,$$

which may be somewhat unenterprising as a rule of inference, but can scarcely lead us astray. Two axioms governing the interplay of $(A\ )$ and $\rightarrow$ commonly employed are:[14]

---

[12]　See above, §2.3.

[13]　Usually known as 'quantifiers'. See below, §4.3.

[14]　Compare §13.3.

G $(Ax)(Fx \rightarrow Gx) \rightarrow ((Ax)Fx \rightarrow (Ax)Gx)$
T $(Ax)Fx \rightarrow Fy,$

which become, when we erase the individual variables and quotifiers,

$$(F \rightarrow G) \rightarrow (F \rightarrow G)$$
$$F \rightarrow F,$$

which again are evident tautologies.

Proof by Erasure

Predicate Calculus		Propositional Calculus
		. . . .
		. . . .
		. . . .
- - - - - - - - - - - - -	translates	- - - - - - - - - - - -
- - - - - - - - - - - - -	into	- - - - - - - - - - - -
- - - - - - - - - - - - -		- - - - - - - - - - - -
- - - - - - - - - - - - -		- - - - - - - - - - - -
- - - - - - - - - - - - -		- - - - - - - - - - - -
- - - - - - - - - - - - -		- - - - - - - - - - - -
- - - - - - - - - - - - -		- - - - - - - - - - - -
- - - - - - - - - - - - -		- - - - - - - - - - - -
- - - - - - - - - - - - -		- - - - - - - - - - - -
- - - - - - - - - - - - -		- - - - - - - - - - - -
$A \wedge \neg A$		$A' \wedge \neg A'$

(The extra dotted lines at top of proof on right are the proofs in propositional calculus of the substitution instances of the tautology $p \rightarrow p$, which we need to prove the lines $F \rightarrow F$ and $(F \rightarrow G) \rightarrow (F \rightarrow G)$ when they occur corresponding to the citation of axioms of predicate calculus in the original proof.)

Once again, as with non-Euclidean geometry, we imagine that there were an inconsistency in predicate calculus. We then should have a proof by erasure of an inconsistency in propositional calculus, for the special axioms of predicate calculus, when erased, become tautologies, which therefore can be proved as theorems of propositional calculus, and the Rule of Generalisation, when erased, leads to a bare repetition of the preceding line in the proof. So any proof-sequence which yielded an inconsistency in predicate calculus would be converted into a somewhat repetitious proof-sequence of an inconsistency in propositional calculus. And similarly for first-order logic.[15]

---

[15] First-order logic is predicate calculus together with an extra symbol, $=$,

Such proofs are *relative* consistency proofs. They establish the consistency of one axiomatic system, granted that of another, which in turn might be established on condition that some further system is. With Descartes' invention of coordinate geometry we can, in fact, show that Euclidean geometry is consistent provided that the arithmetic of the real numbers is. But however far back we go, relative consistency proofs will always depend on the consistency of some system not itself proved consistent by a relative consistency proof.[16] Some absolute consistency proof is needed. And absolute consistency proofs are, in some cases, forthcoming.

A formal system consists of a finite set of symbols and a few rules for manipulating them. Implicit in the concept of a symbol are the rules, "formation rules", for writing the symbols down. I need to write p the right way up—else it would be indistinguishable from b—and in the relevant place on the paper, the tape, or the screen, and usually we place restrictions on which symbols can be placed next each other—17, 1+7, 1×7 and $p \lor q$ are allowed, but not $+\times$ or $\lor \to$. Formation rules pick out a set of well-formed formulae which is typically a subset of all typographically possible concatenations of symbols. The rules of inference entitle us to manipulate well-formed formulae; often an initial set of axioms is given, although some systems of Natural Deduction dispense with axioms altogether. In either case, however, the rules of inference yield certain *pukka* well-formed formulae—the theorems—which must, according to the rules, be allowed.

The question then arises whether abiding by the rules constitutes any real constraint on the well-formed formulae I am allowed to maintain, or whether every well-formed formula turns out to be a theorem. Clearly, if one of the rules of inference was

from the premis $p \lor p \to p$

to infer q

then granted the former as an axiom and the Rule of Substitution I could produce any well-formed formula whatsoever as a theorem.

Being a theorem is important, but will only retain its significance if it is not co-extensive with merely being well formed. The first requirement on a formal system, therefore, is that these two

representing identity, and appropriate rules for its use.

[16] Compare Plato's difficulty (§1.9) in finding an unpostulated starting point from which he could deduce the truth of geometry and everything else.

concepts should be effectively different, and should not characterize precisely the same sets of symbols. Clearly we want the axioms
to be well formed, and the rules of inference to apply only to well-
formed formulae; so the axioms and the well-formed formulae that
can be derived from them by means of the rules of inference, which
together constitute the theorems of the formal system, are a subset of the well-formed formulae altogether. The question is whether
they are a *proper* subset, or are coterminous with them. If the theorems are a proper subset of the well-formed formulae, we say that
the system is "absolutely consistent": if they are coterminous with
them, we say that the system is "absolutely inconsistent". The reason for adopting this terminology is that in propositional calculus
we have as a theorem:

$$\neg p \rightarrow (p \rightarrow q).$$

It follows that if we can prove two contradictory well-formed formulae, say Γ and its negation $\neg\Gamma$, then by simple substitution in
the theorem, we can prove q or any other well-formed formula we
like. Conversely, if every well-formed formula is a theorem, then in
particular, Γ and $\neg\Gamma$ are. So, if a formal system has symbols with
the formal properties of negation and implication, it will be absolutely consistent iff[17] it satisfies the condition of non-contradiction,
or, as we might say, iff it is "consistent with respect to negation".[18]
Absolute consistency thus expresses the requirement of not being
self-contradictory without actually invoking the concept of contradiction or negation. In stipulating that the set of theorems be a
proper subset of the set of well-formed formulae, it is requiring that
to be a theorem is something more than just being well formed.
Were that not so, were every well-formed formula a theorem, then
there would be no *cachet* in being a theorem. In Gilbert's words

> If everybody is somebody,
> Then nobody is anybody.

Absolute consistency can sometimes be established. We can be
sure that propositional calculus is absolutely consistent, because
the axioms are all tautologies, and the two rules of inference yield

---

[17] 'iff' is short for 'if and only if'. See p.xi.

[18] See Alonzo Church, *Introduction to Mathematical Logic,* Princeton, 1956,
§§18, 19, pp.108-110.

only tautological conclusions from tautological premises, whereas other well-formed formulae, such as p, are not tautological. So p, not being tautological, is not a theorem.[19]   Hence propositional calculus is absolutely consistent. It follows also that no contradiction—no well-formed formula of the form $\Gamma \wedge \neg\Gamma$—can be a theorem; nor can $\neg\Gamma$ be a theorem if Γ is. The connexion between the Law of Non-Contradiction and the intelligibility of discourse becomes more apparent.[20]

Having established the consistency of propositional calculus, we can also prove, by erasure, the consistency of predicate calculus and first-order logic. In some other rather rare cases there are other absolute proofs of consistency. But since we cannot prove the consistency of Peano Arithmetic within Peano Arithmetic, consistency proofs for the formalisations of the main mathematical theories can never be absolutely sceptic-proof,[21] and it will typically call for some element of faith on the part of the mathematician when he commits himself to using them.[22]

The requirement of absolute consistency is a requirement that the set of theorems be not too large. We might also wonder whether it was large enough, or rather, whether it was as large as it could be. We characterize a formal system in which the set of theorems is as large as it can be without making the system absolutely inconsistent as being "syntactically complete". More formally, we say that a formal system is syntactically complete iff the result of adding, as an axiom, any well-formed formula that is not already a theorem would be to make the system absolutely inconsistent. Propositional calculus is syntactically complete, but predicate calculus and first-order logic are not, since we can add, for example

---

[19]   Some care is needed in phrasing this argument. Strictly speaking, we should not talk of being a tautology, which is, as we shall see, a semantic concept, but a carefully defined syntactic equivalent. But anyone who might be minded to make this objection, would be capable of seeing how it could be met. See more fully, Geoffrey Hunter, *Metalogic*, London, 1971, pp.81-83.

[20]   See above, §1.8, and below, §7.5.See, further, J.R.Lucas, "Not 'Therefore' but 'But'", *The Philosophical Quarterly*, **16**, 1966, pp.289-307.

[21]   See below, §8.9.

[22]   For further, informal arguments about the consistency of Peano Arithmetic see J.R.Lucas, *The Freedom of the Will*, Oxford, 1970, §28, pp.146-163.

the well-formed formula $(\mathbf{V}x)Fx$, to the axioms of first-order logic and still be consistent.

A further question is whether a formal system is "decidable", that is, whether for any well-formed formula of the system we can automatically tell if it is a theorem. Caution is needed, because the word 'decidable' is used by mathematical logicians in a different way from our ordinary use. We need, in fact, to distinguish a whole series of different sorts of decidability. At one extreme we have a uniform method of fixed length that will tell us in all cases whether or not any particular instance possesses a certain property. Thus with the natural numbers expressed in decimal notation we can tell whether or not any given number is odd by examining the final digit; similarly whether or not it is divisible by five. More often, however, the length of the procedure for getting an answer will depend on the question: the test for a natural number, expressed in decimal notation, being divisible by three is simple, but the number of steps needed increases as the number of digits increase. Similarly in formal logic the formation rules enable us to tell whether any given formula is well formed or not; but the number of steps needed depends on the formula in question. Propositional calculus is decidable in this sense. From any well-formed formula of propositional calculus there is a step-by-step procedure—an algorithm— with its length depending on the well-formed formula in question, which will end by showing either that the well-formed formula is a theorem or that it is not. The same holds good with the *monadic* predicate calculus, that is, the predicate calculus with monadic predicates ascribing properties but no polyadic ones for relations. Once we go beyond this and have polyadic predicates, first-order logic ceases being decidable in this strong sense. But there is a decision-procedure for theoremhood in a Pickwickian sense. We can go through all possible proof-sequences systematically, and see if any of them end up by proving the well-formed formula in question. IF it is a theorem, then sooner or later its proof will turn up, and we shall know that it is indeed a theorem. But if it is not, we may never know, and may go on grinding out proofs, one after another, until kingdom come. First-order logic has one-way decidability, the weakest sort of decidability there is.[23] It is surprising that it is only one-way decidable. We might have expected

---

[23] See below, §8.8.

it to be two-way decidable, though not boundedly so. This would be the case if there were a test both for theoremhood and for non-theoremhood. Then we could alternate between the two tests until one or the other yielded an answer, and we should know either that it was a theorem or that it was not. We should not know how long we would have to go on for, as we can when we test a well-formed formula of propositional calculus. But we could be sure that sooner or later a definite answer would be forthcoming.

We thus have four different sorts of decidability:

1. fixed-length
2. bounded
3. unbounded two-way
4. unbounded one-way

In ordinary parlance only the first two would be accounted decidable. Mathematical logicians, however, use the term in the third sense. Rather surprisingly it turns out that many formal systems are not decidable in this sense. In Chapter Eight it will emerge that the underlying reason is the emphasis on proof, where in pursuit of maximum cogency proofs are constituted of very few sorts of step, repeated a very large—indefinitely large—number of times.

3.5 Meaning and Interpretation

Plato's charge of meaninglessness was countered by interpretation. In the formal development of finite projective geometry[24] the terms 'line', 'point' and 'on' had no meaning beyond that implicitly conferred on them by the axioms: but if we understood them in the ordinary way, the axioms were true, and the rules of inference preserved truth, so that the theorems were true too. The same would hold good in the lunch club interpretation, with a line being interpreted as a lunch, *etc.* An abstract theory acquires meaning by being interpreted or given a model. Just as group theory is exemplified by the rotations of an ice crystal, the transformations of a Rubik's cube, the permutations of the roots of an equation, or the successive changes rung on a peal of bells, so a formal system may have many interpretations, which bring out its axioms as true, its rules of inference as truth-preserving, and hence its theorems as true, and not in the least devoid of meaning. Besides the purely syntactical study of formal systems sketched in the previous sec-

[24] §2.4.

tion, we can consider formal systems semantically, that is, in terms of their models.

The semantic approach develops naturally from a view of logic that understands it not as concerned with the meaning of words and the avoidance of inconsistency, but as the study of the "universal ordinary", articulating forms of valid argument and classifying patterns of inference that hold good irrespective of the topic being argued about. We need to distinguish variables, which are to vary according to topic, from logical constants, which are the same in every case. Having recognised that from the premises:

All mammals are warm-blooded

All whales are mammals

it follows that

All whales are warm-blooded,

we see, further, that from the premises:

All Greeks are intelligent

All Athenians are Greeks

it follows that

All Athenians are intelligent,

and generally that from the premises:

All Bs are Cs

All As are Bs

it follows that

All As are Cs.

A valid inference on this account is one that holds whatever substitutions are made for the variables; it holds good under all interpretations; whenever the premises are true, the conclusion is true also; any model that brings out the premises as true, brings out the conclusion true too. It is represented by the double turnstile $\models$ in contrast to the single turnstile $\vdash$, where, considering only the syntax, we accept as valid only those arguments we have to allow on pain of inconsistency—the condition of being able to communicate at all.

Many inferences are arguably valid on the semantic approach. There are patterns of inductive inference, and perhaps also of moral inference, which are universal, applicable in all sorts of different cases. Reason is inherently universal, and the study of universally applicable forms of reasoning is within the province of logic; and inductive logic, in particular, is illuminating. On the syntactical approach, by contrast, inductive logic is a contradiction in terms. However many white swans we have observed, it is always possible—logically possible—that the next swan we see will be black. There is no inconsistency in allowing that all swans hitherto have been white, while denying that all swans are white. Neither use of the word 'logic' is wrong. The Greek word λόγος (*logos*) is ambiguous, and can mean 'reason', which supports the semantic view of logic as the universal ordinary, what is common to all particular models, but can equally well mean 'word', which supports the syntactic view of logic as the observance of linguistic rules and the avoidance of inconsistency. The difference is reflected in the pervasive difference between syntactic and semantic approaches. At the risk of being called a racist, I shall say that the syntactic approach is typically that of the Scotsman, careful, reliable, cautious and not conceding anything more than he must, while the semantic approach is typically that of the Welshman, expansive,

Syntactic	Semantic
Scotland	Wales
canny	expansive
reliable	error-prone
well-formedness	meaning
uninterpreted calculus	meaningful discourse
form	content
consistency	truth
provable	true
proof theory	model theory
consistent	sound
constructive	Platonist
finitist	infinitist
$\vdash$	$\vDash$

generous, but perhaps a little error-prone—in speaking of all models, one may be letting in unwelcome intruders.[25]

The ontology is lush, but many of the concepts derived from the syntactic study of formal systems are parallelled in semantics. Corresponding to syntactic consistency is semantic soundness: a formal system is sound if every theorem is true in all models. Semantic completeness is a more natural exegesis of completeness than syntactic completeness was. A formal system is semantically complete if every well-formed formula that is true in all models is a theorem. Thus in a system that is sound and complete every theorem is true in all models and every well-formed formula that is true in all models is a theorem. The theorems are all that they ought to be, and every well-formed formula that ought to be a theorem is one. It is a considerable merit of first-order logic that it is both sound and complete and in the opinion of many logicians a demerit of second-order logic that though sound, it is not, so far as intended models go, complete.[26]

3.6 Epistemological Formalism

We are led to Formalism in pursuit of maximum cogency, and many philosophers have thought that only Formalism could give a satisfactory account of mathematical knowledge. But Formalism fails to provide an adequate epistemology.

It fails because absolute validity is purchased at the cost of absolute vacuity. If arguments are to be absolutely ungainsayable it must be inconsistent to affirm the premises and deny the conclusion. But if it is logically impossible to resist the argument, what the argument is excluding is a nothing, and so what the argument is maintaining is empty too.

"Emptiness" is not a charge that bothers Formalists who often say that mathematical argument is the manipulation of "meaningless" symbols. But although we can, on occasion, consider a formal system as an uninterpreted calculus, it is disingenuous to make out that mathematics is *merely* a game, with no concern for truth, or that the symbols mathematicians manipulate are meaningless all the time. In a formal system we may divest the object language of all meaning, but still have to understand the meta-language in

[25] See below §4.6 and §6.4.

[26] But see further below, §13.5n.

terms of which the object language is defined, and the rules of inference promulgated. Even if we construe algebra entirely abstractly, when we say that a quadratic equation has two roots, we are using the word 'two' in its ordinary, meaningful, sense.

Formalists not only have to understand the meta-language, but often covertly appeal to it in order to provide content for their uninterpreted formalisms. Cardinal numbers, we shall see in the next chapter, can be explicated in terms of first-order logic; we can say that there are at least two elephants in Noah's Ark by saying that there exists an x that is an elephant in Noah's Ark and that there exists a y that is not identical with x and is an elephant in Noah's Ark; and thus we seem to have defined 'at least two' in purely formal terms. But when we come to render 'If there are seven apples and five oranges in the dish there are twelve pieces of fruit altogether', we realise that we are essentially having to distinguish twelve different variables, not just x and y, but, say, $x_1, x_2, x_3, \ldots, x_{11}, x_{12}$ and are counting in the meta-language in order to define numbers in the object language. Even if mathematics is evacuated of all meaning, meta-mathematics is "contentful", and in need of explanation, just as much as unformalised mathematics is.[27]

The Formalist fails even to achieve his own objectives. The drive to eliminate all pattern-recognition can never be carried through completely. We cannot altogether replace an implicit know-how by explicit instructions. Even if the Formalist makes do with only two or three Rules of Inference, some ability is called for in recognising the situations in which those Rules apply. Although there may be some advantage on occasion in reducing the number of different sorts of pattern that have to be recognised, there is no point of principle at stake. Epistemological Formalism has to recognise patterns as much as Epistemological Platonism does: it is just that it seeks to make do with fewer.

The Formalist does indeed make do with fewer forms of argument within his formalism, but cannot be so sparing when he comes to apply his formal systems to particular cases. He has to discern the form of the model, and see if the formal system fits it. In some cases it is a matter of great difficulty to recognise patterns aright, and often we misidentify the relevant pattern at first, and only get

---

[27] For a further example see below, §4.7.

it right after our errors have been pointed out.[28] On a clock face
the hour and minute hands coincide at 12 o'clock, and similarly at
five past one, ten past two, five to eleven, *etc.* There is a pleasing
symmetry about these points of coincidence; most people, asked
how many axes of symmetry there are, reply "Twelve", and only
after they have been taken round the clock hour by hour, recognise that they have double counted half past six and twenty five to
seven, and that the group to apply is a cyclic one of order 11, not
12. Such cases abound. We have to exercise considerable *nous* to
recognise that the uninterpreted calculi studied by the Formalist
apply to particular models. But if mathematicians can develop a
reasonably reliable ability to recognise the true form of a model,
then it is difficult to see why they should not proceed directly, as
the Platonists claim, and recognise relevant forms as they come
across them. There is no pre-eminent virtue in reducing all mathematical argument to instances of very few forms of reasoning, if
at the beginning and the end of an argument mathematicians have
to rely on an ability to recognise correctly a much wider variety of
forms.

> Doing Mathematics is like a Game
>
> but
>
> 1. A special sort of game, because a search for truth
> 2. We still need to understand rules
> 3. We still are led to think informally

Finally, Formalism fails to account for the way mathematicians
actually argue and assess arguments. The Formalist is too fussy.
He clutters up the exposition in his anxiety to dot every *i* and
cross every *t*, so much that the reader cannot see the wood for the
trees. He cannot separate the relevant wheat from the irrelevant
chaff, and can give no account of the "depth" of a mathematical
theorem. We value proofs because they are deep, because they
are beautiful, because they are fruitful, because they are ingenious.
These dimensions of assessment are obscured if proofs are construed
as being essentially proof-sequences, no more and no less.

---

[28] See below, §14.4.

3.7 The Logicist Programme

Although Formalism was contrasted with Logicism in Chapter One, they have much in common. They are rivals as regards the justification of their axioms, but thereafter are both committed to arguing *more geometrico*. The development and criticisms of the Formalist programme has helped also the articulation of a logicist programme.

Plato could not go very far along the logicist path, although he had many logicist intuitions, and lectured on The One, which he identified with the Form of the Good, because geometry seemed entirely separate from arithmetic. Descartes' coordinate geometry not only secures the consistency of geometry relative to that of the real numbers, but paves the way for grounding geometry as a particular sort of algebra over the real numbers. If we can give an adequate account of the real numbers in terms of the rationals, and of the rationals in terms of the positive rationals, and of the positive rationals in terms of the natural numbers, and if we could, furthermore, as the Logicists claimed, give an adequate account of the natural numbers in terms of concepts that are purely logical, self-evidently true, and in need of no further justification, then we should have established geometry, and indeed the whole of mathematics, on a satisfactory foundation. Logic, we could reasonably claim, is our ἀρχὴ ἀνυπόθετος (*arche anupothetos*), an unpostulated starting point, from which we can decently derive the whole of mathematics.

Some of the steps are straightforward. We can give an account of the positive rational numbers (the fractions) in terms of the positive whole numbers. Normally we express fractions by writing two positive whole numbers, one (the numerator) above the other (the denominator):

$$\frac{2}{3}, \frac{3}{4}, \frac{5}{12}, \frac{17}{13}, \ etc.$$

but with the understanding that we divide out common factors; that is to say

$$\frac{4}{6} = \frac{2}{3}, \frac{3}{4} = \frac{6}{8} = \frac{9}{12}, \frac{25}{60} = \frac{5}{12}, \frac{68}{52} = \frac{34}{26} = \frac{17}{13}, \ etc.$$

We can define positive rational numbers as ordered pairs of positive whole numbers, subject to an equivalence relation

$$\frac{w}{x} \approx \frac{y}{z} \ \text{iff} \ w \times z = x \times y.$$

(Often, to emphasize the abstract nature of this definition, we write

$$(w, x) \text{ instead of } \frac{x}{y}.)$$

It is easy then to define multiplication of rational numbers, rather more cumbersome to define addition. When we have defined addition, we can introduce negative rational numbers, in much the same way as we introduced fractions, as ordered equivalence classes of pairs of rational numbers, only with a different equivalence relation:

$$(w, x) \approx (y, z) \text{ iff } w + z = x + y;$$

((w, x) represents w minus x, instead of w divided by x).

Other steps are problematic. Dedekind and Cantor define real numbers in terms of sets of a special sort, with difficulties arising over impredicable sets.[29] Moreover, Frege defines natural numbers by means of second-order logic, which is commonly construed nowadays in terms of sets; and Whitehead and Russell reconstruct Frege's definition of natural number explicitly in terms of sets, or "classes" as they call them. We are embroiled with set theory, and set theory is a mess.

Again, we have to tangle with infinity in a more direct way than in geometry. Although there is some involvement with infinity in some geometries, it is rather peripheral; infinity for Euclid is where parallel lines meet; Hilbert's axioms of order and continuity have some implications which involve infinity; but in each case the involvement is neither direct nor very great; infinity in geometry is lurking only at the corner of the eye. In arithmetic, however, we are going straight towards it, and cannot but be aware that it awaits us just over the hill.

And finally, as we shall see in Chapter Eight, Gödel's theorem shows that Elementary Number Theory is incomplete. These are great difficulties, and the logicist programme did not, within its own terms, succeed. Nevertheless, it is illuminating to follow it through; suitably moderated, Logicism does give a satisfactory grounding for mathematics, particularly in its elucidation of the natural numbers.

[29] See below, §15.3.

Logicist Programme of Reduction

1. Euclidean Geometry $\longmapsto$ Cartesian Geometry
2. Real Numbers $\longmapsto$ Rational Numbers (beware)
3. Rational Numbers $\longmapsto$ Positive Rationals
4. Positive Rationals $\longmapsto$ Natural Numbers
   [a +*ve* rational number is an equivalence class of
   ordered pairs of positive whole numbers:
   $3/4 \approx 6/8 \approx 9/12 \approx \cdots$ *etc.*
   $(w, x) \approx (y, z)$ iff $w \times z = x \times y$]
5. Natural Numbers can be axiomatized by Peano's
   five postulates involving three primitive concepts:
   0, successor, number (See below, ch.6.)
6. (i) Frege defines 0, Successor and Cardinal Number
   (needs "concepts": see below, ch.4.)
   (ii) Dedekind defines 1, Successor, Progression of
   Ordinal Numbers (needs 2nd-order logic: see below,
   ch.5.)
7. Whitehead & Russell, *Principia Mathematica*,
   prove Peano's Postulates. (Need Set Theory,
   Axiom of Infinity, Axiom of Choice, Axiom of
   Reducibility)

So for Logicist Programme we need:
equivalence relations, ordered pairs, set theory

Table 3.7.1

Chapter 4
Numbers: The Cardinal Approach

4.1 Etymology

Linguistically, numerals are odd. Often in inflected languages, though not in Russian, they are, with the exception of the smaller ones, indeclinable. In Greek εἷς, δύο, τρεῖς, τέσσαρες (*heis, duo, treis, tessares*) decline, but the rest not. In Latin *unus, duo, tres* decline, but the rest not. In French and German indeclinability begins with *deux* and *zwei*, with only *un, une* and *ein, eine* behaving like adjectives, as in almost every other major language where the words for none and one are declinable, and agree with their noun. In English all the numerals are indeclinable; in German there is a distinction between the use of *ein, eine* as a number asking, or anticipating the question 'How many?', in which use it declines and agrees with the noun, and the use of *eins* as a counting number, where it is indeclinable. Indeclinability is on the increase. The older the language, the more numerals are wedded to their nouns, and have to agree with them, like adjectives; but they are gradually shaking off their etymological shackles, and establishing themselves as free-standing self-subsistent citizens.

Most languages are unsystematic below ten, with the exception of Basque, where the word for nine is *bederatzi* meaning 'one lower', in the same way as *undeviginti* means nineteen in Latin. Nine, ἐννέα (*ennea*), *novem, neuf, neun*, was the new number, and perhaps goes back to a time when our ancestors were beginning to go beyond the numbers they all could see at a glance, and were able to answer 'Nine' when asked 'How Many?' only by resorting to the new method of counting. Eight, ὀκτώ, *octo*, was originally a dual, perhaps expressed by the two hands being held up showing four fingers apiece.

After ten, and especially after twenty, the names become systematic.[1] In Latin and Greek, *undecim, duodecim,* ἕνδεκα, δώδεκα are already on a decimal scheme. Our 'eleven', the German *elf*, is still irregular, but 'twelve' already shows signs of twoness, and thirteen, fourteen, *etc.*, are obviously systematic. After twenty almost every language is regular. The only exception is French, where seventy, eighty, and ninety are expressed periphrastically, like our 'three score years and ten'. The metropolitan French despise the Belgians who say *septante, huitante,* and *nonante,* but it is the metropolitan version that has regressed, while the French spoken on the peripheries, in Belgium, in Switzerland, and in Quebec, has kept the logic that is the pride of the Gallic tongue.

The ordinals are also instructive. 'First', *primus,* πρῶτος (*protos*), are all superlative in form. *Secundus* in Latin and 'second' in English are not formed from the cardinals *'duo'* and 'two', but from *sequor,* I follow. In Greek δεύτερος (*deuteros*), is connected with *duo* but is comparative in form, as is the Latin *alter* which is often used for the "twoth" member of a sequence. 'Third' and *tertius* are not quite standard in form, but from 'fourth' onwards the ordinals are formed systematically from the cardinals. It is noteworthy, and of considerable significance, that although we can use an ordinal form for rather large numbers—'The Old Hundredth', 'One hundred and fourthly', 'The Hundred and Twenty First Psalm'— we tend to use the simple form 'Ps. 100', '104.)' or 'Ps. 121' in which we use cardinal numbers in an ordinal way as counting numbers. Language suggests that smaller numbers have highly individual names and present themselves as predominantly cardinal, large numbers are named systematically and are much more ordinal in feel.

There are many other numerals besides the cardinals and ordinals:

    once, twice, thrice, four times, ...
    whole, half, third, quarter, fifth, ...
    single, double, treble
    single, couple, triple, quadruple, quintuple, ... n-tuple,
    twins, triplets, quads, quins, sextuplets
    twosome, threesome, foursome

---

[1] Most languages are based on the decimal system, although shepherds in the North of England used to count in a Celtic dialect to the base five.

solo, duo/duet, trio, quartet, quintet, ..., octet.

primary, secondary, tertiary, quaternary.

We should also notice the contrast simple/multiple, simplicity/duplicity. Besides the word 'couple' we have 'pair' and 'brace'. Often the appropriate word depends on the social or linguistic context—we play doubles in tennis but row in pairs; we have a couple of hounds, a pair of turtle doves, and a brace of pheasants. In Japanese the principle is extended very far, and the numerals vary systematically with what is being numbered.[2] In English we do not go beyond two in exact numbering, but some of our inexact collective words vary in the same way—a flock of sheep, a herd of pigs, a covey of partridges, a gaggle of geese, a drove of cattle, a team of oxen, a hatch of flies, and a charm of goldfinches.

4.2 The Uses of Numbers

The moral to be drawn is that we use numerals in many different ways. We use them as answers to the question 'How many?', as a means of expressing an order, and as a repetitively enlargeable stock of basically similar names.

The difference between the first and second uses is illustrated by the song "Green grow the rushes, Oh!".

> I'll sing you seven, Oh!
> What are your seven, Oh?
> Seven are the seven stars in the sky...

The first two uses of the word 'seven' are as **counting numbers**: I'll sing you one, I'll sing you two, I'll sing you three, I'll sing you four, I'll sing you five, I'll sing you six, . . *etc.* In its third use, where we say 'Seven are the seven stars in the sky', we are using seven as a cardinal number, answering the question 'How many stars are there in the sky?'. If I am asked 'How many stars are there in the sky?', I can answer 'seven', and this is a different use of the word 'seven' from when I am just counting.

The chorus makes a further important point about the natural numbers:

> Seven are the seven stars in the sky,
> Six are the six Proud Walkers,

---

[2] I am indebted to the Crown Prince of Japan for authoritative confirmation of this fact.

Five are the symbols at your door,
Four are the Gospel Makers,
Three, three are the rivals,
Two, two are the lilly-white boys,
One is one and all alone and ever more shall be so.

And at that point the chorus stops. It cannot go on. We have run out of counting numbers. For, whatever may be the case with ordinary counting upwards, count-downs are always finite. Even with transfinite numbers, so long as I count backwards, I shall always in the end get to an end.[3] The case is very different if I count forwards. Then there is no end to how far I can go. As soon as I have finished 'I'll sing you seven, Oh!' with its chorus, off I go on 'I'll sing you eight, Oh!'. This is a further lesson to be learned from the song. There is no mathematically determined end to the progression of natural numbers, as there is to any regression: although they have a least number, they do not have a greatest number. And yet in fact the song does not go on for ever, but stops when we have reached twelve. So far as mathematics goes, we need not stop there: we could go on to thirteen; we could go on to fourteen; we could go on to one hundred and forty four: but the mind boggles. After twelve, there is a certain repetitiveness about our numbers. It is rather clever to be able to count up to twelve, and shows a certain mastery of the English language, but when we go beyond twelve, it becomes somewhat mechanical. Twelve is, as we claimed in the previous section, the last number with an individuality all of its own.

Besides the cardinal and ordinal uses of numbers, we use them as names when we want to play down the differences between the entities we are naming—criminals are often referred to only as a number, soldiers have a number, as did civilians during the War. We find it offensive, because it suggests that they are qualitatively identical and only numerically distinct, and implies that people are merely units without any individuality of their own. It is not similarly offensive to use numbers to name things. Car registration numbers and telephone numbers use numerals and letters to

---

[3]   This has important consequences for the proof-sequences of §2.3 and §3.4; given any purported proof, I can always work back to the beginning, and thus check every step in the sure knowledge that I shall be able to check them all. So proofs are two-way decidable.

constitute an identifying name or address.

Mathematicians are similarly varied in their use of numerals, although more inclined to the third type of use than the first or the second. Sometimes numerals are used simply as labels, as when we index a set of entities $a_1, a_2, a_3, \ldots$ *etc.* Sometimes they are addresses, as when we use coordinates to label the points of a space. Often they are taken to refer to abstract entities, which may be studied in their own right, or may be used as models, a set of distinct entities which can be shown to satisfy some set of postulates. Sometimes they are clearly ordinal, as when we talk of a second-order differential equation, or solutions of quintic equations. And sometimes they are cardinal, as when we say a quadratic equation has two roots. Often the uses overlap, as when we use real numbers both as coordinates and to indicate the distance from the relevant axes. But the uses do not always overlap, and it is easy to obtain a distorted view of number by concentrating on only one use.

The three primary senses of the words used for natural numbers will be discussed in this and the following two chapters. Numerals can be used to refer to **Cardinal Numbers**, answers to the question 'How many?'. Frege and Russell took cardinal numbers as basic, and hoped by elucidating them to elucidate the nature of all other numbers as well. They can also be used to refer to **Ordinal Numbers**. Ordinal numbers, as we saw in the previous section, can be expressed in two different ways. They can be expressed by the ordinal terms, 'first', 'second', 'third', *etc.*, or they can be expressed simply by counting, 'one', 'two', 'three', *etc.* In the latter case, we may call them 'Counting Numbers' rather than ordinals, but the important thing about them is just the order they have; and they should be regarded as being logically much the same as the ordinals. Dedekind, Cantor, Peano and Kronecker, all took ordinal numbers as basic, and tried to elucidate them as a step to elucidating numbers generally. Numerals can, thirdly, be used **Symbolically**, where we have them formed repetitively, according to some definite rule, rather dully; we have a finite stock of digits, together with some sort of rule, so that we can always go on, forming new expressions, as required. It is the sort of thing computers can be programmed to do, but, so far as finite numbers are concerned, presents none but technical problems of programming expertise. Peano, again, can be seen as protagonist of this approach, although he was dealing not with decimal, nor even with binary, digits, but with unary ones.

Numbers

1. Cardinal	Answers to question 'How many?' natural numbers Nought, One, Two, Three,...	Frege, Russell
2. Ordinal	Place in a list ordinals counting numbers First, Second, Third,... One, Two, Three,...	Dedekind, Cantor, Kronecker (Peano)
3. Abstract	Symbolic $1, 2, 3, ..., 10, 11, ..., 100, ... 1024, ...$ $1,000,000,000,000,000$ 10^{10} $10^{10^{10}}$ 35K	Peano

---

4.3 How Many?

Frege maintained that we should locate natural numbers on the conceptual map by considering cardinal numbers. Cardinal numbers are, he argued, answers to the question 'How many?', in Latin *Quot?*, in Greek πόσοι; (*posoi?*). He further pointed out that in order to ask the question 'How many?', we need to specify *two* variables: that is, if I ask the question 'How many?' I have got to fill it out in two ways, and ask "How many *whats* there are in *what*?".[4] We get different answers if we ask how many books there are in the *Iliad*, or how many lines; how many packs there are in a pile of cards, or how many honour cards in the game of skat. Berkeley, and before him Plato, had noticed the same point, but had wrongly seen it as an argument for subjectivism.[5] For although

---

[4] G.Frege, *The Foundations of Arithmetic*, tr. J.L.Austin, Oxford, 1950, §22, §46,§49,§52, pp.28-29,59-60,62,64.

[5] G.Berkeley, *New Theory of Vision*, §109; *Principles of Human Knowledge*, §xii; *Republic* VII, 522c-526a; and *Hippias Major*, 300e-302e.

it is up to me what question I ask, it is not up to me what the correct answer is. Having asked 'How many books are there in the *Iliad*?', I cannot get as a correct answer 'Twenty three' (although if I want to get the answer 'Twenty three', I can elicit it by asking a different question, *e.g.* 'How many un-boring books are there in the *Iliad*?').

The logical status of the two variables is different. The first is an individual variable, ranging over books, un-boring books, lines, packs of cards, cards, honour cards at skat. The second variable is a predicate variable. It indicates what the individuals have in common that prompts us to ask how many there are. It is books or lines in the *Iliad*, not in the *Odyssey* nor the *Aenead*. It is cards in the pile in my friend's hands, not in the cupboard or in a shop. Logicians make the distinction between individual and predicate variables in formal logic by using lower case letters for the former and capital letters for the latter. The convention is to write the capital letter for the predicate first, and the lower-case letter(s) for the individual variable(s) second. We might use b for books, l for lines, I for in the *Iliad*, O for in the *Odyssey*, and A for in the *Aeneid*. We could then ask 'How many?', or in Latin *Quot?*, in these combinations:

Quot I(b)?	*Quot O(b)?*	*Quot A(b)?*
Quot I(l)?	*Quot O(l)?*	*Quot A(l)?*

and obtain the answers

24	24	12
15,688	12,225	9,896

In the standard predicate calculus as it has been developed by logicians in this century, all the emphasis has been on the predicates, with the individual variables being reduced to the status of mere dummies, rather like the dx in an integration. If we want to express 'All humans are mortal' we do not write it as[6]

$$(Ah)Mh$$

but as

$$(Ax)(Hx \rightarrow Mx).$$

where (Ah) and (Ax) are "universal quantifiers" (or "quotifiers" as we shall be led to call them) binding h and x respectively. Instead

---

[6] For (A) and (V) (normally written ($\forall$) and ($\exists$)) see note on logical symbols on p.xi.

of talking about the noun, 'humans', we use the adjective, 'human', and talk about all beings, not only human ones, saying of each of them that if it is Human, it is Mortal.[7] In a similar fashion we rephrase sentences of the form 'Some humans are Wise' which might naturally be expressed by means of the "existential quantifier", $(\mathrm{V}h)Wh$, as 'Some beings are Human and Wise' $(\mathrm{V}x)(Hx \wedge Wx)$. Whatever their merits for ordinary formal logic, such rephrasings are not helpful for an analysis of number, where we do not want to slur over the difference between individual variables and predicate variables. Instead of the standard predicate calculus, we need to use the "Many-Sorted" predicate calculus developed by Professor Smiley,[8] in which there are many sorts of individual variables, with appropriate rules correlating each individual variable, such as h, for humans (as a noun), with the corresponding predicate variable, such as H, for Human (as an adjective). Thus Smiley has a typical axiom

$$(\mathrm{A}h)Hh$$

i.e. All humans are Human. From this, and other highly acceptable axioms, he is able to develop a predicate calculus which is much more natural and closer to our normal ways of thinking and expressing ourselves than the standard predicate calculus studied by logicians. For our purposes, however, we do not need to follow Smiley's development of the Many-Sorted Predicate Calculus. All we need is the general form of question

$$(Quot\ h)Wh?$$

symbolizing the question 'How many humans are Wise?'; or

$$(Quot\ s)Ps?$$

for the question 'How many honour cards at skat are there in this pile?'; or

$$(Quot\ m)Jm?$$

---

[7] In this passage, for ease of reading, I follow a counter-Germanic convention, giving adjectives a capital initial letter and nouns only a lower-case one.

[8] T.J. Smiley, "Syllogism and Quantification", *Journal of Symbolic Logic*, **27**, 1962, pp.58-72; see also Hao Wang, *Journal of Symbolic Logic*, **17**, 1952, pp.105-116; and Alonzo Church, *Introduction to Mathematical Logic*, Princeton, 1956, pp.339-341.

for the question 'How many moons of Jupiter are there?'; or

$$(Quot\ b)Ab?$$

for the question 'How many books are there in the *Aeneid*?' *etc.*
and possible answers to these questions, which we shall symbolize
in the general form

$$(Q\ h)Wh,\quad (Q\ s)Ps,\quad (Q\ m)Jm,\quad (Q\ b)Ab,\ etc.$$

Q is a sort of quantifier, that is a term of the same logical type as
'some', 'all', 'none', 'no' $(Vx), (Ax),$ ...*etc.* The name 'quantifier'
is unfortunate, as the question to which there are possible answers
is not *Quantum?* (How much?) but *Quot?* (How many?). On
this score, contrary to the general tendency, Latin proves itself a
better philosophical tool than Greek. In Greek the word for 'how
many?', πόσοι; (*posoi?*) and for 'how much?', πόσον;, (*poson?*)
are very similar, whereas in Latin *quot?* and *quantum?* are obviously different.[9] The Greeks knew that there was a distinction to
be drawn, and and were careful in distinguishing the sort of thing,
which they called πλῆθος (*plethos*) a multitude, about which the
question πόσοι; (*posoi?*), *quot?*, 'how many?' could be asked, from
the sort of thing, which they called μέγεθος, (*megethos*) a magnitude, about which the question ποσόν; (*poson?*), *quantum?*, 'how
much?' could be asked. But although they draw this distinction,
and although the Schoolmen were very clear about its importance,
it has been largely obscured in modern thought. In modern logic we
talk about "Quantification Theory", in which we use quantifiers.
But it is "Quotification Theory" we should be studying in logic,
with quotifiers answering our questions 'How many men are mortal?', 'How many pigs can fly?', 'How many undergraduates are
clever?', and 'How many professors are absent-minded?', by the
answers 'All', 'None', 'Some', and 'Not all', respectively. Quantification is something that a quantity surveyor does, and when we
come to consider the application of real numbers to magnitudes,
and are properly concerned with quantifying them and assigning
to them a suitable quantitative measure, we shall need to keep the

---

[9] But Greek does have another word, πηλίκος (*pelikos*), which is specifically
concerned with bulk rather than multitude.

distinction very clear.[10] And so, although it is too late to hope to reform the speech-habits of logicians, I shall be pedantic, and speak of quotification, quotifiers, and quotities throughout.

Let us, then, invent the word 'quotifier', and say that $(Q\ h)$ is a quotifier. Since there are different possible answers to the question 'How many humans are Wise?', we leave at present a blank after the Q, which can be filled by the appropriate numeral when we know the answer to the question. Thus $(Q_{24}\ b)Ib$ is our answer to the question: *Quot I(b)?*, 'How many books are there in the *Iliad*?'. Strictly speaking the individual variables, h and b in the examples above, are redundant, being adequately specified by the h in the Wh and the b in the Ib. But we shall have occasion to use more complex formulae in which there are other bound individual variables, where it will help to indicate which was the relevant individual variable in question; and in any case it is desirable to stress the analogy between

$$(Q\ h)\ \text{and}\ (Q_{24}\ b)Ib \qquad \text{on the one hand,}$$
and $\qquad(Ax)\ \text{and}\ (Vx) \qquad\qquad$ on the other.

Besides the quotifiers studied in formal logic, there are some others, such as 'many', 'most', 'few', and 'a few', which can also be given as answers to the question 'how many?', in addition to the numerical answers which seem most often to be called for. All these should be classed as quotifiers.[11] Although less specific than numerical answers, they are analogous in being of the same logical shape as numbers; or, more illuminatingly, numbers are analogous to them.

Frege calls the complex expression, Wh in our example, which can be read as 'humans who are Wise', or in his examples 'moons of Jupiter', 'horses who draw the king's carriage', 'leaves on a tree', a "concept", but he is at pains to argue that they are not merely creations or attributes of our minds. Concepts are objective (as also are numbers, which are, in Frege's terminology "assigned" (*legen*)

---

[10] In ch.11.

[11] It is worth quoting the sentence: "I am the one who gave his all in the fight of the few against the many", cited by Paul Benacerraf in his "What Numbers Could Not Be", *Philosophical Review*, **74**, 1965; reprinted in Paul Benacerraf and Hilary Putnam, eds., *Philosophy of Mathematics*, 2nd ed., Cambridge, 1983, p.284.

to concepts, or "belong" (*kommen*) to concepts[12] but are not material objects or spatially located ones, nor attributable only to
collections of material objects, as he accuses Mill of supposing. He
quotes Locke and Leibniz, who point out that we can ask and answer numerical questions about non-material objects just as well
as about material ones[13]—How many roots does a quadratic equation have? How many groups are those of order eight? How many
persons in the Trinity? How many figures of the Aristotelian Syllogism? Frege also points out the difference between numbers and
ordinary predicates which might be said to be assigned to, or to belong to, objects. We speak of a tree's having 1000 leaves in a quite
different sense from its having green leaves.[14] From the latter it follows that each leaf is green, but it does not follow from the former
that each leaf is 1000. Arguing the other way, Frege points out that
whereas from 'Solon was wise' and 'Thales was wise' there follows
'Solon and Thales were wise' from 'Solon was one' and 'Thales was
one' there does not follow 'Solon and Thales were one'.[15] A similar ambiguity occurs in English childhood experience. When the
hostess at a children's party says 'Now we are six', she may mean
it individually, that each one of us is six years old, and go on to say
'we are too old to cry', or she may mean it collectively, and go on
to say 'we can form a ring, and play ring o' ring of roses'. *Being six
years old* is logically speaking, an adjective: our together being six
in number is not. The logical grammar of numerals is thus clearly
different from that of ordinary adjectives. Even in languages where
the numeral declines and agrees with the noun, the entailment patterns are like those of the word 'all', *omnes*, πάντες (*pantes*), so
that numerals in these uses should be classed as quotifiers rather
than ordinary adjectives or nouns.

---

[12] G.Frege, *The Foundations of Arithmetic*, tr. J.L.Austin, Oxford, 1950, §46, p.59; §55, p.67; and elsewhere.

[13] *The Foundations of Arithmetic*, §24, p.31; citing John Locke, *Essay on Human Understanding*, II, 16, 1, and G.W. Leibniz, (Erdman ed., pp.8 and 162).

[14] *The Foundations of Arithmetic*, §22, p.28.

[15] *The Foundations of Arithmetic*, §29, pp.40-41.

4.4 Nought

That Frege's arguments lead to the conclusion that numerals are a
sort of quotifier is shown most clearly by his account of the number
Nought. To say that the number of moons of Venus is nought is
simply to say that there are no moons of Venus, which is to say that
there does not exist any moon of Venus, which can be expressed
symbolically:

$$\neg(Vm)Vm) \qquad (\text{or} \quad (Am)\neg Vm)$$

where m stands for moon, and V for orbiting round Venus (to be
distinguished from (V), the existential quotifier). The case for
explaining 'nought' in terms of 'naught' or 'no' or 'none' is over-
whelming. Further support, if any were needed, comes from Frege's
explicit statement that existence is analogous to number, and his
reference to the standard critique of the Ontological Argument.[16]
The core of the criticism is that the Ontological Argument assumes
that existence is a property whereas it is really something expressed
by a quotifier. But if existence is something expressed by a quotifier
and is analogous to number, number must be something expressed
by a quotifier too.

Nought is the cardinal number to begin with: if asked 'How
many moons of Venus are there?' or 'How many stars in the
Pleiades can you distinguish?', I may say 'Nought' but I may well
say 'None'. 'Nought' and 'None' are both possible answers to the
cardinal question 'How many?', and no account of cardinal numbers that excludes them will be satisfactory. Nought thus plays
a crucial role in the cardinal approach. It clinches the argument
for holding that numerals are quotifiers, and it anchors them by
identifying one numeral as one of the quotifiers we are already familiar with. If we can give a recursive definition of each numeral
in terms of its predecessor, then we shall have achieved a general
schema of definition for every one. We can, as it were, sing our
way through the chorus of "Green Grow the Rushes, Oh!", defining each in terms of its predecessor, until our count-down reaches
nought, and then we can define nought in entirely non-numerical
terms. Every other numeral is defined generically as a quotifier,

---

[16] G.Frege, *The Foundations of Arithmetic*, tr. J.L.Austin, Oxford, 1950,
§53, p.65.

but specifically in numerical terms as the successor of an quotifier. But nought is not the successor of any number; instead, it is
equivalent to None, and None is definable in terms of either All or
Some, either, that is, as $(Ax)\neg$ or as $\neg(Vx)$, so that we can give a
completely explicit definition of the nought quotifier, and say:

$(\mathcal{Q}_0)Fx$ is defined as $(Ax)\neg Fx$

'Nought' is not the only word for nought. We talk of absolute
zero, and use the symbol '0' to express a cypher. There are, correspondingly, other conceptual connexions. Absolute zero, 0K, is
that temperature lower than which it is impossible to go. Zero
is the measure of a minimum magnitude, and when we come to
measure theory in Chapter Twelve, minimality is a more important link than none-ness. We can also characterize 0 as the natural
number that is not the successor of any natural number, and as
the Identity element under the operation of addition.[17] Thus if, as
in Chapter Three, we introduce negative numbers as equivalence
classes of ordered pairs of positive numbers, (x, y), subject to the
equivalence relation $(x, y) \approx (z, w)$ iff[18] $x + w = y + z$, we can
introduce 0 as (x, x), or equivalently (y, y), or (z, z), *etc.* We then
have $(z, w) + (x, x) = (z, w)$, for all (z, w). Another characterization, less obvious, but of some theoretic interest, is that 0 is the
"universal element" under multiplication: that is, $0 \times x = 0$ whatever the x. In this it resembles ∞ under addition, the speed of
light in the Special Theory of Relativity, $\top$ under $\vee$ and $\bot$ under
$\wedge$ in propositional calculus, where $p \vee \top$ is $\top$ for all p, and $p \wedge \bot$ is
always $\bot$.[19]

4.5 Quotifiers and Quotities

If we can give an adequate account of nought, we can reasonably
hope to do the same for other numerical quotifiers. Frege sketches
a recursive definition, and shows that it satisfies requirements essentially similar to those of Peano's postulates,[20] but the modern

---

[17] See below, §6.2, §12.7.

[18] Short for 'if and only if'.

[19] See further, §11.7.

[20] G.Frege, *The Foundations of Arithmetic*, tr. J.L.Austin, Oxford, 1950,
§76-§79, pp.89-92.

exposition of David Bostock is simpler.[21] We need to make a distinction between the assertion that there are *exactly* n things of type x that are F and the assertion that there are *at least* n things of type x that are F. The distinction is brought out by the limerick

> There was an old man of Lyme
> Who married three wives at a time;
>   When asked "Why the third?"
>   He replied "One's absurd,
> And bigamy, Sir, is a crime!"

It is fairly easy to give recursive definitions of 'There are at least n things of type x that are F' and 'There are at most n things of type x that are F', which are the concepts we need for defining bigamy and monogamy. We could then give Lyme definitions, and define 'There are exactly n things of type x that are F' as the conjunction of 'There are at least n things of type x that are F' and 'There are at most n things of type x that are F', but we can more economically define 'There are exactly n things of type x that are F' by the conjunction of 'There are at least n things of type x that are F and the denial of 'There are at least n' things of type x that are F', where n' is the next number after n. If there are at least six Proud Walkers and it is not the case that there are at least seven Proud Walkers, then there are exactly six Proud Walkers.

So let us start defining 'There are at least.....things of type x that are F'. The usual existential quotifier $(Vx)Fx$ expresses that there is at least 1 thing of type x that is F. We could write it explicitly as $(V_1x)Fx$. Let us set out this definition formally:

$(V_1x)Fx$ is defined as $(Vx)Fx$

It then is easy to define $(V_2x)Fx$ in terms of $(V_1x)Fx$

$(V_2x)Fx$ is defined as $(Vx)(Fx \land (V_1y)(Fy \land y \neq x))$

We should note in this definition that (Vx) is used on one occasion and (V_1y) on the other, even though we have defined the latter as being exactly the same as the former. The reason for this becomes clear when we generalise and make similar definitions for $(V_2x)Fx$, $(V_3x)Fx$, and generally $(V_nx)Fx$, thus:

$(V_3x)Fx$ is defined as $(Vx)(Fx \land (V_2y)(Fy \land y \neq x))$

Similarly

$(V_4x)Fx$ is defined as $(Vx)(Fx \land (V_3y)(Fy \land y \neq x))$

---

[21] David Bostock, *Logic and Arithmetic*, I, Oxford, 1979, ch.1, §2, pp.9-25.

and, generally,

$(V_{n'}x)Fx$ is defined as $(Vx)(Fx \land (V_n y)(Fy \land y \neq x))$

This last definition can be rephrased in terms of predecessors rather than successors, so as to make it obvious that we are embarking on a "count-down" definition which must come to a conclusion. Let us write n^* for the predecessor of n. Then

$(V_n x)Fx$ is defined as $(Vx)(Fx \land (V_{n^*} y)(Fy \land y \neq x))$

Having now given a general recursive formula for defining 'There are at least n things of type x that are F', we define our numerical quotifiers in terms of there being at least n things of type x that are F, but not n' things of type x that are F. Formally, we first define $(Q_0 x)Fx$:

$(Q_0 x)Fx$ is defined as $\neg(V_1 x)Fx$

(which is the same as $\neg(Vx)Fx$, which in turn is the same as $(Ax)\neg Fx$, as used in our first definition); we then go on to define $(Q_1 x)$ in terms of $(V_1 x)Fx$ and $(V_2 x)Fx$:

$(Q_1 x)$ is defined as $(V_1 x)Fx \land \neg(V_2 x)Fx$

Similarly $(Q_2 x)$ is defined as $(V_2 x)Fx \land \neg(V_3 x)Fx$

and generally: $(Q_n x)$ is defined as $(V_n x)Fx \land \neg(V_{n'} x)Fx$

This completes the formal definition of the numerical quotifiers. The definition is a bit more cumbersome than we might have hoped, but it has none the less achieved our aim of giving an account of the cardinal use of numerals and grounding them in other, non-numerical concepts. To the question "What are numerals?" we answer: "Numerals are quotifiers, that is to say, answers to the question 'How many?', and of the same logical type as 'All', 'Some', 'None', and 'Not all'; and indeed, the numeral 'nought' is just another word for 'none'." But if we were further asked what *numbers* are, as distinct from numerals, we could not answer similarly. As Hunter felicitously puts it:[22]

> Any numerical adjective, but no numerical noun, can be unambiguously defined in the language Q <*i.e.* first-order logic>, interpreted only with respect to the quantifiers, the connectives, and a symbol for identity.

Some further step is needed. Plato, similarly dissatisfied with accounts of how words such as 'just' or 'virtuous' were used in particular contexts, postulated some abstract entity that lay behind their various uses, and eventually, somewhat apologetically, coined

---

[22] Geoffrey Hunter, *Metalogic*, London, 1971, §49, [49.6], p.207.

the word ποιότης (*poiotes*), 'qual-ity' from ποῖος (*poios*), the equivalent of the Latin *qualis*, to mean what he had in mind.[23] We
might likewise say that numbers are "quotities", where quotities
stand to quotifiers as qualities do to adjectives and as substances
do to substantives.

In first-order logic we use two quotifiers, (Ax) and (Vx), and
they are classed along with the truth functors, ¬, ←, &, ∨, ↔, ⊤
and ⊥ (otherwise known as sentential functors, sentential connectives, or logical constants). We can say that there are *sixteen* different binary truth functions, which can *all* be expressed in terms
of negation and disjunction. If truth functions can be counted, and
quotities are like truth functions, then quotities look the right logical shape to be counted too. If we can, so as to be able to say that
there are three prime numbers between 10 and 20, then we are in
effect quotifying over quotities, and treating them as variables, in
which case Quine's *dictum* "To be is to be the value of a variable"
applies, and we are ascribing to quotities high ontological status.[24]
It is a test that qualities pass: "He has three good qualities", we
say in a reference, "loyalty, adaptability and industry"; and we use
the universal quotifier of qualities in Russell's example of the man
who had all the qualities of Napoleon. Quotities and qualities are
in the same case. We can quotify over qualities, and so should be
able to quotify over quotities themselves, being likewise countable;
and in the absence of cogent metaphysical arguments against their
being counted or otherwise quotified over, we should be happy to
accept them as respectable abstract entities with a reasonably clear
conscience.

If we have a whole series of quotifiers:

$$(Q_0\,),(Q_1\,),(Q_2\,),(Q_3\,),\ldots,(Q_{24}\,),\ldots,$$

we can discern a pattern, and pick out the subscripts:

$$0,\ 1,\ 2,\ 3,\cdots,\ 24,\cdots,$$

in much the same way as mathematicians do when they discern
the same group structure in a number of different groups, or the

---

[23] *Theaetetus* 182a.

[24] W.V.O.Quine, *From a Logical Point of View*, Cambridge, Mass., 1953,
chs. 1 and 6; *Methods of Logic*, §38.

similarity between a finite projective geometry and the rules of a lunch club.[25] It is not so copper-bottomed a procedure as a formal logician would like: he may complain that it is merely hand-waving. But the edge of that criticism is turned, by the fact that hand-waving—or at least informal argument—cannot be altogether dispensed with. If the procedure is generally intelligible, and mathematicians seem to be able to be talking about the same things, when they talk about numbers, we need not be greatly put out by hard-line Logicists bewailing our sloppy methods, once we realise that they are themselves, in their desire for absolute rigour, crying for the moon.

But Frege did cry for the moon.

4.6 Frege's Extensions and Sets

Frege drew back from identifying cardinal numbers with quotities, and defined them instead in terms of extensions—*Umfänge*—of concepts. It was a disastrous move, and led to the wreck of his logicist programme. He was led to it because the definition in terms of quotifiers was merely a contextual definition. It enabled us to explain what cardinal numbers were when they turned up in certain contexts, but not to say what they were ἁπλῶς, (*haplos*), simply. We do not use numbers just to answer the question "How many?" but in many other contexts too. We talk about them, and in particular we count them. We need, therefore, to be able to tell them apart from other things and apart from one another.

Frege was concerned with how to exclude interlopers, such as Julius Caesar, from being counted as numbers.[26] It is tempting to take a brusque line. We do not need a definition of number to be able to know that Julius Caesar is not a number: a simple acquaintance with Roman history is enough. Julius Caesar is clearly not a quotity, just as he is clearly not a quality. We do not need an exact definition of a quality in order to know that some things are not qualities, and similarly we do not need to define a quotity—certainly we do not need to replace quotities by extensions or sets—in order to assure ourselves that Julius Caesar is not one of them. Later, however, we shall have to soften our

---

[25] See above, §2.4.

[26] G.Frege, *The Foundations of Arithmetic*, tr. J.L.Austin, Oxford, 1950, §56, p.68.

response. There is a real problem of how to exclude interlopers from the realm of numbers, and as we shall see, there is no answer to that problem within the confines of first-order logic.[27] But the problem is not a categorial one. It is not because we cannot define the category of quotity—answers to the question *Quot?*—that we have problems in delimiting exactly what the numbers are. And so this, though a real problem, is not an argument for taking numbers to be extensions rather than quotities, whatever quotities are.

Frege was much more concerned with the problem of there being different numerical expressions referring to the same number, *e.g.* 'twelve' and 'dozen', or 'hundred' and 'century', in much the same way as 'The Morning Star' and 'The Evening Star' refer to the same planet. Numbers must be, he held, *selbständiger Gegenstände*, self-subsistent objects, and hence capable of re-identification, and so re-identifiable (*wiederkennbare*) on other occasions and under other descriptions.[28] Venus is a self-subsistent object because it can be referred to under different descriptions; it does not matter whether we talk of the Morning Star or of the Evening Star; in both cases we are talking of the one and the same object which exists independently of us. In the same way Frege wants to be able to be sure that however we refer to the number 12, we are referring to the same thing, and so seeks a criterion of identity to enable us to tell when different quotifier expressions such as 'twelve', 'dozen', 'the number of the Apostles', 'the number of eggs in this box', 'the number of old-time pennies in a shilling', 'the number of calendar months in a year', which evidently have a different *Sinn*, connotation, have nonetheless the same *Bedeutung*, denotation. He does this by talking of the *Umfang*, extension, of a concept, and considering the equivalence class of all those extensions of concepts that are *gleichzahlig* (translated by Austin as 'similar', and by others as 'equinumerous') with one another,[29] quoting Hume,[30] to the effect that the numbers assigned to two collections are equal when there

---

[27] See below, §6.4.

[28] G.Frege, *The Foundations of Arithmetic*, tr. J.L.Austin, Oxford, 1950, §56 *ad fin.*, p.68.

[29] See further below, §5.2.

[30] G.Frege, *The Foundations of Arithmetic*, §56 *ad fin.*, p.73, quoting David Hume, *Treatise on Human Nature*, Bk.I, Part iii, Sect.1, in Selby-Bigge's ed., Oxford, 1888, p.71.

is a one–one correlation between the members of each collection;
he defines number in terms of extensions that are equinumerous
to one another. He is able to define equinumerosity in terms of a
one–one mapping, which can in turn be defined in first-order logic.
So he can reasonably reckon that he has succeeded in building the
whole of arithmetic on the sure foundation of logic:

> ... the laws of arithmetic are analytic judgements and con-
> sequently a priori. Arithmetic thus becomes simply a devel-
> opment of logic, and every proposition of arithmetic a law
> of logic, albeit a derivative one ...[31]

But Frege's extensions were unable to bear the weight he wanted to
place on them. His own account of them was not sufficiently clear
or acceptable to be absorbed into the mainstream of philosophical
thinking, and they were construed as classes by Russell, and more
generally as sets. Although it is not a historically accurate representation of Frege's thought, it is reasonable for us to construe the
approach of Frege and Russell in set-theoretical terms, and evaluate the logicist definition of numbers as sets of **equinumerous**
sets. The use of equivalence classes to introduce new mathematical concepts is standard,[32] and has the merit of carrying over to
transfinite numbers.

Naive set theory, however, was shown by Russell's paradox to be
inconsistent.[33] Axiomatized set theory avoids the paradoxes, and
is, so far as we know, consistent, but axiomatic set theory is messy,
and much more mathematical than logical. Books on axiomatic
set theory turn out to be about transfinite arithmetic. It is not
much catch to define the natural numbers in terms of set theory,
and then find oneself diving into transfinite cardinals. It may be a
useful technical exercise, to confirm, what we already believe, that
almost all mathematics can be expressed in set theory, but if our
aim is philosophical illumination, we feel that we have succeeded
only in explaining the obscure in terms of the even more obscure.

The set-theoretical exegesis is open to other objections, some of
which can be countered, but which cumulatively draw us back from

---

[31] G.Frege, *The Foundations of Arithmetic*, tr. J.L.Austin, Oxford, 1950,
§87, p.99.

[32] See above, §3.7, for the introduction of rational numbers.

[33] See below, §12.2.

Frege's way out, and lead us once again, after we have developed the concepts of isomorphism and factoring,[34] to ask what quotifiers refer to, and if they are said to refer to quotities, what quotities really are.

4.7 Paradigm Sets

Frege's criterion of equinumerosity enables us to recognise the same cardinal number exemplified in different collections, but in practice we seldom talk of 'the number of the Apostles', and nearly always talk of 'twelve' and other numerals. Frege explicates them by means of a sequence of paradigm sets:[35]

$$\{0\}, \{0,1\}, \{0,1,2\}, \{0,1,2,3\}, \{0,1,2,3,4\}, \{0,1,2,3,4,5\}, \ldots$$

which have, respectively $1, 2, 3, 4, 5, 6, \ldots$ members, and in effect suggests that we characterize first 0 as the set of all sets equinumerous with the null set, Λ, and then

1 as the set of all sets equinumerous with $\{0\}$,
2 as the set of all sets equinumerous with $\{0,1\}$,
3 as the set of all sets equinumerous with $\{0,1,2\}$,
4 as the set of all sets equinumerous with $\{0,1,2,3\}$,
5 as the set of all sets equinumerous with $\{0,1,2,3,4\}$,
6 as the set of all sets equinumerous with $\{0,1,2,3,4,5\}$, *etc.*

This is a very satisfactory characterization of the successor relation in set-theoretical terms, and one which Cantor generalised to cover transfinite numbers too. If we now express $0, 1, 2$, *etc.* explicitly in terms of Λ, we obtain the following explicit definitions:

0 is the set of all sets equinumerous with the null set, Λ
1 is the set of all sets equinumerous with $\{\Lambda\}$,

---

[34] in §9.2-§9.4 and §9.8.

[35] G.Frege, *The Foundations of Arithmetic*, tr. J.L.Austin, Oxford, 1950, §79, p.92. T.J.Smiley, "Frege's 'series of natural numbers'", *Mind*, **97**, 1988, pp.583-584 points out that Austin wrongly uses 'the series of natural numbers' in §76 and thereafter. The correct rendering is 'the natural series of numbers'. It is natural because it is determined by the successor relation. The numbers are the cardinals, infinite as well as finite. The contrast between the natural series of numbers and the natural series of numbers beginning with 0 is that the former consists of various islands, each infinite number being unrelated to anything but itself, while the latter picks out just the island to which 0 belongs, that is finite numbers.

2 is the set of all sets equinumerous with $\{\Lambda, \{\Lambda\}\}$,
3 is the set of all sets equinumerous with $\{\Lambda, \{\Lambda\}, \{\Lambda, \{\Lambda\}\}\}$,
etc.

This seems very satisfactory, but it is not the sole satisfactory way of characterizing numbers in set-theoretical terms. Instead of using equinumerosity, we might accept type theory, and identify $0, 1, 2, 3,$ *etc.* by $\Lambda, \{\Lambda\}, \{\{\Lambda\}\}, \{\{\{\Lambda\}\}\},$ *etc.* Or, again, we might identify $0, 1, 2, 3,$ *etc.* by $\Lambda, \{\Lambda\}, \{\Lambda, \{\Lambda\}\}, \{\Lambda, \{\Lambda, \{\Lambda\}\}\},$ *etc.* And this ambiguity has been held by Benacerraf to tell against the explication of natural numbers in terms of sets.[36]

When C.P. Snow's novel, *The Masters*, first came out, it was rumoured that the head of a certain Cambridge college was dissuaded only by the most earnest entreaties of his friends from suing Snow for libel, on the grounds that Snow's character Jago was clearly meant to be a likeness of him. If the case had come to court, it would have posed an interesting problem. For there was another head of another Cambridge college who also was convinced that Jago was a portrait of him, and who also was dissuaded only by the earnest entreaties of his friends from suing Snow. Two cases of libel, each claiming that a fictional character is a recognisable portrait of two different people are self-defeating. In the same way Benacerraf argues that since there are more than one set-theoretical representations of the natural numbers, none of them can be *the* representation, and all must be inadequate. He tells the story of two boys, Ernie and Johnny, each brought up by militant Logicists to believe that numbers really were sets, but as it transpired different sets. Ernie is brought up to accept Frege's exegesis, Johnny to accept the first alternative given above. And then they have a schoolboy quarrel about which is right, a question to which there is, in the nature of the case, no definitive answer. If numbers really were sets, there would be a unique set that really was the number in question to the exclusion of all other impostors.

Benacerraf's argument is not cogent against the Frege–Russell account, but only against those set-theorists who identify cardinal

[36] Paul Benacerraf, "What Numbers Could not Be", *The Philosophical Review*, **74**, 1965, pp.47-73; reprinted in Paul Benacerraf and Hilary Putnam, eds., *The Philosophy of Mathematics*, 2nd ed., Cambridge, 1983, pp.272-294.

numbers *as*, rather than *by means of*, particular paradigm sets. After all, what Frege was doing was to introduce an equivalence class.
He identified numbers with an equivalence class of extensions. And
the Logicists have a perfectly good equivalence class, even though
different Logicists choose different paradigms of it. It is the same
as with colour. Ernie and Johnny were both taught to use the word
'yellow', but Ernie was taught that it was the colour of daffodils,
while Johnny was taught that it was the colour of primroses. They
both could use the word in the same way, but if they were of a
disputatious disposition, they could go on quarrelling about what
the word really meant, until they realised that there was no real
point at issue. In a more closely analogous case, if Benacerraf's
argument were valid, we could have two militant rationalists, one
of whom used fractions and the other used decimals. Or again one
mathematician might always use binary notation, and use 100 to
express the number four, and express fractions in "perquartages",
as we sometimes do in percentages, insisting that a half was really
10%. That would be perfectly possible. It does not show that rational numbers are not to be explained in terms of ordered pairs
of natural numbers; it is just that what they are is an equivalence
class of all those that cross-multiply. So, too, with Benacerraf's
boys: their disagreement is not a substantial one; it is not about
the nature of natural numbers, which are equivalence classes of
all those sets that are equinumerous with one another, but rather
about numerals, and is no less surprising than if one of them used
Arabic, and the other Roman, numerals; or if one of them was
speaking in German, and saying *drei*, and the other in Greek, and
saying $\tau\rho\epsilon\tilde{\iota}\varsigma$ (*treis*). Although they indubitably disagree, there is an
underlying agreement. Benacerraf's argument would wean us from
maintaining that a particular natural number just *was* a particular
set, in the same way as we could be shown that the rational number
one-half was not *identical with* the ordered pair $\{1, 2\}$. But a realist could still identify a natural number with a quotity, or indeed,
with an equivalence class of equinumerous sets, just as he identifies
rational numbers with an equivalence class of ordered pairs granted
a suitable equivalence relation.

In Benacerraf's example, the suitable equivalence relation will
not be that of equinumerosity, which Frege and Russell used, but
a more complicated one mapping the numerosity of Ernie's sets
onto the type of Johnny's. Let us, for the sake of completeness, list

the sets of a third boy, Tommy, whose sets are the third sequence
suggested above, of the same type as Johnny's, but not as "thin".

Different Paradigm Sets for Natural Numbers

	Ernie	Johnny	Tommy
0	Λ	Λ	Λ
1	$\{\Lambda\}$	$\{\Lambda\}$	$\{\Lambda\}$
2	$\{\Lambda, \{\Lambda\}\}$	$\{\{\Lambda\}\}$	$\{\Lambda, \{\Lambda\}\}$
3	$\{\Lambda, \{\Lambda\}, \{\Lambda, \{\Lambda\}\}\}$	$\{\{\{\Lambda\}\}\}$	$\{\Lambda, \{\Lambda, \{\Lambda\}\}\}$
...	...	...	...

Table 4.7.1

Although Benacerraf's argument does not refute Logicism, it
none the less points to a weakness. We can best see this if we erase
all the symbols except the right-hand brackets, thus:

Erased Paradigm Sets for Natural Numbers

	Ernie	Johnny	Tommy
0			
1	}	}	}
2	}}	}}	}}
3	}}}	}}}	}}}}
...	...	...	...

Table 4.7.2

It is evident then that all we have really done is to replace the old
symbols, $0, 1, 2, 3$, by a string of right-hand brackets; we are using
unary digits, only writing '}' instead of '1', or '/', *etc.* and open
to the same criticisms as Frege made against his predecessors.[37]
The Logicists, like the Formalists, make out that they are giving

---

[37] G.Frege, *The Foundations of Arithmetic*, tr. J.L.Austin, Oxford, 1950,
§34-§39, pp.44-51.

an analysis of number in purely logical terms, but are having to assume that they have numbers available in their meta-logic.[38]

Benacerraf's argument is right, moreover, in two further respects. It stresses the uniqueness requirement implicit in realism, and it raises the importance of structure. Reality is not plural.[39] And the cardinal approach fails to register the importance of the numbers as an order. The picture we obtain from Frege and Russell is of the equinumerosity criterion being used to pick out large bundles of classes from a huge pool of classes, but each equivalence class constituting a cardinal number being entirely separate from every other cardinal number, not taking into account that if twelve are the twelve Apostles, and one falls out, then eleven will be the number of those who went to heaven. Numbers are by nature not only cardinals saying how many there are in a given collection of items, but ordinals too, whose essence in each case depends on its relations with others, that is, its position in a structure.

Figure 4.7.1 Small boy fishing for numbers in Frege's pool of equinumerous extensions

---

[38] See above, §3.6, and below, §14.9.

[39] See below, §15.2.

Chapter 5
Numbers: The Ordinal Approach

5.1 The Superlative Approach

At the end of the previous chapter we saw that it was a demerit of the cardinal approach that it treated each number individually. Each number was a possible answer to the question 'How many?' and was intimately connected to the things of type a that were F, which it was the number of. We had the picture of fishing in a sea of sets or extensions and netting a shoal of equinumerous ones. The ordinal approach, which was pioneered by Dedekind, taken up by Cantor, and was adopted to some extent by Peano, is not concerned with separate individual numbers, but with whole sequences of numbers. These are specified by properties of order, either by the order in which we count them or as explicit ordinals, 'first', 'second', 'third', *etc.* The protagonists of the ordinal approach are primarily counting men, but it is instructive to recall the etymology of the explicit ordinals, where we noted that in English, German, Latin and Greek, the word for 'first' is superlative in form. So, likewise, are the words 'next' and *nächst* and 'last'. In Latin and Greek *alter* and δεύτερος, words for second, are comparative in form, as are also the English words, 'former' and 'latter'. From a logical point of view, too, orderings are specified by transitive irreflexive relations, of which comparatives are the standard exemplars.[1] The ordinals are a special sort of linear ordering, with superlative properties, that is to say that every subset of them has a lea*st* member, which implies that every member has a ne*xt* member. They are

---

[1] See more fully below, ch.9.

"discrete" orderings, in contrast to the "dense" and continuous orderings, exemplified by the rational and the real numbers, where between any two members there is always a third; discrete orderings are, so to speak, black and white, with each member clearly separated from its neighbours, whereas the others are composed of shades of grey, merging into one another. They also have a direction, being bounded in one direction—the chorus of "Green Grow the Rushes, Oh!" always comes to an end—but not necessarily in the other—the soloist could go on indefinitely. Discrete orderings with a least but no greatest member are said to have order-type ω.[2]

Ordinals can be characterized in terms of comparatives and superlatives, which can, in turn, be reduced to a single ordering relation, itself characterized in an entirely formal way; and it is illuminating to view them as a particular type of ordering.[3] But here we shall follow the account given by the protagonists of the ordinal approach, who were able to define ordinals *without* using ordering relations, needing only 1–1 correlations and proper set-inclusion ($\subset$).

5.2 Dedekind's Successor

Dedekind is a counting man.[4] For him the positive integers are primarily what we count with, not a discrete ordering bounded at one end but not the other. He faces great difficulties in consequence. It is much easier to define the superlative, *next* or *next after*, in terms of the comparative, than the other way about. To define the

---

[2] See E.V.Huntington, *The Continuum,* reprinted by Dover, 1955. The order-type of the negative integers, . . . − 3, −2, −1 is called *ω; the order-types of the rational numbers and the real numbers are called by Huntington, but not by modern authors, η and θ respectively. I shall follow Huntington's usage.

[3] See §9.6.

[4] See R.Dedekind, *Was Sind und Was Sollen die Zahlen?*, tr. W.W.Beman, Dover, 1963, *Essays on the Theory of Numbers*, pp.44ff.; and for a short and incisive account, R.Dedekind, Letter to Keferstein, tr. Hao Wang, *Journal of Symbolic Logic,* **22**, 1957, pp.150-151; reprinted in J. van Heijenoort, *From Frege to Gödel*, pp.98-103. For a brief account, see D.A. Gillies, *Frege, Dedekind, and Peano on the Foundations of Arithmetic*, Van Gorcum, Assen, The Netherlands, 1982, ch.9, pp.59-65.

comparative in terms of the superlative requires the "ancestral", which can be defined only in second-order logic, or by means of set theory. Where the cardinal approach involves quotities (or extensions, or classes, or sets), together with a one–one correlation to determine equinumerosity, the ordinal approach involves sets explicitly together with another one–one correlation, the **successor** function. The ordinal approach has as strong a claim as the cardinal approach to be called logicist, though the reliance on set theory, not known to be consistent, and arguably not part of logic at all,[5] leaves both claims open to dispute.

Like Frege, Dedekind has a problem in excluding unwanted intruders from the numbers as he defines them, and for this again he needs second-order logic or set theory. He has a further problem in grounding his ordinals, not having a natural starting point in nought.

Dedekind defines successor in terms of a one-one (*ähnlich*) correlation (*Abildung*, which can equally well be translated 'mapping', 'function' or 'transformation').Whereas Frege needed a one-one correlation at a crucial point, to define the equivalence class of all those extensions of concepts that are *gleichzahlig*, equinumerous with one another,[6] and thus to determine which cardinals are, or are not, equal to one another, Dedekind uses a one-one correlation to determine which sets are, or are not, finite.

He considers the image of a *Systeme*, a set,[7] K. If the image of K is a *proper* subset of K—that is, if the mapping is *into* but not *onto* the set K—the set is said to be (Dedekind-)infinite. This definition of a set's being infinite is worthy of notice, because it runs counter to the principle that the whole is greater than the part.[8] Dedekind, however, denies the applicability of the principle to infinite sets, and makes it the defining characteristic of a finite set that only for a finite set does the principle hold good. If a set is

---

[5] See below, ch.12.

[6] See above, §4.6.

[7] The translation of *Systeme* as 'set' may not be quite accurate to Dedekind's intentions, since he introduces *Kette* together with the mapping f; in modern parlance, then, we should understand by *Kette* a set *with operations and relations defined on it*, or "relational strùcture". I owe this point to Professor M.A.E. Dummett, of New College, Oxford.

[8] See below, §7.2.

shown to be Dedekind-infinite, the image of the set under the one-one mapping is a *proper* subset, and so there is some member of the original set which is not a member of the subset. Pick[9] any such member—which Dedekind calls the base element—and consider the chain (*Kette*) constituted by the base element, its image, its image's image, and so on. It will constitute a progression of order-type ω. Thus suppose we have the one-one mapping of the positive whole numbers onto the even numbers, given by the correlation:

$$1, \quad 2, \quad 3, \quad 4, \quad 5, \quad 6, \quad 7, \quad 8, \quad 9, \quad 10, \ 11, \ 12, \ 13, \ 14, \ 15, \ 16, \ \ldots$$
$$2, \quad 4, \quad 6, \quad 8, \quad 10, \ 12, \ 14, \ 16, \ 18, \ 20, \ 22, \ 24, \ 26, \ 28, \ 30, \ 32, \ \ldots$$

then there is some number in the original set but not in its image—indeed all the odd numbers are; pick any one, say 3, and consider the sequence:

$$3, 6, 12, 24, 48, 96, 192, \ldots.$$

this is a progression of order-type ω, and is, we are told, just the whole numbers under another name. Just as in geometry we abstract from many isosceles triangles and talk about *the* isosceles triangle, so in number theory we abstract from many progressions, and talk about *the* progression of order-type ω, with which Dedekind identifies the whole numbers.

Dedekind's account of abstraction is given in psychological terms, about performances of the human mind, and is open to Frege's criticisms of "psychologism". Frege argues that when we are talking about the numbers, we do not think we are talking about what men can, as it happens, do, but about something independent of human abilities. Of course, we may be wrong. It may be that there is nothing in common which we are recognising, when we think we detect a common pattern in different progressions, and that our agreement is to be explained away in social or psychological terms. This is a view which a philosopher of a strongly reductionist turn of mind, who is anxious to practise extreme ontological economy might put forward. But it is only a possibility, not an established fact. Although a philosopher may put forward an "error theory" of pattern recognition in much the same way as Mackie

---

[9] We invoke here a Principle of Finite Choice, which has always been regarded as uncontentious in the finite case, but may fail to be legitimate when extrapolated to an infinite number of choices.

puts forward his error theory of moral discourse,[10] the substantial fact is that we speak and behave as if we were able to recognise patterns, and communicate about them, and teach people to recognise patterns they had not been able to recognise before. Hence, although Dedekind uses psychological language, and himself takes up a conceptualist stance on the status of mathematical entities, he is not obliged to, and a supporter of his account of numbers could appeal to the psychological fact of our being able to recognise an order-type common to all progressions as evidence of there actually existing some common pattern we each could recognise, and thus construing abstraction as a logical, rather than merely psychological, operation. Dedekind would then be in no worse case than the early Plato, so far as his use of abstraction went, or than Frege, in having to rely, at a crucial stage, on an ontological principle open to metaphysical criticism.

5.3 And So On

There are serious difficulties Dedekind has to circumvent before this line of argument can be made cogent. In the first place, the 'and so on' is intolerably loose—all right in a hand-waving outline of an argument, but not a proper argument in itself; moreover, although every finite ordinal is excluded by the chain procedure, not every transfinite ordinal is. Besides the order-type ω there is the order-type $\omega + 1$, which might be expressed by the phrase 'ever and a day' and can be pictured

$$1, 2, 3, 4, 5, 6, 7, \ldots, 0$$

that is to say, by the sequence of whole numbers, and then, finally, another number, different from all the earlier ones and after them all. There is also the order-type $\omega + \omega$, which might be expressed by the phrase 'ever and ever' and can be pictured

$$1, 2, 3, 4, 5, 6, 7, \ldots 1, 2, 3, 4, 5, 6, 7, \ldots,$$

that is to say, by the sequence of whole numbers, and then, the sequence of whole numbers all over again. Or, indeed,

$$1, 3, 5, 7, 9, 11, \ldots 2, 4, 6, 8, 10, \ldots,$$

---

[10] J.L.Mackie, *Ethics: Inventing Right and Wrong*, Penguin, 1977, pp.35, 48-49.

that is to say, by the sequence of odd numbers followed by the sequence of even numbers.

Both these orderings will seem all right. To rule these out, Dedekind requires that a sequence must have not some, but all, of the properties possessed by the base element and such that if possessed by any number then possessed by its successor. Thus $\omega + 1$ and $\omega + \omega$ are excluded, because it does not possess the property which ω has, that there is only one number in it which is not the immediate successor of any other number. More precisely, he defines a progression as the intersection (*Gemeinheit*) of all those chains which contain the base element and are such that if they contain any member they contain its image. This, since it is the intersection of all such sets will be the smallest of them, and will therefore exclude all unwelcome intruders. It will be a genuine progression of order-type ω, and has been rigorously defined.

Dedekind is right in claiming rigour.[11] He has achieved two goals. He has excluded all unwelcome intruders, and he has done so without resorting to some vague 'and so on'. As he sees it, he has achieved it by the use of chains, that is, sets which are such that if they contain any member they contain its image, or, in modern terms, sets closed under some particular mapping **f**.

This was one of the most difficult points of my analysis, and its mastery required lengthy reflection. If one presupposes knowledge of the sequence N of the natural numbers and, accordingly allows himself the use of the language of arithmetic, then of course, he has an easy time of it. He need only say: an element n belongs to the sequence N if and only if, starting with the element 1 and counting on and on steadfastly, that is, going through a finite number of iterations of the mapping **f** ..., I actually reach the element n at some time; by this procedure I shall never reach an

---

[11] To form a just estimate of Dedekind's rigour, the reader should work through his *Was Sind und Was Sollen die Zahlen?*, tr.W.W.Beman, Dover, 1963, *Essays on the Theory of Numbers*, pp.44ff. esp. Chs.IV-VI, pp.56-70; but Dedekind's own exposition is not easy to follow at first. and Appendix II may be useful as a guide. He may have had some doubts whether he was rigorous enough, on account of his reliance on "impredicative" definitions. See Alexander George, "The Conveyability of Intuitionism", *Journal of Philosophical Logic*, **17**, 1988, n.31, p.154. See further, §15.3.

element outside of the sequence N. But this way of characterizing the distinction between those elements t that are
to be ejected from S and those elements n that are alone to
remain in is surely quite useless for our purpose; it would,
after all, contain the most pernicious and obvious kind of vicious circle. The mere words 'finally get there at some time',
of course, will not do either; they would be of no more use
than, say, the words *'karam sipo tatura'*, which I invent at
this instant without giving them any clearly defined meaning. Thus, how can I, without presupposing any arithmetic
knowledge, give an unambiguous conceptual foundation to
the distinction between the elements n and the elements t?
Merely through consideration of the chains ...[12]

We should see as equally important his going into set theory, or,
equivalently, second-order logic, and defining the numbers in terms
of the intersection of all those sets that include the base element and
are such that if they contain any member they contain its image.
But granted these two concepts, he has succeeded in characterizing
progressions of order-type ω without presupposing any knowledge
of the natural numbers—which is more than some cardinal accounts
succeed in doing[13] —and without resorting to mere hand-waving,
using phrases like 'and so on' or *'karam sipo tatura'*. But this,
though a great achievement, is not enough.

5.4 Grounding the Ordinals

Even if we have characterized the ordinal progression ω uniquely,
we have not yet given an adequate characterization of the natural
numbers, because we have not anchored the first ordinal number,
0 or 1 as the case may be. Dedekind did not think he needed to do
more. He just defined the natural numbers as having order-type ω.

If in the consideration of a simply infinite system N ordered by a mapping f we entirely neglect the special character of the elements; simply retaining their distinguishability
and taking into account only the relations to one another
in which they are placed by the ordering mapping f, then

---

[12] R.Dedekind, Letter to Keferstein, tr. Hao Wang, *Journal of Symbolic
Logic*, 22, 1957, pp.150-151; reprinted in J. van Heijenoort, *From Frege
to Gödel*, pp.100-101.

[13] See above, §4.7, *ad fin.*

these elements are called *natural numbers*, or *ordinal numbers* or simply *numbers*, and the base element 1 is called the *base-number* of the *number-series* N.[14]

But this is counter-intuitive. There is something more to the natural numbers than simply their order-type. From the cardinal point of view numbers are potential answers to the question 'How many?', and even if we discount their role there, and consider only their ordinal properties, we are concerned not only with the relation of each to the others, but also with the special position of the first one. As Russell pointed out, the sequence $101, 102, 103, 104, \ldots$, which children use when counting in games like hide-and-seek, is just as much an instance of the order-type ω as the usual natural numbers, and yet is not how we think the natural numbers should begin.[15] There is something special about Nought and One, which distinguishes them from 101 or any other number. Nought is the first cardinal number because it is the lowest possible answer to the question 'How many?'; and One is the first ordinal number, because it is the number we begin with when we count.

Counting is easy to do, but difficult to give an articulate account of what it is that we are doing. We can achieve some clarification, if we follow Benacerraf, and distinguish "transitive" from "intransitive" counting.[16] We count intransitively when we just count, as in "One, Two, Buckle my shoe": we count transitively when we count the individuals that possess a certain property or the members of a given set; for example, the strokes of a clock, or the Apostles. The result of counting transitively is to tell us how many individuals there are that possess the property, or are members of the set, in question; that is, it yields a cardinal number. Thus if we can formulate a rule for counting transitively, it will ground the counting numbers, thus far characterized by Dedekind only with respect to their ordinal properties, in some cardinal properties which are not merely relative to the position of an ordinal number in an ordering, but are in some sense absolute. So we ask: "Can we formulate a

---

[14] R.Dedekind, *Essays on the Theory of Numbers*, Dover, 1963, p.68, §73.

[15] Compare Bertrand Russell, *The Principles of Mathematics*, pbk. 1992, §242, p.249; *Introduction to Mathematical Philosophy*, ch.1, pp.7-9.

[16] Paul Benacerraf, "What Numbers Could not Be", *The Philosophical Review*, **74**, 1965; reprinted in Paul Benacerraf and Hilary Putnam, eds., *The Philosophy of Mathematics*, 2nd ed., Cambridge, 1983, pp.274-275.

rule for counting transitively, *e.g.* for counting in a pack of cards the number of honour cards at skat?"

5.5 How to Count

In order to count the number of individuals—a—which possess a certain property—P—we first (STEP 1) determine whether there are *any* such a with property P. There are two possibilities:

Either $(Aa)\neg Pa$ in which case we say 'No a's are P'
(or 'The number of a's that are P is Nought')
STOP

Or $(Va)Pa$ in which case we choose some particular a—call it a'—and count 'One';
GO TO STEP 2

STEP 2 Let Ra be $(Pa \wedge (a \neq a'))$; then count Ra. There are two possibilities:

Either $(Aa)\neg Ra$ in which case we say 'That's all; the number of a's that are P is One';
STOP

Or $(Va)Ra$ in which case we choose some particular a—call it a''—and count 'Two';
GO TO STEP 3

STEP 3 Let $R'a$ be $Ra \wedge (a \neq a')$; then count $R'a$. There are two possibilities:

Either $(Aa)\neg R'a$ in which case we say 'That's all; the number of a's that are P is Two';
STOP

Or $(Va)R'a$ in which case we choose some particular a—call it a'''—and count 'Three';
GO TO STEP 4

and so on. After the first step, each step is similar. If there is no remainder, if that is, the remainder has nothing left in it, we say 'That's all', and repeat the last intransitive counting number we have reached as the cardinal number of the things originally to be counted: if there is still a remainder, we cite the next counting number, picking one individual from the remainder and taking it away, and repeat the process. Since the remainder is diminished by one each time, sooner or later there will be no remainder, and the process will have to stop, and the counting number then reached will be the cardinal number telling us how many there were in the original group. For any remainder R, either $(Aa)\neg Ra$ or $(Va)Ra$;

if the former, we have reached the end; if the latter, since $(Va)Ra$, we can pick one such, say a', and form the new remainder, R', by defining $R'a$ iff $Ra \wedge (a \neq a')$, and continue the process.

The crucial point about transitive counting is that at each stage we count the remainder, which has one fewer members than the last time, so that we can be sure of counting *down* and reaching an end, when there will be no more to be counted. It is thus the *predecessor*, rather than the successor, which is fundamental. We then go on to say that intransitive counting is connected with transitive counting in that the *intransitive successor relation* is the *converse* of the transitive predecessor relation that we use when we count down the cardinal number remaining after having already counted some things with a specified property. Counting— intransitive counting—is the converse of counting down. It is the chorus that really makes the song "Green Grow the Rushes, Oh!"; the soloist takes the converse relation and extrapolates.

5.6   Ordinals and Cardinals

Ordinals are out of step with cardinals. The first ordinal number is 'first', or 'one', German *eins*, if we are simply counting, whereas the first cardinal is 'nought', which alone can be directly defined in terms of non-numerical quotifiers.

Ordinal	First	Second	Third	Fourth	Fifth ...
Cardinal	Nought	One	Two	Three	Four ...

Many difficulties ensue, particularly when we use the cardinals not just to count indivisible individuals, but as part of a wider scheme for measuring divisible quantities. We are puzzled by the nineteen hundreds being the twentieth century, and children and the very old like their age to be recorded not in terms of the cardinal number of whole years they have lived, but the ordinal number of the current year of their life. I reach double figures sooner in my tenth year than if I have to wait until I am ten, just as I make it to my eightieth year even though I die when I am only seventy nine. The Millennium is being celebrated on January 1st 2000, and the Resurrection took place on the third day, although less than 48 hours after the Crucifixion. Ancient historians have particular difficulty in calculating centenaries of events with a date Before Christ. Was 1 B.C. followed by 0 A.D. or by 1 A.D.? Astronomers have rejected the ordinal numeration of the historians and insist on a zero in order to secure mathematical tractability.

Although it is awkward having the ordinals out of step with the cardinals, there are compensations. We are provided with a natural correlation, more or less that of the successor function. It thus yields a set-theoretical definition of successor for *cardinal numbers.*

For One is correlated with First, and there is just one first cardinal number, namely Nought; and

Two is correlated with Second, and there are just two cardinal numbers up to the second one, namely Nought and One; and

Three is correlated with Third, and there are just three cardinal numbers up to the third one, namely Nought and One and Two; and

Four is correlated with Fourth, and there are just four cardinal numbers up to the fourth one, namely Nought and One and Two Three; ... 　　and So On

So, provided we regard Nought as the First Cardinal Number, there are exactly $(n+1)$ cardinal numbers up to the nth cardinal number. Frege used this to define the successor of a cardinal number. If we start with Nought as Λ (or $\emptyset$), we have Ernie's understanding of number, which Benacerraf contrasted with Johnny's.[17] We can avoid the difficulties which that definition encounters, if we do not *identify* the number Nought *with* the null set, but only pick it out *by means of* it. And the successor of a natural number n is not to be identified with the set $\{0, 1, 2, 3, \ldots, n\}$, but can be characterized as the correct answer to the question 'How many cardinal numbers are there in that set?'.

5.7 Conclusion

The ordinal approach has as good a claim as the cardinal approach to be logicist. It seeks to account for the natural numbers in purely logical terms, and succeeds in characterizing the 'and so on', the iteration expressed by the dots in 1, 2, 3, 4, 5, ...: it offers acceptable definitions of (Dedekind-)infinite and (Dedekind-)finite, and it is fair to see in Dedekind the originator of recursive definitions and the father of Recursive Function Theory. The ordinal approach is adequate for all reasonable arithmetic. Moreover the ordinal approach is carried through in a systematic and rigorous fashion;

---

[17] See above, §4.7.

there is no appeal to dubious entities like quotities or extensions, but only to sets, the same as in other branches of mathematics.

These are real merits, but have to be set against some costs and some demerits. The chief cost in Dedekind's presentation is his heavy use of set theory. This, as we shall see more clearly when we come to consider Peano's approach,[18] is an inescapable cost if we are to be effective in excluding all the unwelcome intruders. It greatly detracts from the logical purity of the logicist achievement. In addition, the ordinal approach, as originally put forward, fails to accommodate the use of natural numbers to answer the question 'How much?' and fails to distinguish the counting numbers from other progressions of order-type ω.

These two demerits have been met by softening the purity of the original ordinal approach. We have accommodated the cardinal uses of natural numbers through an exegesis of transitive counting, and elucidated transitive counting in terms of intransitive counting. Intransitive counting is of order-type ω, but is distinguished from other progressions of order-type ω by the peculiar position of the first counting number, One. The rationale of this lies in the use of intransitive counting numbers to count transitively, and ultimately in the fact that Nought is the first cardinal number. So we need in the end to accommodate the cardinal approach as well, but are less heavily committed to quotities than in the purely cardinal approach.

---

[18] See below, §6.2.

Chapter 6

Numbers: The Abstract Approach

6.1 The Third Approach

The Cardinal and Ordinal approaches may satisfy philosophers, but are likely to irritate mathematicians, who seldom think of numbers as closely connected with the rest of our conceptual structure, reasonably referred to by words, 'Nought', 'One', 'Twelve', 'First', 'Second', 'Fifth', but as abstract entities, presented symbolically, '0', '1', '12', *etc.* (where we read '0' as 'O', like telephonists). A purely symbolic account is, we shall see, as unsatisfactory as a purely cardinal or purely ordinal one. In the end we shall be led to the conclusion that there are three distinct, but interlocking facets to our concept of natural number:

1. a cardinal one, as answers to the question *Quot?*, How many?, where the answers can be Nought, One, Two, ... *etc.*

2. an ordinal one, either as adjectives, First, Second, Third, ...*etc.*, or as intransitive counting numbers, One, Two, Three, ... *etc.*, where the numbers form a queue of order-type ω.

3. an abstract one, as entities named by symbolic numerals generated from a finite stock of digits by a rule capable of indefinite iteration, 0, 1, 2, 3, .., 10, 11, 12, .., 100, 101, 102, .., 1000, 1001, *etc.*

These facets are obviously distinct. The connexion between cardinal numbers and ordinal numbers has been shown in the previous chapter. Abstract numbers are related to the other two through

126

the ordinals. They can be seen as an infinite extension of the in-transitive counting numbers, which, in turn, are grounded in the cardinals by the two requirements:

(a) that intransitive counting is connected with transitive counting so that the intransitive successor is the converse of the transitive predecessor we use when we "count down" the cardinal num-ber remaining after having already counted some things with a specified property; and

(b) that the first natural number be the answer to the cardinal question *Quot?* when there is nothing with the property in question, *i.e.*

Quot F x?	gets the answer		
	Nought	IFF	$\neg(Vx)Fx$
	(or alternatively)		$(Ax)\neg Fx$

If we can ground nought and predecessor cardinally, we can then go along with Dedekind and say that the natural numbers are a pro-gression (of "quotities") whose first member is Nought and closed under the converse of predecessor. Similarly, the counting num-bers are a progression of the same order-type, whose first member is One, the successor of Nought, and again closed under successor. And since the iteration of successor is very same-ish, we should assign numerals formally according to some uniform rule, instead of inventing a new name or symbol for each new number. The symbolic representation of numbers captures what is implicit in Dedekind's 'and so on', and is more or less forced on us once we engage on intransitive counting upwards without limit, instead of transitive counting downwards to yield a definite bounded cardinal answer.

6.2 Peano

Although abstract numbers are thus connected with ordinal and cardinal numbers, the connexion is tenuous, and they tend to take off, and wing their way through the realms of mathematical thought as abstract entities, unencumbered by non-mathematical ties. Mathematicians have often been impelled to seek a purely for-mal characterization of the natural numbers in much the same way and for much the same reasons as they have espoused the axiomatic approach to geometry.

Peano was the pioneer. He axiomatized arithmetic. He was a
logician, but not a Logicist.[1] He developed the ancestor of modern
formal logical calculi in order to derive the theorems of arithmetic
from a few basic postulates, but he did not attempt to establish
these as purely logical in character, as Frege and Dedekind did.
Frege, also, was a formal logician, though his *Begriffsschrift* was too
clumsy to be developed by later logicians, but Dedekind expressed
his arguments informally without the aid of any logical calculus.
Frege can be seen as the predecessor of Russell and the theory of
types, Dedekind of Zermelo and set theory, Peano of Hilbert and
formal arithmetic.

Peano derived arithmetic axiomatically from a number of basic
axioms which involve three primitive terms, N the set of counting numbers, 1 unity, or the first counting number on the ordinal
approach, and S the successor function.[2] Of his nine axioms five
were specifically arithmetical in character. They are, in slightly
modernised terminology:[3]

1. $1 \epsilon N$
6. $n \epsilon N \rightarrow Sn \epsilon N$
7. $n \epsilon N \wedge m \epsilon N \rightarrow (n = m \leftrightarrow Sn = Sm)$
8. $((An)(n \epsilon N \rightarrow \neg(Sn = 1))$
9. $((1 \epsilon M) \wedge (n)(((n \epsilon N) \wedge (n \epsilon M)) \rightarrow (Sn \epsilon M)) \rightarrow M \subseteq N)$

[1] This point is due to D.A.Gillies, *Frege, Dedekind, and Peano on the Foundations of Arithmetic*, Van Gorcum, Assen, The Netherlands, 1982, ch.10,
pp.67ff. Gillies gives a careful and illuminating discussion of the similarities
and differences between Frege, Dedekind and Peano, which is only briefly
summarised here.

[2] Peano writes +1 for the successor function; it is equivalent to Dedekind's **f**
in the previous chapter. Peano's own terminology obscures the distinction
between the unary successor function and the binary addition function (or
operation); in many modern treatments the successor of n is written n';
this is convenient, but easily overlooked, especially since the prime is used
for many other purposes too, and has in this book been used to differentiate
between one variable and another.

[3] For the exact original, see J. van Heijenoort, *From Frege to Gödel*, p.94.
Dedekind had earlier enunciated an equivalent axiom set, but only in pri-
vate correspondence. See Hao Wang, "The Axiomatisation of Arithmetic",
Journal of Symbolic Logic, **22**, 1957, pp.145-157; cited by M.A.E.Dum-
mett, *Frege: Philosophy of Mathematics*, London, 1991, p.49, n.6.

These postulates are expressed in terms of set theory, but do not have to be. What are now known as Peano's postulates are normally expressed informally in five propositions. In order to keep in line with the distinction drawn earlier between counting number and natural number, I shall first give an ordinal version closer to Peano's original intention:

Peano's Postulates (Ordinal Version)

1. 1 is a counting number.
2. The successor of any counting number is a counting number.
3. No two counting numbers have the same successor.
4. 1, and 1 alone, is not the successor of any counting number.
5. Any property that holds of 1, and is such that if it holds of any counting number it holds also of the successor of that counting number, **holds of every counting number**

Peano himself took 1 to be the first number, and indeed it is the first counting number. But we have grounded intransitive counting in transitive counting, and transitive counting in cardinal numbers, of which the first is 0; I shall therefore take, as an alternative, but standard, version of Peano's postulates, one starting with 0; but to emphasize the abstractness of Peano's approach typographically, I shall in this section and when citing Peano's postulates write O following the English practice for telephone numbers, which are abstract entities used as labels, but without being used for counting or ascribing cardinal numbers to groups:

Peano's Postulates (Standard Version)

1. O is a natural number.
2. The successor of any natural number is a natural number.
3. No two natural numbers have the same successor.
4. O, and O alone, is not the successor of any natural number.
5. Any property that holds of O, and is such that if it holds of any natural number it holds also of the successor of that natural number, holds of every natural number.

There are several other versions, depending on how the successor function is specified. If it is specified as a one-one mapping, then the third postulate is not needed. We can thus condense Peano's five postulates into an equivalent set of four:

1. O is a natural number.
2. Successor is a one-one map of natural numbers into natural numbers.
3. O, and O alone, is not the successor of any natural number.
4. Any property that holds of O, and is such that if it holds of any natural number it holds also of the successor of that natural number, holds of every natural number.

If, on the other hand, it is not even given that successor is a *function*—that is at least a many–*one* correlation—then we need to split the second postulate into two halves:

2a) Every number has at least one successor, and
2b) Every number has at most one successor.

Many versions state that O is not the successor of any natural number, but fail to stipulate that O alone has no predecessor. To make this clear, we might divide the fourth postulate into two halves:

4a) O is not the successor of any natural number.
4b) O alone is not the successor of any natural number.

It is a useful exercise to try and formulate several different sets of equivalent postulates. Although it is customary to make use of five, as Euclid earlier, and Whitehead and Russell later, did, we can have more, like Peano, or fewer, according to how fully we specify the primitive terms.

It is helpful to picture Peano's postulates as instructions to a boy playing trains as to how he should lay out his track. Postulates nos. 1 and 4a give him some buffers. Postulate no. 2a allows him always to add on another piece of straight rail. Postulate no. 2b rules out his having any facing points. Postulate no. 3 rules out his having any trailing points. Postulate no. 4b rules out his having any other buffers. Postulate no. 5 says that any train starting from the buffers and going on without stopping will eventually traverse every rail he has put down. It excludes there being some entirely separate bit of track, like a circle, as shown in the diagram.

Peano's postulates have great merits. In the first place, they suffice for almost all serious arithmetic, so much so that Elementary Number Theory, sometimes abbreviated E.N.T., is also called Peano Arithmetic, sometimes abbreviated PA. Granted Peano's postulates, we can derive by rigorous formal deductions the whole of counting-number theory. And, secondly, we can do so using only first-order logic. Although Peano himself formulated his postulates in terms of set theory, as Dedekind did, he was not obliged,

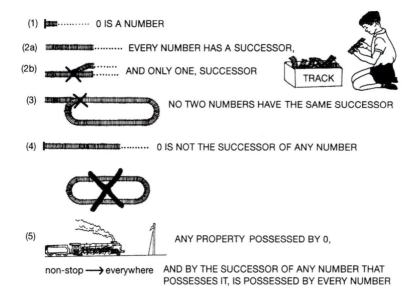

(1) ·········· 0 IS A NUMBER

(2a) ·········· EVERY NUMBER HAS A SUCCESSOR,

(2b) ······· AND ONLY ONE, SUCCESSOR   TRACK

(3) NO TWO NUMBERS HAVE THE SAME SUCCESSOR

(4) ·········· 0 IS NOT THE SUCCESSOR OF ANY NUMBER

(5) ANY PROPERTY POSSESSED BY 0,

non-stop ⟶ everywhere   AND BY THE SUCCESSOR OF ANY NUMBER THAT POSSESSES IT, IS POSSESSED BY EVERY NUMBER

Figure 6.2.1 Playing trains with Peano

as Dedekind was obliged, to use set theory, and was not obliged, as Frege was obliged, to invoke second-order logic. This is because Peano's fifth postulate

Any property that holds of O, and is such that if it holds of any natural number it holds also of the successor of that natural number, holds of every natural number.

can be couched in terms of **any** property, not of all properties. I do not have to wave my hand over all properties or opine that there is some property, I know not what, in order to be able to apply Peano's fifth postulate. It is enough that given a property that holds of O, and is "hereditary", that is if it holds of a natural number it holds likewise of its successor, I can infer that that property holds of every number. Instead of having to consider some universe of all properties, giving rise to serious doubts about their ontological status and whether I can really survey them all, I can confine my attention to particular, given, properties. It is not up to me to know what all the properties are, or might be. It is just that

if you present any property, or come to think of some particular
one, I have a means of telling that that particular one, if it satisfies
the conditions in the antecedent of Peano's fifth postulate, holds
of every natural number. So, by contrast to Frege and Dedekind,

Peano is   1) logically simple, and
                        2) ontologically un-lush.

But, alas!, these merits are not obtained without a cost: it turns
out that

Peano is   non-monomorphic
                        (or non-categorical),

which means that Peano's postulates never succeed in capturing,
in *first*-order logic the *unique* peculiarity of the natural numbers.

6.3 Monomorphism and Non-standard Models

Monomorphism is a difficult concept. A theory is monomorphic
(or categorical, which is easier to pronounce but has misleading
associations with Aristotle's theory of Categories and with Kant's
Categorical Imperative) if and only if all its models—that is to
say all those interpretations of the theory under which its axioms
come out true—are "isomorphic", have the same shape, the same
structure. We can have lots of Dedekind orderings of order-type ω:

1,	2,	3,	4,	5,	6,	7,	8,	9,	10,	...
2,	4,	6,	8,	10,	12,	14,	16,	18,	20,	...
101,	102,	103,	104,	105,	106,	107,	108,	109,	110,	...

but not only are all these sets equinumerous, since there are one-
one mappings between each pair of them, but the one-one mappings also preserve the relation $>$ and the successor function, so
that these orderings are all **isomorphic**. Isomorphism is a generalisation of equinumerosity. Equinumerosity is concerned only with
the cardinality of the sets: isomorphism is concerned with relevant
predicates, relations and functions too.[4] The simplest example
of a non-monomorphic theory is given by the theory of groups.
There are two groups of order 4, whose elements are equinumerous with each other: the cyclic group, $\{c, c^2, c^3, c^4 = I\}$ and the

---

[4] See further, Hao Wang, "Axiomatization of Arithmetic", *Journal of Symbolic Logic*, **22**, 1957, p.154; Alonzo Church, *An Introduction to Mathematical Logic*, Princeton, 1956, pp.329-330; W. and M.Kneale, *The Development of Logic*, Oxford, 1963, pp.387-388, 473, 476.

dihedral group with two generators $\{a, b, ab = ba, a^2 = b^2 = I\}$. These are evidently equinumerous, but not isomorphic; for every element in the latter group is equal to its inverse, but in the former $c \neq c^{-1} = c^3$. To give another example: the rational numbers can be paired with the natural numbers:

$$
\begin{array}{ccccccccccc}
1, & 2, & 3, & 4, & 5, & 6, & 7, & 8, & 9, & 10, & ... \\
1/1, & 2/1, & 1/2, & 1/3, & 2/2, & 3/1, & 4/1, & 3/2, & 2/3, & 1/4, & ...
\end{array}
$$

and so are equinumerous with them,[5] but this correlation does not preserve the relation $>$.

It is not at all obvious that first-order Peano Arithmetic is non-monomorphic. It follows from Gödel's theorem.[6] Gödel's theorem shows that Peano Arithmetic is incomplete: there is some closed well-formed formula—call it G—which is not a theorem of Peano Arithmetic and whose negation is not a theorem either; or, to put it another way, there is some closed well-formed formula which is expressed entirely in terms of Peano Arithmetic but is neither a theorem of Peano Arithmetic nor inconsistent with it. We then consider the two sets of axioms:

$$P_1, P_2, P_3, P_4, P_5, G \qquad \text{and} \qquad P_1, P_2, P_3, P_4, P_5, \neg G.$$

Since these are both consistent, they both (by the Completeness theorem for first-order logic) have models which bring out each

[5] See below, §7.2.

[6] Although Gödel's theorem is itself extremely difficult to prove, and quite difficult even to believe, it is central to the philosophy of mathematics, and will be discussed in Chapter Eight. So it is sensible to argue from that, even though the other proofs are illuminating too. They depend on the Compactness theorem for first-order logic, which trades on the fact that an inconsistency, if it is to be reached at all, must be reached in a *finite* number of steps, so that first-order Peano Arithmetic can never be brought to book on account of infinitely distant infelicities in any of its models. See Alonzo Church, *An Introduction to Mathematical Logic*, Princeton, 1956, §55, p.336; and Hao Wang, "Axiomatization of Arithmetic", *Journal of Symbolic Logic*, **22**, 1957, pp.156-157. It reveals what is wrong with first-order Peano Arithmetic, but is lengthy to prove. See below, §8.7, 16.3.

of Peano's postulates as true, but significantly differ in the truth-value they assign to G (which can be expressed entirely in terms of Peano Arithmetic).

It is difficult to see how there could be a model of Peano's postulates other than the standard one, which we pictured as the boy's railway track starting with some buffers and extending indefinitely far in one direction. This indeed is how the non-standard model starts too. The non-standardness only crops up over the horizon, so to speak, that is, among the transfinite numbers. The non-standard model of Peano Arithmetic starts off with a progression of order-type ω, but then has indefinitely many additional chunks, each of order-type $^*\omega + \omega$, the order-type of the integers, negative as well as positive. The order-type $^*\omega + \omega$ looks like this:

$$.... - 7, -6, -5, -4, -3, -2, -1, \ 1, \ 2, \ 3, \ 4, \ 5, \ 6, \ 7, ...$$

(It can equally well be represented, more cardinally, by $.... - 7, -6, -5, -4, -3, -2, -1, \ 0, \ 1, \ 2, \ 3, \ 4, \ 5, \ 6, \ 7, ...$ Ordinally there is no difference, but in view of the special properties of 0, it is convenient to take the former as our exemplar of order-type $^*\omega + \omega$.[7]) The chunks of order-type $^*\omega + \omega$ in the non-standard model themselves have the order-type η, the dense order-type exemplified by the rational numbers.[8] There is a concertina effect.

$$| + + \cdots \quad \cdots + + + + \cdots + + + + \cdots + + + + \cdots + + + +$$
$$\omega \qquad\quad ^*\omega + \omega \quad\ ^*\omega + \omega \quad\ ^*\omega + \omega \quad\ ^*\omega + \omega$$

Wherever we look, we find a stretch of track of order-type $^*\omega + \omega$, but between any two such stretches, unless they are part of the same chunk, and separated by only a finite number of pieces of rail, there are further chunks, each of order-type $^*\omega + \omega$. That is to say, although locally we are dealing with a discrete ordering, where each bit of track has a next bit of track and a previous bit of track, globally the separate chunks, each of order-type $^*\omega + \omega$, are not discrete; there is no next chunk after any particular one.

It is easy to see that the order-type $^*\omega + \omega$ satisfies Peano's second and third postulates. Hence, within any chunk these two postulates are satisfied. Postulates 1 and 4a are satisfied by the

---

[7] See also above, §5.6.

[8] See above, §5.1, n.2; or below, §9.6.

initial stretch of order-type ω. Postulate 4b is satisfied in that there is only one segment, the initial segment, of order-type ω; none of the chunks has a first element, so that each element is the successor of some other element. Thus the non-standard model satisfies the first four of Peano's postulates. And it can satisfy the fifth; there are models, that is, in which every element, even those in the concertina chunks, possess any hereditary property that the very first number, 0, possesses. So the non-standard model can satisfy all Peano's postulates. But it is clearly not isomorphic with the natural numbers, if only because between any two natural numbers there are only a finite number of intervening numbers, while between some elements of the non-standard model there are an infinite number of intervening elements.[9]

The non-monomorphism of Peano Arithmetic detracts greatly from its claim to give an adequate characterization of the natural numbers in purely formal terms. For, given any formal characterization, there will be, besides the natural numbers which constitute the intended model of Peano Arithmetic, other models which, though they satisfy Peano Arithmetic, differ in some significant way from the natural numbers.

It might seem that if some non-standard model differed from the natural numbers in some significant way, we could use that difference to rule out that non-standard model: and, indeed, we can. But we shall have ruled out only that non-standard model, not all non-standard models. For Gödel's theorem holds not only for Peano's postulates by themselves but for any stronger system constituted by Peano's postulates together with further axioms, so long as they are all consistent with one another. Hence, any such stronger set of axioms must also be non-monomorphic, and thus have non-standard models. So, however much we try to characterize the natural numbers by postulating axioms, we shall always find that we have not succeeded in characterizing them uniquely; besides the intended model of our axioms there are other, unintended ones that satisfy the axioms too, but are significantly different in some relevant respect, and so cannot be represented as being just

---

[9] For a fuller account, see George S.Boolos and Richard C.Jeffrey, *Computability and Logic*, Cambridge, 1980, ch.17, pp.193-195, to whom I am indebted for this exposition; and for discussion see J.L.Bell and M.Machover, *Mathematical Logic*, North Holland, 1977, ch.7, §2, esp. pp. 323-324.

the natural numbers under another name.

It would be all right if instead of picking on characteristic properties one by one, we could invoke them all in one fell swoop, as Dedekind, in effect, does, when he characterizes the whole numbers as the intersection of *all* sets containing 1 and closed under the successor function. The difficulty arises from our formulation of Peano's fifth postulate:

5. *Any* property that holds of O, and is such that if it holds of any natural number it holds also of the successor of that natural number, holds of every natural number.

The word 'any' is proving too restrictive. It would be all right if we could say 'all'. But to do so would require us to go into second-order logic: the formalisation of Peano's fifth postulate in ordinary first-order logic is

$$(FO \land (Am)(Fm \rightarrow F(Sm))) \rightarrow (An)Fn;$$

in this formulation, F is a free variable; we can apply it in any particular case we like, substituting any other predicate variable for F. The generality is implicit rather than explicit. Instead of being an axiom properly so called, Peano's fifth postulate is really an axiom *schema*, a blue-print for constructing axioms on a do-it-yourself basis, as required. But doing it yourself takes time, and there is an implicit restriction in that we can particularise the axiom schema into an axiom only for those predicates *which can be formulated in the language of the logical calculus we are operating with*. We can avoid these restrictions, and achieve a once-for-all characterization of the natural numbers if we avail ourselves of second-order logic and quotify over predicate variables, having instead of $P5$ above,

$$P5' \qquad (AF)((FO\&(Am)(Fm \rightarrow F(Sm))) \rightarrow (An)Fn).$$

Then we shall have excluded all the non-standard models at one pre-emptive blow. If anyone produces a non-standard model, the very feature that makes it a non-standard model will disqualify it from being a model at all: the putative non-standard model will not possess all and only those hereditary properties possessed by O. Whereas in first-order logic I have to produce the characterization of the natural numbers, and you are then free to find some non-standard model that fits my characterization but is different from

the natural numbers in some significant respect, in second-order
logic I can specify at the outset that any acceptable model must
have *all* the hereditary properties possessed by O. The dialogue
between us has a different structure, giving rise to a different logic
for 'all' from that of 'any'. We shall have much occasion later to
use the dialectical structure of argument to elucidate the meaning
of quotifiers and to resolve other problems.[10]

The non-monomorphism of Peano's postulates in first-order
logic thus faces us with a dilemma:

either we stick with first-order logic, which is safe and well known
and fairly well understood, in which case we cannot give a complete formal characterization of the ordinal, or recursive, properties of the counting numbers, and must hold that they are not
only God-given but known even to us by other means than formal
characterization—*e.g.* by ostensive definition: one, two, three, ...
and so on;

or we invoke **second**-order logic with its risk of paradox (or set
theory with its extreme unsimplicity).[11]

This dilemma sharpens our appreciation of the problems Frege and
Dedekind were trying to surmount. It becomes less easy to go
along with the criticisms made of them on the score of their using
second-order logic: at the very least, we shall have to ask "What
is so wrong with second-order logic?", or "Is first-order logic non-
pareil?". We also become more sympathetic to their anxiety to
exclude intruders from the realm of numbers.

---

[10] See below, chs.7, 8, 14.

[11] Compare Thoralf Skolem, *Über die Nicht-charakterisierbarkeit der Zahlen-*
reihe mittels endlich oder abzählbar unendlich vieler Aussagen mit auss-
chliesslich Zahlvariablen, Fundamenta Mathematicae, xxiii, 1934, quoted
and translated by William and Martha Kneale, *The Development of Logic*,
Oxford, 1962, p.476: The number series is completely characterized . . .
by Peano's axioms, if we regard the concept "set" or "propositional function" as something given in advance with an absolute meaning independent
of all principles of generation or axioms. But if one wishes to carry the
axiomatic treatment through consistently, so that reasoning with sets or
propositional functions is also axiomatized, then the unique or complete
characterization of the number series is impossible.

6.4 Immigration Control

Frege was led to abandon the attempt to identify numbers as quotities on the grounds that if he did not know exactly what a quotity
was, he could never decide by means of our simple attempts at
definition "whether the number JULIUS CAESAR belongs to a
concept, or whether that famous conqueror of Gaul is a number or
not".[12] He attempts to rule out this possibility by specifying the
sort of things that numbers must be, namely extensions of certain

Figure 6.4.1 Immigration Control: Frege says "Sorry, Squire!
You have come to the wrong airport. Only if you belong to the
Extension of the Concept 'Equinumerous with some Concept
F' can you be admitted to the Realm of Numbers. You are just
Not Our Type. I shall send you back, to where you belong"

---

[12] G.Frege, *The Foundations of Arithmetic*, tr. J.L.Austin, Oxford, 1950,
§56, p.68.

sorts of concepts, *viz.* the concepts 'equinumerous with the concept
....'. Granted this definition of a number, it should be fairly easy
to establish that Julius Caesar, whatever sort of entity he is, is not
an extension, certainly not an extension of the rather *recherché*
concept 'equinumerous with the concept ....'.

Figure 6.4.2 Customs Control: Dedekind says "I am afraid I
have to examine your baggage very closely, Sir, before I can
let you through. Are you absolutely sure that you possess no
hereditary property which is not possessed by 1? Unless I can
be completely satisfied on that score, I am obliged to refuse
you admission to the Realm of Numbers"

It is fairly easy to exclude Julius Caesar. He is very distinctive,
and there can be little doubt that he is not the right category of
being to be a number. Other things are harder to be sure about.
What about the set 'equinumerous with a set which is a proper

part of a continuum, but cannot be put in one-one correspondence either with that non-denumerable set or with a denumerable one'? If the Continuum Hypothesis is true, there is no such set. But the Continuum Hypothesis is not provable in Zermelo-Fraenkel set theory, nor is its negation provable. Although such a specification of a set has the right sort of profile, and might well "belong to a concept", and so pass at a first glance, it is hard to tell whether it really is the right sort of thing to be a *pukka* number. Frege has set up the wrong sort of immigration control. He can keep out Julius Caesar and similarly undesirable types of being, but cannot know enough about every entity to tell whether it is or is not a genuine number.

Dedekind is equally concerned to exclude undesirable aliens,[13] but more specific in his remedy. He seeks to keep out undesirables not on the grounds of what type of being they are, but by reason of their properties. The counting numbers are what possess all the properties that are possessed by 1 and are hereditary under the successor. Since negative properties count as being properties just as much as positive ones (being single is as much a property as being married), Dedekind's specification is equivalent to saying that the counting numbers are what possess all,[14] and only, those properties that are possessed by 1 and are hereditary under the successor. Intending settlers can be debarred, as in the Channel Islands, if they do not possess enough property, and arrivals can be denied entrance, as more commonly happens, because they are bringing with them some contraband property. So, where Frege established Immigration Control on fundamental genetic grounds, Dedekind set up Customs Control on grounds of property rather than being.

---

[13] R.Dedekind, *Letter to Keferstein* (partly quoted in §5.3), tr. Hao Wang, *Journal of Symbolic Logic*, **22**, 1957, pp.150-151; reprinted in J. van Heijenoort, *From Frege to Gödel*, p.100: "What, then, must we add to the facts above in order to cleanse our system S again of such alien intruders t as disturb every vestige of order and to restrict it to N?"

[14] There are further snares in the word 'all': does it include the property of *being a counting number* itself? The question raises problems about "impredicativity" which may have bothered Dedekind (see above, §5.3, n.16) and has certainly bothered many modern workers in the foundations of mathematics (see below, §15.3).

Figure 6.4.3 Peano 1 says "As long as you are only dealing with me, a first-order official, I cannot refuse you admission, nor any other candidate that starts off with ω and does not have any obvious awkward points about him at which I might stick. I shall give you a visitor's visa, and assume that you will satisfy all our national requirements, and allow me to ascribe to you any hereditary characteristic that is possessed by O."

Peano's response is at two levels. At the lower level, that of first-order arithmetic, he is unable to keep all the undesirables out. Of course, he would be able to exclude some—Julius Caesar, for example, is the wrong logical shape—and he could rule out others for failing at one of the first four posts: a finite cycle, like that of the boy's oval railway track, fails to have any buffers, an element distinguished by having no predecessor; and a finite stretch of straight track fails to satisfy the second postulate, that every number has a successor. But although some entities are evidently unworthy of membership of the realm of numbers and can be deported without more ado, others are not on the face of it disqualified for membership, and would have to be admitted *pro tem*. Only when the resources of higher-order logic are available to scrutinise all their qualifications, will it emerge whether they have some hidden defect that makes them unworthy of full citizenship.

Figure 6.4.4 Peano 2 says "But I am a higher-order official, who can inspect all your qualifications, and I can see that you are not up to our standards. You are none of you, not even $\omega \ldots {}^*\omega + \omega \ldots {}^*\omega + \omega \ldots {}^*\omega + \omega \ldots \ldots$, true-born natural numbers, nor have you got what it takes to become a natural number by adoption or grace. So I am afraid that whatever your abstract mathematical merits, you will never count as one of us."

Once all properties can be taken into account, all at the same time, the picture changes. Although no single requirement that can be specified in terms of first-order logic will exclude all undesirables, there always is some requirement that any particular undesirable will fail to meet. Only *pukka* natural numbers will not fail some test or other, and will get through the whole examination. So by being able to stipulate that candidates, to be successful, must satisfy not just this, that, or the other, requirement, but must satisfy them *all*, higher-order logic can exclude every entity except *bona fide* natural numbers.

6.5   The Fifth Postulate

Peano's fifth postulate is of the greatest importance. Poincaré takes it as the characteristic feature of mathematical reasoning as such, and as what distinguishes mathematical propositions from tautologies and mere analytic truths.[15]

Peano's fifth postulate not only forces a decision on whether it should be formulated in first- or second-order logic, but raises general questions about its status, like the questions already raised about Euclid's fifth postulate and Desargues' theorem, and questions about the Axiom of Choice and the Continuum Hypothesis which we have still to discuss.[16]

In each case our approach to the dubious axiom is the same. We start by a destruction test. We do not merely doubt, as Descartes would have us do, the fifth postulate, but positively deny it, in the hopes of being refuted one way or another, and the expectation of at least learning something from our pig-headedness. So we consider the set of postulates consisting of the first four of Peano's postulates together with the negation of the fifth. At first sight it would seem impossible that such a weird set of postulates could have a model, but when we recall the non-standard model of Peano Arithmetic, we see how a model could be devised. The boy puts a train on his track, an old Southern Railway train, with a green engine and all its carriages green, and sets it going. If Peano's fifth postulate be true, then that train will traverse every stretch of track in due course. But if it is a non-standard model, we, taking a God's-eye view, and able to look beyond the horizon of infinity,

---

[15] Henri Poincaré, "On the Nature of Mathematical Reasoning", *Science and Hypothesis*, New York, 1952, pp.1-20; reprinted in Paul Benacerraf and Hilary Putnam, eds., *The Philosophy of Mathematics*, 2nd ed., Cambridge, 1983, pp.394-402.

[16] See above, §2.2, §2.9, and below, §12.6, §12.7.

might see other trains in the livery of other railway companies, steaming along other chunks of track, with no possibility of any company's train ever getting onto another company's track.

SR   GWR   LMS   LNER   SNCF   CPR

$|++\ldots+++++\ldots+++++\ldots+++++\ldots+++++\ldots+++++\ldots$

ω $^*\omega + \omega$ $^*\omega + \omega$ $^*\omega + \omega$ $^*\omega + \omega$ $^*\omega + \omega$

Of course, we must recognise that these are not the only railway companies, and that between GWR and LMS there are others, B&O (Baltimore and Ohio) say, and that between either of those there are others again, Penn Railroad say, and so on. The order-type of the railways is dense, of order-type $1 + \eta$, whereas the order-type of the rails in the track of any one company is discrete, of order-type ω in the case of the Southern Railway, and of order-type $^*\omega + \omega$ for the rest of them. With such a track, the antecedent of Peano's fifth postulate is satisfied, as are all the other four, but the consequent is false. Hence the conjunction of the first four and the negation of the fifth is not inconsistent, so that the fifth cannot be argued for as being entailed by the first four.

Although Peano's fifth postulate is in the form of an axiom or an axiom schema, it is more natural to regard it as expressing not a mysterious fact, but a principle of argument. Instead of having an axiom schema

$$(FO \wedge (Am)(Fm \rightarrow F(Sm))) \rightarrow (An)Fn$$

we could equally well have a rule of inference

$$FO, (Am)(Fm \rightarrow F(Sm)) \vdash (An)Fn$$

This is how schoolboys are introduced to it. It is often called the Principle of Mathematical Induction. It is an unfortunate name. Inductive arguments have come to be reckoned those that are factual but not deductive. They occur in the natural sciences and in ordinary life, and are contrasted with mathematical arguments on the one hand and legal and moral arguments and interpretative arguments of literary criticism on the other. Mathematical induction is quite different. It would be better if that name were eschewed on account of its misleading associations, and arguments of that form were called **Arguments by Recursion** instead. The fifth postulate is not a complicated implication we are granted as a premise, but a method of argument we are told to use as valid. Rather than wonder whether the fifth postulate is true, we need to ask whether arguments of this form are valid, and if so why.

6.6   *Sorites* **Arithmetic**

The validity of recursive arguments is not simply analytic. That follows from the negation of the fifth postulate being consistent with the other four of Peano's postulates. But it does not follow that it is quite all right to affirm the other four and yet deny the fifth. Although, if I do so, I shall not be trapped in a straight contradiction, I shall escape only by the skin of my teeth, and shall show myself to be thoroughly unreasonable.

Suppose we have just the first four of Peano's postulates, without either the fifth or its negation. Robinson called a carefully formulated version of this arithmetic Q, but let us call it *Sorites* Arithmetic. That is, we have

1. O is a natural number.
2. The successor of any natural number is a natural number.
3. No two natural numbers have the same successor.
4. O, and O alone, is not the successor of any natural number.

Suppose, further, we have the antecedent of the fifth postulate, for some particular property F; that is,

(i) FO, and

(ii) $(Am)(Fm \rightarrow F(Sm))$; then it is evident that, for any particular $n, \vdash Fn$. Suppose, for example, that $n = 8$; then, we could prove it if challenged, thus:

from   (i) $\vdash FO$
from   (ii) $\vdash FO \rightarrow F1$
therefore $\vdash F1$
from   (ii) $\vdash F1 \rightarrow F2$
therefore $\vdash F2$
from   (ii) $\vdash F2 \rightarrow F3$
therefore $\vdash F3$
from   (ii) $\vdash F3 \rightarrow F4$
therefore $\vdash F4$
from   (ii) $\vdash F4 \rightarrow F5$
therefore $\vdash F5$
from   (ii) $\vdash F5 \rightarrow F6$
therefore $\vdash F6$
from   (ii) $\vdash F6 \rightarrow F7$
therefore $\vdash F7$
from   (ii) $\vdash F7 \rightarrow F8$
therefore $\vdash F8$ **QED**

It is clear that we could apply the same line of reasoning to prove $F257$; the proof would start the same and go on until we reached the final line,

from	(i)	$\vdash FO$
from	(ii)	$\vdash FO \to F1$
therefore		$\vdash F1$
from	(ii)	$\vdash F1 \to F2$
therefore		$\vdash F2$
...	...	....
...	...	....
from	(ii)	$\vdash F256 \to F257$
therefore		$\vdash F257$ QED

It would be tedious to fill in the dots, but it could be done, if we had a lot of time and were arguing with an exceptionally stupid man. But anyone else would soon twig what our strategy of argument was, and concede at once, realising that defeat was inevitable, without waiting for the formal proof to grind on to its inevitable conclusion. So, whatever n was chosen, we should be able to prove Fn. And once this was recognised, it would be reasonable for an opponent to concede $\vdash Fn$ generally, and if he conceded $\vdash Fn$ generally it would be as good as conceding $\vdash (An)Fn$.

But this is too quick. We have already seen, in our discussion of the two formulations of the fifth postulate, that there are subtle differences between 'any' and 'all', and that the latter makes a significantly stronger claim than the former.[17] The fact that for any n we have a means of argument for establishing $\vdash Fn$ does not automatically mean that we have established $\vdash (An)Fn$. We must consider carefully.

6.7 Dialogues

The argument turns on a dialogue. In a dialogue there are both points in common and points of difference. There must be some common ground—we cannot argue at all unless we speak the same language, and in fact we need to share more than just a common tongue if we are to be able to get anywhere.[18] But also there must

---

[17] See above, §6.4.

be something in dispute, or neither of us would need to waste breath trying to bring the other to his point of view. The crucial question is how much common ground there is, not only in linguistic competence and shared beliefs, but in goals and aims. If the two parties to the argument share only a common language and adopt only the aim of being able to communicate with each other, then the only thing either must avoid is inconsistency, and the only arguments either will acknowledge as cogent are deductive arguments, since these alone cannot be gainsaid on pain of inconsistency. If that degree of stringency is demanded, then $(An)Fn$ cannot be proved in *Sorites* Arithmetic. If I am stubborn, I need never concede $(An)Fn$, even though you can prove $\vdash Fn$ for any n you care to mention. You show me how you prove $F8$, and I acknowledge that you have proved $F8$. You invite me to pick some other number, but I decline the invitation, contenting myself with the observation that you have proved $F8$, but not $(An)Fn$. You show me how you could set about proving $F257$. I am unimpressed. I observe that there are a lot of dots, and murmur *'karam sipo tatura'*. You in desperation actually write out a proof of $\vdash F257$; I drum my fingers indulgently, and wonder if you would feel like having a crack at $F10^{1000}$. If I play dumb, it is clear that you will never force me to concede $\vdash (An)Fn$, though it is clear, too, that I shall show myself stupid as well as rude.

In what does my stupidity consist? I am achieving my aim of not being proved wrong, and not being forced, on pain of inconsistency, to acknowledge the validity of your contention. But I am achieving that aim at the cost of forgoing the opportunity of ridding myself of error and discovering new truth. Life is short. If my absolutely no.1 objective is not ever to be shown wrong, then perhaps it is worth refusing to recognise that you have got an end-game that must result in your successfully proving $F10^{1000}$, and trusting that we both shall die before I am proved wrong; but it would be a silly objective to have. In playing chess, I resign rather than spin out the game to the bitter end, not because I did not play with the intention of winning or at least avoiding defeat, but because the

---

[18] See J.R.Lucas, "The Philosophy of the Reasonable Man", *The Philosophical Quarterly*, **13**, 1963, pp.104-106; "Not 'Therefore' but 'But'", *The Philosophical Quarterly*, **16**, 1966, pp.306-307; "Philosophy and Philosophy Of", *Proceedings of the British Academy*, LXXII, 1986, pp.260-264.

point of the exercise is not just to win or force a draw, but to do so in an intelligent fashion. It would be childish to spin out each game to the final checkmate, because I could never bring myself to concede unless forced to by the rules.

Once we allow that arguments are not just eristic exercises,[19] but in part co-operative endeavours, in which we share a common desire to know the truth, and that this may outweigh our desire to win the argument, I shall be readier to make a move just for the sake of argument, and quicker to concede in *Sorites* Arithmetic. I shall be willing to name a number, if you invite me to, and I shall acknowledge the force not only of particular proof-sequences actually displayed, but of lines of argument which you can deploy and which I can get the hang of.

Co-operativeness manifests itself in two ways: in making moves, answering questions, accepting challenges, "for the sake of argument"; and in rising from the level of the actual game, with its formal proof-procedures, to a meta-game in which whole strategies of argument and their outcome are considered too. The first has a bearing on the meaning of our standard quotifiers: the second on our understanding of rationality.

The standard quotifiers of predicate calculus are inadequate representations of the subtleties of ordinary language. In English we have not only the words 'all' and 'any', but 'each' and 'every' too. They are grammatically different: 'all' must have a plural noun agreeing with it; 'any' can, but normally governs a noun in the singular; 'each' and 'every' must have a singular noun. The logic of 'any' is peculiarly difficult; 'not any' means 'none' rather than 'not all' or 'not every', and its use in interrogative contexts is similar. It expresses a free variable rather than a bound one.[20] 'Each' differs from 'every' and 'all' in not being susceptible of negation—you can say "Not all the people I know are handsome", or "Not every one is intelligent", but not "Not each....". Greek and Latin draw different distinctions—πᾶς (*pas*), and *omnis* can be used in both singular and plural. Latin has three words for 'some': *nonnullus*, *quidam*, and *nescioquis*, encapsulating different inference patterns, which will be distinguished in the next chapter.[21]

---

[19] Plato, The *Republic*, VII, 539bc.

[20] See Hans Reichenbach, *Elements of Symbolic Logic*, New York, 1947, §21.

[21] §7.5.

Formal logic has hitherto failed to draw these distinctions, partly because, inevitably, it seeks to simplify, partly because it has been "monologous", concerned with the elucidation of continuous pieces of prose put forward by one person, rather than the interchange between two or more.[22] We miss many subtleties if we confine ourselves to one-person monologues, just as we miss most of the point of the theory of games if we consider only one-person games, and neglect the rest. A two-person, "dialectical" approach is illuminating in many parts of mathematics. It elucidates the fine-structure of the quotifiers, and illuminates the concept of infinity, the issues associated with Intuitionism, and the Axiom of Determinacy.[23]

The standard quotifiers in ordinary conversational usage assign choices for subsequent challenges. If I say "Some of my friends are intelligent", and you doubt my assertion, it is up to me to cite just one who is, and I have made my case: if I say "All my friends are intelligent", and you doubt my assertion, it is open to you to cite just one who is not, and you have made your case. The Latin *quilibet* or *quivis* expresses the thought exactly. I have challenged you, and invite you to pick on the worst case you can for my thesis. If you can find a counter-example to my claim, I was wrong, and can now exchange my previous incorrect opinion for a true one: but if you cannot, having done your reasonable best, then that is some ground for supposing I am right, and you will be glad to exchange your previous ignorance for fuller knowledge. Naturally, it depends on our being willing to stick our necks out, and run the risk of being wrong in the course of our attempts to end up being right. But that is the object of a dialogue. If we are engaged in a dialogue, rather than an eristic exercise, then we shall offer and take up challenges not in order to avoid defeat but so as to open up the possibility of achieving truth. I shall construe your claim "All ..." as a challenge which I should not decline merely in order to avoid being defeated.

If we construe the universal quotifier in terms of worst-case analysis, and the existential quotifier in terms of best-case anal-

---

[22] Logicians in Europe, most notably Paul Lorenzen and Kuno Lorenz, of Erlangen, have been more sensitive to the importance of dialogue logic than have English-speaking ones. See *Philosophica*, **35**, 1985.

[23] See below, §7.5, §12.8.

ysis, with the opponent trying to pick on the worst case and the
original proponent trying to select the best case for his claim, the
two quotifiers seem much more on a par, and the lack of particu-
larity, which has often bothered logicians considering the universal
quotifier disappears. We are entitled to argue, as in fact we do,
from particular instances to universal conclusions; there is nothing wrong with generalising, so long as we make sure before we
do so, that we have considered the counter-arguments, and more
especially, those counter-instances most likely to refute our claim.
Argument by generalisation from a typical instance and in formal
logic the rule UI, the rule of Universal Introduction, and also, according to some interpretations, Aristotle's ἔκθεσις (*ekthesis*), capture part of this principle, but they require that the case be typical;
and though often, as in geometry, where no one case is worse than
any other, so that worst-case analysis is typical-case analysis, the
conditions for generalisation from the typical case are met, these
conditions are not met in *Sorites* Arithmetic, where each case is
slightly different. The proof that the angles of an isosceles triangle
are equal is *exactly* the same whatever the triangle you pick, and I
can give a proof-sequence which applies in every case, so that the
conditions for the argument by generalisation are fully satisfied.
But the proof by recursion that 257 possesses the property F is
not exactly the same as, although it is very similar to, the proof
that 8 possesses the property F; it is longer. Nevertheless there is
a great same-iness about it. Once the putative worst case is specified, an exact specification of the proof for that instance can be
given. Provided the courtesies of dialogue are observed, and the
opponent is prepared to attempt to offer a counter-instance, the
argument can proceed, and go through to its conclusion.

But how can we be sure that it will go through to a conclusion?
The opponent is being invited to see that the proponent has a
strategy which will work in every case, but to see this the opponent
has to rise above the level of the rules of the game, and engage in
meta-game thinking, which is not formalised and open to the charge
of hand-waving. After one or two examples of how particular cases
are proved in *Sorites* Arithmetic, the proponent reckons that the
opponent should have got the hang of it, and waves his hand and
says 'and so on'. But is this legitimate? After all, it was just to
get rid of 'and so on's that Dedekind was driven to introduce his
intersections of chains.

Two answers can be made. The deep answer is to maintain that ultimately hand-waving is the basic form of reasoning, and formal proofs are only a special and stylized sub-species of arguments which are for the most part informal and intuitive. Reasoning cannot be completely reduced to rule-following. Even if we formalise as completely as possible, we still have to exercise our *nous* in recognising, for example that

from	(i)	$\vdash FO$
from	(ii)	$\vdash FO \to F1$
therefore		$F1$

is an instance of *Modus Ponens*. We may, for special purposes, lay down rules for deciding special sorts of question, and these decision-procedures may be entirely formal. But they are the exceptional case, and we cannot confine reason to them alone. We not only think in accordance with these rules, but cannot help also thinking about them and assessing their validity and their implications for ourselves, independently of those specific inferences licensed by the rules themselves. And so we cannot help rationality breaking into our rule-bound procedures, and our not only playing according to the game, but making meta-game assessments of what games can be played, and what their outcome must be.

The second answer is a tactical one. Dedekind's objection was to an open-ended 'and so on' with a series of dots extending indefinitely far, and no means of determining whether or not some strange entity was a number or not. We can cut down the range of uncertainty very much by playing the dialectical game more tightly, and, instead of trying to prove to our opponent that we can prove Fn for any n he chooses, inviting him to put forward a putative counter-example and then showing him how we can be sure of refuting at least that counter-example. That is, instead of inviting him to challenge us to prove $F257$, and our then setting off

from	(i)	$\vdash FO$
from	(ii)	$\vdash FO \to F1$
therefore		$\vdash F1$
from	(ii)	$\vdash F1 \to F2$
therefore		$\vdash F2$
...	...	....

```
 . . .         . . .      . . . . . . . . .
from      (ii) ⊢ F256→ F257
therefore      ⊢ F257    QED
```

we invite him to deny our claim that $(An)Fn$, and to produce a putative counter-example. If he then instances 257, that is tantamount to claiming $\vdash \neg F257$. We then argue *Modus Tollendo Tollens*

```
hypothesis     F257
from      (ii) ⊢ F256  → F257
therefore      ⊢ ¬F256
from      (ii) ⊢ F255  → F256
therefore      ⊢ ¬F255
from      (ii) ⊢ F254  → F255
therefore      ⊢ ¬F254
 . . .         . . . . . .      . . . . . .
 . . .         . . . . . .      . . . . . .
therefore      ⊢ ¬F1
from      (ii) ⊢ FO    → F1
therefore      ⊢ ¬FO
```

and this is a contradiction, since we were given FO as one of our hypotheses. The merit of this scheme of refutation is that it is in the form of a regression rather than a progression, running down towards the unmovable buffers, instead of proceeding up towards a movable target. It is an end-game, ending in a straight contradiction, a *reductio ad absurdum*, rather than a recipe for producing positive results. As such it is a little less open to Dedekind's objections. In other dialogues, however, this tactic is not open to us, and the only question is whether reason can be reduced to rules, or always may transcend whatever rules have been laid down.

6.8 Recursive Reasoning

We can now see the rationale of arguments by recursion. Peano's fifth postulate is not entailed by the other four, and the principle of argument by recursion is not a derived rule of inference of *Sorites* Arithmetic. What it does is to entitle us to say in the object language what we could already see to be true in the meta-language. In the object language all we can do is that for any m we can prove $\vdash Fm$; the principle of recursive argument extends this by allowing us to infer, as an additional theorem, $\vdash (An)Fn$. This is an additional theorem, but in this case it extends the theorems of *Sorites* Arithmetic only unobjectionably. (We need to be careful: in Gödel's theorem we can, for any m, prove Gm, but if we were to add $\vdash (An)Gn$, we should land ourselves in inconsistency.[24] We shall then have to distinguish the formal $\vdash$ from the informal 'therefore'.) Hilbert would accept it as a means of proving, compendiously and easily what could be otherwise proved only laboriously and tediously, but without its yielding any theorems about particular finite numbers which could not be proved, equally surely, if more lengthily, without it. We have a three-line proof of $F257$, instead of a three-page one. But we *could* prove $F257$ without the fifth postulate, so we are not running any extra risk of inconsistency by adding it.

We thus have two arguments in favour of arguments by recursion, a negative, Hilbertian one, that no harm will come of it, so we might as well add it, if it will make our proofs easier and shorter; and a positive, dialectical one, that the fifth postulate in some way grows out of the other four, and enables us to say *in* Peano Arithmetic what we could anyhow say *about Sorites* Arithmetic.

It may seem that there is an incompatibility between these two justifications, and that the fifth postulate cannot be at the same time so bland and vacuous that Hilbert can have no objection to accepting it and so important that *Sorites* Arithmetic is somehow defective without it, and needs to be supplemented by it. The answer is that Hilbert is working with a very limited concept of "contentful" (*inhaltlich*), because it is, for him, concerned only with particular finite numbers, and so $\vdash (An)Fn$ does not have any more content than $\vdash Fm$ for each m. For us, however, $\vdash (An)Fn$ does make a greater claim than $\vdash Fm$ for each m. It alters the structure of the dialogue and the subsequent course of argument. 'All' has a higher profile than 'any'. Once the claim of 'all' has been made and allowed, it can be applied to particular instances without more ado, and can be relied on to rule out counter-instances in advance. With 'any', I may be able to prove particular cases one by one, but cannot assume in advance that I have proved them all. The difference was important when we were wanting to rule out non-standard models

---

[24] See below, §8.9.

of Peano Arithmetic, and is likely to be significant wherever we are dealing with different sorts of quotifiers $((An)(Vm)(m > n)$ does not entail $(Vm)(An)(m > n))$, or quotifiers interspersed with modal operators, such as $\diamond$, 'it is possible to find a number such that'. If we can strengthen our ability to establish a claim for *any* into an acknowledgement that it is indeed proved for *all*, we may be able to achieve much more in the subsequent course of argument.

6.9 The Natural Numbers

There are three facets to our concept of natural number, which are linked, but which cannot be subsumed under any one head.

Natural numbers can be answers to the question 'How many?' and must therefore be of a logical shape to fit into quotifiers, which are of the general form $(Q_?s)$. It is reasonable in this sense to say that natural numbers are quotities, although this leaves us with the question 'What are quotities?' to which we do not as yet have a clear or convincing answer.

Natural numbers also have a discrete order, generated by the successor function, or *next after* relation. The successor function defines intransitive counting, and intransitive counting is intimately connected with transitive counting, because that stops when there are no more left. For this reason the discrete order of the counting numbers is anchored by nought's being really the first number, and definable as a quotity in non-numerical terms.

Natural numbers can, however, stand on their own, and be talked about without having to be kept in the context either of the question 'How many?' or of the process of counting. Although they may need to be grounded in answers to the question 'How many?' or the process of counting, they break loose, and can be used without having to be defined contextually. Once we have the decimal notation, we can formulate a rule for generating numerals to name new numbers quite apart from any cardinal or ordinal use we may have for them. Peano's postulates capture much of what we mean by abstract numbers, but characterize them uniquely only if we can avail ourselves of second-order logic. If we confine ourselves to first-order logic, which in the opinion of many logicians is the only portion of logic that is really safe and can really be counted as logic, then Peano's postulates do not characterize the natural numbers uniquely but are satisfied also by non-standard models which differ from the natural numbers in significant respects.

Since we can talk about qualities without their having to be defined contextually, we may tentatively suppose that quotities may be talked about in the same way, and since we can define the nought quotifier in non-numerical terms, and can characterize the predecessor, and hence the successor, function in terms of quotifiers too, we can characterize the natural numbers themselves as **the smallest progression of quotities containing nought and closed under succession.**

From Frege we have taken the importance of nought, and the insight that cardinal numbers are quotities, akin to 'nothing', 'something' and 'everything'. From Dedekind the importance of their being a progression of order-type ω, and their being the smallest such, the intersection of all the innumerable chains, quite beyond the compass of first-order logic. From Peano the systematic and iterative nature of the natural numbers.

Questions about the status of Peano's postulates arise when we approach the abstract numbers axiomatically. Clearly, on the cardinal or ordinal approach the first four are not so much postulates as theorems, or if 'theorem' be too formal a concept, evident truths which can be shown to be true of cardinal or ordinal numbers. The fifth postulate, however, presents some difficulty, as it does not follow from the other four, and informal arguments for its truth seem to beg the question. Rather than see it as an axiom or an axiom schema, we should regard it as enunciating a rule of inference, namely that of argument by recursion. Argument by recursion is a valid principle of inference because it legitimates in the object language inferences we can see to hold in the meta-language. We can bring the point out best by setting the argument in a dialogue between two parties who, though naturally liking to win the argument also want to be right and to know the truth. Because of this commitment each party to the argument is willing to make moves, accept challenges, follow general lines of argument and draw out the implications of strategies of proof, even though he may thereby make himself more vulnerable to refutation than if he played solely to win, or at least to avoid defeat. This is what it is to adopt the "dialectical approach". It is not the only possible one. The practitioner of eristic plays his cards very close to his chest and staves off defeat perhaps until both parties to the discussion are dead. He pays a price. The cost of never being shown to be wrong is not having the chance of being right either. And we reckon it is more reasonable to run the risk of being shown to be wrong than to forgo the possibility of ending up knowing the truth.

"God made the natural numbers", Kronecker is said to have said; "all else is the work of man". Since the word 'number' is used in a variety of senses, it is worth recalling §3.7, §4.2 and anticipating §14.8, and tabulating some of the ways we talk of numbers.

Numbers

1. Natural Numbers   Peano Arithmetic
the smallest progression of quotities containing nought and closed under succession
$0, 1, 2, 3, \ldots, 10, 11, \ldots, 100, \ldots$

2. Counting Numbers

One, Two, Three,...

3. Whole Numbers   (or Integers)
$\ldots -3, -2, -1, 0, 1, 2, 3, \ldots$

4. Rationals   (or Fractions)
$\frac{1}{2}$, $\frac{2}{3}$, $5/7$, $1\frac{7}{12}$, $-\frac{3}{5}$

5. Real Numbers

$\sqrt{2}$, $\sqrt{10}$, π, e,

6. Complex Numbers   (Imaginary Numbers)
$\sqrt{-1}$, $1 + \sqrt{3}i$, $1^{\frac{1}{3}}$, $\cos\theta + i\sin\theta$

It is possible to extend the list further, to include, as well as transfinite numbers (see next chapter), vectors, tensors and quaternions as *soi-disant* numbers.

Chapter 7
The Infinite

7.1 In Defence of Doubt

Once we allow some principle of recursive reasoning, we are landed
with the infinite. There are an infinite number of natural numbers:
for 0 is a natural number, and if anything is a natural number, its
successor is a natural number. So there are natural numbers, and
for any finite number, n, it is demonstrably false that there are
exactly n natural numbers. We feel impelled to allow the question
'How many natural numbers are there?', and the only possible
answer seems to be 'an infinite number'. But we have qualms.
Infinity seems out of this earth. It smacks of Platonism, mysticism
and theology. The word 'infinite' is a negative concept, contrasting
not only with 'finite', in a strict mathematical sense, but with
'definite' and with 'comprehensible'. Often, especially in theology
and ancient philosophy, the Infinite is the Whole, $\tau\grave{o}\ \pi\hat{a}\nu$ (*to pan*),
the Universe, the Absolute, whose logic is difficult and fraught with
inconsistencies. We are wise to be wary.

Although Parmenides, Plato, Augustine, William of Alnwick,
Leibniz, Cantor, Dedekind and most modern mathematicians are
fairly happy with infinity, other philosophers have had doubts.
Aristotle allowed the existence of the potential infinite but denied
the actual infinite, and was followed by Aquinas and most of the
Schoolmen. It is fair to place Weyl and the modern Intuitionists in

that tradition. Locke had considerable difficulty in articulating a coherent and satisfactory account of infinity. Berkeley was deeply criticial of infinitesimals and mathematical infinity generally, and modern Finitists likewise reject every sort of infinity, and try to confine themsleves to finite numbers alone. But infinitistic arguments keep seeping in, and strict Finitists distinguish themselves from their laxer brethren, and still are not stringent enough in their scepticism to escape the strictures of the ultra strict.[1]

It is easy to stifle doubts, and accept the infinite as part of the mathematical exercise, justified by the general success of mathematics. Geometry runs more smoothly if we allow points at infinity: then we can say that two straight lines always intersect, parallel lines meeting at a point at infinity. If we add the symbol ∞ to our other numerical symbols, we are able to discuss series, sums and integrals much more incisively. Once we allow the question 'How many natural numbers are there?' it is illuminating to answer $\aleph_0$. It seems silly to let philosophical scruples deter us from entering Cantor's paradise.

But credulity conduces to inconsistency. Easy acceptance is not on. It is important, though difficult, to articulate the objections to infinity that we are inclined to feel. What tends to happen is that the objections are only half-formulated, and never adequately considered; instead, the mathematician gets used to operating with infinity, and, as it were, represses the doubts he once felt without ever thinking them through properly and either seeing that they are valid and accepting them or seeing that they are not valid and why. As in psychoanalysis, repression causes trouble later on. Many Intuitionists show symptoms of not having come to terms with infinity in their youth, and suffering in consequence from psychological lesions in middle age. The only prophylactic is to give full rein to doubts at the first encounter. Doubt now, doubt bravely: *dubita fortiter* to parody Luther.

---

[1] Terminology varies. Hao Wang (*From Mathematics to Philosophy*, London, 1974, p.52; "Eighty Years of Foundational Studies", *Dialectica*, **12**, 1958, pp.466-497.) distinguished, besides orthodox objectivistic mathematics, three sceptical positions—Predicative set theory, Intuitionism, Finitism—and subsequently distinguished within Finitism, a further, even more sceptical, position, Ultrafinitism. In this chapter the positions distinguished and discussed will be Intuitionism, Lax Finitism and Ultrafinitism.

Doubt bravely. Most sceptics are too timid. They lack the courage of their lack of conviction, and doubt some things, while cravenly believing others, which, according to their lights, are equally open to question. And correspondingly, one cogent counter to scepticism is to disallow selectivity, and deny to the sceptic on grounds of a more complete scepticism the tenets he requires in order to formulate and communicate his doubts.

The cardinal and ordinal approaches to infinity will first be developed, and their difficulties exposed. Intuitionism will then be considered in its own right, and then increasingly sceptical forms of Finitism. Once these are shown not to offer a satisfactory alternative to full-blooded infinitistic accounts, further attention will be given to the difficulties of infinity and ways of remedying them.

7.2 Cardinality

We have seen in Chapter Four that natural numbers are grounded in a certain sort of quotifier which enables us to answer the question 'How many *a*s are *F*?'. These numerical quotifiers can be defined one after another, and form a natural sequence, or progression. The natural numbers are thus adequately characterized. We can, therefore, ask how many there are as we can ask 'How many three-figure numbers are there?'—the question is definite, though the answer is not. But whereas the answer to the latter, 900, is straightforward, the answer to the former must take us into some transfinite realm. For, as Peter of Spain argued, feeling towards the principle of recursion, there is more than one finite natural number, there is more than two finite natural numbers, there is more than three finite natural numbers, and thus by a "ladderlike" inference from these, *et sic de aliis* for any finite natural number there are more finite natural numbers than that.[2] So if we ask the question 'How many natural numbers are there?', no numerical quotifier thus far introduced will give the right answer; it must, therefore, be a new sort of quotifier. We resort to the same tactic as when faced with the questions 'How many times does 5 go into 12?', 'What is left when we take 12 from 7?', 'What is the square root of 2?', and

---

[2] Peter of Spain, *Tractatus called afterwards Summule Logicales*, ed. L.M. De Rijk, Van Gorcum, 1972, p.231, cited by Norman Kretzmann, Anthony Kenny, Jan Pinborg, eds., *Cambridge History of Later Medieval Philosophy*, p.568, n.11.

'What is the square root of -1?'. In each of these cases we extended our concepts so that the question, which previously could not always be given an answer, now can. In the same way, we want to extend our concept of numerical quotifier, so that to the question 'How many natural numbers are there?' we give an answer, and say 'There are $\aleph_0$ natural numbers' (pronounced aleph nought, from the first letter of the Hebrew alphabet).

A key step in the cardinal approach to number was to establish a criterion for the same cardinal number to be applicable in different cases. If I say that the number of natural numbers is $\aleph_0$, how do I tell whether the number of negative integers, of positive rationals, of real numbers, is $\aleph_0$ too? Frege's answer is that the number of negative integers is the same as the number of natural numbers iff they are equinumerous (*gleichzahlig*) with each other, that is to say iff there is a one-one mapping between the negative integers and the natural numbers, so that to each negative integer there corresponds one and only one natural number. But then there is a problem: whereas a finite multitude is never equinumerous with a proper subset of itself, infinite multitudes characteristically can be. If we pair off each natural number with its double, thus:

0	1	2	3	. . .	. . .
0	2	4	6	. . .	. . .

we establish a one-one mapping between the natural numbers and the even numbers. So we have to say that there are $\aleph_0$ even numbers as well as $\aleph_0$ natural numbers, even though the even numbers are a proper subset of the natural numbers. Similarly the pairing

0	1	2	3	. . .	. . .
1	2	3	4	. . .	. . .

shows that there are $\aleph_0$ counting numbers even though the counting numbers are a proper subset of the natural numbers.

Even more paradoxical is Cantor's proof that there are **only** as many rational numbers as there are integers. Although, as we shall shortly see, we cannot pair off the positive rationals in their natural order of size with the positive whole numbers (the counting numbers), we can do so if we rearrange them, expressed as fractions, in the form m/n, where m and n are natural numbers in an array:

1/1	2/1	3/1	4/1	. . .	. . .
1/2	2/2	3/2	4/2	. . .	. . .
1/3	2/3	3/3	4/3	. . .	. . .
. . .	. . .	. . .	. . .	. . .	. . .
. . .	. . .	. . .	. . .	. . .	. . .
. . .	. . .	. . .	. . .	. . .	. . .

This array will more than include all the positive rational numbers (since 1/2, 2/4, 3/6, which all represent the same rational number, will occur separately and be counted separately). Although we still could not establish a one–one pairing if we considered each row, one after another, nevertheless if we count along successive diagonals, taking first 1/1, and then 2/1 and 1/2, and then 3/1, 2/2, 3/1, where in each diagonal the total of the numerator and the denominator is the same, we shall reach every member of the array in due course, and can thus set up a one–one correspondence between the members of the array and the natural numbers. Hence the cardinal number of the positive rationals is the same as that of the natural numbers; and a further extension of the argument shows that so is the cardinal number of all the rationals, positive and negative, together with nought. Such a conclusion seems highly counter-intuitive. We are denying the truism that the whole is greater than the part: by accepting Frege's, Dedekind's and Cantor's definition of equinumerosity, we are led to the paradoxical conclusion that the whole is also equal to the part. But a thing cannot be both greater than and equal to another: if infinity leads to this conclusion, it is absurd, and the whole concept must be rejected.

Many philosophers have accepted that conclusion. John Philoponus used it against the Aristotelian thesis that the world had always existed, and so did many of the Schoolmen; essentially the same argument is used by Kant and has been put forward again in recent years.[3] Others, however, have sought to evade the apparent

---

[3] See Richard Sorabji, *Time, Creation and the Continuum*, London, 1983, chs. 13, 14 and 15 for ancient and mediaeval discussions of infinity. See G.J.Whitrow, "The Age of the Universe", *British Journal for the Philosophy of Science*, **5**, 1954-5, pp.215-225, and **29**, 1978, pp.39-45, esp. p.41. See also K.R.Popper, *British Journal for the Philosophy of Science*, **29**, 1978, pp.47-48 and J.Bell, *British Journal for the Philosophy of Science*, **30** 1979, pp.161-165.

paradox. Nicole Oresme and Albert of Saxony anticipated Galileo and Newton, and simply denied the applicability of the relations *less than* and *equal to* to infinities. Such a response is not open to us. We are already committed to some sense of *equal to* in the relation of equinumerosity we have used to define the equivalence classes from which we abstract cardinal numbers; and we could hardly call them *numbers*, if the relation *less than* were altogether inapplicable. Henry of Harclay allowed the applicability of these relations, but questioned what exactly the part-whole relation was. William of Alnwick began to distinguish different ways in which one infinity could be greater than another, and Gregory of Rimini did distinguish the *greater than* of proper set inclusion from the *greater than* of having a higher cardinality.[4] Gregory was right. Ordering relations, as we shall see in Chapters Nine and Ten, constitute a whole family, as do equivalence relations, so that we need to distinguish different orderings and different equivalences, and although proper set inclusion is incompatible with the set-equality defined as $A = B$ iff $A \subseteq B \wedge B \subseteq A$, it does not follow that it is incompatible with set-equality defined as equinumerosity. Once it is recognised that *equinumerous with* and *less than* belong to different families, the paradox is resolved.[5] Indeed, instead of being a paradox, it can be used as an alternative definition of infinity. Dedekind defined an infinite set as one that was equinumerous with a proper subset of itself.[6] Infinity thus defined comes to the same thing as the recursive approach adopted in this chapter, though it is not quite trivial (and requires the Axiom of Choice) to establish the equivalence.

We might suppose that since infinite sets can be equinumerous with proper subsets of themselves, all infinite sets were equinumerous with one another. But this is not so: there is more than one infinite cardinal. Cantor showed that it was impossible to list all the *real* numbers between 0 and 1, one after another in an infinite list. Of course, they can be ordered. Given any two distinct real numbers we can say that one of them is greater than the other. But that does not give us a list, because there is always another between them—the case is similar to that of the rationals which

---

[4] See Norman Kretzmann, Anthony Kenny, Jan Pinborg, eds., *Cambridge History of Later Medieval Philosophy*, pp. 567-573.

[5] See below, §9.5.

[6] See above, §5.2.

cannot be listed while in their natural order. Nevertheless there might be another ordering which was a list—*i.e.* there was a first, a second, a third, ... *etc.* with nothing between the first and the second, or the second and the third. But Cantor showed it to be impossible. Every real number can be expressed as an infinite decimal, and *vice versa*. Some—those ending in 0 recurring or 9 recurring can be expressed in two ways; thus .9999... is the same as 1.0000... In all such cases he fixes on the 0 recurring form. Suppose then we did have a list of all the real numbers between 0 and 1. It would have the general form:

$$
\begin{array}{cccccc}
.a_{11} & .a_{12} & .a_{13} & \cdots & .a_{12} & \cdots \\
.a_{21} & .a_{22} & .a_{23} & \cdots & .a_{22} & \cdots \\
.a_{31} & .a_{32} & .a_{33} & \cdots & .a_{32} & \cdots \\
\cdots & \cdots & \cdots & \cdots & \cdots & \cdots \\
\cdots & \cdots & \cdots & \cdots & \cdots & \cdots \\
.a_{n1} & .a_{n2} & .a_{n3} & \cdots & .a_{n2} & \cdots \\
\end{array}
$$

where a_{11}, *etc.* are digits, either $1, 2, 3, 4, 5, 6, 7, 8, 9$, or 0. By his method of diagonalization he then constructs a new number $.b_1 b_2 b_3 \ldots b_n \ldots$ which he showed was not in the list. The rule was to define b_n in terms of a_{nn} but so as to be different from it. If a_{nn} was $0, 1, 2, 3, 4, 5, 6, 7$ or 8, b_n was $a_{nn} + 1$: if a_{nn} was 9, b_n was 0. So $b_n \neq a_{nn}$. And in that case the number $.b_1 b_2 b_3 \ldots b_n \ldots$ cannot occur in the proffered list. It cannot be the first one, because $b_1 \neq a_{11}$: it cannot be the second one, because $b_2 \neq a_{22}$: it cannot be the third one, because $b_3 \neq a_{33}$: and so on down the list, it always fails to be the nth one on the list because it differs from it in its nth digit. Thus there is no way of correlating the real numbers between 0 and 1 with the counting numbers $1, 2, 3, 4, \ldots$ *etc.* Since there are evidently at least as many real numbers as counting numbers, and they are not equinumerous, it follows that there must be more real numbers than there are counting numbers, that is, the number of real numbers is greater than $\aleph_0$. We say that the number of real numbers, the cardinal number of the continuum as it is sometimes called, is **non-denumerable**. Further, if every decimal of the form $.c_1 c_2 c_3 \ldots c_n \ldots$ represents a real number between 0 and 1, there must be $10^{\aleph_0}$ real numbers between 0 and 1. For there are 10 possible choices for the first digit after the decimal point, 10 for the second, and so on, *ad infinitum*. Equally, we could have used the binary notation, expressing each real number between 0 and

1 as $.d_1 d_2 d_3 \ldots d_n \ldots$ where d_i could take only the values 1 and 0. So, on this reckoning there are $2^{\aleph_0}$ real numbers between 0 and 1, with what would have seemed previously the paradoxical conclusion that $10^{\aleph_0} = 2^{\aleph_0}$.

That there should be these two infinities is not altogether surprising. The Greeks had distinguished two, the infinite by addition and the infinite by division. They called the former the infinitely big, and the latter the infinitely small. It is ironic that Cantor has led us to the opposite conclusion, with the continuum, which we reach by infinite division, having a larger cardinality than the natural numbers, which were the paradigm of infinite bigness.

One might wonder whether these were the only two infinities there were, or whether there were others besides; more specifically, whether there are any between the natural numbers and the continuum, and whether there are any beyond the continuum. Cantor believed that the answer to the first question was No, and spent much of his life trying to prove "the Continuum Hypothesis", as it was called, to wit that there is no cardinal number between $\aleph_0$ and $2^{\aleph_0}$. We now know that the Continuum Hypothesis can neither be proved nor be disproved within standard axiomatizations of set theory. Cantor proved that the answer to the second question was Yes. He considered the "power set", that is to say, the set of all the subsets of a given set, and showed that it could not be equinumerous with the original set: the assumption that there was a one–one mapping from the original set to the power set led to an inconsistency. He thus established that the cardinal number of the power set was always greater than that of the original set, or in general terms that $2^{\aleph} > \aleph$. Some care is needed in defining *greater than* and *less than* between cardinals. We cannot simply use $\subset$, proper set inclusion, as we can with finite cardinals. Instead, we need **first** to pick out the equivalence classes of equinumerous sets, and **then**, among these, the quotient set of sets under the equivalence relation of equinumerosity,[7] use $\subset$, proper set inclusion, to order these equivalence classes. In effect, we are defining a new relation on sets, and saying that X has a lower cardinality than Y, iff X is properly included in Y **and** X is **not** equinumerous with Y; or formally (and clauses in correct order)

---

[7] See below, §9.5.

$$X \prec Y \quad\quad \text{iff} \quad\quad (X \subset Y) \wedge (X \not\equiv Y).$$

It is clear that this definition works both for finite cardinals and for $\aleph_0$. It is natural to extend it from sets having a cardinality to cardinal numbers themselves, and reckon that one cardinal is less than another iff there is a set having the first cardinality which is not equinumerous with a set having the second cardinality, but is properly included in it.

There is thus an infinite succession of infinities. Whether there are any others, between adjacent members of this succession, that is, whether there is an $\aleph$ between $\aleph_\alpha$ and $2^{\aleph_\alpha}$ is again an open question. The hypothesis that the answer is No is the claim of the General Continuum Hypothesis. We are naturally led also to wonder how many cardinal numbers—how many $\aleph$s—there are. But to this question no answer can be given. The cardinal number of all cardinal numbers is an incoherent concept. In which case, as Dummett observes, we are hardly entitled to press the question 'How many natural numbers are there?' or to posit $\aleph_0$ as an acceptable answer. Even on the simple cardinal approach, the critics have a strong case, and we cannot take infinity for granted without considering and meeting their objections.

7.3 The Mostest

Although most mathematicians first come across infinity as a useful symbol, ∞, or as the cardinal number of the natural numbers, the approach in terms of some ordering relation is more profound, since infinity, coming from the Latin *finis*, an end or a boundary, is, like the other concepts used in discussions of infinity, such as limit, bound, or extreme, susceptible of analysis in terms of some ordering relation. In the Middle Ages the Schoolmen defined the infinite in terms of *maius*, the Latin comparative of *magnum*, meaning 'greater than'.[8] And Cantor was led to develop transfinite arithmetic in order to make sense of successive operations iterated without end, but nevertheless tending towards some sort of limit. He considered the topological operation of taking the derived set of a given set, which could be indexed by a single dash or a subscript $_1$,

---

[8] Thomas Bradwardine, *Tractatus de Continuo*, cited by Norman Kretzmann, Anthony Kenny, Jan Pinborg, eds., *Cambridge History of Later Medieval Philosophy*, p.567, n.8.

and then of taking the derived set of the derived set, which could be indexed by a double dash or a subscript $_2$, and so on, *ad infinitum*. It seemed reasonable to consider the set that would result from *all* these operations having been done, and to assign to it the index ω so that ω could be said to come after all the other indices. It makes sense. Moreover we can assimilate the way in which such a limit number comes after all its predecessors to the way in which an ordinary number comes after its predecessor. We can define 4, the successor of 3, in terms of the set $\{0, 1, 2, 3\}$:[9] and we can define ω, the successor of the whole numbers, as the ordered set $\{0, 1, 2, 3, 4, \ldots\}$.

The difficulty arises as soon as we start talking of the limit as something definite. The limit of 'more' is 'most'. If it is more than all (other) members, it is the most. But could not there then be something more than it? If ω is admitted as a definite ordinal number, a "limit ordinal" coming after $0, 1, 2, 3, 4, \ldots$ can we not have $\omega + 1$ coming after ω? It seems that there is an ineradicable inconsistency in attempting to comprehend that which is necessarily not bounded in one completed whole. Whatever is said cannot be the last word on the topic, and must in the nature of the case be overtaken by the further development of the ever developing incomplete process.

This objection was first formulated by Aristotle, and was much considered in the Middle Ages.[10] Aristotle argued against the "actual" infinite and was willing to allow only the "potential"

---

[9] See above, §4.7 and §5.6.

[10] Many of Aristotle's arguments are physical, and seek to show that no infinite substance actually exists in nature. The theologians, particularly St Augustine (*De Civitate Dei*, XII, xviii, 19.), were concerned with God's unbounded power and knowledge, quite independently of the contingent restraints of physical reality. The only limitations on the power of an omnipotent God are conceptual limitations. The Schoolmen discussed whether there was any logical or conceptual impossibility in the actual infinite as opposed to physical arguments against it (see Norman Kretzmann, Anthony Kenny, Jan Pinborg, eds., Cambridge *History of Later Medieval Philosophy*, Cambridge, 1982, pp.566-569.) In a later age still, Georg Cantor viewed the actual infinite, and the whole of transfinite arithmetic, from a theological standpoint (see Michael Hallett, *Cantorian Set Theory and Limitation of Size*, Oxford, 1984, pp.9-11, 14, 21-24, 35-37).

infinite.[11] His conceptual argument rested upon a distinction in definition. The infinite is not, as is customarily thought, that which has nothing outside it, but that which always has something outside it: οὐ γὰρ οὗ μηδὲν ἔξω (*ou gar hou meden exo*), but ἄπειρον μὲν οὖν ἐστιν οὗ κατὰ τὸ ποσὸν λαμβάνουσιν αἰεί τι λαμβάνειν ἐστιν ἔξω (*apeiron men oun estin hou kata to poson lambanousin aiei ti lambanein estin exo*).[12] Bradwardine and many of the Schoolmen rendered his thesis as saying that the infinite was not *tantum quod non maius* but *non tantum quin maius*[13] in preference to the literal rendering *non enim cuius nihil est extra, sed cuius semper aliquid est extra*, and some, making the crucial distinction between multitudes and magnitudes, said that an infinite multitude was not *tot quod non plura* but *non tot quin plura*.[14]

We can express Aristotle's thesis in symbols, if we take ἔξω, (*exo*), outside, to be representable by $>$: it is not

$$(Vx)\neg(Vy)(y > x)$$

but $\quad (Ax)(Vy)(y > x)$

The former can be rewritten

$$(Vx)(Ay)\neg(y > x)$$

which, granted a linear ordering for $>$, is equivalent to

$$(Vx)(Ay)(x \geq y).$$

The former thesis thus claims that there is a superlative, a $>$est, a "mostest", an all-embracing all; whereas Aristotle denies this, and

[11] *Physics* III, §4-§8, $202^b30 - 208$, esp. $207^b27 - 34$; *Metaphysics*, K, 10, $1066^a35 - 1067^a37$, *De Caelo*, I, §5-§7, $271^b - 275^b$.

[12] *Physics*, III, 6, $207^a7 - 9$.

[13] Thomas Bradwardine, *Tractatus de Continuo*, cited by Norman Kretzmann, Anthony Kenny, Jan Pinborg, eds., *Cambridge History of Later Medieval Philosophy*, p.567, n.8.

[14] Anneliese Maier, "Diskussionem über das aktuell Unendliche in der ersten Hälft des 14 Jahr-hunderts", in Maier, *Ausgehendes Mittellalter*, Vol I, 1964-7, pp.41-44; cited by Norman Kretzmann, Anthony Kenny, Jan Pinborg, eds., *Cambridge History of Later Medieval Philosophy*, p.567n7.

says that however much there is, there is always more. Aristotle is arguing for a comparative rather than superlative account, a more-than rather than a mostest doctrine of infinity. It is clear that the order of quotifiers is crucial. As he sees it, there are two different concepts, on the one hand a metaphysical and theological one, and on the other a conceptual and mathematical one. When we are talking about the Whole, τὸ πᾶν the Universe, or God, it is appropriate to say that it is not included in, enclosed in (we should note Aristotle's spatial word ἔξω (*exo*), outside) or surpassed by, anything else, and so is not comprehended, not bounded. To say that God is infinite is to say that He is unbounded and incomprehensible. To say that the Universe is infinite, although it may now be construed as saying that the measure of some aspect of it—its volume, its duration, its mass—is infinite in the mathematical sense, often means rather that it is not a closed system, that it is not subject to external constraints or external boundary conditions, because, by definition, it includes all such, and every condition is already taken into account. The logic of the word 'universe' is a simple exercise in the superlative mode. There is some ordering relation—usually the part–whole relation—and the universe is the maximum. In theology the relation is ontological: there are greater and less degrees of reality, giving rise to a great chain of being, with God conceived as the most real, the ultimate reality, as in St Anselm's definition, *id quo maius nequeat cogitari*, that than which a greater cannot be thought of. The contrast between the Anselmian absolute, as we may call it, and Aristotle's comparative concept is expressed by the reversal of the order of the quotifiers and the use of the strict asymmetrical ordering relation $>$ instead of the antisymmetrical $\geq$. The two are clearly incompatible. If for every x there is a y that is greater than it,

$$(Ax)(Vy)(y > x),$$

then any candidate for being the Anselmian absolute will be surpassed by some other entity, and so will forfeit its claim to maximality.

So$\quad$ $(Ax)(Vy)(y > x) \vdash \neg(Vx)(Ay)(x \geq y).$

We thus have a straight inconsistency between Aristotle's doctrine of the potential infinite and the Anselmian account of the actual infinite, and it might seem that the former was to be preferred. Intuitionism offers a coherent philosophy of mathematics allowing only the potential infinite.

7.4 Characterization of Intuitionism

Intuitionism was first propounded by L.E.J. Brouwer,[15] who was himself greatly influenced by the philosophy of Kant. It was considerably developed, and modified, by Heyting and Beth. In our own time it has been practised by Bishop[16] and Troelstra,[17] and its chief protagonist has been Michael Dummett.[18] Dummett has been influenced more by Wittgenstein than by Kant, and modern discussions of Intuitionism have been carried on in terms of a theory of meaning, which, it is argued, reveals the invalidity of certain classical principles of logic when infinite sets are involved, notably the Principle of Bivalence, or, equivalently, the Law of the Excluded Middle, and, concomitantly, the Law of Double Negation.[19]

Intuitionism can be seen as a version of conceptualism. Mathematics exists in minds, and is manifested in the activity of mathematicians. Like musical composition, it is invention, not discovery. The emphasis is on proving—the analogue to making music—rather than on what is proved—the score. Musicians form a community of those who love making and listening to music, and mathematicians also constitute a community, of those who love noticing proofs and sharing them with others.

Metaphysically, Intuitionism is cheap, like conceptualism, without being crassly reductionist, as Formalism often seems to be. Intuitionists see themselves as offering an alternative and better

---

[15] L.E.J.Brouwer, *Collected Works*, Volume I: *Philosophy and Foundations of Mathematics*, ed. A.Heyting, Amsterdam, 1975.

[16] E.Bishop, *Foundations of Constructive Analysis*, McGraw-Hill, 1967.

[17] A.S.Troelstra, "Aspects of Constructive Mathematics", in J.Barwise, ed., *Handbook of Mathematical Logic*, North-Holland, 1977, pp.973-1052.

[18] M.A.E.Dummett, *Elements of Intuitionism*, Oxford, 1977; and "The Philosophical Basis of Intuitionistic Logic" in M.A.E.Dummett, *Truth and Other Enigmas*, Duckworth, 1978.

[19] In addition to the works already mentioned, the reader may find it convenient to consult P.Benacerraf and H.Putnam, *Philosophy of Mathematics: Selected Readings*, 2nd ed., Cambridge, 1983, pp.52-61, 77-129.

answer than the Formalists to the question "If not Platonic Realism, then What?"; and answer not in terms of what is drawn on paper or blackboard, but what goes on in mathematicians' minds, and the collective experience of the community of mathematicians.

> ### If not Platonic Realism, then What?
> #### Intuitionism?

The Intuitionists are not committed to some platonist realm of entities over and above those of the familiar world. They do not have to posit the existence of Numbers, or Sets, or any other abstract objects, only people, who think and talk. And they do not have to make out that mathematics is merely the study of marks on paper, or inscriptions on a blackboard: the marks are merely the means of communicating what is in the mathematician's mind. The one claim that the Intuitionist must make is that there are valid proofs, and that these can be seen to be such by other competent mathematicians.

The emphasis the Intuitionists lay on the activity of the mathematical community is a welcome antidote to Plato's ban on all operational terms,[20] and the solipsistic tendencies of most classical accounts. The emphasis on sharing proofs focuses attention on one of the distinguishing characteristics of mathematics. These are real merits. But Intuitionists are unwilling to accept the logic of these emphases. For all their talk of the mathematical community, they are unwilling to accept the general view of the mathematical community as regards their own contentions. Most mathematicians accept classical arguments as valid. Intuitionists beg to differ. It makes sense to disagree with everybody else, if there is some objective standard of truth, independent of what any, or every, one thinks. On that basis, it is perfectly legitimate to hold the great majority of mathematicians mistaken in their acceptance of the Law of the Excluded Middle. But on that basis, too, mathematics is not simply constituted by the communal activity of mathematicians, but aspires to some truth independent of what mathematicians actually do, and in the light of which what they actually do can be corrected. Intuitionists are faced with a dilemma. Either

---

[20] See above, §2.7.

mathematical practice is corrigible or it is not: if it is corrigible, then what is claimed in a putative proof can be different from the proof itself; if it is not corrigible, then the mathematics mathematicians actually do is classical, not intuitionist, and Intuitionists can no more argue that classical mathematicians are wrong to argue as they do than a jazz pianist can argue that Bach is wrong to compose as he did.

Activity is important in mathematics, but is importantly different from musical activity. In music, if it seems right, it is right: in mathematics, the constraints are more rigid, and the object of the operation is external to the operation itself. If by extending a line, I can construct a proof, or by simplifying an equation, factorise and extract its roots, well and good. But always there is an end-result the mathematician is trying to achieve; and it is natural to characterize this as the discovery of truth rather than the creation of beauty.

Proving is not the only mathematical activity. Mathematicians also calculate and solve problems. And although proofs are often shared, Intuitionists too easily assume that everyone can recognise a mathematical proof when he sees one. But most people cannot, and many otherwise intelligent men, like Hobbes, have been gravely mistaken in their judgement that some proof was valid when it was not. Although the feeling of compellingness of mathematical argument is an important feature, an exegesis of mathematical theorems exclusively in terms of their proof, is misconceived. It is easy to understand Pythagoras' theorem, and use a 3-4-5 triangle for marking out tennis courts, without being able to prove it. There are said to be forty-seven proofs of Pythagoras' theorem, but they are all proofs of one and the same theorem, not proofs of forty-seven different propositions. For many years in the last century it was believed that the Four Colour Theorem had been proved by Kempe, until Heawood pointed out a flaw in the putative proof, but mathematicians were able to explain to school boys what it meant, and still can, even though very few people understand the modern proof, if indeed it is a valid one. Similarly, many people understand Fermat's Last Theorem, though only a few can follow Andrew Wiles' proof of it.[21] The logic of 'p is true' is different from that of 'I have a proof of p'. If p is true, it always was true; if Fer-

---

[21] But see further below, §14.3.

mat had not discovered a valid proof of his last theorem, it would none the less still be true, even though he could not have written truthfully that he had a proof of it. Unless a mathematician could understand the proposition to be proved independently of its actually being proved, he could not conduct an intelligent search for a proof. Mathematicians are not interested in proofs alone, but are primarily interested in them on account of the propositions they establish as true. The final argument for insisting on a fundamental distinction between a proof and what a proof actually proves, must be left to the next chapter, where Gödel's theorem establishes beyond doubt that truth outruns provability.

7.5   Proofs and Dialogues

The emphasis laid by Intuitionists on proofs rather than on what is proved explains the most controversial and characteristic tenet of Intuitionism, namely the denial, where infinite sets are involved, of the Principle of Bivalence (p is either true or false) and the Law of the Excluded Middle (It is necessarily the case that either p or not-p). Since in ordinary propositional calculus the Law of the Excluded Middle is inter-derivable with the Law of Double Negation, $\neg\neg p \vdash p$, the Intuitionist also denies that. If we are talking about proofs, then the fact that I have not proved a proposition goes no way towards proving that I have disproved it. To maintain otherwise would be like the Irishman who was accused of stealing a pig, and produced seven witnesses who had not seen him do it. We have

'I have not proved p' does not entail 'I have proved (not-p)'

It is tempting to follow a suggestion originally made by Gödel to re-interpret Intuitionist statements as being really about provability. If we use a "dictionary", due to McKinsey and Tarski,[22] every thesis of intuitionistic propositional calculus becomes a thesis of $S4$; so if we construed the Intuitionist mathematician as talking about

---

[22] J.C.C.McKinsey and A.Tarski, "Some theorems about the sentential calculi of Lewis and Heyting", *The Journal of Symbolic Logic*, **13**, pp.1-15; discussed by A.S.Troelstra, in Kurt Gödel, *Collected Works*, vol. I, New York, 1986, pp.296-299. Gödel's original paper is printed there, pp.300-303; and also in J.Hintikka, ed., *The Philosophy of Mathematics*, Oxford, 1969, pp.128-129. See also A.N.Prior, *Past, Present and Future*, Oxford, 1967, pp.25-27.

proofs rather than propositions proved, it would make good sense. When he asserted p for a simple propositional variable, he would be saying that he had a proof of p, that is, that p is provable. When he asserted $\neg A$, for any well-formed formula, he would be saying that he had proof of $\neg A$, that is that $\neg A$ is provable. When he asserted $A \vee B$, for any well-formed formulae, he would be saying that he either had a proof of A or had a proof of B. When he asserted $A \wedge B$, for any well-formed formulae, he would be saying that he both had proof of A and had a proof of B. When he asserted $A \rightarrow B$ he would be saying that if he had a proof of A, he would *eo ipso* have a proof of B. If we construe the box of modal logic as expressing the 'is provable' of the Intuitionist, Gödel's translation seems natural.

But though classical mathematicians can accommodate within their own terminology what the Intuitionist seems to them to be trying to say, the Intuitionist will have none of it. Although admittedly concerned with proofs, he claims to be talking about what can be proved, and is propounding a radical reconstruction of its logic; and though classical mathematicians regard it as perverse to deny these generally accepted laws of thought, they cannot convict him of inconsistency. It is possible to formulate a version of propositional calculus in which the Law of the Excluded Middle is not a theorem, or equivalently, in which it is not permissible to use the Law of Double Negation to infer p from $\neg\neg p$. A consistency proof for the intutionistic propositional calculus is available—proof by erasure will clearly work—and we can similarly formulate a provably consistent intuitionistic predicate calculus. More generally, intuitionistic mathematics can be developed without any apparent inconsistency, and can be considered as a piece of formal mathematics in its own right without regard to the substantive claims of Intuitionism. Equally, the Intuitionist is unable to convict the classical mathematician of inconsistency either. Gödel and Gentzen have each shown independently that the consistency of intuitionist arithmetic implies the consistency of classical Peano Arithmetic.[23] It is a stand-off. Neither side can show the other to be completely wrong.

---

[23] Paul Bernays, "Sur la Platonisme dans les mathématiques", *L'Enseignment Mathématique*, **34**, 1935, pp.52-69; tr. in Paul Benacerraf and Hilary Putnam, *Philosophy of Mathematics: Selected Readings*, 2nd ed., p.271.

It should be noted that the Intuitionist is not alone in calling at least some of these theses in question. Aristotle raised the problem of "Future Contingents" in his discussion of tomorrow's sea battle, and in the controversy that has raged ever since about the correct resolution of the problem, it has been often suggested that perhaps the Principle of Bivalence does not always apply, and in particular not to contingent statements about the future.[24] Though to deny the Principle of Bivalence is not manifestly absurd, it still seems strange in a mathematician. Benenson put forward an argument by dilemma to show that an irrational number raised to the power of an irrational number may be itself rational.[25] For consider $\sqrt{2}$ raised to the power of $\sqrt{2}$,

$$\sqrt{2}^{\sqrt{2}}$$

Call it x. Then x is either rational or irrational: if it is rational, then the case is proved; if it is irrational, consider x raised to the power of $\sqrt{2}$,

$$\left(\sqrt{2}^{\sqrt{2}}\right)^{\sqrt{2}}$$

By the usual rules for exponents, it is equal to $\sqrt{2}$ raised to the power of $(\sqrt{2} \times \sqrt{2})$, namely 2. So once again we have an irrational number raised to the power of an irrational number yielding a number that is rational.

The Intuitionist denies the force of this argument. The only time a mathematician should say

$$\sqrt{2}^{\sqrt{2}} \text{ is rational}$$

is when he has a proof of it. And the only time a mathematician should say

$$\sqrt{2}^{\sqrt{2}} \text{ is irrational}$$

[24] Aristotle, *De Interpretatione*, ch.9, tr. J.L.Ackrill, *Aristotle's Categories and De Interpretatione*, Oxford, 1966, pp.50-53, 132-142; N. Rescher, "Truth and Necessity in Temporal Perspective", in R.M.Gale, ed., *The Philosophy of Time*, London, 1968; Gilbert Ryle, *Dilemmas*, Cambridge, 1954, ch.2, "It Was To Be"; J.R.Lucas, *The Future*, Oxford, 1989.

[25] See M.A.E.Dummett, *Elements of Intuitionism*, Oxford, 1977, pp.9-10.

is when he has a proof of that. And the only time a mathematician should say p or q is when he either has a proof of p or has a proof of q. We therefore have no warrant for saying either

$$\sqrt{2}^{\sqrt{2}} \text{ is rational}$$

or

$$\sqrt{2}^{\sqrt{2}} \text{ is irrational}$$

and, according to the Intuitionist, the proof fails.

The Law of the Excluded Middle, which underlies Arguments by Dilemma, is inter-derivable with the Law of Double Negation. which better illustrates the issues between Intuitionist and Classical logic. Classical logic is dialectical in its underlying style, and views argument as a cooperative pursuit of truth. I make a claim and issue a challenge. I invite you, *for the sake of argument*, to counterclaim. 'Do you deny it?', I ask. If you do, I shall show you that you are wrong. If not, I claim to have the undisputed mastery of the field. But of course, you might question without denying. You might just say 'Prove it' without picking up my challenge. But if you accept first that my claim is intelligible apart from having been proved, and secondly that I am a serious operator who would not put forward frivolous claims, you will be prepared to cooperate, and either put up a counter-thesis for consideration or shut up, and accept my word for it. And if having tried to gainsay me you find you cannot on pain of inconsistency, then you must let my claim pass without more ado.

Of course you could refuse to cooperate, and I could not convict you of inconsistency if you did. But I should not want to pursue such a policy for myself, and I doubt if you would. If Euclid has an argument by *reductio ad absurdum*, I want to follow it out and discover new truths about geometry. Although by refusing to suppose the opposite I could foil his winning the truth-game, I should do so at the cost of myself forgoing some knowledge of the truth. Rather than do that, I am prepared to stick my neck out, and see what happens. Maybe I shall provide the premise for a *reductio ad absurdum*, and see that your claim cannot be controverted on pain of inconsistency, and acknowledge that if I cannot gainsay it, you must be allowed to assert it.

The Law of Double Negation arises from the concept of contradiction, which goes beyond the minimal concept of negation that

stems from the concept of inconsistency that is a necessary condition of a formal system if it is not to be a trivial one, in which to
be a theorem is nothing more than to be a well-formed formula.[26]
Contradiction is a prerequisite not of a formal logical system, which
is essentially a monologue, but of ordinary language and any dialogue which is carried on between two persons. If we have any
communication between two autonomous agents, it is essential that
either should be able to say 'No' to the other, and contradict what
he has been saying. For there is no point in talking, if there is
no possibility of disagreement. Communication is only necessary
between different, finite, fallible centres of knowledge and ratioci-
nation, where each may know some things and have thought out
some things right, but each may be ignorant of some things, and
is liable to have got some things wrong. Under such conditions it
is always possible that one communicator will wish to dissent from
what another communicator has said, and will need to use a word
like 'No' by means of which he can contradict him. But those who
contradict are also finite, fallible centres of knowledge and ratio-
cination, who may be ignorant of some things, and are liable to
have got some things wrong. They may need to be contradicted in
their turn, so that the record may be set straight again, and their
foolish negation annulled. If a person contradicts me, and I am
not persuaded to change my mind, I shall want to contradict his
contradiction, and re-affirm my original assertion. Thus, although
in a logistic calculus which is being used by only one person the
requirement of consistency does not yield the Law of Double Negation, in a natural language, which is used to listen to as well as
to talk with, it is essential that there should be a principle of cancelling, and of cancelling cancellations. It is a dialectical necessity
between two persons symmetrically placed, and enjoying parity of
epistemological esteem.

Since mathematics, too, is something that is argued about by
more than one person, mathematical statements can be assessed
by hearers as well as asserters, and I can return your service by a
denial, and you can play back a counter-denial, and we can keep up
a volley of denials and counter-denials. Of course, a player might
refuse to volley. He might hit the ball down, instead of returning it
across the net. He might reject his opponent's non-acceptance of his

---

[26] See above, §3.4.

claim, without reinstating it positively. But then the truth-game would peter out. Rather than force a draw, each player extends his claim, exposing himself to the risk of being proved wrong in the hope that either his or his opponent's claim will be found to be right. Truth on this view is not merely a matter of assertibility conditions but also of aspirations, and the Principle of Bivalence represents not an unwarranted assumption that we know what we do not know but an entirely respectable hope that we may know it, coupled with a willingness to play the truth-game in that spirit which will best enable finite beings of limited abilities but unlimited aspirations to discover as much truth as possible.[27]

The Intuitionist's rejection of the Law of Double Negation thus reveals him as occupying a special epistemological position of disparity, in which he does not accept the normal rules of dialectical discourse. In simple cases, like Benenson's argument for there being some irrational number which when raised to the power of an irrational number results in a rational one, where only some singular proposition is involved, his position seems implausible, and almost perverse. In most cases, however, it is where infinite sets are involved that the Intuitionist is unwilling to countenance the Law of Double Negation or Principle of Bivalence; and here his argument is stronger. We do not at present know whether it is in fact true or whether it is in fact false, but it must be one or the other. The Intuitionist demurs. Classical mathematicians, he says, are working with a fundamentally wrong model in mind, supposing that they can inspect each one of the infinite number of even numbers, and see if any are not the sum of two primes, in which case Goldbach's conjecture is false, or that none are not the sum of two primes, in which case all are, and Goldbach's conjecture is true. But there is no surveyable set of the even numbers, and hence there is a difference between genuine existence proofs, which are constructive, and those purported ones that depend on *reductio ad absurdum*. If we came across an even number which was not the sum of two primes, we should have falsified Goldbach's conjecture in a very definite and indisputable way. We would have established that there was a number, and could also say what it was. If, however, we merely devised a proof that showed that Goldbach's conjecture led to an

---

[27] The last three paragraphs are taken from J.R.Lucas, "Mathematical Tennis", *Proceedings of the Aristotelian Society*, 1984, pp.68-69.

inconsistency, we should have established less; it would be more difficult to persuade the determined sceptic, who kept on saying "Show me". If we were writing up our proofs in Latin, we should use the words mentioned in the previous chapter, and express the first result by the words *quidam numerus*, 'a certain number is even and not the sum of two primes', a number we could specify if we wanted, but are not so doing in order to cut out irrelevant detail. In the second case all we could say would be *nonnullus numerus*, 'it is not the case that no number is even and not the sum of two primes'; if asked, we should have to come clean and admit that we did not know which the number was, and we might forestall the question by using the Latin *nescioquis*, 'some number, I know not which, is even and not the sum of two primes'. There is a real difference in the force of the existential quotifier which is obscured in standard classical treatments, but can be accommodated in a dialectical account of the quotifiers: *quidam* invites the question 'Which one?'; *nescioquis* forestalls it; *nonnullus* is non-committal.

The difference between the different Latin renderings of the existential quotifier becomes important in mathematics when the quotification is over an infinite domain. If the domain is only finite, we could in principle go over each case one by one, and either find that it was not a case in point and pass on, or find that it was, in which case we should know not only that there was such a case, but which it was. We cannot do this in the infinite case, and in the eyes of the Intuitionist that fact constitutes a profound difference.

$(Vx)F(x)$ is not the same as
$F(a_1) \lor F(a_2) \lor F(a_3) \lor F(a_4) \lor \ldots \lor F(a_n) \lor \ldots$
Intuitionists think this is **very important**

For them the infinite is always only a potential infinite, and never an actual one. Not only can we never actually survey it, but we cannot conceive of it as surveyable even by God. Classical mathematicians are fond of taking the God's-eye view, and suppose that God can survey an infinite totality as easily as we can finite ones. But this, according to the Intuitionist, is a profound mistake. God can no more survey an infinite totality than He can alter the past. Infinite totalities are not there for Him to survey. They do not exist. They cannot exist. They are a contradiction in terms.

It is difficult to argue theology with an Intuitionist, and our grip on ontology is still weak. But existence is not only a profession of ontological commitment. It is also a counter in argumentative discourse. In mathematics its most important function is to license talk. If I start talking about the greatest prime number, it is the same as if I start talking about the present king of France, or Ryle's youngest son. My discourse, though grammatical and consistent, fails to carry information because it fails to refer to anything. Rather than hear me out as I go rabbiting on, you interrupt, and say "But there is no greatest prime number". That is a conversation stopper. Once it has been alleged that there is no object that my purported referring term refers to, I must either meet the allegation and give it the lie, or else shut up. I cannot go on talking about nothing at all.

In ordinary conversational discourse it is easy to interrupt, and we need take no special pains to guard against failure of reference because should reference fail we shall soon be interrupted and brought to heel. Mathematics, however, is much more monologous. If you are reading my book, you cannot interrupt. Since I cannot argue from your silence that my referring attempts are being successful, I need to anticipate possible interruptions and deal with them in advance, so that if you were minded to interrupt, you would find the point already dealt with. I forestall your "But it does not exist", or, more colloquially, "But there isn't one", by an existence proof. Once I have proved that the nine-point circle exists, I can go on to talk about it and its centre and say that the latter is on the Euler line with complete confidence that I cannot be faulted on the score of talking about nothing at all. Equally if I am disposed to talk about Brouwer's fixed point, I can cite his Fixed Point theorem to ward off the counter that it does not exist, even though it is a non-constructive existence proof. If someone were to prove that Goldbach's conjecture was true, we should thereafter give short shrift to the computer buff who wanted us to give him a grant while he searched for a counter-example: and *per contra* if it were proved that Goldbach's conjecture leads to an inconsistency, then it would be a reasonable proposal to program a computer to find a counter-example.

What is at issue betwen the Intuitionist and the classical mathematician is the validity of inference patterns. The Intuitionist allows the *quidam* inference

$$F(a) \vdash (\mathrm{V}x)F(x),$$

which is the Existential Introduction rule of some systems, but not the *nonnullus* inference

$$\neg(\mathrm{A}x)\neg F(x) \vdash (\mathrm{V}x)F(x),$$

which classical logic also allows, as, so to speak, a pre-emptive strike, whereby it is shown that the objection, "There is no such instance", cannot be maintained. Whereas in the first, the *quidam*, dialogue, I claim that there is an instance, and, if you challenge me, I can say which it is, in the second, the *nonnullus*, dialogue, I counter-challenge you: "Do you maintain that there is no such instance?", I ask. "If you do, I shall show that you are wrong: if you do not, because you cannot, you are no longer in a position to question my original assertion."

The argument, like that with the *Sorites* Arithmetician in Chapter Six, is an argument by challenge, in the context of a cooperative search for truth. In §6.7 the cooperative arguer was prepared to hazard a counter-*example*, and thence be shown that that led to inconsistency, and thus to be convinced that no counter-example was sustainable, and the universal claim must, therefore, be allowed: here the cooperative arguer needs to hazard a counter-*thesis*, in order to be convinced that the counter-thesis is untenable, and thus that the original claim in undeniable. The only way of saying that I cannot say *quidam* is to say *nullus*, and if you say this, I can show you that you are wrong.

The fine-structure of the existential quotifier can thus be displayed by the different dialogues that warrant its use. Best of all is the straightforward *quidam* rule:

$$F(a) \vdash (\mathrm{V}x)F(x).$$

If I could find an even number that was not the sum of two primes, say $10^{11} + 2$, then I should have disproved Goldbach's conjecture in the best way possible, so that even the Intuitionists were satisfied. When I said that there was an even number that was not the sum of two primes, and they asked "Which one?", I could answer them by saying which it was. If, however, I could merely show that the assumption that there was an even number that was not the sum of two primes led to inconsistency, I should lose the first round, having failed to answer their question. But if we were keen to know the truth, we should go on to a second round, which would give you a chance of winning the game, by showing that *if* I had tried to take up your challenge, I should have been bound to fail; that is, you attempt to show that *any* example I care to choose (from your point of view *quivis*: from mine *quivolo*) will prove fatal to my original contention. If you win this round, you win the game. I can no longer claim *nonnullus*, if *quivolo* has been refuted. If, however, you do not win the second round, the game continues to a third round, with *nonnullus* still in the field. In this third round I force you to take the initiative again—this time, since examples have not got either of us anywhere, in terms of a universal proposition as counter-thesis. Although I had not, as it happened, produced an instance of an even number that was not the sum of two primes, your counter-thesis that I could not, in principle, do so, is shown to be itself untenable. It would be unreasonable of you to try and shut down my research programme of looking at even numbers to see if they were the sum of two primes. Although, as of now, I have not succeeded in identifying any such number, or even ascribing any properties to it, I have answered the question *an sit*, and shown that it exists and is talkable about, even though I have not, as yet, answered the question *qualis sit*, or said anything significant about it.

7.6 Verificationist Arguments for Intuitionism

The emotional pressure towards Intuitionism is a general queasiness about actual infinities and platonism generally, but it is argued for, in its modern version, on the basis of a verificationist theory of meaning. Words in general, it is claimed, have meaning only in virtue of the way they are used, and the sentential connectives of propositional calculus can only acquire their meaning through the rules laid down for assertang the complex propositions they are used to build up. If assertability conditions alone are constitutive of meaning, then it is the conditions under which mathematical propositions can be legitimately asserted—that is, when they are proved—which alone determine their sense, and in particular the sense of the sentential connectives.

The key thesis is that assertability conditions alone are constitutive of meaning. It is supported by a rhetorical question:

> How are we supposed to be able to *form* any understanding of what it is for a particular statement to be true if the kind of state of affairs which it would take to make it true is con-

ceived, *ex hypothesi*, as something beyond our experience,
something which we cannot confirm and which is insulated
from any distinctive impact on our experience?[28]

There is a sense that the classical mathematician is claiming some
sort of acquaintance with entities he has no knowledge of, and that
only by confining discourse to what we have a firm grasp of, can
we avoid talking nonsense.

Another argument is the Manifestation Argument, which depends on Wittgenstein's emphasis on the identity of meaning and
use. Wright understands this as establishing that to "understand
an expression is to know how to use it properly, and the proof
of such knowledge is that one does actually so use it".[29] Wright
has an extremely stringent standard of proper use. He concedes
that someone might manifest many signs of being able to use some
expression—

> No doubt someone who understands such a statement can
> be expected to have many relevant practical abilities. He
> will be able to appraise evidence for or against it, should
> any be available, or to recognize that no information in his
> possession bears on it. He will be able to recognize at least
> some of its logical consequences, and to identify beliefs from
> which commitment to it would follow. ... In short: in these
> and perhaps other important respects, he will show himself
> competent to use the statement. But the headings under
> which his practical abilities fall so far involve no mention of
> evidence-transcending truth-conditions.[30]

Only if the classical mathematician can specify exactly the conditions under which he would say that Goldbach's Conjecture had
been proved or refuted, will he have manifested a proper understanding of what that conjecture states.

Wright distinguishes a third argument, the argument from nor-
mativity. "Meaning is normative. To know the meaning of an
expression is to know, perhaps unreflectively, how to appraise uses
of it; it is to know a set of constraints to which correct uses must

---

[28] Crispin Wright, *Realism, Meaning and Truth*, Blackwell, Oxford, 2nd ed.,
1992, p.13.

[29] p.16.

[30] p.17.

conform. Accordingly, to give the meaning of a statement is to
describe such constraints; nothing has a claim to be regarded as an
account of a statement's meaning which does not succeed in doing
so." And, Wright argues, the realist's truth-conditional conception
has indeed no such claim.[31] For, according to the realist, what the
statement means is the same, whether or not it can be actually
verified, and therefore is not constrained by whatever it might be
that would verify it. It is as if the meaning were represented by
one of two small boxes, identical in appearances, but one containing a beetle made of something that vaporises instantly if the box
is opened. The realist's claim to mean something by an expression, independently of whether or not it can be verified, is like the
claim to be thinking of the box with the beetle when in fact there
is no discernible difference between the two boxes. And in such a
situation we have Wittgenstein's authority for saying that that is
a meaningless claim.

All these arguments are based on theories of meaning. But arguments from meaning should always be treated with caution. It is
very easy to devise a theory of meaning, thinking of a few paradigm
examples, and then, finding that other locutions cannot be accommodated within it, to dismiss them as meaningless. Many theories
of meaning are vitiated by apparently taking for granted a correspondence theory of truth. 'Snow is white' is true, they say, if and
only if snow is white, and from this they infer that mathematical
statements are made true by their corresponding to the appropriate
mathematical states of affairs. "How are we supposed to be able to
form any understanding of what it is for a particular statement to
be true", asks Wright, "if the kind of state of affairs which it would
take to make it true is conceived, *ex hypothesi*, as something beyond
our experience, something which we cannot confirm and which is
insulated from any distinctive impact on our experience?"[32] But
there is no *state of affairs* that makes mathematical statements
true, in the way that there, arguably, is in the case of snow's being
white, or the cat's being on the mat. Although sometimes, even in
mathematics, we can extend Tarski's account of truth to enable us
to construct models of theories, the model is being devised to bring
out the desired formulae of the theory as true: the real direction

[31] p.24.

[32] p.13.

of truth-conferring is from the theory to the model, rather than *vice versa*. We cannot argue from our sometimes making use of semantic approaches to a general correspondence theory of truth. For many kinds of discourse—moral discourse, literary criticism, some parts of physics, most of philosophy and metaphysics—the correspondence theory of truth is inapplicable.

The Acquisition Argument carries little weight. Empiricist philosophers often have difficulty in accounting for our formation of concepts. That has always been a difficulty for empiricism. There is also room for a psychological enquiry into the way we learn mathematical concepts. But whatever its outcome, the fact remains that we are able to use mathematical terms in a way that seems to make sense to most mathematicians. We do not need direct acquaintance with some mathematical state of affairs to enable us to learn by ostensive definition what some mathematical proposition means. Rather, having learned on other, perhaps simple, occasions what the meaning of the constituent terms is, we can understand what the new complex must mean also. I come to understand Goldbach's conjecture not by knowing some state of affairs, but by knowing, as I think, the meaning of *every, even, number, sum, two, prime number*. Of course, I may deceive myself. The Intuitionist may persuade me that I do not really know the meaning of *every* in this context. But he has to show it. *Prima facie*, the word *every* is well understood, and the suggestion that we need to make out afresh on each new occasion of using it a justification for its use in the new context is not a suggestion we should take seriously.

The Manifestation Argument is likewise unpersuasive. Wittgenstein identified meaning with use. It is not clear that he was right to do so, but certainly someone cannot be said to understand an expression unless he knows how to use it properly. The anti-realist argues that since, *ex hypothesi*, there are no circumstances in which there is conclusive evidence for an "evidence-transcendent state of affairs", there can be no practical occasion for the assertion of the expression, and hence no grounds for believing that it is really understood. But our understanding is not so limited that we can only understand what we sometimes know. We engage in many speculations about the beginning and end of time, the possibility of spaces disconnected from our own, about the nature of God, about life after death, without ever being able to make warranted assertions about them. Wright himself concedes as much; but, according to Wright, it is not enough, for "the headings under which his practical abilities fall so far involve no mention of evidence-transcending truth-conditions". It is difficult to see what lack is being bemoaned. Goldbach's conjecture is a conjecture. I know what would falsify it—the instancing of some even number with a list of all the primes less than it, and the difference between the even number and each member of the list, with some factor of that difference. This, of course, is not an exact specification—if a particular even number were so specified, then the conjecture would be no longer a conjecture, but false. Much more so, I cannot specify what a proof would look like. I might not be able to understand it even if it were instanced, any more than I can understand the proof of Fermat's Last Theorem. But I have an unspecific idea of what a proof might be like. In putting forward Goldbach's conjecture I am putting forward a *hypothetical*: under certain, not exactly specified, conditions I should withdraw it, recognising it to be false, and under other, even less exactly specified, conditions, I should accept it as definitely true. I do not need to be able to specify these conditions exactly in order to manifest my ability to use the expression meaningfully. It would be absurd to make such a demand. In other realms of discourse—science, history, morals—we often make assertions and entertain hypotheses which may be subsequently confirmed or refuted by considerations not then known to us. Thirty years ago cosmologists were arguing for continuous creation without having then any idea of the echoes of the Big Bang which have subsequently refuted their hypothesis. If being able to use an expression properly is construed as being able to specify exactly the conditions under which it would be conclusively verified or falsified, then hardly any expressions are ever used properly, or are even meaningful.

There is much confusion over hypotheticals and possibilities. The Intuitionist discounts hypotheticals, and seeks to restrict possibilities to the actual. But this is not how we normally use words. When I make an assertion, I stick my neck out. However well warranted it may be, I am taking on the risk of being wrong. It may well be the case that thus far, under a wide range of conditions, whenever there has been an event of type A, there has subsequently been an event of type B, so that I am amply justified in making the causal claim that A causes B. I still may be wrong. New evidence, or a deeper understanding of science, may falsify my assertion. Its meaning cannot be constituted by its assertability conditions, but must take into account also the conditions under which I *might* subsequently *have to* withdraw it, or, alternatively, be entitled to claim that I had been vindicated further. These conditions are fuzzy-edged. They are not tightly specified in advance. We often do not know what we should say if such and such an eventuality should arise, though sometimes, if it does arise, we are fairly clear what the right response is, and do not think it is simply a matter of arbitrary choice on our part how we should respond.

Once it is recognised that meanings are not fully determinate, and that we do not have to cross all bridges in advance of setting out on a journey, other Intuitionist arguments lose their appeal. A mathematical proposition may be not effectively decidable, without being absolutely and always so. We distinguish between the difficult-to-discover beetle in the box, and the logically undiscoverable one. In the latter case I am rationally suspicious, and do not see that there is any difference between the two boxes which could justify my choosing one rather than the other; but if the difficulty is merely a technical one, I can imagine its being overcome—a sufficiently sensitive determination of the moments of inertia would in fact differentiate between a box with a beetle in it and a box with the same material as part of the lining—and then it is reasonable to mean one box rather than the other.

We can allow that the meaning of a word is given by its use, in a sufficiently wide sense of 'use', which includes not only actual use in clearly defined situations, but hypothetical use in conjectural ones. In particular, it includes not only Introduction Rules but Elimination Rules, and the use of sentences in argument and conjecture as well as in warranted assertions, and the relations between sentences and the words they are composed of. The meaning of the word 'or' is not given just by the introduction rules for $\vee$, but at the very least by the vel-elimination rule as well, which would license the argument by dilemma that Intuitionists refuse to accept. So too, the meaning of the word 'every' in Goldbach's conjecture is given not only by the proof of the conjecture, should there be one, but by it consequences. If I believe Goldbach's conjecture to be true, I shall not spend time programming a computer to search the even numbers for one that is not the sum of two primes, whereas if I had a non-constructive proof of its negation, I might well.

7.7 Selective Scepticism

Many of the arguments in favour of Intuitionism fail. Often underlying them there seems to be an exercise in selective scepticism. The Intuitionist professes himself unable to understand what the classical mathematician is saying, or doubtful about the validity of classical arguments, often insinuating that the classical mathematician is working with a wrong picture of what he is doing. It is difficult to defend oneself against such a charge. G.E. Moore was able to reduce his opponents to speechless confusion by asking them exactly what they meant when they used some common word. It is something we are characteristically unable to do. Satisfactory definitions are hard to articulate, and often cannot be given at all. It does not follow that we do not know the meaning of the words we are using. It is one thing to know how to use a word, quite another to know, and to be able to say, how that word is used. *Knowledge how* does not depend on *knowledge that*, but on the contrary, *knowledge that* often is only true in as much as it encapsulates an unarticulated *knowledge how*. Nothing follows from the fact that the classical mathematician is typically unable to give any account of the meaning of the basic logical connectives he uses. I may well be reduced to spluttering, as I attempt to explain the meaning of the word 'not' to someone who professes not to understand, but all that shows is that he is a better gamesman than I, not that I do not know the meaning of the word 'not'.

The best tactic is counter-attack. The classical mathematician cannot make the sceptic understand something he does not want to understand, nor acknowledge the force of an argument he does not want to acknowledge, and it is a lost labour to try and answer the sceptic's questions to the satisfaction of the sceptic. It is much more effective to turn the sceptic's own doubts against himself, and show that if we are to be really scrupulous in what we claim to understand and what arguments we are prepared to regard as acceptable, we must abandon not only the classical arguments the sceptic does not like, but the arguments he cherishes as well.

Intuitionists are vulnerable to the more extreme forms of unbelief practised by stricter finitists, who deny even the potential infinite, and accept not what could in principle be done but only what is in actual fact done. Alexander George calls them the

"Actualists".[33] Actualists do not know what Intuitionists mean by a proof, and are not willing to extrapolate from actual procedures to in principle effective procedures. Like the classical mathematician, the Intuitionist reckons that

$$(10^{(10^{(10^{(10+1)}}+1)} + 1)$$

is either a prime number or else has factors. The Intuitionist thinks that this is a different case from Goldbach's conjecture, because although nobody has ever worked the sum out, it is clear that in principle someone could: we have an "effective procedure" for doing so. The classical mathematician is quite willing to concede this, and more also, but the Actualist is not. The number is not one that has ever been entered on a computer, and until it has been actually done, he is unwilling to concede that the calculation could be done.

In ordinary computer logic or recursive function theory we are able to characterize an effective procedure as one which will terminate in a finite number of steps. But what do we mean by 'finite'? The classical mathematician knows, the Intuitionist knows, but the Actualist cannot easily be told. The concept of finitude cannot be expressed in first-order logic, which is the logic computers can understand. It is only in second-order logic that we can express what it is to be finite, and hence what it is to be an effective procedure;[34] but second-order logic is not itself completely axiomatizable, and hence does not itself have an effective procedure for

---

[33] Alexander George, "The Conveyability of Intuitionism", *Journal of Philosophical Logic*, **17**, 1988, pp.133-156. For the "Actualist" position, see P. Bernays, "On Platonism in Mathematics", in P.Benacerraf and H.Putnam, *Philosophy of Mathematics: Selected Readings*, 2nd ed., Cambridge, 1983, pp.258-271; Crispin Wright, "Strict Finitism", *Synthese*, **51**, 1982, pp. 204, 208-210; and R.Gandy, "Limitations to Mathematical Knowledge", in D. van Dalen, D.Lascar, J.Smiley, eds., *Logic Colloquium '80*, North Holland, Amsterdam, 1982, pp.129-146.

[34] This is somewhat surprising, since in §5.2 we were able to express in first-order logic that there are infinitely many individuals possessing a given property. In order to show that a set is (Dedekind-)infinite, it is enough to specify *one* one–one function mapping the set into a proper subset of itself. But it is much more difficult either to tell or even to formulate the thesis that a set is *not* infinite: for we need to be sure that there does not exist

determining which of its well-formed formulae are true. Though the classical mathematician can be reasonably happy with second-order logic, the Intuitionist ought not to be—at least, if he is happy with second-order logic, he has little reason for cavilling at the classical mathematician's notion of truth as something that goes beyond our ability to give an effective procedure for recognising it. And if, *per contra*, he insists on disbelieving the classical mathematician, he is equally vulnerable himself to even more radical scepticism. He has started down a slippery slope that has Ultrafinitism at the bottom.

7.8 Ultrafinitism

We may ask what is wrong with the strongest version of Actualism, Ultrafinitism as we have called it. The answer is "Nothing—only it is not mathematics"; indeed, with the advent of computers it has become a highly relevant discipline. We are concerned to know not what might in principle could be done, but what our own actual computer does, and if we are wise, we are chary of hand-waving assurances about the potentialities of the hard- and soft-ware the salesman has on offer, and do not believe that anything can be done unless it actually has been done. This is good computational sense: but it is not mathematics. Although a computer engineer might refuse the question whether

$$(10^{(10^{(10^{10+1})}+1)} + 1)$$

is composite or prime, on the grounds that it was too big to be entered into his computer, or the prime-number program was too long and required more memory than he had available, it would be difficult for him to refuse to answer the question whether it is even or odd. Unmanageable though

$$(10^{(10^{(10^{10+1})}+1)} + 1)$$

may be in some respects, it is perfectly manageable in others. We do not have to pair off a sequence of strokes, and see whether at the

any such one–one function mapping it into a proper subset of itself, and that may require an extensive search to carry it through properly, and must require our being able to speak of *all* one–one functions even to formulate it. See further below, §13.5.

end we are left with one over, as the only means of telling whether a number is odd: we can tell at once from the decimal representation of it.[35] And just as we can tell at once from the way it is presented to us that

$$(10^{(10^{(10+1)}+1)} + 1)$$

is odd, we cannot be sure that we shall never have some simple algorithm that will determine in a few lines whether it is prime or not. Whether a number is manageable or not depends not just on the number but the question we are asking about it, and the means at our disposal for answering that question; that is to say, manageability is not something definite, given by the capacity of computer hardware, but depends also on our questions and purposes.

Ultrafinitism is a legitimate discipline, but not the only one. It is perfectly proper, as a Cartesian exercise, to avoid making any leaps, to be very sticky about allowing that something could be done in principle, and to insist that it actually be done in practice, before conceding that it can be done at all. Only the actual proves the possible beyond all shadow of doubt. *Ab esse valet consequentia posse*, and no other proof of possibility is as ungainsayable as actuality. The extreme actualist position is the most cautious possible, bar that of refusing ever to allow anything. He does admit that some things can be done, but only when they have actually been done.

But there is a price to be paid. By restricting the possible to the actual, the Actualist leaves out the characteristic feature of the possible, namely that more things are possible than actually happen. The realm of the possible is for him no other than the realm of the actual. He ceases to be able to understand the mathematician who is trying to tell him about what can be done, and is confined to the more boring bits of autobiography—just those moves which he, with the aid of his computer has, as it happens, actually accomplished.

Besides the restriction in scope, there is a restriction is knowledge. Knowledge is inherently risky. When I claim to know something, I am staking my credit on its being true, and could turn out to be wrong and to have to eat my words. Similarly, when I

---

[35] This point is convincingly made by Mark Steiner, *Mathematical Knowledge*, Cornell University Press, 1975, pp.16-19 and ch.1, §II, pp.41-70. See further below, §14.3.

try and find something out, I could get it wrong, and be misled
in my enquiries into believing something false. The only way I
can be sure of not having to eat my words is to say nothing, and
the only way I can avoid being misled is not to try to find out.
Goldbach made a conjecture. He could have been wrong: possibly
being wrong is the price of possibly being right and propounding
something that is true. In general mathematicians want to know
the truth—so much so, that they are willing to run the risk of being
wrong in their search for it. Of course, if they are wrong, that is
bad, and they withdraw the claim they had made, and eat their
words with red faces. But they are not prepared, in their efforts
to avoid error, to avoid it by saying nothing at all, or by adopting
the safest possible rules of inference. They are in the knowledge
business, and knowledge characteristically outruns brass-bottomed
certitude. In general—outside mathematics—when I lay claim to
know, what I claim to know is logically more than the grounds I
have for claiming it, as when on the evidence of your statement
today, I say I know that you will be at the meeting tomorrow. In
mathematics our rules of inference are of a different, non-empirical
and very stringent, kind, but they too are intended to lead to truth
and not mere warranted assertibility, and so are not necessarily the
safest and most restrictive rules possible.

Ultrafinitism is not mathematics, because it is more concerned
with safety than with truth. It remains a perfectly respectable exercise. We are not always seeking after truth, and may on occasion
sacrifice knowledge for greater security. In the law courts the jury
is told not to seek after truth but to decide whether the accused
has been proved guilty beyond reasonable doubt. Engineers are
required to build in large margins of safety into their calculations.
As regards purely numerical computations, the Actualists are the
accountants, who double-check every calculation, and make sure
that the figures add up correctly, and never embark on speculations whether

$$(10^{(10^{(10+1)}+1)} + 1)$$

is prime or not. Mathematicians think accountancy is boring. Perhaps that is the reason why it is much better paid.[36]

---

[36] See further D.Dantzig, "Is 10*(10*10) a Finite Number?", *Dialectica*, **9**,
1956, pp.273-277; and Crispin Wright, "Strict Finitism", *Synthese*, **51**,
1982, pp.272-282.

7.9 Lax Finitism

The boundary drawn by Wang between manageable and unmanageable numbers is unsatisfactory from a theoretical point of view. For one thing, it depends on technology, and shifts as better hardware is developed. For another, and more importantly, it is vulnerable to new formalisms and new methods of proof, which may make what was previously unmanageable and unsurveyable amenable and perspicuous. Once we have the decimal notation, we have available certain methods of proof which make previously horrendous problems easy to solve. We can tell at once that

$$10^{(10^{(10+1)}+1)}$$

is even, and that

$$(10^{(10^{(10+1)}+1)} + 1)$$

is odd, as is also

$$(10^{(10^{(10+1)}+1)} - 1),$$

and that the first and last of these numbers are composite. Other notations are feasible, other methods of proof possible. We are therefore always being tempted to go beyond the limits set by our specification of acceptable methods, and help ourselves to new insights, which show us new truths we can see to be true though they cannot be established by the acceptable methods specified thus far. And thus the Lax Finitist, who confines himself to computable quotifier-free methods, is led to acknowledge a potential infinity of cases.

The temptation can be resisted. But it is difficult to give a satisfactory rationale for resistance. For the crucial concepts are only available to those who are not restricted to the specified methods. *Infinita sunt finita*: there are an infinite number of finite numbers, and the concept of a finite number can be defined only in second-order logic. If I understand finitude, I can resolve to use only finitary methods; but only if you and I both understand finitude, will you be able to take in why I restrict myself to some methods of proof, and refuse to allow others. But since to understand finitude involves being able to understand infinitude too, and to define the concept of a finite number requires the generous resources of second-order logic, it is implausible to give as a reason for restricting ourselves to finitary methods that we cannot understand any others. Either we restrict ourselves by a series of arbitrary *fiats*, without giving any general characterization at all, or, in explaining what we are doing, we show that the reason why we are doing it cannot be that we could not understand anything more. We cannot say what the limits are, unless we are already able in our thinking to go beyond them.

7.10 Actualising Potentiality

There are, indeed, difficulties in the concept of infinity. But if we are to be consistent sceptics, we must abandon mathematics altogether for the different discipline of computer studies. We need, therefore, to return to infinity, and try and resolve the difficulties. Aristotle's account of the two incompatible concepts of infinity reveals three areas of ambiguity: the concept of a **limit**, which in turn involves the range of the **quotifiers**; and, thirdly, the **modalities** involved.

Plato and Aristotle found the infinitely small more difficult to doubt than the infinitely large,[37] and we can get a better grip on infinity if we think of lower limits and infinitesimals. However slowly I am going, I can always go slower, for so long as I am not standing still—in which case I am not *going* at all—I am moving with a speed greater than zero, and so there is another speed, also greater than zero but less then mine, at which I could be going; and, more generally, for any extension with a given magnitude there is another extension with a smaller, and so there is no extension of smallest magnitude. Yet a point, although not itself an extension, is a lower bound to all extensions.[38] It seems natural to extend the domain of the relation $<$ so that a point as well as an extension can be said to have an extension which is less than that of the given extension, and to extend the range of the quotifier (V) so that it ranges over points as well as extensions. If we signal these changes by writing (Vs) whose universe of discourse is S, a proper superset of X, the universe of discourse of (Ax), we can affirm both the converse of Aristotle's comparative thesis

$$(Ax)(Vy)(y < x)$$

and a counter-Anselmian superlative thesis

$$(Vs)(Ay)(s \leq y).$$

---

[37] *Physics*, III, 4, 203^{a}15, III, 6, 206^{b}27 and III, 7, 207^{a}25.

[38] See above, §2.5. See further below, §12.5.

To alter the universe of discourse over which a variable ranges, is often to alter the ontology. A state of rest is different from a state of motion: a point is different from an extension. We may have qualms about the ontological status of states of rest and points, but the two accounts of infinity cited by Aristotle are no longer *inconsistent* with each other. Once we allow the existence of point-like lower bounds which are themselves of a different status from the extensions they are bounding, we cannot in principle disallow the existence of upper bounds, likewise of a different status from the entities they are bounding. Instead of speeds, we might consider their reciprocal, slownesses, as we might call them, measured in hours per mile, or hours per inch. For each finite speed, there would be a corresponding finite slowness, and corresponding to the state of rest as the limit of minimum speed, there would be a state of infinite slowness as the limit of maximum slowness. A number greater than all the finite numbers could similarly be spoken of without inconsistency, so long as it was not itself a finite number.

Thus far we have shown that the Anselmian view of the infinite is not ruled out as being simply inconsistent with Aristotle's account, but we have not given any argument to justify Cantor's claim that any potential infinity presupposes a corresponding actual infinity.[39]

Aristotle elucidated modality in temporal terms. Although he is sometimes careful to distinguish logical from temporal priority, he often construes successor, ἐφεξῆς (*ephexes*), or, occasionally, ἐφεξῆς ὕστερον (*ephexes husteron*), in temporal terms.[40] In particular the Greek word τέλειον suggests a temporal succession of tasks accomplished. He draws attention to the close relation between τὸ ὅλον (*to holon*), the whole, and τὸ τέλειον (*to teleion*), the complete, and τὸ τέλος (*to telos*), the end; and the latter has even stronger temporal overtones in Greek than in English—Herodotus regularly uses τελυτέω, (*teleuteo*) to mean 'die'. There is a suggestion that an infinity is always becoming, "an ever increasing sequence" and therefore never complete, always potential, and therefore never actual. But that suggestion depends on the temporal metaphor, and otherwise is unconvincing. Although 'before' and 'after' do define

---

[39] Michael Hallett, *Cantorian Set Theory and Limitation of Size*, Oxford, 1984, §1.1, p.7.

[40] *Physics* V, 2, esp. 227ᵃ4; *Metaphysics*, K, 12, esp. 1068ᵇ35

an order, it is not the only order: there are many other order-ings defined by other ordering relations, which do not need to be, and sometimes cannot be, explained in temporal terms, but which may be unbounded. Nor need modality be construed temporally. Although there are temporal modalities, there are non-temporal modalities too. We should, if we can, avoid importing temporal elements into our exegesis of infinity. Although a purely temporal account is inappropriate, an operational one, *pace* Plato,[41] is not. As with quotifiers, an exegesis in dialogue terms is illuminating, and shows how Aristotle's purely potential infinite leads on to an actual infinite.

The development of the infinitesimal calculus required an exact exegesis of the infinitely small. Although non-standard analysis has vindicated the infinitesimals that Newton and Leibniz used, it was the epsilon-delta account, in terms of a universal and ex-istential quotifier, that really explained infinitesimals and made them respectable in the eyes of rigorist mathematicians. Nor was it enough that points should be the limits of smaller and smaller extensions; a tangent might touch a curve in two coincident points, but two coincident points would not determine the slope of a line. It was necessary, rather, to consider the slope of chords, and de-termine their limit as their end-points approached each other. In saying that the slope of, say, $y = x^2$ at the point $(1, 1)$ was 2, I am claiming that however close to 2 you require me to get, I can find values of dx and dy such that the chord between the points $(1, 1)$ and $(1 + dx, 1 + dy)$ has a slope within the limits you have specified. More generally, infinite sequences can be assigned limits, which can be explained in terms of quotifiers, which in turn can be explained in terms of a dialogue, where an existential quotifier represents a choice I am allowed to make, the best instance I can put forward to make my case, and a universal quotifier represents a choice my adversary is allowed to make, the worst instance he can cite against my case. But we share rationality. Just as in *Sorites* Arithmetic, it would be unreasonable to argue every case, so with limits of infinite sequences, the underlying rationale can be under-stood by both parties, and the general point will be conceded by the adversary, who is more concerned to acknowledge truth than to escape dialectical defeat by forcing an agnostic draw.

---

[41] See above, §2.7.

The transition from the potential to the actual is a feature of rationality, if modal operators are elucidated in terms of a game, played between two rational truth-seekers, who, being rational, stand back, and consider the meta-game. If meta-gamely the object of the game is the discovery of truth, then certain strategies and certain concessions will be rational for both parties. The Aristotelian potential infinity is actualised by being acknowledged by both sides as being always and necessarily available. Once my adversary realises that whatever natural number he chooses, I always can choose its successor, it is no longer just something I *can* do, but something he *must* accept. Seen from my point of view, the stress is on the 'can': seen from his point of view, the stress is on the 'always'. A perpetual possibility on my part is for everyone else an actual constraint. Whereas in the physical world there is an important difference between what can exist and what actually does exist, in discussing concepts and games and mathematical manoeuvres we are already discussing possibilities, and so what necessarily can be is. Once we have shown that we must be able to go one step further, we are in a position to envisage all those further steps actually taken.

7.11   All

Tensions still remain, arising from Cantor's two definitions of successor. Cantor modified the successor relation so that ω could be said to come next after all the finite numbers.[42] Thus by modifying the simple successor relation, where each successor has a unique predecessor, to $\succ$ which allows ω to be the successor of all its predecessors, we can affirm both

$$(Ax)(Vy)(y > x)$$

and

$$(Vw)(Ay)(w \succ y),$$

where w is a different sort of number, and $\succ$ is a slightly expanded version of $>$. But the two-pronged definition of $\succ$ raises difficulties. With derived sets it was possible not only to consider the set that would result from all the operations having been done, but then

---

[42] See above, §7.3.

to consider the derived set of that set. We cannot similarly consider slower and slower speeds, or successively smaller extensions. If the limit of an infinite sequence of nested extensions is a point, the point is a *terminus ne plus ultra*. We approach it as $n \to \infty$, but attach no further sense to $\infty + 1$. If pressed, we should simply say that $\infty + 1 = \infty$. You cannot move more slowly if you are at rest, and correspondingly your slowness cannot exceed infinity. For Cantor, however, although $1 + \omega = \omega$, $\omega + 1$ does not; ω has a successor, $\omega + 1$, which is turn is succeeded by $\omega + 2$, $\omega + 3$, ... *etc.* ... and then $\omega + \omega$, *ad infinitum*. Every ordinal has a successor, either the next after its predecessor, or the ordered set of all its predecessors. Granted the two-pronged nature of ordinal ordering, it is not surprising that the ordinal or all the ordinals is an inconsistent concept. The trouble lies in the word 'all'. There is a parallel between universality, expressed by the universal quotifier ($\mathrm{A}x$), and necessity, $\square$, and between necessity, $\square$, and inference, $\vdash$.[43] If, as will be argued in the next chapter, mathematical inference cannot be completely formalised, but is inherently extensible and fuzzy-edged, it follows that the concept of necessity, some uses of 'all' and some applications of the universal quotifier are inherently extensible and fuzzy-edged too. In Cantor's development of transfinite arithmetic there is a tension between the word 'all', which has a superlative import, and captures the sense of the infinite being the "mostest", and the word 'next', which has a sense of "more-than-ness", implicit in Aristotle's exegesis of infinity, which seems to deny the possibility of the superlative. If both of these are combined in the definition of ordinal succession, there is an obvious and ineradicable inconsistency in attempting to comprehend that which is necessarily not bounded in one completed whole, the ordinal of all ordinals, or the cardinal number of all cardinal numbers. Whatever it is said to be cannot be the last word on the topic, and must in the nature of the case be overtaken by the further definition of further successors. We may modify the concept of successor to reach into the transfinite, and sometimes it may provide a useful characterization of mathematical operations. But we need to keep tight tabs on 'all' if we are to avoid inconsistency, and restrict its range to what has *already* been defined, and not allowed to range over ordinals or cardinals not yet precisely characterized.

[43] See below §12.8, §15.3.

In a dialogue neither side has, as a matter of right, the last word. Sometimes we can ascend to a meta-dialogue, and see that it would be counter-productive if one side persisted; but that cannot be taken for granted. For, as we shall see in the next chapter, proofs cannot be completely formalised, and however fully we have specified what it is to be a proof, some proofs can be devised which do not fall under our specification thus far, but nevertheless commend themselves to us as cogent. And so, when we engage in argument, our 'all's are only 'all, thus far's; and it is open to our respondent to go a step further, and make a new move, which we had not thought of before. We cannot talk of all cardinal numbers, all ordinal numbers, or all sets, because the very way we introduce these terms precludes our being able to exclude the possibility of further ones, not hitherto envisaged, and so not covered by our 'all' thus far.

Chapter 8
The Implications of Gödel's Theorem

8.1   *Pons Asinorum*

Gödel's theorem holds for any **first**-order theory that formalises the ordinary arithmetic of the natural numbers—in particular it holds of first-order Peano Arithmetic—and proves that it is **incomplete** and **undecidable**.

Gödel's theorem is one of a cluster of incompleteness theorems— Tarski's theorem, Church's theorem, Turing's theorem, the Kleene-Church theorem, Löb's theorem—which have unexpected and profound implications both for mathematics in particular and for our understanding of reason and reality in general.

Gödel's proof is difficult. It represents the *Pons Asinorum* of mathematical logic. It can be mastered only by careful study and much rumination. There are many expositions, none of them easy, few of them altogether satisfactory. Different readers approach the proof at different levels of sophistication, and with different demands for being shown the wood as a whole, or the trees in detail. In the next four sections I shall attempt to give an overview, showing the general strategy, and indicating areas of difficulty, but not properly proving that they can be overcome. Many readers may find some other exposition more helpful.[1]

---

[1] For a good technical exposition, see George S. Boolos and Richard C. Jef-

8.2 The Flavour of the Gödelian Argument

Gödel's theorem is a variant of the Epimenides, or Liar, Paradox. Consider the statement 'This statement is untrue': if it is true, then it is untrue; and if it is untrue, then it is true. Normally we are not greatly bothered by such a statement. We naturally ask 'What statement?', remembering that Russell was able to escape his paradox by deeming self-referential class specifications meaningless,[2] and refuse to accept that a statement has been made until the statement being referred to has itself been completed.[3] But Gödel has blocked this escape route, because, granted the resources of *Sorites* Arithmetic, he was able to devise a means whereby we can code well-formed formulae into numbers, **and** some properties of, and relations between, well-formed formulae into properties of, and relations between, numbers. In the case of the Liar Paradox it is not the 'this' but the 'true' that has to go: Tarski's theorem says that a formal logistic theory cannot contain a predicate possessing the properties of our 'true', for if it did, it would lead to a straight contradiction. Gödel's theorem, however, avoids paradox in a different way: it replaces Tarski's 'true' by the more definite and down-to-earth 'provable-in-the-system': 'provable-in-the-system' *can* be formalised, but since it is not the same as 'true', a well-formed formula can be not provable-in-the-system and still true. Indeed, if we think about it, we see that it must be. The formula cannot be provable-in-the-system, for if it were, then, being provable-in-the-system, it would be true, and being true, what it asserted would be the case, that is, that it was not provable-

frey, *Computability and Logic*, 2nd ed., Cambridge, 1980, 3rd ed., Cambridge, 1989, chs. 14 and 15. A very full exposition, with concessions to the non-numerate is given by James R. Newman and Ernest Nagel, *Gödel's Proof*, London, 1959. P.J. FitzPatrick, "To Gödel via Babel", *Mind*, 1966, pp.332-350, gives the best account of the translation problem, which I shall deal with in §8.4. A.W.Moore, *The Infinite*, London, 1990, ch.12, §2, pp.174-178, gives a fresh approach. See also J.N. Crossley and others, *What Is Mathematical Logic?*, Oxford, 1972, ch.5; Hao Wang, *Reflections on Gödel*, MIT, 1987; S.G.Shanker, *Gödel's Theorem in Focus*, London, 1988; Raymond Smullyan, *Forever Undecided: A Puzzled Guide to Gödel*, Oxford, 1988.

[2] See below, §12.2, §12.3.

[3] See Gilbert Ryle, "Heterologicality", *Analysis*, XI, 1950-51, pp.67-68.

in-the-system, which would be a contradiction. Equally, it cannot be false, for if it were false, what it asserted, namely that it was unprovable-in-the-system, would not be the case, and so if it were false, it would be provable-in-the-system, and hence true, which again would be a contradiction.

There are three crucial themes in this argument: reference, translation and diagonalization. These will be discussed in the next three sections.

8.3   Gödel Numbering

Gödel was able to block the ban on self-reference by his scheme of Gödel numbering, which enabled him to code every well-formed formula into a natural number, and thus to refer to it indirectly. Gödel's own system of Gödel numbering is easy to understand, though difficult to operate.[4] Every natural number can be factorised in terms of its prime factors. Thus $360 = 2^3 \times 3^2 \times 5^1$, which we could express succinctly as $\{3, 2, 1\}$. Gödel goes the other way. If we have a formula, and can give each type of symbol used a natural number, we can code the formula as a sequence of numbers, which in turn can be coded uniquely as the natural number that results from taking these numbers as indices of prime factors in their natural ordering. Peano Arithmetic is expressed by means of a finite number of symbols. Typically we need the brackets, the sentential connectives, the quotifiers, a stock of propositional variables, of individual variables, of predicates (including dyadic predicates for expressing relations), one particular individual—nought— and one particular function—the successor function, S. These can be arranged in an order, and can be correlated with the odd prime numbers, $3, 5, 7, 11, 13$, *etc.*

(	)	$\rightarrow$	$\neg$	A	p	x	F	$'$	0	S
3	5	7	11	13	17	19	23	29	31	37

Any formula, whether or not it is well formed, is a string of symbols each of which can be represented by some prime number or another. Each such string can then be expressed as a single (though astronomically large) number, by forming the product of the odd prime factors in order, each being raised to the power of

---

[4] There are many others, which make the mathematical working easier, but the general scheme more difficult to grasp.

the number assigned to the symbol that comes in that order in the string. Thus, the formula

$$\neg\neg p \rightarrow p,$$

which has five symbols, and so could be expressed with the aid of the first five odd prime numbers, namely $3, 5, 7, 11, 13$, and would be expressed by the natural number

$$3^{11} \times 5^{11} \times 7^{17} \times 11^7 \times 13^{17}$$

Such a number is enormous, but it is evident that every string of symbols can be thus expressed as a single number. We might reasonably hope that it would prove possible to express the property of a string of symbols being a well-formed formula as a corresponding property of the Gödel number of that string. This indeed is possible. Moreover, Gödel showed that it was possible to express the rule of substitution as a relation between the Gödel numbers of the two well-formed formulae involved, and also the rule of generalisation, and again the rule of *Modus Ponens* as a three-term relation between the Gödel numbers of the premises and the Gödel number of the conclusion. Clearly we can specify the Gödel number of each axiom of some given system.

Gödel devised one other coding facility. He needed to code not only strings of symbols but strings of strings of symbols, in order to be able to handle *sequences* of well-formed formulae, and thus to characterize *proof sequences*. We can conveniently do this by reserving the factor 2 for Gödel numbers of sequences of Gödel numbers, themselves the Gödel numbers of (invariably well-formed) formulae. Thus suppose it turned out that the Gödel number of $\neg\neg p \rightarrow p$ was 999 (of course, in fact it is much, much larger than that), and we had a proof of

$$\neg\neg\neg\neg p \rightarrow p,$$

whose own Gödel number was 1729 (again, it is much, much larger than that), the first line of which was $\neg\neg p \rightarrow p$ as an axiom, then the proof sequence would have as its Gödel number a number beginning $2 \times 3^{999} \times \ldots$ and ending, say, with 37^{1729}. With this notation, Gödel enables us to refer to sequences in general, and to express the property that a Gödel number must have if it is to be the Gödel number of a sequence that is a **proof** sequence. Granted that, it is relatively easy to define a two-term predicate of natural numbers that holds between two Gödel numbers when, but only when, the first is the Gödel number of a proof sequence whose last line is a well-formed formula whose Gödel number is the second number of the pair.

> An imaginary, and much simplified case:
>
> the Gödel number of the proof sequence is
> $2 \times 3^{999} \times 5^{1025} \ldots 37^{1729}$,
>
> the proof predicate would be
> $Pr(2 \times 3^{999} \times 5^{1025} \ldots 37^{1729}, 1729)$.

If we can carry through the coding so as to assign to every well-formed formula a Gödel number, **and** represent all the syntactical properties of well-formed formulae by means of arithmetical predicates—and it is a big IF—then we have found a way round the ban on self-reference, which was invoked to fault the simple formulations of the Liar Paradox, and can try to reformulate it in objection-proof terms.

8.4 Translation

It is easy to see that Gödel numbering enables us to **refer**, difficult to prove that it can **represent**, or **translate** the meta-logical features needed for Gödel's argument. As we saw in §8.2, Tarski's theorem shows 'true' is untranslatable into any formal system. The difference between the sentence uttered by the Liar and that constructed by Gödel is that the former is 'This statement is un**true**' whereas the latter is a coded way of saying 'This statement is un**provable**'. The former would lead to a straight contradiction IF 'true' could be expressed in terms of properties of, or relations between, Gödel numbers, and thus shows that 'true' cannot be so expressed: the latter, however, can be expressed, provided we confine 'provable' to what can be proved **within a specified formal system**, whose formation rules and rules of inference have been antecedently laid down; in that case, we avoid inconsistency by acknowledging a distinction between wide-ranging open-ended truth on the one hand and closely-defined and tightly-tied-down provability-within-a-given-formal-system on the other.

The 64,000-byte question is

Is such a translation feasible?

Gödel showed that it was. Granted the resources of a suitably formalised version of *Sorites* Arithmetic (SA), in which there was a first natural number and the successor function, and in which addition and multiplication, were defined by **recursion**.[5] The box below gives these two recursive definitions.

Recursive Definitions of Addition and Multiplication

Addition	Multiplication
$n + 0 = n$	$n \times 1 = n$
$n + Sm = S(n + m)$	$n \times Sm = (n \times m) + m$

These are **Primitive** Recursive Functions: they are functions which can be calculated by a computer. Other functions, such as exponientiation and factorial, which can be generated by certain legitimate means from these, are also Primitive Recursive functions. The Theory of Recursive Functions is complex and finicky, and of some importance for computer scientists. The over-all moral is important, but the details need not concern us here. It is helpful to compare Recursive Function Theory with an axiomatic treatment of Propositional Calculus, with the initial stock of primitive recursive functions being like the axioms, and the rules for generating new primitive recursive functions as the rules of inference. Gödel defined Primitive Recursive **predicates** and Primitive Recursive **relations** similarly. Almost all predicates and relations needed for translating important syntactical properties of Peano Arithmetic into properties of Gödel numbers are Primitive Recursive.

---

[5] Modern treatments use Robinson's Arithmetic Q; Q is "distinguished by the simplicity and clear mathematical content of its axioms" (George S. Boolos and Richard C. Jeffrey, *Computability and Logic*, 2nd ed., Cambridge, 1980, 3rd ed., Cambridge, 1989, p.158, quoting Tarski, Mostowski and Robinson). Its chief merit is that, although in other respects a weak language, it is tailor-made to have all recursive functions representable in it.

Clearly, if multiplication is, then being a prime number is; and if exponientiation is, then being the product of prime factors raised to various powers must be also. We have an algorithm—a mechanical rule—for telling whether a string of symbols is a well-formed formula, so it is likely that we should be able to translate it into a test for telling whether a natural number was the Gödel number of a well-formed formula. It is not obvious that the three rules of inference—the rule of substitution, the rule of generalisation and the rule of *Modus Ponens*—can be represented by Primitive Recursive Relations between the Gödel numbers of the premises and the Gödel numbers of the conclusions, but if we follow all Gödel's detailed working, we shall be convinced that they can. If that be granted, then it is obvious that Gödel numbers of the axioms can be specified individually, so that we could check whether a sequence of Gödel numbers was such that every one was either a Gödel number of one of the axioms that have been individually specified, or a Gödel number of a substitution-instance of an earlier one, or a Gödel number of a generalisation of an earlier one, or the Gödel number of a well-formed formula that follows by *Modus Ponens* from two well-formed formulae whose Gödel numbers come earlier in the sequence. Again, it is a laborious task to check in detail that this can be done, and that given some **sequence** with a Gödel number $2 \times 3^n \times 5^m \times 7^l \ldots$ the property of being a **proof** sequence is Primitive Recursive. But it can be done, and it is reasonable to take the word of competent mathematicians that it has been done. This much granted, the last steps are relatively easy. The property of being the largest prime factor of a given (even) number is clearly Primitive Recursive, as is that of being the exponent of the largest prime factor of a given (even) number. Hence the relation $Pr(x, y)$ is Primitive Recursive, where $Pr(x, y)$ is the relation that obtains between x and y, where x is the Gödel number of a proof sequence having as its last member the well-formed formula whose Gödel number is y; that is to say x is the Gödel number of a "proof" of y.

We have thus advanced the argument of the last section, and shown that Gödel numbering not only enables us to refer to well-formed formulae and sequences of well-formed formulae, but enables us also to represent as a Primitive Recursive relation the crucial syntactic relation of being a proof of a particular well-formed formula within a specified formal system.

To go to the more general provability-within-a-specified-formal-system, we need to add a quotifier, $(\mathbf{V}x)$, to obtain $(\mathbf{V}x)Pr(x,y)$; and then the predicate is no longer **Primitive** Recursive, on account of the unbounded range of $(\mathbf{V}x)$, though it retains a general sort of recursiveness, in as much as IF it does hold in a particular case, a computer, by working through each value of x in turn, would sooner or later find the value of x for which it did hold, and hence establish the fact that it did. For the sake of definiteness we work not with the wide-ranging $(\mathbf{V}x)$, but a μ-operator, the **least** x such that . . . . Such a predicate is called **General** Recursive; General Recursive Relations and General Recursive Functions are defined similarly. Often the 'General' is omitted, and recursive predicates/relations/functions are those that can be defined by some recursion schema, together with some innocuous operations such as substitution, and the use of a "μ-operator", which picks out the first number, if there is one, that satisfies the specified predicate, relation, or function.

We have thus vindicated the claim that thanks to Gödel numbering we can not only refer to well-formed formulae, but characterize meta-logical truths about them in arithmetical terms. Once we are assured of the adequacy of the translation—of the representability of the proof-predicate in computer-speak (that is, in some suitable formalisation of *Sorites* Arithmetic)—Gödel's argument is under way.

8.5 Diagonalization

Gödel looks like being able to refer to well-formed formulae without having actually to quote them, and to express within a formal system the meta-logical property of being unprovable-in-that-system. But it is not evident that he can actually construct a Gödelian formula G with just the tricky internal structure needed for the argument. Might he not be forever trying to tread on his own tail?

Gödel is in fact able to construct a well-formed formula with the necessary properties by means of a Diagonalization procedure that is similar in spirit to Cantor's proof that there are more real numbers than there are natural numbers:[6] the details are a mathematical *tour de force*, but not philosophically difficult. What is philosophically difficult is the integration of these manoeuvres into one coherent argument, making use of the peculiar features of G.

---

[6] See above, §7.2.

REFERRING   Gödel Numbering
TRANSLATION   Recursive Function Theory
SELF-REFERENCE   Diagonalization

G has to be regarded both as a formula in a calculus and as a proposition with content, making a statement about a natural number. And we also need to be able to talk about G, making precise meta-logical statements about its status—whether it is well-formed, whether it is provable within a tightly specified formal system. It is difficult to keep track of these shifts of standpoint. One useful aid is to follow a device of FitzPatrick,[7] and distinguish the different uses of symbols by using different natural languages: Latin; French; and English.

Latin is the formal system we are interested in, in this case Peano Arithmetic. (Latin is a dead language, which we study but do not normally use, though we can: a formal system may be studied as an uninterpreted calculus, though it can be interpreted, and used to express content-ful propositions.)

French is a meta-language for meta-logic. (French is a living language, which we do not just study, but *use* to make very precise statements *e.g.* about Latin syntax.)

English is for real. We make true statements in it, and can (sometimes) tell that a statement is true (*e.g.* 'Two and two makes four'). Moreover, as English linguistic chauvinists like to make out, and Frenchmen deny, English is at least as rich as French: every statement in French can be translated into English. Or, more mathematically, English must contain the whole of *Sorites* Arithmetic (SA). (Of course, it may contain more; if the system under study in Latin is Peano Arithmetic (PA), it will need to contain that; in which case, since *Sorites* Arithmetic (SA) is contained within Peano Arithmetic (PA), it will certainly be rich enough. If English is rich enough to translate Latin adequately, it is rich enough to translate French.)

    Gödel was able to construct a well-formed formula, G, and considered it as a well-formed formula of a system of first-order Peano Arithmetic (PA)—a Latin sentence. We may ask, meta-logically,

[7] See P.J. FitzPatrick, "To Gödel via Babel", *Mind*, 1966, pp.332-50.

> Gödel needs to view the Gödelian sentence in three ways:
> 1. as a string of symbols—a formula—being used according to certain specified syntactic rules, but with no interpretation attached.
> 2. as making a statement in a meta-language about formulae.
> 3. as making a statement about natural numbers, like 'Five and seven make twelve' (only, much more complicated).

whether or not this string of symbols is derivable as a theorem of Peano Arithmetic. It would be like asking a French classicist whether a string of Latin words was good Latin or not. We can also consider this string of symbols as a meaningful expression, and ask whether or not it is true. It would be like asking a historian whether a statement in a letter by Cicero was true or not. We have, in effect, translated from Latin into English, and assessed the truth of the proposition expressed in the English translation. If we ask the two questions, the answers are, surprisingly, different: if we ask whether G is true, the answer turns out to be Yes; but if we pose the question in French, *Est la formula G dérivable de Peano Arithmétique?* the answer turns out to be *Non*.

$$PA \not\vdash G.$$

La formula G n'est pas dérivable de Peano Arithmétique.

The reason for the answers' being different emerges if we translate again from French into English, which we can do, thanks to Gödel numbering, so that instead of being a French statement about Latin syntax, it is an English statement about a certain natural number, namely: g, the Gödel number of G, to the effect that there is no number x, such that x is even (i.e. x is the Gödel number of a **sequence**), x has the proof property (enormously complicated to spell out in simple arithmetical terms), and the index of the largest prime factor of x is g. This is a statement in English, and since it is a statement about natural numbers, and their properties, and the relations between them, expressed in *Sorites* Arithmetic (SA), it can be translated into Latin, that is to say, the formal language of Peano Arithmetic, which contains *Sorites* Arithmetic (SA). If we do this, we find that, because of the peculiar way Gödel has constructed G, the Latin translation turns out to be G itself. We can express this in English (and hence also in Latin, if we *use* it, instead of merely talking about it), using the semantic turnstile,

$$\models G$$

as a claim of ordinary **informal** arithmetic that G is true.

Gödel has constructed G to be of the form $\neg(\forall x)(Pr(x,g))$; where g is the Gödel number of G. If we ask French questions about it, we have to say *La formula G n'est pas dérivable de Peano Arithmétique*, or, in symbols, $PA \not\vdash G$, but if we translate it into English, and ask if it is true, we have to say it is, $\models G$, since any other view would, as we argued earlier, lead to a contradiction. Hence, provided Peano Arithmetic is consistent, G, though true, is not provable in Peano Arithmetic. So Peano Arithmetic is **not semantically complete**.

Moreover, a further argument shows that $\neg G$ is not derivable as a theorem of Peano Arithmetic: *la formula ¬G n'est pas dérivable de Peano Arithmétique*, or in symbols $PA \not\vdash \neg G$. It follows that we could add G, not itself already a theorem, to Peano Arithmetic without inconsistency. Hence Peano Arithmetic is **not syntactically complete**; and also, since G can be neither proved nor disproved in it, Peano Arithmetic is **undecidable**.

Latin	G?
French about Latin	$PA \not\vdash G$
French about Latin	*La formula G n'est pas dérivable de Peano Arithmétique*
English	$\neg(\forall x)Pr(x,g)$
Latin in use or English	$\models G$

The crucial step is the translation from French into English, that is from meta-logical propositions about well-formed formulae into arithmetical propositions about natural numbers, ascribing to the number g a complex predicate of the form $\neg(\forall x)(Pr(x,g))$. The predicate $Pr(x,g)$ is defined, very complicatedly, in terms of *properties of natural numbers* and *relations between natural numbers*. It is a simple question of arithmetical fact whether or not a particular number has this property. And then in the particular case of whether g has the property, it turns out, thanks to the way G was constructed, that the (English) translation of (the French) $PA \nvdash G$, i.e. $\neg(\forall x)(Pr(x,g))$, is just the proposition G in Latin, considered as a true statement of arithmetical fact. So G is True, i.e. $\models G$, iff $\neg(\forall x)(Pr(x,g))$ iff $PA \nvdash G$. The syntactic relation $PA \nvdash G$ is viewed **meta**-logically as a true assertion about PA, which translates, via Gödel numbering, into a true assertion about a particular number, g, namely the assertion G, where G is a fully interpreted statement about ordinary natural numbers, independently of any formalisation of arithmetic. We can not only use French to talk about Latin, but translate from French into English, with all the important French terms having adequate representations in English. *La formula G est dérivable de Peano Arithmétique* translates into $\neg(\forall x)Pr(x,g)$, i.e. G is PA-unprovable, and if this were false in English, the French *La formula G n'est pas dérivable de Peano Arithmétique* would have to be false too, so that *La formula G est dérivable de Peano Arithmétique* and $\vdash_{PA} G$, so that in Peano Arithmetic we could derive false propositions, and Peano Arithmetic would be unsound and inconsistent.

8.6 Conditions

Gödel's proof works only under certain conditions. It applies only to consistent systems.[8] If a system is inconsistent, then we can prove both A and $\neg A$, and from these two premises we can, granted some standard rules and theses of propositional calculus, derive any well-formed formula whatsoever, and so, in particular, the Gödelian formula G. Gödel's proof applies only to formal systems, systems, that is, which have fully spelt-out formation rules, axioms and rules of inference. They must be not only fully, but *finitely*, specified, so that after a finite number of steps it will be clear whether or not a sequence of symbols is well formed, whether or not a well-formed formula is an axiom, whether or not a well-formed formula follows from one or two others in virtue of a particular rule of inference.

---

[8] Originally to prove $PA \nvdash \neg G$ Gödel needed ω-consistency, but Rosser improved Gödel's proof so as to need only ordinary consistency. See J.B.Rosser, "Extensions of some theorems of Gödel and Church", *Journal of Symbolic Logic*, **1**, 1936, pp.87-91. See also further below, §8.11.

It is essential also, if a theory is to contain the means for some form of Gödel numbering, that it should include the natural numbers together with the operations of addition **and** multiplication. Peano Arithmetic and *Sorites* Arithmetic contain both because they contain the successor function, and addition and multiplication can be implicitly defined, as we have seen, by suitable axioms involving just the successor. Rather surprisingly, neither addition by itself nor multiplication by itself is enough. Presburger has shown that if we have only addition but not multiplication, the theory *is* complete and decidable. Similarly Skolem showed that if we have only multiplication but not addition, the theory is, again, complete and decidable. Even more surprisingly Tarski has shown that geometry and the elementary algebra of real numbers, *with* addition and multiplication, but *without* the general notion of natural number, is complete and decidable.[9] These results are surprising, and call for some explanation. The reason why Gödel's theorem does not apply is that in these theories we are thinking of the numbers in some other way—*e.g.* as an infinite Abelian group with addition as the composition function: they are not *counting* numbers, an endless succession of individually distinct entities, capable of being used for coding without ever being in any danger of running out. Once we have the natural numbers as counting numbers, we are subject to Gödel's theorem, because there is a potential infinity of natural numbers, and Dedekind-infinite sets can be correlated with a proper subset of themselves. But we need only a potential, not an actual, infinity of natural numbers. Gödel's theorem holds not only of Peano Arithmetic, but of the simpler *Sorites* Arithmetic. Essentially, that is, we can address Gödel's argument to a computer. We do not need to invoke the hand-waving arguments of Chapter Six to avail ourselves of the principle of recursive reasoning, in order to prove Gödel's theorem: it applies even within

---

[9] M.Presburger, "Über die Vollständigkeit eines gewissen Systems der Arithmetik ganzer Zahlen, in welchem die Addition als einzige Operation hervortritt", *Sparawozdanie z I Kongresu matematyków krajów slowianskich, Warszawa, 1929*, Warsaw, 1930, pp.92-101, 395. T.Skolem, "Über einige Satzfunktionem in der Arithmetik", *Skrifter Utgitt av Det Norske Videnskaps-Akademi i Oslo*, I. Mat.-Naturv. Klasse, 1930, no.7, Oslo, 1931. These and other results are conveniently summarised by Geoffrey Hunter, *Metalogic*, London, 1971, p.260.

the austere limitations of *Sorites* Arithmetic, with no commitment to any actual infinity.

Although Gödel's theorem does not hold for unnaturally weak formal systems, it does hold for all stronger first-order ones, no matter how much we strengthen them. It seems at first surprising: a stronger system, surely, should be more decidable and more complete. But, as we shall see with first- and second-order logic,[10] it does not follow, for as we strengthen a system, we increase not only its resources for answering questions, but the number and type of question that may be asked of it. Contrariwise, however, the restriction to first-order logic *is* essential. If we strengthen logic on that front, we can no longer prove Gödel's theorem. One of the consequences of Gödel's theorem is that *second*-order logic is *not* finitely axiomatizable, not the sort of logic a computer can be programmed to do.

8.7 Corollaries and Consequences

Gödel's theorem yields many further results, some of which can be argued for independently, but which are conveniently seen as corollaries and consequences of Gödel's theorem. They are summarised below.

Corollaries

1. Peano Arithmetic is not syntactically complete
2. Peano Arithmetic is not negation-complete
3. Peano Arithmetic is not decidable
4. Peano Arithmetic is not semantically complete

Further Consequences

5. Peano Arithmetic is non-monomorphic.
6. Tarski's theorem
7. Church's theorem
8. Turing's theorem
9. Gödel's second theorem

Some of these results need little discussion: others need amplification in the next two sections. Gödel's theorem has some immediate corollaries. It shows first that Peano Arithmetic (and

---

[10] See below, §13.5.

Sorites Arithmetic) is not **syntactically complete**. For we can add G, which is not a theorem of Peano Arithmetic, to PA, the conjunction of the axioms, without making $PA + G$ inconsistent It shows similarly that Peano Arithmetic is not **negation-complete**. For neither G nor $\neg G$ are theorems of Peano Arithmetic. It shows thirdly that Peano Arithmetic is not **decidable** For we cannot **tell** within Peano Arithmetic **whether or not** G or $\neg G$ are theorems. And fourthly it shows that Peano Arithmetic is not **semantically complete**: for $PA \nvdash G$ though $\models G$.

These immediate results are really just different ways of looking at Gödel's theorem. They give rise to further, less obvious, consequences. Since neither $\vdash_{PA} G$ nor $\vdash_{PA} \neg G$ neither $PA \cup \neg G$ nor $PA \cup G$ is inconsistent, and so each has a model. Hence, as we argued in Chapter Six,[11] PA has two models, in one of which G obtains, and in the other of which $\neg G$ obtains, so that the two models are not isomorphic with each other, and Peano Arithmetic is non-monomorphic.

It should be noted, however, that this result, though it follows from Gödel's theorem, does not depend on it. We could have proved it from the Compactness theorem for first-order logic. It is only that since we were going to prove Gödel's theorem anyhow, it was more economical to use it to give us this result also.[12]

In proving Gödel's theorem, we glimpsed also a proof of Tarski's theorem, which shows that we cannot represent within Peano Arithmetic any predicate that has the characteristic properties of 'true'. For then the Liar Paradox would be unfaultable, and we should have shown how we could always derive a contradiction within Peano Arithmetic, which is to say that Peano Arithmetic is inconsistent. So, provided Peano Arithmetic is consistent, 'true' cannot be represented within it.

---

[11] §6.3.

[12] See above, §6.3, n.6.

8.8 Church's Theorem and Turing's Theorem

Gödel's theorem yields Church's theorem, that first-order logic is undecidable; that is, not two-way decidable in the sense of §3.4. For SA has its own Gödelian formula; suppose that first-order logic were decidable: then the well-formed formula $SA \rightarrow G$ would be decidable, and so we could tell whether or not $SA \vdash G$, that is, whether or not $\vdash_{SA} G$, contrary to Gödel's theorem.

Church's theorem is surprising. We might naturally suppose that first-order logic, being complete, was also decidable. Indeed, with the aid of Gödel numbering, we can number not only all well-formed formulae, but all sequences of well-formed formulae that constitute valid proofs in first-order logic, and work through them one by one to see if they happen to be a valid proof of any particular well-formed formula we are interested in. In this way, given sufficient time, we shall find a proof, *if any exists*. We do have **one**-way decidability. What we lack is any way of telling that a particular well-formed formula of first-order logic is **not** a theorem. We could go on grinding out proof after proof of other well-formed formulae, in each case finding that it was not the proof we wanted, but never knowing that it was 100% certain that the next proof we looked at would not be the sought-after one. We lack a definitive test for **non**-theoremhood. That is not to say that we cannot often show of a particular well-formed formula, A say, that it is not a theorem. If we have already proved $\neg A$, then, since we know that first-order logic is consistent, we can be sure that there is no proof of A. But first-order logic is not negation-complete, though it is semantically complete. Even though every well-formed formula that is true under all interpretations is a theorem, there are many well-formed formulae, such as $(\mathrm{V}x)(\mathrm{V}y)(F(x) \wedge F(y) \wedge (x \neq y))$, which are true under some, but not under all, interpretations, so that neither that well-formed formula, since it does not hold in a one-membered universe, nor its negation, which does not hold in a two-membered universe, is a theorem.

Church's theorem forces us to distinguish one-way from two-way decidability, and the bounded and fixed-length versions of the latter, as in §3.4.

The discussion has been entirely in terms of well-formed formulae and theoremhood. It is easier to grasp the importance of what is at issue that way, but it is also, as we have now seen, easy to be misled. Mathematical logicians therefore move away from well-formed formulae to their Gödel numbers, and consider, abstractly, sets of numbers, where they call those sets of numbers that are two-way decidable "recursive", and those that are only one-way decidable "recursively enumerable". The Gödel numbers of theorems of propositional calculus are recursive; the Gödel numbers of theorems of first-order logic are recursively enumerable; and the Gödel numbers of non-theorems of first-order logic are not recursively enumerable; the Gödel numbers of theorems of Peano Arithmetic are recursively enumerable; and the Gödel numbers of non-theorems of Peano Arithmetic are not recursively enumerable.

The elucidation of decidability has been in terms of there being a *method* for deciding questions. Gödel's theorem gave rise to much discussion of what constituted a method, and the concept was elucidated in terms of a fool-proof method which a computer could be programmed to follow. Turing produced a specification of what it essentially was to be a computer, in his definition of a "Turing machine". A Turing machine can be identified with a program for an idealised computer. Notoriously, some programs do not work, but get into a loop, and just go on running without ever arriving at a result. It would be nice to have a program to check programs and eliminate all those that would not reach a conclusion. It would be nice, but we cannot have it. That is what Turing showed. Turing's theorem is an analogue of Gödel's: it states that there is no general procedure for deciding whether or not a given procedure will itself end in a definite decision, one way or the other. Note that Turing's theorem does not show that we cannot ever weed out dud programs—we can and do—but we cannot devise a *program* for weeding out them *all*. In this it closely resembles Church's theorem. Like Church's theorem too, it does not show that we cannot have a procedure for selecting all those programs which do work. We can—given enough time. Given enough time, we can run each program, and those that are such as sooner or later to arrive at a result sooner or later will. But at no time can we argue from the fact that a program has not been completed yet to the conclusion that it never will. And although we may have our suspicions that it never will, and in *some* cases may be able to spot a loop, we have no *method* which will always identify a program as non-terminating if in fact it is.

In our computer age many people find Turing's theorem more accessible than Gödel's, and prove Gödel's as a corollary of Turing's. But Gödel's raises further questions of truth and provability which are of great philosophical interest. I therefore concentrate on Gödel's theorem, and leave Turing's theorem, together with Löb's theorem, which is of considerable importance in mathematical logic,[13] and turn to the final consequence of Gödel's first theorem I shall discuss, namely Gödel's second theorem.

8.9 Gödel's Second Theorem

Gödel's second theorem highlights one crucial assumption made throughout the proof of his first theorem, that Peano Arithmetic is consistent. Granted that premise, Gödel had been able to argue in proving his first theorem not only that the Gödelian formula, G, was unprovable-in-Peano-Arithmetic, but that it was actually true. This argument was a strict deductive argument, and could be formalised in first-order logic, to yield a formal proof of G granted the consistency of Peano Arithmetic. The premise that a formal system is consistent *can* be formalised in a formal system: we cannot hope to escape *à la* Tarski by holding that consistency, like truth, cannot be expressed formally. After all, once we have expressed in a formal system what it is for a well-formed formula to be provable-in-that-system, we can say that there is no well-formed formula such that both it and its negation are provable; and indeed, it is sufficient to state simply that there is *some* well-formed formula which is not a theorem,

$$(\mathrm{V}a)(WFF(a) \wedge \neg(\mathrm{V}m)(Pr_{PA}(m, a))),$$

where a is the Gödel number of a formula A, and $WFF(a)$ expresses in arithmetical terms that A is well formed, and $Pr_{PA}(m, a)$ is the proof predicate of the formal system PA expressing the fact that m is the Gödel number of a proof in Peano Arithmetic of A. Let us abbreviate it as $Cons(PA)$. Then we can formalise the informal argument of the proof of Gödel's first theorem and say

$$\vdash_{PA} Cons(PA) \to G,$$

---

[13] For an account of Löb's theorem see George S. Boolos and Richard C. Jeffrey, *Computability and Logic*, 2nd ed., Cambridge, 1980, 3rd ed., Cambridge, 1989, ch. 16, esp. pp. 187-188; see also ch. 15 for an illuminating survey of other results, but seen as stemming from Turing's theorem rather than Gödel's.

and thus, IF we had a proof of $Cons(PA)$, that is, if

$$\vdash_{PA} Cons(PA),$$

we should, by *Modus Ponens*, have a direct proof

$$\vdash_{PA} G.$$

But this is the direct contradictory of Gödel's first theorem,

$$\nvdash_{PA} G.$$

So IF we had a proof of the consistency of Peano Arithmetic, we should end up with an inconsistency.[14] That by itself is not quite enough to prove that we cannot have a proof of the consistency of Peano Arithmetic—it could be the case that Peano Arithmetic *was* inconsistent, in which case, paradoxically there would be a proof of $Cons(PA)$, since there would be a proof of *every* well-formed formula, including $Cons(PA)$. What we have instead is the slightly weaker result that

IF Peano Arithmetic **is** consistent, then we cannot **prove that** it is, *within Peano Arithmetic*.

That is Gödel's second theorem.

It is important to note the italicised condition. Only formal proofs within Peano Arithmetic (and hence within any weaker system) are excluded. We can in fact prove that Peano Arithmetic is consistent by transfinite induction: this was done by Gentzen.[15] But the principle of transfinite induction is not one that is available in Peano Arithmetic itself. We may also be able to argue for the consistency of Peano Arithmetic informally, and to this, again, there is no objection. All that is excluded by Gödel's second theorem is there being a formal proof within Peano Arithmetic itself. That is, indeed, a remarkable result, but it does not mean that we must utterly despair of the consistency of arithmetic, or take up an attitude of resolute agnosticism to the question.

---

[14] In which case, paradoxically, we could prove every well-formed formula to be a theorem, including that asserting that PA was consistent. In §12.10 many axioms of Zermelo-Fraenkel set theory are reported to be proved consistent provided ZF is itself, but ZF can be proved consistent only if it is not!

[15] G.Gentzen, "Die Wiederspruchfreiheit der reinen Zahlentheorie", *Mathematische Annalen*, **112**, 1936, pp.493-565; tr. in M.E.Szabo, ed., *The Collected Papers of Gerhard Gentzen*, London and Amsterdam, 1969.

8.10   Mechanism

Gödel's and Turing's theorems establish certain limitations on formal systems and computer programs. Gödel's theorem goes further, and shows that although the Gödelian formula, G, was unprovable-in-the-system, it was none the less true. That seems to suggest that the mental powers of an ordinary mathematician go beyond the formal inferences of a formal system, and cannot be simulated by a computer, no matter how sophisticated its programming. Alternatively, we might argue directly from Tarski's theorem, that since truth cannot be adequately expressed in a formal system, and since we evidently possess the concept of truth, we cannot be just the embodiment of some formal system. The mechanist, who wishes to deny this, would be reduced to denying that we really have a concept of truth at all. Some are prepared to maintain just this, but then have difficulty in claiming that mechanism is true.

These arguments have been developed in detail, and have been accepted as cogent by some, and vehemently rejected by others.[16] Much of the controversy turns on what exactly is meant by a machine, and by mechanism. Often also the critics have misunderstood the structure of the argument. Just as Gödel does not produce an absolutely undecidable well-formed formula, but only, after having had a formal system specified, works out a well-formed formula which is unprovable-in-that-system, so the philosopher arguing against mechanism, does not produce something that no machine can be programmed to do, but only offers a scheme of disproof, whereby any claim to represent a mind by a particular machine can be shown to fail for that particular machine.

The issues raised by this controversy are of considerable philosophical interest generally—it makes quite a difference to determinist and materialist views of the mind, if no mechanist account of the mind can be adequate: but that discussion belongs to meta-

---

[16] The original article was "Minds, Machine and Gödel", *Philosophy*, **36**, 1961, pp.112-127; and the argument was set forth more fully in J.R.Lucas, *The Freedom of the Will*, Oxford, 1970. The most noteworthy recent supporters of the argument are Dale Jacquette, "Metamathematical Criteria for Minds and Machines", *Erkenntnis*, **27**, 1987, pp.1-16; and Roger Penrose, *The Emperor's New Mind*, Oxford, 1989, and *Shadows of the Mind*, Oxford, 1994.

physics or the philosophy of mind, and here we need to confine ourselves to questions bearing on the philosophy of mathematics. These are first and foremost the nature of proof, and, stemming from that, the nature of mathematical knowledge.[17]

8.11 Gödel's Theorem and Provability

Gödel's theorem shows that for any reasonable system, L, some well-formed formulae are true which are not provable-in-L. Not only are they true, but we can see that they are true. Nor is this seeing some *recherché* sense-experience: rather, it is the result of careful argument. Gödel's theorem is proved. An intelligent man can follow his proof, and be rationally convinced by it that the Gödelian formula, G, is true. In some sense of 'prove' G is proved to be true. Gödel's theorem thus suggests that mathematical truth outruns provability-in-any-formal-system, and that beyond provability-in-any-particular-formal-system there are further possibilities of proof.

In Chapter 6 we were led to extend *Sorites* Arithmetic by the rule of recursive reasoning, but the implication of Gödel's theorem is more profound. Gödel originally needed ω-consistency to prove $PA \not\vdash \neg G$ on the strength of being able, for any m, to prove Gm. But we need to walk warily: if we were to allow ourselves to prove-in-the-system $\vdash ((An)Gn$, we should land ourselves in inconsistency. We have to distinguish the formal $\vdash$ from the informal 'therefore' (which we symbolize as $p \;\; \Vdash q$ in §13.3). This is puzzling. "Why", the reader may ask, "was it all right in Chapter 6 to allow a general licence to infer from for EACH $m, \vdash_L Fm$, to $\vdash_L ((An)Gn$, but not here to infer from for EACH $m, \vdash_L Gm$, to $\vdash_L (An)Gn$?" The answer is that the method of proof is different in the two cases. The premises in the former case, $\vdash_L Fm$, were proved for each successive m, by recursion, in a fairly standard

---

[17] Since the views expressed in this section are highly controversial, it is only fair to refer the reader to criticisms of the Gödelian Argument, which are listed by Chalmers at

http://www.artsci.wustl.edu/~philos/papers/chalmers.biblio.4.html

In particular there are many in *Journal of Behavioral and Brain Sciences*, **13:4**, 1990, and **16:3**, 1993. Judson C. Webb, *Mechanism, Mentalism and Metamathematics; An Essay on Finitism*, Dordrecht, 1980, is a sustained attack on the arguments given here.

way, like, though not *exactly* like, the proofs of $\vdash_L Ft$ for particular instances of t. But in the case of the Gödel formulae, although for each m, $\vdash_L \neg Pr(m, g)$, the proof is not the same in each case: it is not a straightforward standard generalisation, nor a recursive proof, but a global *Reductio ad Absurdum*. Working out the proof predicate will be different in each case, but we can be sure that in each case it will turn out not to be a proof of G.

Three stages of generalisation:

1. Standard generalisation;
   from $\vdash_L Ft$ infer $\vdash_L (\forall x)Fx$
   from $\vdash_L$ for ANY $\vdash_L$ ALL

2. Proof depends on case, but in a standard way;
   from for EVERY m, $\vdash_L Gm$ infer $\vdash_L (\forall n)Gn$;
   from $\vdash_L$ for EVERY $\vdash_L$ ALL

3. Proof depends on case, but in a non-standard way;
   from for EVERY m, $\vdash_L Gm$ infer that $\vdash Gm$ holds generally,
   but do not infer $\vdash_L (\forall n)Gn$;
   from $\vdash_L$ for EACH do not infer as a theorem of L, $\vdash_L$ ALL although the informal inference from EACH to ALL *is* valid.

Of course we could formalise the proof of Gödel's theorem, but only in *another* formal system, which would in turn have proofs which were not formalisable in it. However far we go in formalising Gödelian proofs, and adding them to formal systems, the new system will still be subject to the Gödelian style of argument, which will yield yet further well-formed formulae that cannot be derived in the new system, but can never the less be seen to be true.

The "incompletability of mathematics", as it may be called, is well expressed by Myhill.

> Gödel's argument establishes that there exist, for any correct formal system containing the arithmetic of natural numbers, correct inferences which cannot be carried out in that system.[18]

---

[18] J.Myhill, "Some Remarks on the Notion of Proof", *Journal of Philosophy*, LVII, 1960, p.462.

It is of great significance. In the first place it tells against Formalism. We cannot give a satisfactory account of provability or mathematical truth in terms of the syntactic properties of any formal system adequate for arithmetic. Even *Sorites* Arithmetic is incomplete, and contains well-formed formulae that are unprovable-in-*SA*, but can be proved and seen to be true from outside *Sorites* Arithmetic. The whole programme of accounting for mathematical inference in formal, syntactic terms alone, loses credibility: and we feel impelled to look elsewhere for the inwardness of mathematical endeavour. Post argues,

> For the entire development should lead away from the purely formal as the ideal of a mathematical science, with a consequent return to postulates that are to be self-evident properties of the new meaningful mathematical science under consideration.[19]

Gödel's theorem has been taken to imply that we simply have an innate ability to recognise a valid proof when we see one, much as the Intuitionists claim. But what Gödel's theorem shows is only that the concept of proof cannot be completely formalised, not that it cannot be formalised at all. In fact, Gödel's theorem argues against Intuitionism. Intuitionists, as we saw,[20] lay great emphasis on mathematicians' activity in actually proving theorems, and construe truth in terms of provability, from which it would follow that the Principle of Bivalence—that every proposition is either true, or else false—is questionable. But once we recognise that truth outruns provability, the validity of the Principle of Bivalence can no longer be impugned on those grounds, and the intuitionist critique of classical logic loses its edge.

More generally, the fact that mathematical truth outruns provability within a formal system argues for the creativity of mathematical inference, and perhaps its objectivity, but poses problems about the logic of argument. Kant argued that moral actions and moral judgements must be universalisable, and it has seemed to many modern philosophers that this is a requirement of rationality

[19] E.L. Post, "Recursively Enumerable Sets of Positive Integers and their Decision Problem", *Bulletin of American Mathematical Society*, **50**, 1944, p.416, fn 100; quoted by Robin Gandy "The Confluence of Ideas in 1936", *The Universal Turing Machine*, Oxford, 1988, p.96.

[20] §7.4.

generally. But if every inference is valid only if it is in accordance
with some maxim, it would seem that reason must be entirely rule-
governed. The resolution of the difficulty lies in distinguishing the
order of the quotifiers. The version of universalisability espoused
by Kant and his modern successors, requires that there be some
rule which every action (in the case of Kant) or every inference (in
modern accounts) accords with:

there is a *Rule* such that for every *Inference*

(*Inference* accords with *Rule*),

(V *Rule*)(A *Inference*)(*Inference* accords with *Rule*),

and this requirement is one that Gödel's theorem shows to be not
always satisfiable. All that rationality really requires is the weaker
condition:

for every *Inference* there is a *Rule* such that

(*Inference* accords with *Rule*),

(A *Inference*)(V *Rule*)(*Inference* accords with *Rule*).

We cannot formulate in advance rules of inference that will cover
every valid inference: but given an inference, we can detect the
hitherto unformulated principle it exemplifies. Inferences are necessarily not essentially one-off, in the way that some choices are,
and the particular configuration of individual objects in space. It
is not that some particular Gödelian formula just happens to be
true but unprovable: the argument that establishes its truth can
be used to establish the truth of other well-formed formulae, and
if some putative Gödelian formula does not have its truth established, we are entitled to ask "Why?", and have some difference
pointed out to us, to distinguish its case from the ones where the
argument does apply. Universalisability is a real requirement of
rationality, but less rigid than commonly supposed, allowing us to
take a more generous view of the nature of mathematical truth.[21]

---

[21] See, more fully, J.R.Lucas, "The Lesbian Rule", *Philosophy*, 1955, XXX,
pp.195-213.

Gödel's Theorems show:

1. First-order Peano Arithmetic is not decidable
2. First-order Peano Arithmetic is not complete
3. First-order Logic is not decidable
4. First-order Peano Arithmetic has non-standard models (see §6.3)
5. Second-order Peano Arithmetic is not recursively axiomatizable
6. Second-order Logic is not recursively axiomatizable
7. First-order Peano Arithmetic cannot be proved consistent by the methods of First-order Peano Arithmetic alone
8. Truth outruns provability
9. Verificationist arguments against the Principle of Bivalence are invalid
10. However much proofs are formalised, there are further proofs not fully formalised, but evidently cogent
11. Hilbert's Programme cannot be carried through to a successful conclusion
12. Reason is creative
13. Synthetic *a priori* truths are possible

Chapter 9
Transitive Relations

9.1 Logic

Thus far the logic out of which mathematics has developed has been primarily that of quotifiers. But the study of equivalence relations, ordering relations, one-one, and many-one, relations should be counted as part of logic. Frege made use of the relation of equinumerosity to show that different numerical expressions referred to the same thing, the same natural number.[1] Dedekind characterized the counting numbers in terms of their order.[2] The logic of relations is indubitably a part of logic.

Relations can be characterized in different ways. Many-one and one-one relations give rise to functions, and in particular to mappings, themselves establishing homomorphisms and isomorphisms. These will be discussed in §9.3, after considering the equivalence relations they characteristically generate. **Equivalence** relations are **transitive** and **symmetric**, and it is in terms of these features that relations are most illuminatingly classified. We can have relations that are symmetric but not transitive, such as *spouse*, *other than*, and *different from*; but of greater interest are the **ordering** relations, that is those that are transitive and asymmetric.

[1] See above, §4.7.

[2] See above, §5.2.

> **Query**
>
> Could there be a
> transitive, non-symmetric,
> *non*-reflexive relation?

We can further disjoin an equivalence relation with an ordering relation to form an **antisymmetric** relation, such as *being the same age as or older than*. Antisymmetric relations are transitive and non-symmetric. They are characterized by the three axioms,

1. $(x \overset{\scriptscriptstyle\leq}{\sim} y \wedge y \overset{\scriptscriptstyle\leq}{\sim} z) \to x \overset{\scriptscriptstyle\leq}{\sim} z$
2. $x \overset{\scriptscriptstyle\leq}{\sim} x$
3. $(x \overset{\scriptscriptstyle\leq}{\sim} y \wedge y \overset{\scriptscriptstyle\leq}{\sim} x) \to x \approx y$

Conversely, we can define both equivalence and ordering relations in terms of antisymmetric relations. It is tempting to do so, both for the sake of economy, and because the logicians' $\to$ and entailment, $\vdash$, are antisymmetric.[3] Nevertheless, it would be an unwise course. We should be wary of a logical economy that is not reflected in our ordinary understanding. The officialese *on or before* sounds awkward because we do not naturally disjoin the two types of relation. For the sake of clarity, too, it is better to distinguish them. It is dangerously easy to confuse "strict" orderings, characterized by means of asymmetric irreflexive relations, with "quasi" orderings, characterized by means of antisymmetric relations. And finally, in particular and conclusively, we need to take every reasonable step to secure ourselves against confusing identity, $=$, with the more general equivalence relation $\approx$.[4] For these reasons we shall, where possible, avoid antisymmetric relations in favour of equivalence relations and ordering relations, properly so called.

For a typology of possible
relations see table on p.444.

---

[3] It is unfortunate that the standard logical symbolism, $\to$, $\supset$ and $\vdash$ obscure this, and half suggest that they are asymmetric. But it would be too cumbersome and finicky to write $\overset{\to}{\sim}$, or $\overset{\to}{-}$, *etc.* in general, though we shall in §9.11 where confusion is particularly likely.

[4] See below, §9.2.

9.2   Equivalence Relations

Equivalence relations are much used in modern mathematics. They
are used to introduce new, abstract entities, as they were in Chapter Three to explicate rational and negative numbers in terms of
ordered pairs of natural numbers.[5] The theory of groups can be
seen as a natural generalisation of equivalence relations, as also, in
a different way, category theory. Much of the theory of measurement depends on equivalence classes, and they will be needed when
we develop an account of magnitudes.

Equivalence relations are transitive. They differ from ordering
relations in that whereas an equivalence relation is also symmetric and therefore reflexive, an ordering relation is asymmetric and
irreflexive. More formally we may define a relation R as being an
equivalence relation iff

1. If xRy and yRz then xRz, and
2. if xRy then yRx.

It follows, in any domain in which an equivalence relation holds at
all, that it is reflexive; that is

3. xRx.

When a relation is transitive, symmetric and reflexive, it is often
written $x \sim y$, or $x \approx y$, or $x \equiv y$.

There are many equivalence relations: *contemporary, colleague,
compatriot, co-religionist, comrade*; that is, *being the same age as,
being in the same institution as, being a citizen of the same country
as, having the same religious affiliation as, being in the same situation as*. Equivalence relations capture the sense of 'being the same
as', 'being similar to', 'being like'. Often there is a special word,
usually constructed from the Latin, *co-, com-*, or *con-*, but we can
make any equivalence relation we want by specifying the respect in
which we are the same: I can ask whether I am the same height
as you, or the same weight as you, although, since these are not
scientifically, socially, morally, or emotionally, important concepts,
we do not have special words to say that I am co-altitudinous, or
componderous, with you.

It follows that we can treat equivalence relations in two ways.
We can treat each one individually, call it R, or S, or T, and say
that R, or S, or T, is a dyadic two-term relation which happens to
be an equivalence relation, *i.e.* it happens to be the case that R,

---

[5] §3.7.

or S, or T, is transitive, symmetric and reflexive, but this is, so to
speak, a one-off property of the particular relation under consideration. Alternatively we can consider the whole family of equivalence
relations, recognising that there are particular members, such as R
and S and T, but concentrating our attention on the family characteristics. In that case, rather than pick on a particular R, S, or
T, we use some generic symbol, such as $=, \sim, \approx, \equiv$. Unfortunately
logicians often forget that $\approx$, or any other sign of equivalence, is
an incomplete symbol, unless we indicate, either contextually or
explicitly, which equivalence relation is under consideration. The
same is true of ' *is the same as* '. If you are asked if you are the
same as me, you do not know how to answer. You say 'Am I the
same *what?*'. Once you are told—'the same age', 'the same height',
'the same sex'—you can answer the question, but if the respect in
which we might be the same is left unspecified, you can only say
'I am the same as him in some respects, and different from him in
others'. We can express this by saying '— is the same as . . .' is not,
as it seems, a dyadic, two-term relation, but a triadic, three-term
one: '— is the same as . . . in respect of - - -'. Similarly, when we
formalise, we should not say simply

$$x \approx y$$

but

$$x \approx_r y$$

where the subscript $_r$ indicates the respect in which x and y are
said to be equivalent. We use a lower-case letter to indicate that
it is referring to a respect, and not directly to a relation. That is
to say,

$$x \approx_r y$$

is to mean the same as

$$x R y$$

where R is an equivalence relation; and although it might be tempting to write the former

$$x \approx_R y,$$

to do so would slur over the distinction between relations and respects. If R stands for the particular equivalence relation '— is
contemporary with . . .' then r stands for 'age': if I am contemporary with you, I am the same age as you; but 'age' is of a different
logical type from 'contemporary with'.

The fact that equivalence relations are triadic seems obvious enough, but we often overlook it, and then are easily misled. If the question is asked whether I am the same height as you, it is not enough to consider you and me and whether we are the same or not: the question is whether we are the same *height*, and not whether we are the same weight, same age, or same nationality. Once the respect is specified, we have a particular equivalence relation which is dyadic, transitive and symmetrical, and can be handled quite easily. But if it is not specified, confusion abounds. In political discourse egalitarians often argue that since all men are equal in some respects—we all are men, we all are mortal, death is the great equaliser—they are equal without qualification, and so ought to be treated the same in every respect, and be given the same income, the same education, the same opportunities, the same everything. If we always specify respects, such fallacies can be avoided. The facts that we are all men, all mortal, all sentient beings, all rational agents, are relevant facts, and are grounds for serious political argument, but the argument as normally stated or implied is invalid because it assumes what is really a triadic, three-term relation to be merely a dyadic, two-term one. Arguments are needed (which sometimes can be given) why sameness in one respect is evidence, or a ground, for sameness in some other respect. The only general thesis in politics we can properly propound is that any two people are the same in some respects, different in others.

Mathematicians are more careful. But it is useful even for them to distinguish different sorts, and even different degrees, of sameness. On the whole we distinguish being the same as from being similar to by using the latter where the points of resemblance are few and the former where they are many. Similar triangles have their angles the same but not their sides. If their sides also are the same, and their orientation too, we use a stronger word, in this case 'congruent', with the slightly weaker 'counterpart' for two triangles with their angles the same and the lengths of their sides the same but of opposite parity, that is with one being the mirror image of the other. The extreme case of being the same in all respects, is identity. But although we can be happy to say that *a* is identical with a, we have difficulty as soon as we use different names for one and the same thing, for someone might then know one of them but not the other, and not know, for example, that Tully was identical with Cicero; in which case there would be some property of Tully—*e.g.* being known as the author of Tully's *Offices*—not

possessed by Cicero. Clearly something has gone wrong, and we
exclude such "referentially opaque" properties. But it is difficult
to draw the line, and often we say that a is identical with b, in
the weaker sense of qualitative identity rather than strict numerical identity. We need, therefore, to be careful in saying that a is
the same as b in *all* respects, for there is considerable unclarity as
to what exactly constitutes a respect, and therefore how far 'all
respects' extends. For the present it is enough to require that the
respects be specified, and to note that for the most part 'being similar to' implies that there are fewer respects in which resemblance
is claimed than 'being the same as'.

Further snares lie ahead. Perhaps I went to the same school as
you, and you went to the same school as Peter: it does not follow
that I went to the same school as Peter. You went to different
schools, an early nursery school where you romped with me, and
a big proper school where you got to know Peter and other people
who would be useful to you in later life. Schools are not like weight
or height. Mathematical physicists sometimes are confused because
they think that simultaneity is like being the same weight as, instead of seeing that being simultaneous in one frame of reference is
like possessing characteristics shared with fellow-Wykehamists, and
being simultaneous in another frame of reference is like possessing
characteristics shared with fellow-Etonians. 'At the same school
as', or 'at the same time as', denotes not one but a whole family of
equivalence relations, each picking out a different equivalence class
manifesting different common characteristics.[6]

There are many, many possible equivalence relations. At one
extreme we have identity (normally written $=$, though we could
express it as $\approx_i$) which each individual bears to itself alone. At the
other we have the universal relation, which each individual bears

---

[6] For fallacious arguments involving the concept of simultaneity in the Spe-
cial Theory, see H.Putnam, "Time and Physical Geometry", *Journal of
Philosophy*, **64**, 1967, pp. 240-247; reprinted in H.Putnam, *Mathematics,
Matter and Method. Philosophical Papers*, I, Cambridge, 1979, pp.198-205;
C.W.Rietdijk, "A Rigorous Proof of Determinism Derived from the Spe-
cial Theory of Relativity", *Philosophy of Science*, **33**, 1966, 341-344, and
"Special Relativity and Determinism", *Philosophy of Science*, **43**, 1976,
pp. 598-609; John W. Lango, "The Logic of Simultaneity", *Journal of
Philosophy*, **66**, 1969, pp.340-350. See further fn.38 in §9.8 below

to every other. We can use a quality, expressed by a monadic predicate, to generate an equivalence relation. If $Q(x)$ and $Q(y)$, then we can say $x \approx_q y$, that is, that x and y resemble each other in both possessing the property Q.[7] Normally we use a determinable, sex, colour, shape, and say that I am the same sex as you, rather than that I am the same as you in that I am male, but that locution is possible, and is sometimes insisted on. Indeed, given any class of individuals, each of which possesses some property in common, we can define a corresponding equivalence relation. This, in effect, is what is done when it is argued that all men are equal because they all are men. They are all equal to one another *in respect of* humanity. Given any class, say that of prime numbers, we can characterize the members as bearing an equivalence relation, that of "equi-primeness" to one another. We can express this by saying $x \approx_p y$ iff x is prime and y is prime, and there is no objection to our doing so, provided we take care not to drop the subscript p, and assume that since x is equi-prime with y, x is equal to y. In this case there is only one equivalence class. We could, at the cost of considerable artificiality, take several, quite different classes, and provided they were mutually disjoint and jointly exhaustive, construct an equivalence relation which would generate just that partition. In the domain of natural numbers we might partition the composite numbers by reference to their smallest factor—thus having all the even numbers except two, then all the odd numbers divisible by three except three itself, then all the remaining numbers whose least divisor was five, except five itself, and so on. It is an instructive exercise to define the corresponding equivalence relation. Other exercises can be constructed, but soon become tedious.

Given any equivalence relation, $\approx_a$, *being contemporary with* we can (in this case only roughly, with considerable ambiguity over marginal cases) separate a population into "age-groups", that is, people who are all contemporary with one another. These age-groups are equivalence classes. All the members of a particular age-group have something in common—namely their age. Age is just that which all members of a given age-group have in common. It is the common property of each equivalence class. Similarly with

---

[7] P. Simons, *Parts*, Oxford, 1987, ch.9, §9.3, p.335, uses the symbolism $xFFy$ if their common bond is the fact that $Fx \wedge Fy$

weight, height, and a whole range of other abstract entities. Weight depends on balancing. Balancing, if done properly, is a symmetric, and within reasonable limits, a transitive relation. It therefore can separate out equivalence classes of bodies which balance against one another, and each such class is said to be a class of things "having the same weight".

In this way age, or height, or weight, or rational number, can be generally defined. If we have a particular equivalence relation $\approx_r$, then the equivalence relation will divide up any domain, X, of individuals into a "partition", as it is called, of mutually disjoint and jointly exhaustive equivalence classes: $A, B, C, ...,$ etc. So that

if x is a member of A, then y is a member of A iff $x \approx_r y$.

Instead of introducing new letters, $A, B, C, ..,$ etc., we can define the equivalence class of any particular individual, say x, which we write $[x]_r$ and say that y is a member of $[x]_r$ iff $x \approx_r y$. Thus in ordinary speech instead of saying that Bernard is *contemporary with* me, I can say that he is *a contemporary of mine*. Once we have partitioned a domain into equivalence classes, we can distinguish the generic respect from particular specifications of it. If 'is contemporary with' is given by the relation T, then 'being the same age as' will be expressed

$$x \approx_t y$$

and there will be as many distinguishable age-groups when the domain of human beings is partitioned by the relation $\approx_t$ into equivalence classes. So t would be age generally, and particular ages would be indicated by $[x]_t$ where $[x]_t$ and $[y]_t$ refer to the same particular age if $x \approx_t y$, and to different ages if $\neg(x \approx_t y)$.

Each specific equivalence relation generates a set of mutually disjoint and jointly exhaustive equivalence classes, each one of which can be seen as having some property in common, and the whole family of equivalence classes as being particular specifications of some generic respect. We can then consider the set of equivalence classes as a set in its own right, which we can write $\langle X/\approx \rangle$. Such a class is called a "quotient class". When we come to measure physical magnitudes in Chapter Eleven, we shall need to establish some underlying equivalence relations which tell us what things are equal, as regards weight, or duration, or length, or angle, and then form the quotient class, and establish a linear order between different weights, or durations, or lengths, or angles. We shall look at the conditions under which this can be done in §9.8.

9.3 Functions

Functions are normally regarded as definitely mathematical, rather than logical, concepts. But they can be explicated in terms of many-one relations, and thus have logical roots. A function assigns to each value of the "argument" a unique resultant value. Usually both the arguments and the resultant value are numbers, but they do not have to be: truth-functions map truth-values into truth-values.

A function corresponds to a relation between the argument(s) and the resultant value, with the proviso that the resultant must be unique. That is, if xRy and xRz, then $y = z$. There is no similar restriction on the arguments: if xRy and zRy, then it does not follow that $x = z$. Often there is more than one argument: we can easily have a function from the ordered pair $(x; y)$ to some resultant value. The resultant value can also be an ordered pair, but that is less common.

Functions are essentially many-one relations, and many includes one: that is, we consider as functions those relations, where not only if xRy and xRz, then $y = z$, but the other implication, if xRy and zRy, then $x = z$, does also hold. These are one-one, or "bi-unique", functions. They evidently have inverses, since if y bears the relation R to x, x bears the converse relation R^{-1} to y, and is unique in doing so.

Functions are transitive. If x bears a many-one relation R to y, and y bears a many-one relation S to z, then x bears some many-one relation to z, since to each x there is a unique y, and to each y there is a unique z, so that to each x there is a unique z.

Most naturally we think of functions of functions as constituting a discrete relationship,[8] but that does not have to be so, and we can have families of functions, $f_n(x)$, where n is a dense or continuous parameter. The best example is the causal transformation over time t, of a system of particles, where the nth particle has position q_{nx}, q_{ny}, q_{nz}, and momentum p_{nx}, p_{ny}, p_{nz}, and there is a general law of evolution, giving the position and momentum of each after time t, granted that of them all initially. This can be seen as a function of phase space into phase space, but is parametrized continuously rather than discretely.

Functions give rise to "morphisms". The simplest case is Frege's

---

[8] See below, §9.6.

gleichzahlig, 'equinumerous'. In that case we are concerned only with quotity, the question 'How many?', and know that if a one–one function holds between one set and another, the answer must in each case be the same. More generally, we consider not only a set of individuals, X, but various properties, monadic—qualities—and polyadic—relations—that they have. Two "relational structures", $\langle X, Q, R \rangle$ and $\langle X', Q', R' \rangle$, are "isomorphic" if and only if there is some one–one function f from X onto X' such that if $x' = f(x)$, and $y' = f(y)$, then $Q'(x')$ if and only if $Q(x)$, and $R'(x', y')$ if and only if $R(x, y)$. The definition can be generalised to have more than one quality Q, more than one relation R, and further relations which are not merely dyadic, but obtaining between three or more individuals; it is convenient also to include functions separately from relations, so that we consider

$\langle X; Q_1, Q_2, \ldots; R_1, R_2, \ldots; f_1, f_2, \ldots \rangle$ being isomorphic to $\langle X'; Q'_1, Q'_2, \ldots; R'_1, R'_2, \ldots; f'_1, f'_2, \ldots \rangle$. The underlying idea is that the one–one function not only correlates individuals, but maps features, so that if any two individuals share a feature, or stand in some particular relation to each other, then their opposite numbers will also share some corresponding feature, or stand in some corresponding relation to each other.

Besides isomorphisms, we can consider the particular case where the function is from a set onto itself: this is called an automorphism. We also consider, the more general case, with many–one, instead of one–one, functions. Such functions do not have inverses, and the morphisms they give rise to are called homomorphisms instead of isomorphisms. The definition of a homomorphism is like that of an isomorphism, except that the 'if and only if' is weakened to an 'only if'. Two relational structures, $\langle X, Q, R \rangle$ and $\langle X', Q', R' \rangle$, are homomorphic if and only if there is some many–one function f from X onto X' such that if $x' = f(x)$, and $y' = f(y)$, then $Q(x)$ only if $Q'(x')$, and $R(x, y)$ only if $R'(x', y')$.

Every relational structure is isomorphic with itself, but typically morphisms hold between relational structures that are not identical, and then the question arises as to what the interrelation between function and sameness is: what functions preserve what samenesses, and *vice versa*? We can see relational structures as the natural generalisation of sets, and isomorphisms as the generalisation of cardinal number. Morphisms pick out deep similarities between relational structures, and these can be regarded as the underlying object of mathematical concern.

Category theory adopts this very abstract approach, dealing
with very general features, and very general classes of functions
and transformations.[9] On this approach the fundamental objects
of mathematical interest are structures, rather than objects. Similarity of structure is often elusive and difficult to pin down—like
covariance rather than simple invariance: category theory encour-
ages us to view mathematics not as about abstract entities, but as
revealing the interconnectedness of things. "Category theory is like
a language in which the 'verbs' are on an equal footing with the
'nouns'."[10] In modern times we can see Dedekind, with his ordinal
characterization of the natural numbers, as a precursor;[11] though
the thought that mathematics is a science of structures goes back
to Plato, with his study of παραδείγματα (*paradeigmata*), ideal
patterns.[12]

9.4 Identity in Difference

The search for underlying samenesses raises problems. Equivalence
relations generate equivalence classes all of whose members are, in
the relevant respect, the same, and thus seem to obliterate individuality. We therefore need to retain identity, and consider the
interplay of *two* equivalence relations, combining a general $\approx_r$ with
the identity $=$. We may, for example, think of the ways in which a
regular shape, say an ice crystal or hexagon, can be moved, rotated,
or reflected so as to look exactly the same.

Figure 9.4.1 The figure on the left looks the same as the figure
on the right

---

[9] For a brief account, see J.L.Bell, "Categories, Toposes and Sets", *Synthese*,
51, 1982, pp. 293-337; or, even briefer, his *Toposes and Local Set Theories*,
Oxford, 1988, ch.8, Epilogue, pp. 235ff.

[10] J.L.Bell, *Toposes and Local Set Theories*, Oxford, 1988, p.236

[11] See above, ch.5, esp. §5.2.

[12] See further below, §14.3, §15.6.

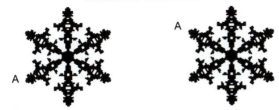

Figure 9.4.2 The figure on the left is not identically the same
as the figure on the right

Thus the figure on the left in Figure 9.4.1 above looks the same
as the figure on the right and under the relation $\approx_l$ would be placed
in the same l-equivalence (looks-equivalence) class. But if we also
have the relation of identity, and can identify the individual elements of the structure, we may distinguish them. This iswhy, in
giving our account of geometries in Chapter Two, it was not enough
to characterize them in terms of the Euclidean or some other group
(§2.7), or define them only implicitly by a set of axioms (§2.3), but
needed also to give some independent characterization of points
and lines (§2.5).

In this way we are preserving individual identity in the l-
equivalence class, and can distinguish between different members
that are l-equivalent. In the theory of groups, the operators of any
group always combine to form another operation of that group; this
ensures that taken as a whole they are transitive: to every operator
there is an inverse; this ensures that they are symmetric: and, in
consequence, there is always an identity operator in the group; this
secures reflexivity. Any set of functions, transformations, operations, or mappings, which is such that

1. any two can be compounded to form a third,
2. the associative law holds,
3. there is an identity,
4. to each one there is an inverse,

is called a "group". We can thus view the theory of groups as
being a natural elaboration of our theory of equivalence relations,
in which we have both a general equivalence relation and the most
exclusive one of identity. A Hegelian would describe it as a development of the theme of identity in difference. A physicist would say
it was giving the "fine-structure" of an equivalence relation. The
equivalence relation expresses what is common to all those things
that can be transformed into one another by transformations of the
group: and each transformation of the group characterizes what is

peculiar to the relation of one thing to some particular other thing. Thus the theory of groups should be seen as grounded in the logic of sameness and difference rather than in that of the quotifiers. Of course group theorists use numbers, and have special theorems about groups with a prime number of elements, and the sub-groups of groups with a divisible number of elements, and classify infinite groups separately from finite ones. But their chief concern is with distinguishable differences within some over-arching similarities. Plato might have portrayed the theory of groups as the progeny of the Form of the Like and Form of the Unlike.

Difference is more difficult than sameness. *Being different from* is a symmetric relation, like being the same as, but is non-transitive and irreflexive. As with equivalence relations, we can consider either particular difference relations, which are dyadic, two-term, or a general difference relation $\neq$, which is a triadic, three-term relation, and needs to have the respect in which the difference obtains specified, $\neq_r$ *etc.* But because they are non-transitive, difference relations are more difficult to treat generally than equivalence relations, and we concentrate on a subclass of them, those that are in fact transitive, that is to say, the ordering relations, to which we now turn.

9.5 Ordering Relations

Ordering relations are, like equivalence relations, fundamental. Dedekind used a special type of discrete ordering relation in his ordinal characterization of the natural numbers, and the magnitudes we measure are inherently ordered. The concepts of *finite* and *infinite*, as we saw,[13] and of *limit* and *boundary*, as we shall see, are to be elucidated in terms of some ordering relation, and so too are the neighbourhoods that form the basis of topology.[14]

Ordering relations are, like equivalence relations, transitive, but asymmetric and irreflexive, instead of symmetric and reflexive. All English phrases ' —er than', express relations that are irreflexive, and, with one exception, asymmetric and transitive. [The one exception is 'other than', which shows that the fundamental force of 'than' is irreflexive; so too the use of 'than' with 'else', and the Americans' urge to say 'different than'; the Greek $\mathring{\eta}$ (e) is the

---

[13] §7.3.

[14] In ch.10.

same, being used both after comparatives and after ἄλλος (*allos*).]
The transitive asymmetric irreflexive relations expressed in the —
er form are the standard, though not the only, way of expressing
ordering relations. Either of the latter conditions implies the other.
That is, an ordering relation may be defined as one that is transitive and irreflexive, and therefore asymmetric, or preferably, since
more systematically, as one that is transitive and asymmetric, and
hence irreflexive; more formally,
a relation R is an *ordering relation* iff
1. If xRy and yRz then xRz, and
2. if xRy then $\neg yRx$.
It follows, in any domain in which an ordering relation holds at all,
that it is irreflexive; that is
3. $\neg xRx$.
An ordering relation is often written $<$, or $>$, and read 'less than',
or 'greater than'.[15]

     Ordering relations are, like equivalence relations, triadic, and
we need to specify, either implicitly in the context or explicitly by
a subscript, the respect in which something is greater than or less
than another—am I greater than you in weight, in height, or in
age? So we should write

$$>_w, >_h, >_t, <_w, <_h, <_t, \ldots etc.$$

Fortunately, however, we are better protected by linguistic usage
from overlooking the respect in which things are ordered than the
respect in which things are the same: fewer confusions arise, and
so we shall be readier to drop the subscript. Where we need to

---

[15]   E.V.Huntington, "A Set of Postulates for Real Algebra, Comprising Postulates for a One-Dimensional Continuum and for the Theory of Groups",
Transactions of the American Mathematical Society, **6**, 1905, p.18, n.,
points out that *greater than*, and *less than* have connotations of quantity which are inappropriate here, and suggests that *below* and *above*, or
before and *after*, are preferable. The point is well taken, though the spatial
and temporal connotations of *below* and *before* can also mislead: *precedes*,]
symbolized by $\prec$, is perhaps the least loaded term. In this section we shall
continue to use the familiar $<$, but hereafter, as we come to need the distinction between metrical and purely ordering concepts, we shall tend to
use $\prec$.

distinguish only a few ordering relations, besides $\prec$, we can use $\ll$, $\prec\!\!\prec$, or $\subset$, to supplement $<$.

The converse of an ordering relation, unlike that of an equivalence relation, is a different relation. It is usually expressed by $>$, $\succ$, $\gg$, $\succ\!\!\succ$, or $\supset$. For the sake of uniformity, we mostly use the *less than* form. The converse of an ordering relation is necessarily not the same as the ordering relation itself, but it is often very similar, and has the "mirror image property",[16] whereby general features of $<$ are also features of $>$.

Although grammatically the comparative is formed from the positive, the logical dependence is the other way about. The positive adjectives, such as 'great', 'big', 'large', 'tall', 'old', 'fast', 'small', 'little', 'short', 'young' and 'slow', are the simplest, and the comparatives, 'greater', 'bigger' *etc.*, are formed from them. Logically, however, the comparative is the basic form, and both the positive and the superlative are formed from the comparative.

Plato, when he first put forward the theory of forms, thought that every adjective denoted some abstract universal. 'White' denoted the colour white, 'square' denoted the square shape, and similarly 'great' denoted the property of greatness, 'big' of bigness, 'little' of littleness. But then there was a paradox. Simmias was big in comparison with Socrates, little in comparison with Phaedo: my fourth finger is big in comparison with my little finger, little in comparison with my middle finger: a very beautiful ape would be hideous as a human. Plato at first thought these puzzles showed the unreliability of the senses, which could easily be bamboozled into seeing inconsistent properties present in the same thing at the same time: but later realised his mistake, and that the puzzles were puerile, and evaporated once we recognised that the positives were back-formations from the logically more primitive comparatives. Words like 'great', 'big' and 'little' do not denote qualities or ascribe properties in the way that words like 'white' or 'square' do. To say that the middle finger is big is to say that it is *bigger than* most of the others: to say that Socrates is short is to say that he is shorter than most men. Only if the range of comparison is explicitly stated or evident from the context do we know what is meant by saying Socrates is short. He is short *for* a man, but not short

---

[16] I take this term from C.L.Hamblin, cited by A.N.Prior, *Past, Present and Future*, Oxford, 1967, p.35.

for a boy: indeed he is taller than most boys. How much shorter than the average man or taller than the average boy someone needs to be in order to be short or tall is not clear. A man who was only very slightly shorter than the mean, or median, man in his group of comparison, would not be accounted short or tall. Statisticians might reckon that an individual needs to be more than one standard deviation beyond the mean to be accounted short or tall. But this is to impute more precision than ordinary men normally will admit.

Superlatives are relevant to ordering relations, and, more obviously than positives, derive from the comparative. The first, the last, the greatest, the least, the most, and in particular the next, play a crucial role in distinguishing the various global and local structures that different sorts of ordering have.

9.6 Macrostructure and Microstructure

Orderings may be classified by reference to their global, or their local, structure. As regards their global, macro-, structure, they may be characterized first as either linear or partial. They may also be characterized as either having extremal elements or as being serial. And the local, or micro-, structure of some orderings is discrete, while others are dense, some being not merely dense but continuous. We need furthermore to distinguish the strict orderings generated by the ordering relations properly so called, from the quasi-orderings generated by antisymmetric relations, which are reflexive.

An ordering $\langle X, \prec \rangle$, consisting of the relation $\prec$ on a set X, is linear[17] if the relation is "connected", that is, if the ordering relation always holds between any two distinct elements. Provided x and y are distinct, either $x \prec y$ or $y \prec x$; which is often reformulated as the "law of trichotomy":

$$(Ax)(Ay)((x = y) \vee (x \prec y) \vee (y \prec x)) \text{ holds.}$$

Given any two elements, either the one is higher than the other, or the other than the one, or they are boththe same. Either my

---

[17] The word 'linear' is used in many different, though related, senses by mathematicians. Some readers may prefer to use 'connected' of orderings, in order that they may not be confused with linear transformations.

birthday is before yours, or yours is before mine, or they are both the same.

There are many examples of partial orderings: the relation '— is divisible by . . . ', or in the Special Theory of Relativity the relation of *being after*, or *causal influenceability* as it could more accurately be termed. Partial orderings may be characterized, by an axiom of Robb's:[18]

For every element x, there is another element y such that neither $x > y$ nor $y > x$.

Figure 9.6.1 In the Special Theory of Relativity two events may be neither before nor after each other: A is neither before nor after B, though both A and B are before D and after C.

Robb's axiom, however, requires also that the ordering be non-serial, and secures only "global non-linearity", being satisfied by orderings that are not "locally non-linear".

Figure 9.6.2 If an only child marries a single parent and they then have one child, who in turn has an only child, the order generated by *descendant* is globally non-linear, but with locally linear sub-orderings.

---

[18] A.A.Robb, *The Absolute Relations of Time and Space*, Cambridge, 1921, Postulate V, p.17; or *Geometry of Time and Space*, Cambridge, 1914 and 1936, p.27. It is worthy of note, though not for discussion here, that with the aid of very few other axioms Robb is able to derive the Special Theory of Relativitiy as the instantiation of his "conical order".

We need to strengthen Robb's axiom by requiring that it apply within the range of predecessors of each element.

$$(Ax)(Ay)(Vz)(y \prec x \to z \prec x \land \neg(z = y \lor z \prec y \lor y \prec z))$$

The partial orderings hereafter considered will all be locally non-linear.

Superlatives are relevant to ordering relations in two ways: whether there are extreme elements that are the first or the last, the highest or the lowest, with respect to the order in question, and whether within the ordering there are next elements. In ordinary usage the greatest is the one which is greater than all the others, the biggest the one which is bigger than all the others, the least the one which is less than all the others. On reflection we recognise that sometimes there may not be a single one that outstrips all the others, as when two boys come first-equal in a form order. It is useful to distinguish a strict maximum which alone is greater than everything else from those elements in an ordering that are merely maximal, that is to say that each of them is not exceeded by any other element, even though it does not itself exceed the other maximal elements. In some orderings no element is maximal, and however far we go, there is always another element that is more than the one in question. Such an ordering is called serial: formally, an ordering, $\langle X, \prec \rangle$ is *serial* iff $(Ax)(Vy)(y \prec x)$. It is possible for an ordering to be serial, with no maximum element in one direction, but not in the other. There is no greatest, or last, natural number, but there is a least, or first,[19] one. The integers,

$$\ldots\ldots -6, -5, -4, -3, -2, -1, 0, 1, 2, 3, 4, 5, 6, \ldots\ldots$$

with the order-type $\omega^* + \omega$, have neither a greatest nor a least element, and thus constitute a serial ordering for both $\prec$ and $\succ$.

If every element of an ordering $\langle X, \prec \rangle$ has a next, the ordering is *discrete*; equally, if every element of an ordering has an immediate predecessor. These two conditions are not quite the same: if we consider all the even numbers followed by all the odd numbers, every number has a next number, but 1 has no immediate

---

[19] It is customary, though not mandatory, to confine the terms 'first' and 'last' to linear orderings, and use 'greatest' and 'least' more generally for partial orderings.

predecessor. Ordinals are another, very slightly different, type of discrete ordering; they are a generalisation of Dedekind's progression ω.[20] An ordinal is an ordering $\langle X, \prec \rangle$ in which every (proper or improper) subset has a *first* element, and the elements of such an ordering are said to be **well-ordered** by the ordering relation. Well-ordered sets are easily shown to be linear. They are almost the same as those that always have a next element, but the latter condition is satisfied by the integers, with order-type $\omega^* + \omega$, which is not an ordinal, since it does not have a first member. Well-orderings lack the mirror-image property.[21]

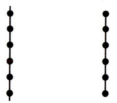

Figure 9.6.3 Hasse diagrams representing discrete linear orderings, with and without extremal elements.

If every element in an ordering $\langle X, \prec \rangle$ is to have no next, then it must always be the case that between every element and its putative next element there is a third, that is,

$$(\mathrm{A}x)(\mathrm{A}y)(x \prec y \rightarrow (\mathrm{V}z)(x \prec z \wedge z \prec y)).$$

Such an ordering is called "dense". An example is the rational numbers, with the order-type η.[22] The classification is not exhaustive. An ordering could be in some parts dense, in others discrete. Nevertheless, all the orders we shall be concerned with are either dense throughout or else altogether discrete.

It is natural to see a discrete ordering as paradigmatically superlative, and a dense one as paradigmatically comparative. The strict superlative is uniquely referring. It picks out one maximum velocity, one tallest man, one least natural number, one first in a

---

[20] §5.2.

[21] See the previous section, §9.5.

[22] E.V.Huntington, *The Continuum and Other Types of Serial Order*, Dover, 1955, ch.IV, §44, p.35.

series, one next, one last. The comparative, by contrast, does not pick out just one (except when there are only two, as in 'the former' and 'the latter'), but could be used of any one of the many that stand in the specified relation to a given one. It gives an order, but nothing more. Given any two things, it may be able to place them in order, but does not of itself say how many there are in between, or whether they are next or near each other. We can say that one thing comes after another in a given order, but not that it succeeds it (in the sense of being its successor, the next after).

The tension between the comparative and discrete ideals of ordering admits a profound resolution: dense orderings may be not just dense, but also **continuous**. Continuous orderings combine, in a manner of speaking, the virtues of both the dense and the discrete. They are dense—between any two elements there is a third, so that there is, in a sense, always more ordering going on—but they have the virtue of a discrete ordering in maintaining some sort of next-ness.

Prima facie this is a contradiction. But as often in mathematics, *prima facie* contradictions are resolved by a shift in meaning.[23] In this case it is the word 'next' that has to change its meaning. Although it is not possible for two *elements*[24] to be next each other— that is tantamount to discreteness—an element can be next to, that is to say, a "limit point of", a *set* of elements, or of a *portion*, or of a *region*, or of an *extension*.

It is a difficult distinction, and one that Hume missed. His arguments against the continuity of time and space are not only epistemological. Besides Zeno's argument against infinite divisibility, he adduces an argument from succession.

> 'Tis a property inseparable from time, and which in a manner constitutes its essence, that each of its parts succeeds another, and that none of them, however contiguous, can ever be co-existent. For the same reason, that the year 1737 cannot concur with the present year 1738, every moment must be distinct from, and posterior or antecedent to another. 'Tis certain then, that time, as it exists, must be compos'd of indivisible moments. For if in time we could never arrive at an end of division, and if each moment, as it

---

[23] See above, §7.3 and §7.10.

[24] Compare Aristotle, *Physics*, Δ, 10, 218ᵃ18.

succeeds another, were not perfectly single and indivisible, there would be an infinite number of co-existent moments, or parts of time; which I believe will be allow'd to be an arrant contradiction.[25]

Three words are crucial: 'succeeds', 'another' and 'contiguous'. The word 'succeeds' could mean a one–one relation—that is, a relation in which to each moment there is exactly one moment that succeeds it, and exactly one moment that it succeeds—or a many–many relation—that is, we could say of every moment in 1738 that it succeeds every moment in 1737. In the former sense it defines a discrete ordering. The successor to any moment is the next after it, and there is no moment after it and before its successor. In the latter sense, however, it is compatible with an ordering's being not discrete but dense. Hume equivocates between the two. At the conclusion of his argument he is taking 'succeeds' as being equivalent to 'posterior' and correlative with 'antecedent'. In that sense it is an arrant contradiction to suppose time to be composed of an infinite number of moments which are neither posterior nor antecedent to one another. But at the start of his argument he is taking 'succeeds' as a one–one relation, like the 'successor' of modern mathematics. Only so will it establish his contention that time is discrete. But there is no warrant for supposing that the moments of time must be successive in that sense. For, the fact that given only two distinct moments of time one must be after the other, it does not follow that one must be next after the other. Hume has smuggled in an assumption of nextness by his double use of 'succeeds'.

The equivocation is made more compelling by a parallel one in the use of 'another', which may mean 'some other' or may mean 'a particular other'. The former sense does not pick out a particular moment as *the* moment that a given moment succeeds. In that sense all that Hume is saying is that for each moment there is at least one (and in fact many) moments which it succeeds. And this is true, and carries with it no suggestion of discreteness. But the use of the singular—'another'—carries with it the implication of uniqueness, that for each moment there is one and only one moment which it succeeds. And this would yield the conclusion

[25] *A Treatise of Human Nature*, Bk I, Part II, Sect II; in Selby-Bigge edn. p.31. Compare Aristotle, *Physics*, E, 1, 231^{b}10 – 18.

that time was discrete.

The word 'contiguous' comes from the Latin *tango*, I touch. Each moment is contiguous to another if it is in contact with it, and touches it. But if it touches it, there cannot be any moment between, or it would separate them. So contiguity as a relation between moments implies discreteness. And contiguity seems called for, else we separate moments (and similarly points in space) into a discontinuum. Some sort of togetherness is called for if we are to characterize the unity of time (and similarly of space), and contiguity seems to express this requirement. And so it does, but not as a relation between moments. Instead of one moment being contiguous to another moment—which must yield discreteness—one moment is contiguous to an interval, and *vice versa*. Every moment is contiguous to those intervals of which it is the limit, or bound, or boundary, and conversely every interval is contiguous to those moments that are its limits or bounds. In this way we can characterize the togetherness of the continuum without reducing it to a discrete "contiguum".

Continuous orderings reconcile the comparative merits of denseness, shown by the rational numbers, where it is always possible to squeeze another in, and we never reach an end of divisibility, with the superlative merits of the natural numbers, which know their neighbours, and have no gaps in their ranks. They achieve this, by changing the focus, and not concentrating on individual elements alone, but considering other, less atomized, entities as well. In our general survey of orderings, we shall need to be directed by comparable guidelines, though first considering the paradigm, the continuum of the real line, defined ultimately in terms of the real numbers.

9.7　The Continuum

Eudoxus almost succeeded in giving a satisfactory account of the continuum, but it was not until Dedekind and Cantor that a really rigorous treatment was finally achieved. Dedekind's account turned on the least upper bound of certain sets of rational numbers: Cantor's on nested intervals of rational numbers converging to a limit.

Dedekind considered the rational numbers in their natural order, and particular partitions of them into "Dedekind cuts". A Dedekind cut was a partition of the rational numbers in which

every member of the left-hand set was less than any member of
the right-hand set. A real number was defined as a Dedekind cut
of rational numbers. Since the rational numbers are dense, there
could not be both a greatest member of the right-hand set and a
least member of the left-hand set, for then there would be some
number between them, which would not be a member of either, so
that they would not together constitute a partition after all. The
three remaining possibilities are that the left-hand set should have
a greatest member, or that the right-hand set should have a least
member, or that neither the left-hand set should have a greatest
member, nor the right-hand set should have a least member. In
either of the two former cases, the Dedekind cut would correspond
to a rational number; that is, it would define a rational real number:
and in the last case would constitute a specification of an irrational
real number. Thus if we define a Dedekind cut by saying that every
rational number whose square is less than 2 is to belong to the left-
hand set, and every rational number whose square is greater than,
or equal to, 2 is to belong to the right-hand set, there will be no
rational number that is the greatest of the left-hand set, or the
least of the right-hand set, and we can *identify* the Dedekind cut
as the irrational real number $\sqrt{2}$.

In a very similar spirit Cantor defined a real number as the
limit of a sequence of nested intervals of rational numbers. Cantor's approach is closer to our normal way of representing irrational
numbers by an infinite decimal. Essentially, instead of depending
on a least upper bound, it invokes a limiting lower bound that is,
once again, of a different ontological type from the members of the
sequence, according to our normal reckoning, but is identified with
that sequence for the purpose of definition. In either case, real
numbers are defined as special classes of rational numbers, themselves equivalence classes of positive rationals, which in turn are
equivalence classes of natural numbers. Real numbers can thus
be grounded in the natural numbers, which, the Logicists hoped,
could be completely defined in terms of formal logic alone.

The arithmetization of analysis has been enormously successful. It has enabled mathematicians to free analysis from all spatial
and temporal intuition, to give a coherent account of the continuum, and to handle, with rigour and precision, the difficult notions
of *continuity, function of a real variable, differentiation* and *integration,* and to avoid the confusions and inconsistencies into which
philosophers had previously fallen. But for all its virtues, the arith-

metical approach secures rigour at the cost of obscuring other conceptual features. The continuum is explicated in terms of the real numbers, themselves complicated constructs involving the algebra of the natural numbers. But the continuum is not in itself an arithmetical or algebraic concept—witness the fact that it has been thought about most commonly in relation to time, where the senses of order and connectedness are paramount, and that of number remote, if not altogether absent. In order to reveal the conceptual links between the foundations of mathematics and logical concepts other than the quotifiers, we need to carry through, with no disrespect to Cantor and Dedekind, a counter-programme of the De-arithmetization of Analysis, in which we seek a more austere approach, without reference to numbers, rational or real.

Alternative approaches abound. We can use fields. For, as Birkoff and MacLane put it,[26] "There is one and (except for isomorphic fields) only one complete ordered field", which is, indeed, isomorphic with the real numbers without being so by definition. But a field has a lot of structure. It has two operators, addition and multiplication, each with its own identity element, zero or unity, and hence is implicitly committed to numerical concepts; our intuitive notions of togetherness and separation seem more primitive and non-numerical.

We can, up to a point, give accounts in terms of ordering relations alone.[27] Root works with points and a single triadic relation *a is between b and c*.[28] With a dense ordering we can abstract from

[26] G.Birkoff and S.MacLane, *A Survey of Modern Algebra*, New York, ch.IV, §5, Theorem 7, p.99. See also L.Fuchs, *Partially Ordered Algebraic Systems*, Pergamon, 1963, ch.VIII, §6, pp.139-140; Claude Burrill, *Foundations of Real Numbers*, New York, 1967, ch.7, p.108, Th.7.

[27] E.V.Huntington, *The Continuum and Other Types of Serial Order*, Cambridge, Mass., 1917; pbk, New York, 1955, ch.V, §54-§65, pp.44-57; and E.V.Huntington, "A Set of Postulates for Real Algebra, Comprising Postulates for a One-Dimensional Continuum and for the Theory of Groups", *Transactions of the American Mathematical Society*, 6, 1905, pp.18-22; and O.Veblen, "Definition in Terms of Order Alone in the Linear Continuum and in Well-ordered Sets", *Transactions of the American Mathematical Society*, 6, 1905, pp.165ff.

[28] R.E.Root, "Limits in Terms of Order", *Transactions of the American Mathematical Society*, 15, 1914, pp.51-71.

Dedekind cuts and lay down a Lowest Upper Bound property. If every linearly ordered dense set has a least upper bound, then the ordering will be not merely dense but continuous. Prior cites from Cocchiarella a postulate that secures that a dense temporal order be continuous:[29]

$$CGp\,CHGCGpPGpHGp$$

or more familiarly

$$(Gp \to (HG(Gp \to PGp) \to HGp)),$$

where G means 'it always will be the case that ... ' H means 'it always has been the case that ... ' P means 'it sometime was the case that ... '.[30] The key is the back step from Gp to PGp; if any situation which is always going to obtain must have been going to do so at some earlier time, then in continuous time it must always have held good, though not necessarily in a merely dense temporal ordering. Thus in a merely dense temporal ordering a situation might obtain for all instants after $\sqrt{2}$, and at each of those instants Gp would be the case, and it would be true also that PGp, without its having to be the case that p or Gp at any instant before $\sqrt{2}$. But if $\sqrt{2}$ is admitted as a temporal instant, then since p obtains *ex hypothesi* at all later instants, Gp holds at $\sqrt{2}$ and hence PGp at earlier instants. A merely dense ordering has gaps, such as $\sqrt{2}$, which prevent the start of a situation's obtaining being shunted ever further back to extend over all time. A continuous ordering, like a discrete ordering, is "gapless". The Lowest Upper Bound characterization of continuity combines the superlative merit of discrete orderings with the comparative merit of dense ones by picking on the unique limit which is greater than all the (infinitely) many members of a set, and which, therefore, can be said to be next-them-all, though not next any one of them.

---

[29] A.N.Prior, *Past, Present and Future*, Oxford, 1967, p.72. See also §13.4 below.

[30] Tense logic can be seen as a special case of modal logic, in which the Browerian axiom does not hold (nor axiom T), and we can therefore distinguish between the modal operators and their inverses. Cocchiarella's Continuity Postulate then becomes $(\Box p \to (\Box^{-1}\Box(\Box p \to \diamond^{-1}\Box p) \to \Box^{-1}\Box p))$.

The account of the continuum given thus far is entirely non-numerical. But a further condition is needed to secure gapless linearity, the property of being "Archimedean", which is most easily understood by contrast with orderings that are non-Archimedean. The points on the square, ordered by putting those with a lower x-coordinate before those with a larger one, and when the x-coordinates were the same, by putting those with a lower y-coordinate before those with a larger one is a non-Archimedean ordering. Although we normally take it as indisputable that time is ordered Archimedeanly, some mystics and writers of fiction have envisaged a non-Archimedean time, in which aeons of understanding or experience are "injected" into a single instant of our ordinary time.[31] Archimedes distinguished such non-Archimedean orderings from ordinary linear ones by means of a metrical criterion. Excluding non-Archimedean orderings without benefit of measurements is difficult. Huntington cites a postulate of linearity for the bounded real numbers originally due to Cantor.

The class K contains a denumerable subclass R in such a way that between any two elements of the given class K there is an element of R.[32]

This condition is easily seen to be satisfied by the real line, since the rational numbers furnish a sufficient separation of the real numbers, while being, somewhat surpisingly, denumerable; but it is too arithmetical to be entirely satisfactory; in the absence of a more abstract and intuitive characterization, the de-arithmetization of analysis remains incomplete.

9.8　The Marriage of Equivalence with Order

We often have to consider ordering and equivalence relations in the same logical breath. Indeed, it is only when we could intelligibly speak of something's being greater or less than another, that we may properly speak of their being equal.

---

[31]　See more fully, J.R.Lucas, *A Treatise on Time and Space*, London, 1973, §7, esp. pp.38-40.

[32]　E.V.Huntington, *The Continuum and other types of serial order*, Cambridge, Mass., 1917; pbk, New York, 1955, ch.5, §54, p.44; O.Veblen, *Transactions of the American Mathematical Society*, **6**, 1905, pp.165-171.

In developing a theory of measurement, we characteristically use arguments of the form x balances against y, y is heavier than z, so x is heavier than z. We take *balancing against* to be an equivalence relation, and assume that it must be compatible with *being heavier than*, writing the one as $x \approx_w y$, and the other as $y >_w z$. But this is not in all cases so: proper set inclusion, we have already seen,[33] is not compatible with equinumerosity, and $\subset$ has seemed insignificant and has given way to $\subseteq$ in transfinite set theory. *Per contra*, if we are to retain some sense of *being less than* among equinumerous infinites, so that we shall be able to say that one is a proper part of the other, we must, as Gregory of Rimini observed,[34] distinguish a different sense of *being less than*, in which a part is, indeed, less than that of which it is a part; and this in turn will determine what sort of equivalence relations are compatible with it.[35] We need to think explicitly about the conditions under which the ordering and the equivalence relation involved are compatible with each other.

Equivalence relations can be based on order, just as they can on qualities, represented by one-place predicates.[36] In general, x and y are R-equivalent iff everything that stands in the relation R to x stands in the relation R to y, and *vice versa*. If R is an ordering relation, $<$, we can express it formally,

$$x \approx_< y \quad \text{iff} \quad (\mathrm{A}z)((z < x) \leftrightarrow (z < y)).$$

This is evidently a symmetric relation, and easily shown to be transitive. The equivalence relation defined by $<$ is not necessarily the same as that defined by $>$. I have the same descendants as my wife, the same ancestors as my brother and sisters. Evidently then $\approx_<$ is not the same as $\approx_>$ (which could also be written $\approx^<$). But, although the equivalence relation generated by a relation is not necessarily the same as that generated by its converse, very often it is, and we need the two to be the same if the equivalence

[33] §7.2.

[34] Gregory of Rimini, *Comm. Sent*, Lib 1, dist 42-44.Q.4:f.173^v; cited and translated in Norman Kretzmann, Anthony Kenny, Jan Pinborg, eds., *Cambridge History of Later Medieval Philosophy*, p.572.

[35] See further below, §11.3 and §11.4.

[36] See above, §9.2.

relation is to be generally compatible with the ordering relation. Granted that

$$x \approx y \;\; \text{iff} \;\; (Az)((z < x) \leftrightarrow (z < y)) \;\; \text{iff} \;\; (Az)((z > x) \leftrightarrow (z > y)),$$

it is straightforward to show that

$$x \approx y \;\wedge\; y < z \to x < z$$

and

$$y < x \;\wedge\; x \approx y \to y < z.$$

The equivalence relation generated from an ordering relation is not the only compatible one. The identity relation, $=$, is always compatible with any ordering relation. It represents the limiting case, when the equivalence relation generated by an ordering relation is the most stringent possible; evidently it will be the same for both the relation and its converse, and fully compatible with both. Often there are other compatible equivalence relations: they play an important role in the theory of measurement, which we shall discuss in Chapter Eleven.

Granted a compatible equivalence relation, we can operate with a modified law of trichotomy. If I am neither older nor younger than you, it follows that I am the same age, but not that I am identically the same person. With age and height and weight and many other magnitudes, we do not have the strict law of trichotomy[37]

$$(Ax)(Ay)((x = y) \vee (x \prec y) \vee (x \succ y)),$$

but the modified one,

$$(Ax)(Ay)((x \approx y) \vee (x \prec y) \vee (x \succ y)).$$

The modified law of trichotomy does not always obtain, and errors arise from assuming that it does. It is illuminating to take an example from social life, because our emotions are involved, and we see therefore in sharper relief how they are perceived. Many people are class-conscious, and classes are equivalence classes between which there is some ordering relation. At first we are inclined to think that the ordering relation is linear, that of any two people

---

[37] See above, §9.6.

one must be superior to the other unless they are both of the same class. But are you the social superior, the social equal, or the social inferior of an American Congressman? Both you and he are the social inferior of the Queen, and the social superior of a taxi-driver at London Airport. But you would hesitate to claim or concede social superiority, and yet would also hesitate to admit him as social equal because social equals have something in common, and you have nothing in common with him. We are torn. One definition of equality is based on order and negative—not being either superior or inferior—the other is in terms of some positive feature shared by all who are equal. Some egalitarians are moved negatively, by a dislike of anyone's being better than anybody else, others are inspired positively by a sense of having much in common with others. A very similar confusion occurs in the Special Theory of Relativity. Instead of shifting from simultaneity in one frame of reference to simultaneity in another, a new concept of topological simultaneity is defined: two events which are neither before nor after one another—neither is in the light-cone of the other—are said to be "topologically simultaneous", and from this definition and the assumption that topological simultaneity is an equivalence relation, it is easy to derive bizarre conclusions about time, necessity and free will.[38]

Where the modified law of trichotomy does obtain, we can reduce it to the strict one by "factoring out" the equivalence relation $\approx$ and the equivalence classes it generates to form a quotient class.[39] Clearly, if two members of the original set $\langle X \rangle$ are ordered by the relation $<_t$, their respective equivalence classes, $[x]_t \ldots$, will

---

[38] See references in §9.2, above, fn.6. Similar fallacies have been based on a concept of ET-simultaneity; see E.Stump and N.Kretzmann, "Eternity", *Journal of Philosophy*, **78**, 1981, pp.428-458; reprinted in T.V.Morris, ed., *The Concept of God*, Oxford, 1987, pp.219-252. For further discussion, see Howard Stein, "On Einstein-Minkowski space-time", *Journal of Philosophy*, **65**, 1968, pp.5-23; and "A note on time and Relativity Theory", *Journal of Philosophy*, **67**, 1970, pp.289-294; see also R.Sorabji, *Necessity, Cause and Blame*, London, 1980, pp.114-119; R.Torretti, *Relativity and Geometry*, Oxford, 1983, §7.3, pp.75-89; and J.R.Lucas and P.E.Hodgson, *Spacetime and Electromagnetism*, Oxford, 1990, §2.9, pp.65-67. See also below, §11.3.

[39] See above, §9.2.

be ordered in a similar way by $>_t$ (with a bold subscript t to indicate that the relation, holding in a different domain, is formally a different relation). Formally,

$$[x]_t <_t [z]_t \text{ iff } x <_t z.$$

What we have done is to alter the domain of our relation from that of people, $\langle X \rangle$, to that of age-groups, the abstract entity common to all those who are the same age as one another, which we should then express as $\langle X/ \approx_t \rangle$. People cannot be strictly ordered by age, because I may, besides being either older or younger than you, be the same age: ages, by contrast, are strictly ordered; the time of my birth was either earlier or later than the time of your birth, or else exactly the same time. In this way, then, the modified law of trichotomy can be reduced to a strict one. Where the quotient class obtained by factoring out the compatible equivalence relation is itself a linear ordering, the modified law of trichotomy holds, and no confusion will result from defining the equivalence relation negatively. It is very obvious; so obvious, indeed, that we can slip into confusion as we slide from the quasi-linear ordering of weighty material objects to the genuinely linear ordering of weights.

9.9 Converse Transitivity

In the previous section an equivalence relation was defined in terms of a strict ordering relation. This suggests a comparable definition of a further quasi-ordering relation again in terms of a strict ordering relation. We can generate from one ordering relation $<$ a further quasi-ordering relation $\overset{<}{\sim}_\prec$:

$$x \overset{<}{\sim}_\prec y \text{ iff } (Az)(z \prec x \rightarrow z \prec y).$$

The new relation $\overset{<}{\sim}_\prec$ cannot be precisely the same as the relation $<$ which generated it, since $\overset{<}{\sim}_\prec$ is antisymmetric, while $\prec$ is asymmetric, but we can compare it with $\overset{<}{\sim}$, and in some cases, it will indeed be the case that

$$(x \overset{<}{\sim}_\prec y) \leftrightarrow (x \overset{<}{\sim} y),$$

that is,

$$x \overset{<}{\sim} y \text{ iff } (Az)(z \prec x \rightarrow z \prec y).$$

This condition parallels the ordinary transitivity condition

$$(x \prec y) \wedge (z \prec x) \rightarrow (z \prec y);$$

we might call it "converse transitivity", and in this case, "converse transitivity from below",[40]. to distinguish it from the comparable condition

$$x \overset{\succ}{\sim} y \text{ iff } (\mathrm{A}z)(z \succ x \rightarrow z \succ y),$$

which we might call "converse transitivity from above". Converse transitivity from below and converse transitivity from above are not necessarily the same, as the spouse/sibling example shows,[41] and it is possible to construct other examples in which one or the other or both conditions do not hold.

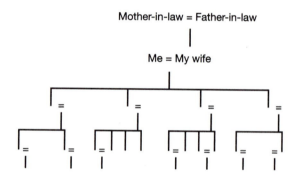

Figure 9.9.1 If I am strictly monogamous, all my descendants are descendants of my father-in-law, but I am not descended from him.

Nevertheless, there is a certain naturalness about them. Although ordering relations are asymmetric, they often have the mirror-image property, so that everything true of $\prec$ is, *mutatis mutandis*, true of $\succ$. In that case, $\approx_{\prec}$ is the same as $\approx_{\succ}$, and then converse transitivity from below and above must also hold. For paradigmatic orderings, therefore, we stipulate that they generate

---

[40] P. Simons, *Parts*, Oxford, 1987, ch.1, §1.4, p.28, calls this the *Proper Parts Principle*

[41] See above, §9.8.

a single equivalence relation, which is factored down to identity, and they are conversely transitive.

If our concern is with the ordering, it is natural to factor out any compatible equivalence relations, and consider just the order of the quotient class of the equivalence classes. We can then classify them with regard to their macro- and micro-structure, according to whether they are upper- or lower- directed, or both, and whether they have most, least, and next, elements. Two paradigm orderings emerge: one is upper- and lower- directed, and has most, least, and next, elements; it is exemplified by the lattice generated by the proper set inclusion relation, $\subset$, of set theory. the other is only upper directed, and is serial and dense; it is exemplified by the tree generated by the *proper part of*, $\prec$, relation of mereology.

9.10   Paradigm Partial Orderings

Partial orderings can be divided into further types, according as to whether any two elements have some third element higher than (or preceded by) both or some fourth element lower than (or that precedes) both. In the former case it is said to be "upper-directed": in the latter case it is said to be "lower-directed". If both conditions hold, the ordering is said to be *directed*, or to possess the "Moore-Smith property".[42]

Figure 9.10.1 Hasse diagram representing a directed ordering (one possessing the "Moore-Smith property").

If the ordering is directed and not serial, and has both a maximum and a minimum element, it is a **lattice**.

---

[42] L. Fuchs, *Partially Ordered Algebraic Systems*, Pergamon, Oxford, 1962, pp.1ff.

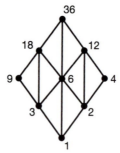

Figure 9.10.2 A lattice—the factors of 36

If it is only one-way directed—if there is just either always an element higher than (preceded by) any given two elements, or always one lower than (that precedes) each of them, but not always both—then the ordering is a tree.

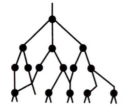 

Figure 9.10.3 Directed Orderings and Trees. Note that the definition given does not exclude branches subsequently reuniting, as occasionally happens with lime trees, illustrated in the right-hand figure.

A tree may have a maximum and minimal (or a minimum and maximal) elements, but need not; and similarly, it may be dense (and even continuous), but may also be discrete. It may be that two elements may be neither the one higher than the other nor both lower than some third element nor both higher than some fourth one, although either or both of these conditions may hold for other pairs. We might call such an ordering a "thicket".

It is illuminating to consider paradigm partial orderings, taking into account the distinction between directed and non-directed orderings, in addition to the distinctions already drawn between serial and non-serial, and discrete and dense (or even continuous), ones.

The paradigm orderings are those that are completely non-linear and possess the mirror-image property, and are conversely transitive. Trees do not possess the mirror-image property, and so will be considered only as special cases of thickets. It is natural, though not necessary, to associate directedness with there being a maximum and minimum, and hence with non-seriality. And again, it is natural, though not necessary, to associate there being a most and a least with their being a next. Paradigm partial orderings, therefore, are on the one hand those that are directed, having a maximum and minimum and discrete, and on the other those that are not directed, serial rather than having extremal elements, and dense (or even continuous) rather than discrete.

9.11   Lattices and Set Theory

Lattices are paradigm orderings, and, apart from linear orderings, the simplest. If there is always *an* element lower than or identical with any two elements, there cannot be a number of minimal elements, and it is natural to posit a single *lowest* or a *least*. Similarly, if there is always *an* element higher (or more) than or identical with any two elements, it is natural to posit a *highest* or a *most*. Hence, if we are to take the directed option, it is natural to stipulate that such orderings should not have merely extremal elements, and should not be serial, but should be complete lattices, and have a maximum and a minimum element, and to add to this the further superlative excellence of discreteness. Granted discreteness, it is unproblematic to identify a *lowest* upper bound and *highest* lower bound to every pair of elements in the lattice. The least upper bound of x and y is called the **join** of the two elements, and the highest lower bound is called the **meet**. They are represented by $x \cup y$ and $x \cap y$ respectively.

Instead of defining the join and meet, $\cup$ and $\cap$, in terms of an ordering relation, we can characterize them in terms of their mutual relations, and then define the antisymmetric relation, $\preceq$, giving rise to a quasi-ordering. We could equally well define its converse, $\succeq$; lattices can have the mirror-image property. The following four axioms characterize a lattice:

L1 $\qquad\qquad x \cup x = x \quad$ and $\quad x \cap x = x$

L2 $\qquad\qquad x \cup y = y \cup x \quad$ and $\quad x \cap y = y \cap x$

L3 $(x \cup y) \cup z = x \cup (y \cup z)$ and $(x \cap y) \cap z = x \cap (y \cap z)$

L4 $(x \cup y) \cap x = x$ and $(x \cap y) \cup x = x$

We can then define $x \preceq y$:

$$x \preceq y \quad \text{iff} \quad x \cap y = x$$

Paradigm lattices have two further properties: they are distributive, and they can be complemented. The meet of one set with the join of two others is the same as the join of the meet of the one set with one of the others and the meet of the one set with the other: in symbols

L5 $x \cap (y \cup z) = (x \cap y) \cup (x \cap z).$

And similarly the join of one set with the meet of two others is the same as the meet of the join of the one set with one of the others and the join of the one set with the other:

L5$'$ $x \cup (y \cap z) = (x \cup y) \cap (x \cup z).$

Not all lattices are distributive: the lattice of Hilbert spaces under the relation *subspace of* is not distributive, and much effort has been expended on trying to devise a "quantum logic" to mirror this feature.

If a lattice has a maximum element **I**, and a minimium element **O**, they will act as identity and universal elements for the operations $x \cap x$ and $x \cup x$:

$$\mathbf{I} \cap x = x \quad \text{and} \quad \mathbf{O} \cup x = x$$
$$\mathbf{I} \cup x = \mathbf{I} \quad \text{and} \quad \mathbf{O} \cap x = \mathbf{O}$$

Complementation can be defined in terms of maximum and minimum elements. Each set, x, has a complement, x', such that

$$x \cup x' = \mathbf{I},$$

and

$$x \cap x' = \mathbf{O}.$$

A lattice that is complemented and also distributive is "orthocomplemented", that is, its complement is unique, and satisfies the further two conditions:

$$(x')' = x$$
$$x < y \leftrightarrow y' < x'.$$

Complementation is like negation. Essentially, we have defined complementation in terms of $\cap$ and $\cup$, and these two symbols in terms of the quasi-ordering relation $\preceq$ and the word 'and' of ordinary English.[43]

A complemented distributive lattice is called a "Boolean lattice". Set theory is the paradigm of Boolean lattices. It orders sets by means of an irreflexive subset relation, $\subset$, or quasi-orders them by means of an antisymmetric subset relation, $\subseteq$. There is a minimum set, the null set, Λ,[44] and, with some qualms, a maximum, $\mathbf{V}$.[45] The null set exists by stipulation rather than as an expression of our untutored thought. In our natural way of thinking we should say that the sets of Roman Catholic priests and matriarchs had no intersection, that there was no set which was a subset of them both. We could have a workable set theory in which there was no null set, and we used only the fused phrase 'is null' of the intersection of two sets when they had no non-empty intersection. As it is, we *postulate* the *existence* of the null set, and deem it to be a subset of every set, thereby securing the lattice property, that every two sets have a meet, that is, a set less than or identical with them both.

Since Peano, we have been careful to distinguish the proper subset relation, $\subset$, from the relation of set membership, $\in$, and individual members from singleton sets. But the distinction is not intuitively clear, and in transitive set theory, set membership is transitive as well as the subset relation. If we work with transitive set theory, we often lay down an axiom of regularity, or an axiom of foundation, which secures, in the absence of a null set, the existence of minimal elements. We are then working with a discrete, non-serial tree, rather than a lattice. From the present point of view, however, we do not need to consider set membership at all. We lay down a lattice structure, with the null set, Λ, as the minimum element, and the singleton sets next above it, being those sets whose

---

[43] See further, J.L.Bell and M.Machover, *A Course in Mathematical Logic*, North Holland, 1977, ch.4, §1, pp.125-129.

[44] There are many different representations of the null set, or empty set: $\emptyset$ is typographically close to 0, but sometimes mistaken for a Danish ø, or a Greek ϕ. Here we align our symbol with $\wedge$, $\cap$, (Ax), and $\bigcap$, and think of Λ as the intersection of all sets, and the universal set, $\mathbf{V}$, as the union of all sets, analogously with $\vee$, $\cup$, (Vx), and $\bigcup$. Sometimes, instead of Λ, $\bigwedge$ is used, and instead of $\mathbf{V}$, $\bigvee$, which is logical, but typographically awkward.

[45] See above, §7.11.

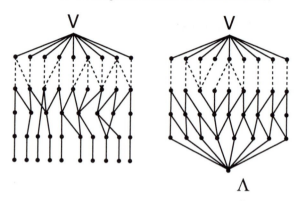

Figure 9.11.1 On left: Transitive Set Theory, with Axiom of
Regularity (Axiom of Foundation) but no Null Set. On right:
Standard Set Theory quasi-ordered by $\subseteq$, showing the singleton
sets on the level above the null set.

only subsets are themselves and the null set.

Set inclusion is conversely transitive from below and above.
From this it follows that if we start with the strict ordering relation
of proper set inclusion, $\subset$, we can define identity by means of the
equivalence relation generated by $\subset$. Equivalence from below is
expressed by the Axiom of Extensionality. Normally we formulate
the axiom in terms of set membership, $\in$, and lay down

$$x = y \leftrightarrow (\mathrm{A}z)(z \in x \leftrightarrow z \in y),$$

but if, instead, we consider proper set inclusion, $\subset$, we have

$$x = y \leftrightarrow (\mathrm{A}z)(z \subset x \leftrightarrow z \subset y).$$

Similarly, equivalence generated from above yields

$$x = y \leftrightarrow (\mathrm{A}z)(x \subset z \leftrightarrow y \subset z).$$

On the face of it, this is a relational thesis: but relations can be
construed monadically, though at the cost of much reduplication,
and then equivalence from above is seen as a version of Leibniz'
Law of the Identity of Indiscernibles

$$x = y \leftrightarrow (\mathrm{A}F)(F(x) \leftrightarrow F(y)),$$

with $F(*)$ in place of $* \in z$.

9.12 Trees and Mereology

The logic of the relation *is a part of* has been studied, sometimes under the title "Mereology" (from the Greek μέρος (*meros*), a part), sometimes under that of "The Calculus of Individuals".[46] Often the questions addressed have been ontological, and many different systems have been developed, to take account of different metaphysical intimations. We can approach mereology in two ways. We can idealise the transitive irreflexive relations we have been discussing so as to produce a paradigm of ordering, or we can articulate our everyday concept of being a part of, as exhibited in the ordinary use of the word 'part', itself reflecting the metaphysical assumptions we, often unconsciously, have been making. The approaches are not exclusive. Our ordinary use is influenced by ideas of what ideally ought to be the case, and our logical paradigms can be developed in different directions to satisfy alternative *desiderata*. Such concerns we shall at first leave on one side, developing a formal paradigm to exemplify the comparative ideal, so as to be able, in the next two chapters, to consider how far it is possible to ground the concepts of topology and a theory of measurement in ordering relations.

Set theory operates with a partial ordering, conversely transitive from above and below, and has a maximum and a minimum, thus being a lattice, and is distributive and complemented. The opposite paradigm is likewise a partial ordering, everywhere non-linear, and conversely transitive from above and below, having the mirror-image property, but, instead of being discrete, we want it to be at least dense, and perhaps continuous, and instead of having a maximum and minimum, we want its ordering relation, together with its converse, to be serial. It is natural to go further, and

---

[46] Much of the early work was done in Poland, notably by Leśniewski, Lejewski and Tarski. See also N.Goodman and H.S.Leonard, "The Calculus of Individuals and its Uses", *Journal of Symbolic Logic*, 5, 1940, pp.45-55. A.N.Whitehead, *An Enquiry Concerning the Principles of Natural Knowledge*, Cambridge, 1919, §27.2, pp.101-2; his line of thought has been developed by T. de Laguna, "Point, Line and Surface, as Sets of Solids", *Journal of Philosophy*, 19, 1922, pp.449-461; David Bostock, *Logic and Arithmetic*, vol.2, Oxford, 1979, ch.2, §4, pp.112-130; and J.E.Tiles, *Things that Happen*, Aberdeen, 1981, §8. An excellent survey of the different mereological systems is to be found in P.Simons, *Parts*, Oxford, 1987, ch.2, pp.46-100.

deny that it is directed; if the ordering is to have the mirror-image property, it will be neither upper- nor lower-directed. Distributivity, therefore, becomes a hypothetical issue, and complementation likewise does not feature in the comparative paradigm.

We consider a relational structure, $\langle X, \prec \rangle$, where $\prec$ is intended to capture the sense of *proper part of*,[47] which together with its converse, *having as a proper part*, or in Whitehead's terminology, *extends over*, ranges over a field of portions, parts, regions, or extensions.[48] As with set theory, we stipulate that there shall be converse transitivity from below and above:

$$x \preceq y \text{ iff } (Az)(z \prec x \overset{\rightarrow}{-} z \prec y),$$

and

$$x \preceq y \text{ iff } (Az)(x \prec z \overset{\rightarrow}{-} y \prec z).$$

We go further and stipulate that the equivalence relations generated by $\prec$ shall both be just the identity, that is,

$$((Ax)(Ay)(Az)(z \prec x \leftrightarrow z \prec y) \rightarrow x = y)$$

---

[47] Hereafter *is a part of* will be taken to mean *is a proper part of*. Although, for the reasons given in §9.1, I take the strict ordering generated by the asymmetric $\prec$ as fundamental, it is often convenient to work with the derived antisymmetric relation $\preceq$, like $\subseteq$ in set theory. And exceptionally, I shall sometimes write $\overset{\rightarrow}{-}$, instead of $\rightarrow$, in order to bring out the antisymmetry of implication. The reader should also note that Bostock works with an antisymmetric *proper or improper part of* relation, which he writes as $\subset$. In quoting him, I have rewritten this as $\preceq$. Simons uses an irreflexive relation, $\ll$, which I rewrite as $\prec$, and an antisymmetric $<$, which I rewrite as $\leq$.

[48] No term is altogether apposite: 'portion' is reminiscent of canteens; 'part' is idiomatically unexceptionable, but awkward in the context of the relation *part of*; S.Leśniewski, "Podstawy ogólnej teoryi mnogości", *Prace Polskiego Kola Naukowe w Moskwie*, Moscow, 1916, used *przedmiot*, 'object'; 'lump' (used by Menger), 'chunk' (used by Veblen) and 'piece' (used by Moore) have too materialistic connotations; many English writers have used 'individual'; 'extension' would be the best term for *res extensa* and extended magnitudes, but that carries with it connotations of connectedness we have not as yet justified, and invites confusion with the Axiom of Extension in set theory, and so later I shall use 'region' as the least misleading term I can think of. In this chapter I shall use 'portions'.

> Compare, in set theory,
>
> $$x \subseteq y \text{ iff } (Az)(z \subset x \overset{\rightarrow}{-} z \subset y)$$
> $$x \subseteq y \text{ iff } (Az)(x \subset z \overset{\rightarrow}{-} y \subset z)$$

and

$$((Ax)(Ay)(Az)(x \prec z \leftrightarrow y \prec z) \to x = y),$$

which is to say $\approx_{\prec}$ and $\approx^{\prec}$ are both the identity relation, $=$.
We may call these the Axiom of Constituents and the Theorem
of Envelopes,[49] regarding them as analogies with the Axiom of
Extensionality and the Identity of Indiscernibles in set theory. The
Axiom of Constituents has a materialist tinge. Things are just what
they are made up of, with no allowance for supervenient graces.
But that is the logic of portions. Considered as a portion, I am
just so much carbon, so much oxygen, so much hydrogen, so much
nitrogen, *etc.* No reckoning is made of my social accomplishments,
my spiritual aspirations, or my political correctitude. The airline
operator is not interested in such things: only my weight might
concern him, and minds and souls have no weight. The Axiom of
Envelopes likewise focuses attention away from organic wholes and
relational structures, and considers a portion simply as that, and
not with respect to its significance in some wider scheme of things.
My liver may play a key role in my metabolism, but is counted
only in respect of its contribution to my overall weight.

Converse transitivity from below and above offer a justification
for these axioms, and seem desirable features in their own right,
again suggesting a certain metaphysical slimness characteristic of
the *part of* relation. Later, however, their absence will be a crucial
feature of a stronger, topological, relation.[50]

The *part of* relation is dense:

$$(Ax)(Ay)(x \prec y \to (Vz)(x \prec z \wedge z \prec y)).$$

---

[49] Only one of these is an axiom, the other being a theorem, granted that
the equivalence relation has the mirror-image property. But for expository
purposes, it may be easier to construe them both as mirror-image axioms.

[50] §10.8.

The *not discrete—no minimum—not a lattice* inference is reasonable, though not watertight, and guides us to lay down that $\prec$ shall
be serial:

$$(\mathrm{A}x)(\mathrm{V}y)(y \prec x).$$

Every part, no matter how small, has a proper part that is smaller:
there are no minimal elements—no atoms. The mirror-image property requires that $\succ$, too, shall be serial, that is to say, that there
shall be no maximal portions. In order not to be a lattice, a partial
ordering must be not both upper- and lower-directed. If we deny
the Big Bang, and the possibility of a Big Crunch, Robb's conical
ordering for the Special Theory would be directed, though serial in
both directions, and thus without extremal elements. Simons offers
a stronger version that Robb's axiom of non-linearity, which also
secures that the partial ordering be not lower-directed.[51] It stipulates that if one element is below another, then there is a third
element also below it, without there being any fourth one below
them all:

$$(\mathrm{A}x)(\mathrm{A}y)(x \prec y \rightarrow (\mathrm{V}z)(z \prec y \wedge \neg(\mathrm{V}w)(w \prec z \wedge w \prec x))).$$

The antecedent of the conditional is always satisfied, since the ordering is serial in the upward direction and so we are saying that
for every portion, there is another that is "disjoint" from it, which
is to say that it does not overlap it at all.[52] The mirror-image
requirement stipulates that the ordering should also be not upper-
directed. In many presentations, however, though two elements
do not always have a meet, they do always have a join, so that
the system is upper-directed, and lacks the mirror-image property.
Nevertheless, for the sake of purity, we stipulate the mirror image
of Simons' axiom, but leaving out the antecedent (already secured
by upward seriality):

$$(\mathrm{A}y)(\mathrm{V}z)(y \prec z \wedge (\mathrm{V}w)(y \prec w \wedge \neg(w = z \vee w \prec z \vee z \prec w))).$$

[51] P.Simons, *Parts*, Oxford, 1987, p.28: SA3 "The Weak Supplementation
Principle".

[52] David Bostock, in his *Logic and Arithmetic*, vol.2, Oxford, 1979, p.113,
uses the word 'discrete', as do others who write in this field; but that word
is standardly used in a different sense in mathematical logic.

It is convenient to have formal definitions of overlapping and being disjoint. Let us symbolize *overlaps* by $\circ$, and say:

$$x \circ y \text{ iff } (\mathrm{V}z)((z \prec x) \wedge (z \prec y)).$$

Let us symbolize being disjoint by $|$, and say

$$x \mid y \text{ iff } \neg(x \circ y),$$

that is,

$$x \mid y \text{ iff } \neg(\mathrm{V}z)((z \prec x) \wedge (z \prec y)).$$

These permit more succinct and perspicacious formulation of some of the axioms, further economy often being possible, by reason of the presence of other axioms, such as seriality and denseness. With their aid the pure paradigm of a partial ordering that has the mirror-image property is dense, serial, everywhere non-linear, conversely transitive from above and below, and not necessarily directed, is expressed by the following axioms:

Pure Paradigm

'$\prec$' primitive; '$=$', '$\preceq$', '$\circ$', '$|$' defined

A 1	$x \prec y \wedge y \prec z \to x \prec z$	Transitive
A 2	$\neg(x \prec x)$	Irreflexive
A 3	$x \prec y \to (\mathrm{V}z)(x \prec z \wedge z \prec y)$	Dense
A 4 (i)	$(\mathrm{A}x)(\mathrm{V}y)(x \prec y)$	Downwards Serial
A 4 (ii)	$(\mathrm{A}x)(\mathrm{V}y)(y \prec x)$	Upwards Serial
A 5	$(\mathrm{A}x)(\mathrm{A}y)(\mathrm{A}z)(z \prec x \leftrightarrow z \prec y) \leftrightarrow$	
	$(\mathrm{A}x)(\mathrm{A}y)(\mathrm{A}z)(x \prec z \leftrightarrow y \prec z)$	Mirror Equivalence
D 1	$x = y$ for $(\mathrm{A}x)(\mathrm{A}y)(\mathrm{A}z)(z \prec x \leftrightarrow z \prec y)$	
D 2	$x \circ y$ for $(\mathrm{V}z)(z \prec x \wedge z \prec y)$	
D 3	$x \mid y$ for $\neg(x \circ y)$, *i.e.* $(\mathrm{V}z)(z \prec x \wedge z \prec y)$	
D 4	$x \preceq y$ for $x \prec y \vee x = y$	
A 6	$(\mathrm{A}x)(\mathrm{A}y)(x \prec y \to (\mathrm{V}z)(z \prec x \wedge z \mid y))$	
	Locally Non-linear and Not Downward Directed	
A 7	$(\mathrm{A}x)(\mathrm{A}y)(\mathrm{V}z)(\mathrm{A}w)(x \prec y \to (x \prec z \wedge \neg(y \prec w \wedge z \prec w)))$	
	Not Upward Directed	
A 8 (i)	$(\mathrm{A}x)(\mathrm{A}y)(\mathrm{A}z)((z \prec x \to z \prec y) \to x \preceq y)$	
	Conversely Transitive from Below	
A 8 (ii)	$(\mathrm{A}x)(\mathrm{A}y)(\mathrm{A}z)((x \prec z \to y \prec z) \to y \preceq x)$	
	Conversely Transitive from Above	

Our everyday concept of being a part of does not fully conform to the ideal paradigm, and has been articulated in different directions. Some mereologies are lattices.[53] Others differ from set theory only in having no minimum. They are perfectly possible formal systems—we may wish to avoid a minimum, null element for other reasons than a dislike of superlatives. Many mereologies have minim*al* null portions. Pythagoras' definition of a point, given in §2.5, is that of a minimal portion that itself has no parts.[54] In metaphysics atomism requires such a mereology. But atoms, in spite of their name, have an uncomfortable tendency to be split. Even if, in the current state of particle physics, there are quarks or quarklets which owing to a lack of funds have not yet been split, physicists are able conceptually to unglue them, and imagine their being split if only high enough energy were available. Logical atomism is not a contradiction in terms, but is discrete, not dense, and in not being serial runs counter to a human urge ever to go further in the search for a deeper understanding.

The argument from non-discreteness to non-seriality has seemed less compelling in the upward direction; we often have intimations of there being some whole, some universe, which comprehends everything.[55] Even without that assumption, it is often laid down that the ordering be upper-directed.[56] In either case we may call the structure tree-like, though we must be careful to allow lime-like trees, in which portions, though different, may yet overlap. In such cases the *part of* relation lacks the mirror-image property. But in our ordinary thinking we are much more concerned whether two portions overlap or are disjoint than whether or not there is some further portion which they both are parts of. Only in special circumstances do we ask whether they are both part of the same portion—only when they are mutually disjoint and jointly

---

[53] M.Bunge, "On Null Individuals", *Journal of Philosophy*, **63**, 1966, pp.776-778, propounds a lattice mereology in which there is a null portion (*cf.* the null set) that is a part of every portion.

[54] For a clear account of such a "classical extensional mereology", see P. Simons, *Parts*, Oxford, 1987, ch.1, §1.5, pp.37-41. See earlier, A.Tarski, *Logic, Semantics, Metamathematics*, Oxford, 1956, pp.333-334n.

[55] See further, M.K.Munitz, *Existence and Logic*, New York, 1974, pp.191ff.

[56] A.N.Whitehead, *An Enquiry Concerning the Principles of Natural Knowledge*, Cambridge, 1919, §27.2 (vi), p.101.

exhaustive of it, as well as satisfying some further condition of togetherness, yet to be elucidated.

Mereologists are as much interested in portions as in the *part of* relation, and want to be able to identify particular portions. It is not enough to know that two portions overlap, they want to be able to talk about *the* overlap. They supplement the comparative language of *part of* with the superlatives 'greatest' and 'least'. The "product", $x \odot y$, of two portions, x and y, that overlap, is the highest lower bound of x and y,

$$z = x \left(\cdot \right) y \quad \text{if and only if} \quad (Aw)(w \prec z \leftrightarrow (w \prec x \wedge w \prec y)).$$

With highest lower bounds and lowest upper bounds, further economies of axiomatization are possible. With some unfairness to each, it is possible to view Whitehead, Bostock and Simons, as developing a canonical mereology, which takes more account of our actual concept of being a part of than the idealized paradigm, while still offering logical coherence and clarity. It does not have the mirror-image property, but is dense, serial, everywhere non-linear, conversely transitive from above and below, and not downward directed.

Whitehead's presentation is deliberately informal.[57] He worked with a transitive irreflexive relation K, 'covers', equivalent to $\succ$. Bostock works with an antisymmetric relation, and combines the axioms expressing the transitivity, antisymmetry and converse transitivity from below of $\preceq$ into a single axiom,

P1 $$x \preceq y \leftrightarrow (Az)(y \mid z \rightarrow x \mid z).$$

> Compare, in set theory,
> $$x \subseteq y \leftrightarrow (Az)((z \cap y = \Lambda) \rightarrow (z \cap x = \Lambda))$$

[57] Whitehead has been much criticized for being slipshod. See V.F.Sinisi, "Leśniewski's Analysis of Whitehead's Theory of Events", *Notre Dame Journal of Formal Logic*, 7, 1966, pp.323-327. But Whitehead was not concerned to give a rigorous account—something that the author of *Principia Mathematica* could have done perfectly well, if he had wanted to. Rather, he was concerned to convey the general lines of an approach. There is a trade-off between rigour and intelligibility. Both are good. But it is captious to criticize Whitehead when he seeks to secure the latter, on the grounds that he has failed to secure the former.

Bostock strengthens Whitehead's axiom of upper-directedness by a further one:

P2 $(Vx)(Fx) \wedge (Vy)(Ax)(Fx \rightarrow x \preceq y)$
$$\rightarrow (Vy)(Az)(y \mid z \leftrightarrow (Ax)(Fx \rightarrow x \mid z)).$$

This axiom posits a Lowest Upper Bound property. Provided we have a non-empty family, F, of portions, all of which are proper or improper parts of some portion y (so that in effect y is an upper bound, so far as the *part of* relation is concerned), then there is a maximum portion z, which is disjoint from all but only those portions which do not overlap any member of the family F. Whitehead's axiom secures that for any two branches of the tree, there is a bigger branch they are both branches of: Bostock's secures that there is a node, a final point of branching. More formally, Whitehead's posits the existence of an upper bound, Bostock's of a lowest upper one (and for any number, not just two).

Simons separates out his axioms for transitivity and irreflexivity, and then secures local non-linearity by his Weak Supplementation Principle:

SA3 $x \prec y \rightarrow (Vz)(z \prec y \wedge z \mid x)$

He is then able to show, by simple but ingenious derivations, that both local non-linearity and converse transitivity from below follow from an axiom stating that if two portions overlap, then there is a unique product.

SA6 $x \circ y \rightarrow (Vz)(z = x \odot y).$

This he calls *Minimal Extensional Mereology*.

The axioms in the box on the opposite page could be formulated differently. We could, for instance define identity in terms of equivalence from below; but that would weaken the analogy with the Axiom of Extensionality in set theory. Bostock's and Simons' own formulations are more elegant and economical, but make it less evident where they are departing from the pure paradigm. There are many other axiomatizations, not all of them equivalent. They articulate different understandings of the concept of *portion* and *being a part of*. These concepts, like that of a set, are not clearcut, and it is by considering different axiomatizations that we are helped to decide what we ought to mean when we use these terms.

Applied Mereology

Whitehead-Bostock-Simons

'$\prec$', '$=$' primitive; '$\preceq$', '$\circ$', '$|$' defined

A 1	$x \prec y \wedge y \prec z \rightarrow x \prec z$	Transitive
A 2	$\neg(x \prec x)$	Irreflexive
A 3	$x \prec y \rightarrow (Vz)(x \prec z \wedge z \prec y)$	Dense
A 4 (i)	$(Ax)(Vy)(x \prec y)$	Downwards Serial
A 4 (ii)	$(Ax)(Vy)(y \prec x)$	Upwards Serial
A 5	$(Ax)(Ay)(Az)((z \prec x \leftrightarrow z \prec y) \leftrightarrow x = y)$	Axiom of Constituents

D 1 $x \preceq y$ for $x \prec y \vee x = y$

D 2 $x \circ y$ for $(Vz)(z \prec x \wedge z \prec y)$

D 3 $x \mid y$ for $\neg(x \circ y)$, i.e. $(Vz)(z \prec x \wedge z \prec y)$

A 6 $(Ax)(Ay)(y \prec x \rightarrow (Vz)(z \prec x \wedge z \mid y))$

      Locally Non-linear and Not Downward-directed

A 7 $(Ax)(Ay)(Az)((z \prec x \rightarrow z \prec y) \rightarrow x \preceq y)$

      Conversely Transitive from Below

A 8 $(Ax)(Ay)(Az)((x \prec z \rightarrow y \prec z) \rightarrow y \preceq x)$

      Conversely Transitive from Above

A 9 $(Ax)(Ay)(Vz)(x \prec z \wedge y \prec z)$ Upward-directed

A 10 $(Ax)(Ay)(x \circ y \rightarrow (Vz)(z \prec x \wedge z \prec y$
     $\wedge(Aw)(w \prec z \leftrightarrow w \prec x \vee w \prec y)))$ Unique Product

The full strength of *Classical Extensional Mereology* is achieved by replacing SA6 by the *General Sum Principle*:

SA24 $(Vx)(Fx) \rightarrow (Vw)(Ay)(y \circ w \leftrightarrow (Vz)(Fz \wedge y \circ z))$;

but this is inconsistent with the partial ordering being upwardly serial. All that Whitehead would allow is a *Binary Sum Principle*, guaranteeing not only the existence for any two portions of a node, that is, a minimal portion of which they were each a part, but one that had no other parts disjoint from those two.

If we posit the existence of a lowest upper bound and a sum, we are securing the mirror image of there always being a maximum product, if two portions overlap at all. But neither thesis is to be taken for granted if we are dealing with some sorts of portions.

Two areas may be entirely separate, and not combine into a single region, and even if they intersect, their common portions may be themselves separate.[58]

With the Lowest Upper Bound and Highest Lower Bound, mereology verges towards a discipline concerned with limits and boundaries, where we deal not merely with the *portions* that are parts of some whole, but the *regions*, or *extensions*, which, sharing a boundary, are unseparated parts and together constitute one continuous extent. The study of these constitutes the discipline of topology; and also is a precondition of a satisfactory account of measurement, in which we systematically assign numbers to portions of various sorts.

—o0o—

A Typology of Relations

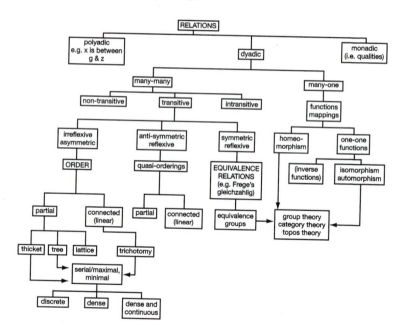

Chapter 10

Prototopology[0]

10.1 Togetherness

Togetherness is a key notion in philosophy generally as well as in mathematics. The Great Chain of Being binds the disparate levels of Reality into One Coherent Whole, and togetherness is a mark of being integrated into a single unity. The *part of* relation is a simple mereological one, as sketched in Chapter Nine, §9.12, but the concept of *being a whole* is stronger than a simple correlative of *being a part*. The theory of measurement depends on there being some extensive magnitudes for which the measure of the whole is the sum of the measures of the parts. In the next chapter (§11.4), we shall need the thesis that two regions are parts of one connected, or unseparated, whole, if they share a common boundary; but though we can often recognise their doing this in practice, we have also to give a theoretical account. Togetherness is the chief concern of topology, and is taken for granted in geometry.

Plato had many dark sayings in his later dialogues, the *Parmenides* and especially the *Philebus*, about τὸ πέρας (*to peras*) and τὸ ἄπειρον (*to apeiron*) and about the more and the less and

---

[0] Throughout this chapter I have drawn heavily on the work, and the patience, of David Bostock, who has let me see much unpublished work of his own, and on innumerable occasions has pointed out the loopholes in my latest arguments and definitions.

the Great and the Small, and Aristotle seems sometimes to be engaged in what we might describe as prototopology.[1] He and his successors puzzled long over the continuum, particularly with regard to the nature of time. The Greeks had a sense of the present, τὸ νῦν (*to nun*), *both* dividing the past from the future, *and* joining them together in a single united time.[2] Although the past and future are disjoint, with the present instant between them, yet they are connected, because the present instant is next them both. The continuum, because it is gapless has that sense of connectedness, which a merely dense ordering lacks; συνεχῆ μὲν ὧν τὰ ἔσχατα ἕν (*suneche men hon ta eschata hen*), those things are continuous whose extremities are one.[3]

Kant was the first to recognise the importance of *Analysis Situs*. But it was mathematicians, concerned to give a rigorous treatment of functions and of irrational numbers, who finally elucidated the concepts of continuity and connectedness, which can be taken as the key concepts of topology, and the rigorous explication of togetherness.

10.2 Axiomatic Approaches

In most modern treatments topology is introduced axiomatically, in terms of open sets or closure operators. Topology is presented as an enrichment of set theory, to which we add some further term, such as *open set*, and further axioms governing its use. The open sets form a family of sets, closed under union and finite intersection. Various other axioms of separation are added to obtain stronger and stronger topologies. Alternatively, instead of having a special property of sets, that of their being open, we may have a special operator, such as closure, which operates on sets to form sets, perhaps the same, perhaps different, which are said to be the closure of the original sets.

Either approach has its merits, and either can reasonably be regarded as a natural extension of existing mathematics. The first ap-

---

[1] See especially, Kenneth M. Sayre, *Plato's Late Ontology*, Princeton University Press, 1983; M.J.White, *The Continuous and the Discrete*, Oxford, 1992, and Bostock's article cited in n.22.

[2] *Physics*, IV, 220a4-13.

[3] *Physics* VI, 1, 231a20. Bostock takes this as a definition of 'connected', rather than 'continuous'.

proach has the virtue of conceptual simplicity—essentially it adds
to set theory only the monadic property of a set's being open—and
the rules, though complicated, have the merit of underscoring the
distinction between finite and infinite. The second approach involves an operator, which is slightly more *recherché* than a simple
property of sets, but the axioms, which are due to Kuratowski, are
more intuitive, and show a striking similarity to those governing
the modal operators in **S4**. If we take a set's being included in
another set as being like one proposition's implying another, then
the closure operator is like the ◊ of modal logic, or what comes to
the same thing, necessity, □, is like the interior operator, which is,
so to speak, the dual of the closure operator.[4] If we think of the
necessity operator as cutting out the penumbra of uncertainty, the
parallel with the interior operator is illuminating.[5]

These approaches to topology suit different philosophical concerns and different metaphysical standpoints. A family of special
sets, closed under finite conjunction and infinite disjunction, and
whose complements were not in general members of the family,
would appeal to a Leibnizian with a strong sense of the importance of positive monadic predicates, though not regarding negative predicates as referring to real qualities. Finite conjunctions of
positive predicates would refer to complex qualities, instantiated
by some open set, potentially capable of an infinite membership;
but infinite conjunctions of positive predicates would individuate
some particular unique monad. Disjunctions of positive predicates,
whether finite or infinite, would specify open, though perhaps not
very natural, sets, clearly capable of infinite membership. A Leibnizian approach would be suitable for a jurisconsult, considering
legal cases, some of which very closely resembled one another, while
others were fairly far from them, and clearly separate. More generally, the distinction between finite intersections of open sets, which
are themselves open, and infinite intersections of open sets, which
may be closed, parallels a distinction in the logic of argument,

---

[4] Some care is needed, because the topological analogue of implication, →,
is being-a-subset-of, ⊆, not being-a-superset-of, ⊇. Since the interior of
a set is always included in it, and a set is always included in its closure,
□ has to be compared with the interior operator, and not, as might have
been supposed, the closure operator.

[5] See further, §13.3, §13.4.

which countenances any finite number of objections or reformulations, but regards a critic who goes on raising objections or shifting his stance *ad infinitum* as merely captious, a sceptic to be ignored rather than a substantial opponent to be taken seriously.[6]

The axiomatic approaches bring out clearly the separate assumptions we commonly make about togetherness, and also show deep structural similarities between topology and other disciplines. Nevertheless, they fail to characterize topology adequately. The basic axioms highlight some features but leave out others, and have to be supplemented by a succession of further, often somewhat *ad hoc*, axioms whose rationale is far from self-evident. And even then, we find that the characterization is still too wide, and we have to specify that it is the "standard topology" we have in mind. It would be better if, instead of postulating axioms, we could develop the crucial concepts of topology in terms of ordering relations alone, as the natural reconciliation of the comparative ideal of denseness with the superlative one of nextness.[7]

10.3 Whitehead's Programme

In the second decade of this century Whitehead attempted to ground topology and geometry in mereology, using "Extensive Abstraction" to define nearness.[8] If he had succeeded, we would have had a fourth volume of *Principia Mathematica*.

Whitehead worked with an informal version of the mereology outlined at the end of the previous chapter.[9] He laid down postulates which secure that $\succ$ and $\prec$ are dense and serial, and that $\succ$

---

[6] See J.R.Lucas, "The Lesbian Rule", *Philosophy*, **30**, 1955, pp.195-213; and "Philosophy and Philosophy Of", *Proceedings of the British Academy*, **72**, 1986, pp.261-262.

[7] For an early plea to develop topology on these lines, see K.Menger, "Topology without Points", *Rice Institute Pamphlets*, **27**, 1940, pp.80-107.

[8] A.N.Whitehead, *The Principles of Natural Knowledge*, Cambridge, 1919, §30, pp.101-106. I am indebted to T.J.Smiley, Fellow of Clare College, Cambridge, for drawing my attention to this.

[9] See above, §9.12; Whitehead's system is presented concisely and rigorously by P. Simons, *Parts*, Oxford, 1987, ch.2, §2.9.1, pp.81-86. Whitehead himself talks of 'events', $a, b, c, \ldots$ *etc*. But this term, though appropriate in view of his empiricist programme, is awkward for the present purpose, and will be replaced by 'region'; similarly, Whithead's relation *extends over*,

is (lime-)tree-like.[10] "Abstractive classes" were a generalisation of
Cauchy sequences and a predecessor of modern filters and directed
sets, which could be used to define limits of regions in the same
way as Cantor used nested intervals to define point-like real numbers. Whitehead defines an "abstractive class" as a set[11] of nested
regions. That is, a set of regions is called an abstractive class, when

1. of any two of its members one is a proper part of the other, and
2. there is no region which is a proper part of every extension of
   the set.[12]

Part of Whitehead's motive in promoting the method of Extensive Abstraction was metaphysical. He was at that time working very closely with Russell, and hoped that abstractive classes
would serve the purpose of grounding the mathematical concepts
of point, line and surface, in four-dimensional regions— "events"—
which could be understood in safely empiricist terms. But there
were further, conceptual, goals his programme might well be able
to achieve, which are of greater concern to us here.

Abstractive classes converge to limits, which might be boundaries, and in particular the common boundaries which two extensive magnitudes must share if they are to constitute together one
unseparated whole.[13] Abstractive classes offer also a prospect of
distinguishing limit elements of different dimensionality, and thus
of defining dimensions, and distinguishing the points, lines and
surfaces, and carrying out suggestion (ii) in §2.5 of grounding geometrical concepts topologically. And granted that we could define
points by means of abstractive classes, they could do duty for neighbourhoods, or open sets, and thus enable us to develop standard
point-set topology.

Whitehead's key notion is that of one abstractive class's "covering" another abstractive class. If Φ and Ψ are abstractive classes,
Φ is said to cover Ψ iff every member of Φ has some member of Ψ

symbolized as aKb. which is naturally interpreted as *has as a proper part
of itself*, $\succ$, will be rephrased in terms of $\prec$.

[10] See above, §9.6.

[11] Whitehead does not explicitly require that the set be countable (*i.e.* of
cardinality $\aleph_0$), though he implicitly assumes it.

[12] p.104.

[13] See below, §10.4.

being part of it; in symbols

$$\Phi \text{ covers } \Psi \quad \text{iff} \quad (Ax)(x\varepsilon\Phi \;\rightarrow\; (Vy)(y\varepsilon\Psi \wedge y \prec x)).$$

Clearly covering is a transitive and reflexive relation. We shall symbolize it by $\supseteq$.[14] When Φ covers Ψ and Ψ covers Φ, they are said to be mutually covering each other, and mutual covering is an equivalence relation. We might hope then to define limit elements, such as points, lines, or surfaces, as equivalence classes of abstractive classes that mutually cover one another; and among such equivalence classes of abstractive classes, to characterize points as those associated with abstractive classes which do not cover any abstractive class that does not also cover them; and similarly lines as those associated with abstractive classes which cover, without being covered by, abstractive classes associated with points, but otherwise do not cover any abstractive class that does not also cover them; and similarly surfaces as those associated with abstractive classes which cover, without being covered by, abstractive classes associated with points and lines, but otherwise do not cover any abstractive class that does not also cover them. We could avoid some imperfection by further stipulating

3. no initial segment of an abstractive class specifies it uniquely.

We might also hope to have the points constituting a Hausdorff space (or T_2-space) and to be able to define two regions being pointwise connected if there were some abstractive class such that every one of its members overlapped with both regions, and two regions being completely connected if there were some abstractive class such that some of its members did not have as a part any region that did not overlap with either region. In this way we could reasonably hope to give definitions of limit elements, dimension and connectedness, in terms of generalised Cauchy sequences of regions, or some other sort of regions, using just the relation of *part of* or its converse *having as a part of*. We should have achieved our aim of giving a non-arithmetical foundation to analysis and topology, in terms of mereology alone, itself characterized as a relational structure exemplifying a paradigm dense, serial, tree-like ordering relation.

---

[14] Here we depart from our normal rule of having "less than" ordering relations, in order to avoid the risk of confusion with the set-theoretical relation $\subseteq$.

10.4 Failure

Unfortunately Whitehead's programme failed. His definition did not exclude "pathological abstractive classes" which converge to a point that is outside, or on the boundary of, the regions of the abstractive class. The best example is the set of open intervals $(0, \delta_n)$, where δ_n tends to 0; this set satisfies Whitehead's definition, but fails to characterize the point [0] uniquely, since the set of open intervals $(-\delta_n, 0)$ also converges to 0, although no member of either set is a part of any member of the other. Similarly, the set of closed intervals $[0, \delta_n]$ also fails to characterize the point [0] uniquely, since the set of closed intervals $[-\delta_n, 0]$ also converges to 0, although no member of either set is a part of any member of the other.[15]

With the loss of punctiformity goes uniqueness. Different equivalence classes of mutually covering abstractive classes can be associated with the same point. Instead of a one–one relation, we have a many–one relation, and we therefore can no longer use abstractive classes to define points, because there is no longer a unique way of associating equivalence classes of abstractive classes with particular points. Besides the difficulty of *identifying* points, we are faced with a further difficulty of *characterizing* them. We have lost minimality. With genuine, that is to say non-pathological, abstractive classes, we can distinguish those equivalence classes that are associated with single points from those that are associated with other limit elements by their not covering any abstractive class that does not in turn cover them. But once we admit pathological abstractive classes, we can, except when confined to only one dimension, construct ever further ones, converging to the same point, which are covered by, but do not cover, other abstractive classes that also converge to the same point. For example, the interiors of the semicircular segments of radius $1/n$ converge to the centre, as do

---

[15] Bostock gives a further type of pathological abstractive class that needs consideration, namely the intervals

$[0, \infty], [1, \infty], [2, \infty], \ldots$.

It seems reasonable to claim that these classes are excluded by the requirement that successive members be nested within their predecessors at every boundary. But there may be doubts about taking ∞, and its analogues in non-linear cases, as definite boundaries. Since, however, we are concerned with classes converging to nothing, it might be acceptable to stipulate that the first member of the class be finite or bounded.

also quarter sectors, each one of which is a part of a corresponding semicircular one. For any convergent family of sectors, each subtending an angle θ at the centre, there is another family of sectors, each subtending an angle $\theta/2$, which is covered by it but does not cover it. There is thus no minimal abstractive class which can be defined as converging to a point. Punctiformity cannot be defined in terms of abstractive classes alone.

Figure 10.4.1 The Piece of Cake. We can have a series of pieces of cake converging to the centre. But then we can have a set of smaller pieces of cake converging to the same point.

We are also unable to eliminate other awkward cases. An abstractive class may tend towards a limit in a number of unexpected ways. Although no region is a proper part of all the members of an abstractive class, the limit may be non-minimal. A succession of members of an abstractive class might all encompass a hairline crack, thus giving rise to a "whisker", which could serve to make two widely separated regions be accounted together. Only if we have punctiformity, can we rule out whiskers, and other higher-dimensional limits, and have a workable test for connectedness and separation.

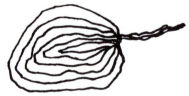

Figure 10.4.2 A pathological abstractive class need not converge to an ordinary boundary, but may include "whiskers" which extend in untoward directions.

We lose not only our criterion for distinguishing points from lines and higher-dimensional limit elements, but our criterion for distinguishing an abstractive class that converges to a single point from one that converges to two separate ones, and thus our ability to use abstractive classes to pick out connected regions from disconnected ones. The intervals $[-2, -1]$ and $[1, 2]$ are, by any standard, disconnected, but the abstractive class whose members are $(-\frac{1}{2} - \frac{1}{n}, -\frac{1}{2} + \frac{1}{n}) \cup (\frac{1}{2} - \frac{1}{n}, \frac{1}{2} + \frac{1}{n})$ has all its members overlapping $[-2, -1]$ and $[1, 2]$, and so they would have to count as connected. Of course, we should not accept $(-\frac{1}{2} - \frac{1}{n}, -\frac{1}{2} + \frac{1}{n}) \cup (\frac{1}{2} - \frac{1}{n}, \frac{1}{2} + \frac{1}{n})$ as a proper unseparated region. But unseparatedness is just what we are trying to define, and we cannot assume it as part of our explication without being open to accusations of arguing in a circle.

Whitehead may have been thinking in a circle. He seems to take it for granted that regions are connected. He does not discuss the problem of pathological extensive abstractive classes, but having introduced Extensive Abstraction, he does not use it to define connectedness; instead, he defines two regions' being connected in terms of a third region's overlapping them both without having any part disjoint from them both,[16] and later adopted an approach of de Laguna.[17] The fourth volume of *Principia Mathematica* was never written.

10.5 Pointed and Linear Hopes

Whitehead's programme was very ambitious. Apart from its metaphysical, empiricist, aims, it sought to define limit elements, and then points and hence lines and surfaces, all with the aid of abstractive classes, converging on limits not themselves being regions at all. Before abandoning it altogether, it is worth reviewing the resources that might be available for carrying it through.

Abstractive classes failed to characterize points, through the failure of the minimality condition. But we have other characterizations of points. A point can be characterized as having no size, or as able to be a boundary but not to have one, or as having no

---

[16] "Two events [regions in my terminology] x and y are 'joined' when there is a third event [region] z such that (i) z intersects both x and y, and (ii) there is a dissection of z of which each member is a part of x, or of y, or of both." §29.1, p.102.

[17] T. de Laguna, "Point, Line and Surface as Sets of Solids", *Journal of Philosophy*, **19**, 1922, pp.449-461.

parts.[18] Having no size, is too metrical for our present purpose;
we have not yet assigned measures to portions, or regions, and
when we do, we shall need the thesis that points, and other limit
elements, have zero size, as a substantial thesis, not a definitional
stipulation.[19] "Able to be a boundary but not to have one" is already topological, and is not available unless we can characterize
'boundary' in some independent way. We could alter our mereology to accommodate partless points; we could have a mereology
which was less thoroughly comparative, and in which the *part of*
relation, $\prec$, was not serial. But there is a metaphysical price to be
paid. We are easily led then by Zeno-esque arguments into confusion and atomism. Many philosophers in the ancient world and
the middle ages were torn between infinite divisibility and the apparently necessary existence of indivisibles. But even if we were
willing to pay the metaphysical price, we should still be unable to
distinguish genuinely punctiform abstractive classes from pathological ones. Although we could rule out the set of open intervals
$(0, \delta_n)$, where δ_n tends to 0, we should still be left with the set of
closed intervals $[0, \delta_n]$, which together with the set of closed intervals $[-\delta_n, 0]$, converges to the limit $[0]$, and is covered by, but does
not cover, the genuinely punctiform abstractive class $[-\delta_n, \delta_n]$.

But still, we should like abstractive classes to work, and it would
seem that they should, since they proved eminently successful in
the case of the real lines. Indeed, the programme of generalising
the account of the linear continuum given in the previous chapter
(in §9.7) has met with considerable success. It is possible in any
partially ordered system to define successively
(1) least upper bounds and greatest lower bounds
(2) limits superior and limits inferior
(3) limits
ensuring their existence by completing the partially ordered system in a determinate way.[20] The Dedekind cut for rational numbers has been generalised to arbitrary partially ordered sets.[21] But

---

[18] §2.5.

[19] §12.5.

[20] G.Birkhoff, "Moore-Smith Convergence in General Topology", *Annals of Mathematics*, **38**, 1937, pp.39-56, esp.§8, pp.55-56.

[21] H.MacNeille, "Extensions of Partially Ordered sets", *Proceedings of the National Academy of Sciences*, **22**, 1936, pp.45-50.)

bounds are not boundaries. What is wrong with pathological abstractive classes is that the boundaries of successive members overlap, and whereas in a linear continuum a finite interval has only two end-points, which can be individually specified as being different from the end-points of other intervals under consideration, with a partially ordered set there are indefinitely many opportunities for boundaries to coincide, and no way of stipulating that they shall differ.

Linearity, then, is more promising, since we can characterize linearity in terms of order, and can define boundaries, limits and continuity in a one-dimensional linear ordering: Cantor's intervals can be specified as nested, Dedekind's sets have unique lowest upper and highest lower bounds. We might hope to define a set of abstractive classes that was linear, and would distinguish pathological abstractive classes, whose successive members would "intersect" some such linear segment all at the same "point", from genuinely punctiform abstractive classes, for which every such linear segment would "intersect" successive members at different "points". But although we can define suitable linear segments that are continuous and connected according to the defined linear order, they need not be continuous and connected according to the basic mereological part/whole ordering. Continuity and connectedness are relative

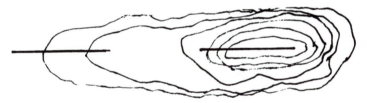

Figure 10.5.1 A gappy linear segment, e.g. $[1, 2) \cup [3, 4]$ gives a false negative with a genuinely punctiform abstractive class.

to ordering. A continuous connected interval of the real line can be mapped by one-one functions into intervals that are discontinuous and disconnected, and also, more suprisingly, into intervals that are, according to the natural ordering of the interval, continuous, but not connected according to the original ordering.[22] Dedekind

---

[22] See David Bostock, "Aristotle on Continuity in *Physics* VI", in L.Judson, ed., *Aristotle's Physics: A Collection of Essays*, Oxford, 1991, pp.180-188, esp. p.186.

and Cantor were able to formulate their definitions because the rational numbers had their own intrinsic ordering, with respect to which bounds and limits could be defined. The mereological ordering by itself, though intrinsic, is not linear: other orderings, though linear, are not the same as the mereological ordering, and continuity and connectedness with respect to them does not secure continuity and connectedness mereologically.

Bostock shows that the problem is insurmountable. For any genuinely punctiform abstractive class can be transformed into a pathological abstractive class by a mapping that preserves mereological ordering. Suppose for example we have a 2-dimensional genuinely punctiform abstractive class converging to the point $(1, 0)$: if we transform the plane so that all points to the right of the vertical line $x = 1$ are displaced one unit upwards, while the rest of the plane is unaltered, the genuinely punctiform abstractive class becomes pathological, while the *part of* relation, $\prec$, remains unaffected.

10.6 Alternatives

From an empiricist point of view, it would be no objection that we were taking unseparatedness and boundedness for granted. Frege, after the discovery of Russell's paradox, and the failure of his logicist programme, thought that perhaps mathematics rested on certain fundamental geometric intuitions, and unseparatedness (or connectedness) could well be one of them. We are able to recognise bounded unseparated regions when we see them, and it would be quite acceptable to do as Whitehead did, and define two regions being connected in terms of there being some region that overlapped them both without having any part disjoint from them both. We might simply start with a family of bounded unseparated regions, and confining ourselves to them, give definitions in terms of them alone, ruling out of court the clever counter-examples that we can construct with the aid of topological notions. It could be argued that we could not conceive the counter-examples unless we were already able to recognise the standard cases for what they were. The sceptic can often attack some common notion of ours, but if he can do so only by presupposing that we are already in possession of it, his doubts do not stick. We just do have certain notions of connectedness, continuity, extension and magnitude, and they neither can be given nor need any further justification or explication.

In this approach orthodox mereology is restricted to bounded *connected*—that is, pathwise connected—portions, that is to say, *regions* in our terminology. But in ordinary mereology, even if we start with regions, the rules for intersections and unions give rise to portions that are disconnected:

Figure 10.6.1 Two regions intersect in two separate portions.

it is necessary, therefore, to modify the postulates of orthodox mereology to secure that no disconnected part intrudes itself. Granted this restriction, we could go on to develop topology as the General Theory of Bounded Extensions (*i.e.* Connected, or Unseparated Portions). This approach is useful in articulating what our concept of a region really involves, but since it is not closed under the normal mereological operations of union and intersection, it seems awkwardly *ad hoc*.

Instead of restricting the portions to connected regions, we may add explicit assumptions to the axioms of mereology, in order to provide an underlying topological structure, or modify them so as to characterize some key topological concept. The next two sections will explore each alternative.

10.7   Mooreology

Whitehead's Extensive Abstraction could not be rehabilitated, because mereology alone did not provide enough structure. R.L. Moore sets out to provide a structure of portions or "pieces" as he calls them, which will perform something of the same function as the family of open sets postulated by topologists.[23] He works with a transitive irreflexive relation, *being embedded in*, together with an axiom postulating a sequence of sets of portions, $G_1, G_2, G_3, \ldots$ such that for each n, $G_{n+1} \subset G_n$, and for any portion g, there is

---

[23] R.L.Moore, "A Set of Axioms for plane analysis situs", *Fundamenta Mathematicae*, **25**, 1935, 99.13-28.

for each n a portion belonging to G_n that is part of g. Or formally, $(Ag)(AG_n)(Vx)(x \in G_n \wedge x \prec g)$. Furthermore, if $k \prec h$, there is a G_m such that every portion which belongs to G_m and overlaps k is part of h. Or formally,
$$(Ak)(Ah)(k \prec h \rightarrow (VG_m)(Az)(z \in G_m \wedge z \circ k \rightarrow z \prec h)).$$
Essentially Moore is imposing a granular structure with a succession of sets of ever more finely grained portions, so that every portion, no matter how small, has some grain as a part of it, and provided we choose a set of sufficiently small grains, if one portion is embedded in another, all the grains that overlap the smaller will be themselves embedded in the larger. It is clear that this last postulate rules out pathological abstractive classes; each portion is given, as it were, a coating of ball bearings, which separate its boundary from that of any portion in which it is embedded.

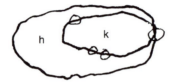

Figure 10.7.1 The portion k cannot have a common boundary with h in which it is embedded, since then some grains overlapping k would also only overlap h, instead of being embedded in it.

Whitehead's abstractive classes defined grains of ever smaller size, but not uniformly over the whole space. Moore has smaller and smaller portions everywhere, *and* sets of them, the sets being more or less ordered by "size", so that sufficiently small grains are everywhere available, to come between any portion and another it is embedded in. It might seem at first that Moore had smuggled in some metrical concept of size, but this is not so. He does not need to secure that each grain in a set is of the same size, but only that for sufficiently large m the portions belonging to G_m will be sufficiently small.

From these axioms alone, Moore is able to derive the key axiom of Point Set Theory, indeed, of a metric topology. Further, somewhat less intuitive, postulates are needed to secure arc-wise connectivity, compactness and the whole of Point Set Theory.

One may wonder whether much has been gained by postulating sets of suitably diminishing portions instead of sets of open sets.

Admittedly a lot of postulating is going on in this case, as in standard presentations of topology. But the idea of increasingly small portions is less arcane than that of open sets. And our experience of the world is much more of chunks than of individual items. Rather complicated conceptual structures are required if we are to articulate our experience into an experience of separate things. Sometimes this is necessary, but we are in danger of distinguishing too much, and we are truer to our experience if we start with comparative relations and from them develop superlative ideals of discreteness, rather than the other way round.

10.8 More Mereology

Instead of positing sets of portions, we may try and formulate axioms for slightly stronger mereology, which will allow us to develop topological concepts, or we may simply adjoin to an existing mereology some further, topological, concept, such as *pathwise connectedness*. Granted this concept, Bostock is able to define two regions being connected at only one point, and thence the concept of a point as the unique connexion of two regions that are pathwise connected at only one point.[24] Having defined points, he can go on to develop topology as the General Theory of Bounded Extensions (*i.e.* Connected, or Unseparated Portions). His approach is useful in articulating what our concept of a region really involves, and interesting in showing how points can be introduced and identified in an entirely new way.

Somewhat similarly, Clark and Röper add a new primitive—x *connects with* y, which Röper symbolizes by ∞—to the concepts of orthodox mereology, and postulates governing its use.[25] Clark defines x *is separate from* y, $x][y$, as $\neg x \infty y$; x *just touches* y, xTy, as $x \infty y \wedge x|y$; and x *is a firmly inner part of* y, $x \prec\!\prec y$, as $x \prec y \wedge \neg (Vz)(zTx \wedge zTy)$; and has five axioms:
A1 $x \infty x$.

---

[24] In an unpublished monograph "Points".

[25] Bowman L. Clark, "A Calculus of Individuals Based on Connection", *Notre Dame Journal of Formal Logic,*, **22**, 1981, pp.204-218, esp. pt I, pp.204-208; and "Individuals and Points", *Notre Dame Journal of Formal Logic*, **26**, 1985, pp.61-75. A useful summary is given in P. Simons, *Parts*, Oxford, 1987, §2.10.2, pp.94-98. Peter Röper, "Region-based Topology", Forthcoming.

A2 $x\infty y \to y\infty x$.

A3 $(\mathrm{A}z)(z\infty x \leftrightarrow z\infty y) \to x = y$.

A4 $(\mathrm{V}z)(z \prec\prec x)$.

A5 $(\mathrm{A}z)((z\infty x \to z \odot x) \wedge (z\infty y \to z \odot y)) \to (\mathrm{A}z)(z\infty x \cap y)$.[26]

Röper, working with a somewhat different mereology, also has five axioms:

A1   If $\alpha\infty\beta$ then $\beta\infty\alpha$

A2   If $\alpha \neq 0$ then $\alpha\infty\alpha$

A3 $0 \cancel{\infty}\alpha$

A4   If $\alpha\infty\beta$ and $\beta \leq \gamma$ then $\alpha\infty\gamma$

A5   If $\alpha\infty(\beta \vee \gamma)$ then $\alpha\infty\beta$ or $\alpha\infty\gamma$

He also needs a further concept, that of a region's being *limited*, which he characterizes by a further five axioms. He is then able to introduce points as equivalence classes of limited ultra filters, and within his region-based topology define the concepts of traditional point set topology, and prove its characteristic theses. Bostock is able to achieve the same, using his definition of a point, and then defining what it is for a point $[x, y]$ *to be at no distance from* a region a, which he symbolizes as $[x, y]\infty a$. He needs only one postulate,

B $a\infty b \leftrightarrow (\mathrm{V}x)(\mathrm{V}y)([x, y]\infty a \wedge [x, y]\infty b)$.

On this approach, topology becomes a special sub-theory of mereology, with one additional primitive, governed by appropriate axioms.

Instead of adding a new primitive term and appropriate axioms, we may seek to strengthen the *part of* relation, as Moore does, but instead of characterizing *being embedded in*,[27] which can be symbolized by $\prec\prec$, by extra existential axioms, do so directly.[28]

[26]   Taken from Simons, pp.95, 96, but with changes of terminology and symbolism.

[27]   Other writers have used *being a firmly inner part of*, or *being an inner part of*, or *being an internal part of*, or *being nested within*, or *being wholly within*, or simply, *being within*.

[28]   J.E.Tiles, *Things that Happen*, Aberdeen, 1981, §8, n.4, pp.40ff. and 53ff. A useful summary is given in P. Simons, *Parts*, Oxford, 1987, §2.10.2, pp.93-94. See also K.Menger, "Topology without Points", *Rice Institute Pamphlets*, **27**, 1940, §§3-5, pp.84-96; J.Nicod, *Foundations of Geometry and Induction*, London, 1930, ch.4, pp.36-49; Wald, *Ergebnisse v. Math. Kolloquium, Vienna*, **3**, 1932, p.6.

We may, indeed, hope that *being within* will enable us to rule out pathological abstractive classes, and define *punctiform* abstractive classes, which converged to, and adequately characterized, a definite point, since in the pathological abstractive classes the successive members, although proper parts of all their predecessors, were not within any of them. But although we can, indeed, thus exclude the pathological cases noted in §10.4, there are other Zenoesque ones which are not so easily excluded. Bostock instances an analogue to the "Pieces of Cake" counter-example. Within the two-dimensional region around the point [0,0], there are a series of holes getting progressively smaller and closer together as they approach [0,0] as a limit. We can construct a succession of such regions, each within its predecessor, and converging towards [0,0], but there would be many different such abstractive classes converging to [0,0], yet neither covering, nor being covered by, one another. And in the general case there would be no minimality: for any given punctiform class, one could construct another, full of Zeno-esque holes, which it covered, but was not covered by. A one-dimensional example can be constructed from a series of portions, $P_1, P_2, \ldots P_m, \ldots$, where P_m consists of the interval

$$(-\frac{1}{2^m}, \frac{1}{2^m})$$

minus a succession of holes

$$(\frac{1 - \delta_m}{2^n}, \frac{1 + \delta_m}{2^n})$$

where

$$\delta_m = (\frac{1}{3} - \frac{1}{2^{m+1}}).$$

Of course the portions P_1, P_2, etc., are, in one dimension, highly fragmented. But without a definition of unseparatedness, we are not entitled to rule them out.

We may be able to circumvent the Zeno-esque objection, but should not, in any case, be unduly grieved by a further failure to carry out Whitehead's original programme. We can reverse Röper's original definition, and define *being in contact* and *unseparatedness* in terms of *being within*. One region is separated from another if and only if it is within a region that is itself disjoint from the other.

We therefore need to consider how far we can go in characterizing *being within*. We characterized the *being a part of* relation as

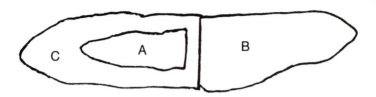

Figure 10.8.1 A, being within C, which is disjoint from B, is separate from C.

a partial, dense, serial ordering. Exactly the same conditions hold of the *being within* relation. Although we took it that that condition adequately characterized the *being a part of* relation, we did not consider whether it did so precisely. There was, however, one further feature of the *being a part of* relation, converse transitivity, which is not possessed by the *being within* relation. If every part of x is a part of y, then x is either itself identical with y, or a part of it:

$$(Az)((z \prec x) \rightarrow (z \prec y)) \rightarrow (x \prec y).$$

Similarly

$$(Az)((x \prec z) \rightarrow (y \prec z)) \rightarrow (y \prec x),$$

expressing converse transitivity from above, holds of $\prec$, the *part of* relation. But neither condition holds of $\prec\prec$, *being within*.

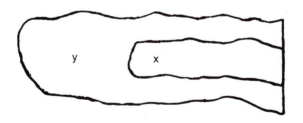

Figure 10.8.2 Every portion within x is also within y, but in this case x is not within y, though it is part of it.

We can thus distinguish *being a part of* from *being within* by purely formal means. We have two transitive, asymmetric, dense, serial, relations, one always implying the other, so that whenever the latter holds, the former does too:

$$x \prec\!\!\prec y \rightarrow x \prec y,$$

though not *vice versa*. Moreover, following the terminology of §9.8, the two relations are *compatible* with each other, that is to say,

$$x \prec\!\!\prec y \wedge y \prec z \rightarrow x \prec\!\!\prec z \wedge x \prec z$$

and

$$x \prec y \wedge y \prec\!\!\prec z \rightarrow x \prec z \wedge x \prec\!\!\prec z.$$

But one of them is conversely transitive, and the other not.

	Axioms for *Being Within*	
	'$\prec\!\!\prec$' primitive; '$=$', '$\preceq$', '$\prec$', '$\circ$', '$\mid$', '$\parallel$', '$\bowtie$' defined	
A 1	$x \prec\!\!\prec y \wedge y \prec\!\!\prec z \rightarrow x \prec\!\!\prec z$	Transitive
A 2	$\neg(x \prec\!\!\prec x)$	Irreflexive
A 3	$x \prec\!\!\prec y \rightarrow (\mathrm{V}z)(x \prec\!\!\prec z \wedge z \prec\!\!\prec y)$ Dense	
A 4 (i)	$(\mathrm{A}x)(\mathrm{V}y)(x \prec\!\!\prec y)$	Downwards Serial
A 4 (ii)	$(\mathrm{A}x)(\mathrm{V}y)(y \prec\!\!\prec x)$	Upwards Serial
A 5	$(\mathrm{A}x)(\mathrm{A}y)(\mathrm{A}z)(z \prec\!\!\prec x \leftrightarrow z \prec\!\!\prec y) \leftrightarrow$	
	$(\mathrm{A}x)(\mathrm{A}y)(\mathrm{A}z)(x \prec\!\!\prec z \leftrightarrow y \prec\!\!\prec z)$	
		Mirror Equivalence
D 1	$x = y$ for $(\mathrm{A}x)(\mathrm{A}y)(\mathrm{A}z)(z \prec\!\!\prec x \leftrightarrow z \prec\!\!\prec y)$	
D 2	$x \circ y$ for $(\mathrm{V}z)(z \prec\!\!\prec x \wedge z \prec\!\!\prec y)$	*overlaps*
D 3	$x \mid y$ for $\neg(x \circ y)$, *i.e.* $(\mathrm{V}z)(z \prec\!\!\prec x \wedge z \prec\!\!\prec y$	
		is disjoint from
D 4	$x \preceq y$ for $(\mathrm{A}z)(z \prec\!\!\prec x \rightarrow z \prec\!\!\prec y)$	
		is a proper or improper part of
D 5	$x \prec y$ for $x \preceq y \wedge \neg(x = y)$ *is a proper part of*	
D 6	$x \parallel y$ for $(\mathrm{V}z)(x \prec\!\!\prec z \wedge z \mid y)$ *is separate from*	
D 7	$x \bowtie y$ for $\neg(x \parallel y)$ *is connected with*	
A 6	$(\mathrm{A}x)(\mathrm{A}y)(y \prec\!\!\prec x \rightarrow (\mathrm{V}z)(z \prec\!\!\prec x \wedge z \mid y))$	
	Locally Non-linear and Not Downward Directed	
A 7	$(\mathrm{A}x)(\mathrm{V}y)(y \prec x \wedge \neg(y \prec\!\!\prec x))$	
	Not Conversely Transitive from Below	

If we axiomatize a system based on $\prec\prec$, *is within*, not only many of the axioms, but many of the definitions, come out the same. Because the ordering is dense and serial in both directions, whenever there is a portion that is a part of another portion, there will also be a portion that is within it. So the definitions of overlapping and being disjoint can be expressed in terms of either, and likewise the axioms of local non-linearity and non-downward-directedness. We can use equivalence to define identity, and converse transitivity to define $\preceq$, *is a proper or improper part of*, and then $\prec$, *is a proper part of*. The definitions of *is separate from* and *is connected with* are what we wanted the stronger relation for, but the axioms thus far do not rule out $\prec\prec$ being interpreted as simply $\prec$. That interpretation is ruled out by there being no converse transitivity from below. The axioms given in the box neither prescribe nor proscribe the mirror image property. It would be implausible to have converse transitivity from above, or to deny Mirror Equivalence, but the system might well be upward-directed. When we are dealing with regions, rather than with mere portions, it seems more plausible; and instead of stipulating that it be upwardly serial, we might well posit a whole space, within which all other regions were nested. Questions about the existence of mereological sums and products fade into the background, as we are able, with some refinement of the concept of connectivity, to specify precisely the conditions under which two regions can together form an unseparated whole, whose measure should be precisely the sum of the measures of its parts.

Chapter 11
Magnitude and Measure

11.1 *Quantum?* and *Quot?*

Sets can be counted: portions only measured. Measuring is very like counting, so much so that we often overlook the differences, and the Greeks, as we saw,[1] had only one stem for asking 'how many?', πόσοι (*posoi*), or 'how much?', πόσον (*poson*), in contrast to the Latin *quot?* for the former and *quantum?* for the latter. They were none the less able to distinguish πλῆθος (*plethos*), multitude, from μέγεθος (*megethos*), magnitude, and we distinguished quotity from quantity, and should correspondingly distinguish the natural numbers that we ascribe to multitudes from the numerical measure of magnitudes. Just as we ask the question *Quot?*, 'How many?', of a multitude, and the answer is a quotity, or natural number, so we ask the question *Quantum?*, 'How much?', of a magnitude, and the answer is a quantity, or numerical measure.

Unfortunately, we often fail to draw the distinction firmly, and our usage is confused. Even Aristotle defines time as the ἀριθμός (*arithmos*), positive whole number, of change when he should have said it was the μέτρον (*metron*), measure. In ordinary usage the words 'quantity' and 'magnitude' are ambiguous. Although we sometimes use 'quantity' as an abstract term for 'howmuchness', analogous to 'quality' meaning 'whatsortness', and sometimes use 'magnitude' to indicate the kind of 'How much?' we are asking about, whether it is expense, weight, or area, *etc.*, we often also use them as generic terms for that of which the 'How much?' question

---

[1] See above, §4.3.

is being asked. A recipe may tell us to take a quantity of flour, much as a pollster may be told to question a number of voters. Astronomers describe stars as being of a certain magnitude, and we may say it was the magnitude of the current that caused the fire. The confusion is due, in part, to the ways in which 'How much?' questions and answers differ from 'How many?' ones; and the argument of this chapter will show how our usage needs to be refined. For the present I need only to fix on generic terms, such as 'amount', 'chunk', 'dollop'. In contrast to the discrete 'individuals', 'members' and 'elements' of set theory, I shall use the words 'portion' and 'extension': I shall use the word 'portion' generally and mereologically of anything about which, in respect of some magnitude or other, the question 'How much?' can be asked and some quantitative answer given, and 'extension' for those portions which can form unseparated wholes.

11.2 The Point of Measuring

Why do we make measurements? Because we seek a certain sort of reliable description. Although often we are content with subjective impressions, often, indeed, preferring them, because they are more vivid and illuminating, we also suspect impressionistic accounts, because they depend on the judgement of the person making them, and are liable to prejudice, error and bias. If we are anxious to avoid the danger of being wrong, we go through a *procedure* whereby our answers will be checked, and made reasonably proof against error. It is this, rather than the use of a numerical vocabulary, which is essential to measurement. If I say I mind about the outcome of an election only half as much as I do about Oxford's losing the boat race, I have not made a measurement. Estimates are not measurements, although they are indubitably numerical, because they are not proof against error. If I guess that the window is two yards wide, I am quite likely to be a few inches out, whereas I shall be accurate to within an inch if I use a tape-measure. This is important when I come to buy curtains or curtain rail. If I measure the window, I can be reasonably sure that the curtain rail, when I come to put it up, will be long enough; and that if I order the curtains by post, the amount of material cut off by the draper will be no different from what would have been cut off if I had done it myself. And so, although on other occasions we may prefer less impersonal descriptions, and may describe the windows

as spacious and the wine sauce as intriguing, on those occasions
when our concern is to minimise subjective error we fall back on
procedures where a competent observer can scarcely go wrong.

Measurement, then, is a way of obtaining a standardised description based on a systematic procedure. It is a mapping according to some rule into some abstract entity. Usually it is in terms
of the rational real numbers, but we should not exclude, as simpler
cases, a mapping into the integers, the elements of the periodic table, or even the two-membered ranges $\{N, S\}$, $\{+, -\}$, or $\{\top, \bot\}$,
and, as more complicated cases, vectors and tensors. Formally we
construe measurement as a mapping into some set of abstract entities in accordance with some systematic procedure that reflects
significant similarities among the things measured.

Measurement is not only a mapping into some set of numbers,
but a *systematic* one. It is the requirement that they be systematic which distinguishes the measurements of ordinary life and the
natural sciences from the measures postulated by mathematicians
in their measure theory. Mathematicians take the God's-eye view,
and say "Let there be a measure function **f** defined from a set of
sets into the real numbers." But although God could assign measures by arbitrary *fiat*, such detailed power is beyond mere human
capacities, and if we are to assign measures, it must be by means
of some general system.[2]

Measurement is general in another way too. It is not just a
mapping, but a *many*–one mapping, unlike a coordinate system,
or the assignment of numbers to houses in a street, which, although
systematic, does not constitute a proper measurement. A many–
one mapping involves equivalence classes—all the many things that
are mapped into one and the same number. These equivalence
classes cannot be arbitrary if the measurement is to be systematic.
What is measured must have some sort of feature, property, quality
or relation, which could in principle be possessed by some other
thing. If two things are labelled with the same number they should
have something in common beyond the bare fact that they have the
same number assigned to them, and if two things are labelled with
different numbers, one of the ways they differ should correspond to
the way in which the numbers differ. If the weight of this butter is
four ounces and the weight of that butter is four ounces, then either

[2] See further below, §11.6

will be as good as the other for making pastry with. Were it not so, we would not use weights in recipes. So, generally, if two things have the same numerical measure, they are similar in some other significant respect. Measuring does not just impose similarities, but presupposes them. It is a fact of great importance. It means that far from being a matter of simple observation, measurement is highly theory-laden.

11.3 Equivalence Structures

Measurement presupposes objective similarities much as biologists and chemists assume the existence of species and natural kinds. Similarities are equivalence relations, equivalence relations betoken groups, and groups indicate symmetry.[3] The symmetries and equivalence classes presupposed by practical measuring processes have a profound influence on our theory of measurement. Our normal ways of measuring length and angle presuppose the invariance of rigid rods and protractors, which in turn carries with it a commitment to our space having constant curvature, and if we accept, as we normally do, that lengths and angles are invariant under translations and rotations—that is, under transformations of the proper Euclidean group—we are committed to a Euclidean geometry for space.[4] This is, in part, an empirical question, vulnerable to observational refutation, but not entirely so. If space did not have constant curvature, at least approximately, rigid transport would be impossible, and not only our theory of measurement would be invalidated, but many of our normal assumptions and everyday practices would be impossible. To this extent our assumptions about rigid rulers and protractors are deeply rooted in our metaphysic of nature.

Time is different. We cannot lay off an hour of yesterday's time against an hour of today's, and check that their durations are equal. Instead of rigid transport with its Euclidean implications, we rely on periodicity, compendiously expressed by exponential functions of imaginary arguments, and hence with a faint foretaste of Minkowskian timelikeness. We assume that certain periodic processes mark out isochronous intervals, and that 3,600 swings of a pendulum yesterday took up as much time as 3,600 swings of a pen-

---

[3] See above, §9.2, §9.3, §9.4.

[4] See above, §2.7.

dulum do today. We could be wrong. Early clock-makers were, and much effort has gone into eliminating adventitious sources of error that led to the duration of periodic processes being different under different conditions obtaining at different times. More profoundly, we take for granted the fortunate fact that "there is a unique basic rhythm of the universe",[5] and that periodic processes depending on the conservation of angular momentum—the diurnal rotation of the earth—and those depending on gravity—pendulum clocks, the earth's annual orbit round the sun—and those depending on quantum mechanics—the oscillations of a hair-spring, a quartz crystal, or a caesium atom—all cohere and yield the same isochronous intervals.

In our standard procedures for weighing objects we again have to make assumptions which are outside the realm of logic, but not simply a matter of observation. We assume that the process of weighing does not affect the weight, that the weight is not altered by moving objects around, that the earth's gravitational field is fairly uniform, that space is uniform and homogeneous, that the force exerted by the pans on the arms acts only through the point of contact, that the torque exerted by each pan depends only on the force and the length of the arm, and that the arms are equal in length. All these assumptions could be denied without inconsistency. But they are reasonable, and constitute extra-logical grounds for there being the objective similarities that measurement presupposes.

A similarity implies an equivalence relation, $\approx_r$, and hence also a partition of what is being measured into equivalence classes, all the members of each one of which have some property in common, like being the same age, or having the same weight. The question then arises about the relations between members of different equivalence classes. There is, typically, some ordering relation, *being bigger than*, *being older than*, *being further than*, and this needs to be compatible with the equivalence relation.

The requirement of compatibility between the equivalence relation and the ordering relation is secured, as we have seen,[6] if the equivalence relation is generated from the ordering relation,

[5] G.J.Whitrow, *The Natural Philosophy of Time*, 1st ed., Edinburgh, 1961, p.46.

[6] §9.8.

and is the same in both directions. Conceptually, it is an intuitively plausible condition, but empirically it is difficult to verify. We find it easier to define a symmetric relation negatively, and then check that, within the limits of experimental accuracy, it is also transitive. Thus we construe a balance as telling us whether either body is heavier than the other,[7] having little difficulty in verifying that *being heavier than* is a transitive relation, which we may symbolize $>_w$. If the two bodies balance, then neither is heavier than the other. It is an empirical fact, though one deeply grounded in the homogeneity and isotropy of space, and the truths of Newtonian mechanics, that the relation of balancing against each other is, within the limits of experimental accuracy, transitive.[8] We idealise, in order to exclude cases where marginal inaccuracies might add up to produce counter-examples, and argue that the relation $(x \not>_w x') \wedge (x' \not>_w x)$, being evidently symmetric, must be an equivalence relation, and must be compatible with $<$, since if $x >_w y$ and $(x \not>_w x') \wedge (x' \not>_w x)$ it would lead to an inconsistency unless also $x' >_w y$; and similarly if $x >_w y$ and $(y \not>_w y') \wedge (y' \not>_w y)$, it would lead to an inconsistency unless also $x >_w y'$.

Granted an equivalence relation that is compatible with the ordering relation, we can factor it out and obtain essentially the same ordering relation holding between the equivalence classes as held between individual members.[9] Besides the relation of $>_w$, *being heavier than*, or *weighing more heavily than*, holding between in-

---

[7] Most people take it as obvious that if one thing balances against another, they weigh the same because *balancing against* is an equivalence relation. But it is not. An equivalence relation is reflexive, and no material object can be placed in both pans of a balance at once. The same holds of two objects being at the same temperature if no heat flows from one to the other, or of two forces being at the same electric potential if no current flows, or of two forces being equal in magnitude, if, when opposed, they result in no acceleration, or of two solids being equally hard if neither will scratch the other. In all these cases logical exactitude requires us to adjoin identity in order to secure a genuine equivalence relation.

[8] That this is an empirical fact can be seen by comparing the case in the Special Theory, cited in §9.8, n.38, where the negatively defined "topological simultaneity" was not a transitive relation.

[9] See above, §9.2, §9.5.

dividual material objects, there is also the corresponding relation, shown with a capital subscript, $>_W$, which holds not between individual material objects but between weights, that is to say equivalence classes of individual objects that all balance against one another; in ordinary English we should read $>_W$ as *being greater than*, since we say that one weight is greater than another, rather than that it is heavier than, or weighs more heavily than another.

Formally we say that if X is the set of material objects, $X/\approx_w$ is the set of weights, and

$$[x]_w >_W [y]_w \quad \text{iff} \quad x >_w y.$$

In each case a system of measurement needs not only an equivalence relation but an ordering relation that is compatible with it, which enables us not only to establish a many–one mapping between what is being weighed and the abstract features each of the equivalence classes has in common, but to arrange those features or those quotient classes in a strict linear order, representing differences of degree between relevantly similar things.

Actual comparisons remain difficult to carry out in practice. Equivalence classes themselves cannot be weighed in balances, or measured with voltmeters: we can deal only with particular instances of an equivalence class. And often there are difficulties in comparing them—we cannot easily lay off a period today against one yesterday afternoon. Only in favourable circumstances can one portion be compared with another. Measuring instruments are contrived to create such circumstances, and to use the relevant equivalence relation to pick out some paradigm portions which are equivalent to those we want to compare, and which can themselves be compared. For two portions, x and y, and some magnitude q, we may well not be able to compare them directly, and tell whether $x <_q y$ or not, but we can find two other portions, z and w, such that $z \approx_q x$ and $w \approx_q y$, and either $z <_q w$, or $w <_q z$, or $z \approx_q w$. The characteristic circumstance in which we can be confident of making one of these judgements, is when z is a part of w, or w is a part of z, or z is identical with w. Our confidence in making such a judgement is based on the principle that

(1) The whole is greater than the part.

or, in symbols: for a magnitude, Q,

$$\text{if } z \prec w, \quad \text{then } z <_q w,$$

which, although not necessarily or universally true, is nonetheless valid in most cases. Portions of which this holds are paradigms and constitute a measure of the magnitude in question.[10]

11.4 Addition Rules

Although, occasionally, we can establish only an *order*, as with Mosh's degrees of hardness, typically we seek to establish a *scale*. In order to have a scale, we need to be able to say by how much one thing is greater than another, and thus require some sort of addition rule. Many rules are possible: a few are purely derivative; as Campbell points out, we do not directly add densities or degrees centigrade.[11] In some cases we tend to take it for granted that some operation counts as adding: putting two objects together on the pan of a balance *obviously* results in a total mass or weight that is the sum of them. But how obvious? Is it obvious that putting two resistances in series results in a resistance which is their sum? If we think it is, we have to explain why putting them in parallel yields a conductance (the reciprocal of a resistance) which is the sum of their individual conductances. Obviousness depends on theory. Even with the balance, there is, as we have seen, some theory involved in ascribing equality, and so, too, in applying an addition rule. Granted some general assumptions, we argue that the two bodies in the one pan have masses, which in a gravitational field exert forces on the arm of the balance at the point from which the pan hangs, and two forces acting on the same point in the same direction are simply added; because accelerations are, and these because velocities (as we normally suppose) are, and these ultimately because distances and durations are. Weights, therefore, are additive. So far as mass itself is concerned, it is as much a question of stipulation as of discovery. Newton postulated that there was a "quantity of matter" which could be summed. At

---

[10] Compare G.F.B.Riemann, Inaugural Lecture, "On the Hypotheses which Underlie Geometry", *Gesammelte mathematische Werke*, 2nd ed., Leipzig, 1892, p.272; tr. and quoted, N.Bourbaki, *General Topology*, Paris, 1966, p.163. "Measurement consists of superposition of the magnitudes to be compared, hence in order to measure, we need some means of using one magnitude as a yardstick for another. the absence of this we can compare two magnitudes only if one is part of the other."

[11] See N.R. Campbell, *Foundations of Science*, New York, 1957, pp.276-283.

one level we can say simply that Newton has been vindicated by experimental tests of Newtonian mechanics. But there are deep theoretical commitments in the additivity of mass and of energy which themselves reflect a need for invariance over time, itself an ultimate exemplar of an extensive magnitude.

Thus, ultimately, as we press back in our justifications of measurement, we come down to the addition of some *extensive* magnitude—the magnitude assigned to some sort of extension, such as length, time, angle, area, or volume.

We add extensive magnitudes on much the same grounds as we order them. To the doctrine invoked in the previous section, that the whole is greater than the part, we add

(2) The whole should be, measure-wise, exactly the sum of its parts.

Both theses are intuitively acceptable, but they cannot be claimed to be logical truisms. We may on occasion be led to reject them: velocity in the Special Theory is a case in point. Intuitively it would seem obvious that velocities were extensive magnitudes. If you are moving away from me with velocity u, and Peter is moving in the same direction with velocity v with respect to you, then we naturally suppose that he must be moving away from me with velocity $u + v$. But the Special Theory bids us adopt the different composition rule,

$$u \oplus v = \frac{u + v}{1 + \frac{uv}{c^2}}$$

The justification for adopting this composition rule, and not the simple additive one $u + v$, is connected with the adoption of the velocity of light as the unit, and lies deep in the Special Theory. Granted that the composition rule satisfies certain intuitively acceptable conditions, we can always regraduate the physical magnitudes involved, so as to have the regraduated magnitudes simply additive. In this case there is a certain function of velocities, "rapidities", or "pseudo-angles", as they are sometimes called, which are simply additive, and we are led to look askance at velocities as the simple extensive magnitudes we once thought they were, and instead, regard rapidities as the fundamental magnitudes. *Per contra* the fact that energy, *vis viva*, when it was first taken to be a physical magnitude, was found to be simply additive helped us regard it, and hence also mass, as a fundamental magnitude that is thought of as extensive.

Although in any particular case we may be led by theory to change our views about what is an extensive magnitude, we should not be able to give an ultimate justification for any measurements, unless there were some magnitudes we acknowledged to be extensive, and for which the principle that the measure of the whole was the sum of the measures of the parts did in fact hold. It is reasonable, then, to allow these principles as presumptively valid, and to accept them in the absence of objections in the particular case, and to recognise that there is some sense of 'extension' and 'being part of' in which they are true in virtue of what we mean by those terms.

We cannot add disparate lengths, intervals, angles, areas and volumes, *etc.*, any more than we can compare them. It is only if they adjoin without overlapping that they constitute a whole whose measure is the sum of the measures of the parts. We need some criterion of togetherness that enables us to tell when two extensions together constitute an unseparated whole. Such a criterion is not mereologically available as a matter of course. We may be able to invoke some topological condition, as when we reckon that two areas with a common boundary constitute one unseparated whole; or that two volumes of the same liquid in the same container can be regarded as a single volume: but the Greeks were already queasy about the measurement of areas, and we want to make as few extra assumptions as possible.

In the case of linear extensions we do have a criterion of togetherness. Even if in a fairly arbitrary way we assign rational real numbers to an extension and those extensions that are parts of it, subject only to condition 1 of the previous section, that the whole is greater than the part, we have enough of an ordering to constitute a continuum with definite bounds and limits. We can assure ourselves that the interval between one end of a foot rule and the six inch mark adjoins that between the six inch mark and the other end. Of course we want more. We want rigid rods to lay off equal intervals, and an initial arbitrary assignment of rational real numbers would have to be regraduated to secure suitable isometries. But that can be done. It can be done not only for lengths, but for durations and angles, both of them being subject to a natural linear ordering, as well. Areas are more difficult. But granted that triangles between the same pair of parallel lines, and having the same base, are equal in area, we can reduce the measurement of

area to that of length, and volumes similarly. Provided we can find
some paradigm that is linear and satisfies condition (1) in §12.3, we
can pick out those extensions that together form an unseparated
whole, and apply the principle that measure of the whole should
be exactly the sum of the measures of its parts.

Granted that there are extensions and extensive magnitudes,
and that we can recognise them, the justification for the way we
measure them seems very simple. We have an extra-logical equivalence relation, which assures us that some rigid ruler lays off
equal lengths, some protractor equal angles, some clock marks off
isochronous intervals, and we use these equivalence relations to
find an equivalent to what has to be measured on some standard
measure where parts and wholes are easily compared. I cannot directly compare an hour yesterday with a minute today, but, granted
that a pendulum or balance wheel or caesium atom always has the
same period of oscillation, I can reckon that yesterday's hour has
the same duration as one today, and that today's minute is just as
long as fifty nine others which together make up the hour. Duration just is a measure of intervals such that a subinterval has a less
measure and the measures of two mutually exclusive and jointly
exhaustive subintervals add up to the measure of the whole interval. The magnitude is defined in terms of the relevant $\prec$ relation
and addition rule. For almost all practical purposes that is enough.
The rational numbers will give us all that we need to express all the
measurements we actually make to any desired degree of accuracy.

11.5 Limits and Zero

There remains one further difficulty to be overcome before we have
a satisfactory theory of addition. In order to provide a criterion for
togetherness, so that two non-overlapping parts should constitute
an unseparated whole, we had to concern ourselves with boundaries, or limits, and once we recognise the existence of limits, we
feel uneasy about how they should enter into our metrical book-
keeping.

Consider our measuring two pieces of string with a foot rule,
finding they are each six inches long, and concluding that they
together amount to twelve inches. The equivalence relation $\approx_l$
causes no trouble. Within the limits of experimental accuracy we
can confirm that either bit of string will lay off against either the
first six inches or the second six inches. When, however, we be-

come sensitive to limits, we distinguish the closed intervals, $[0,6]$, $[6,12]$ and $[0,12]$, which include their end-points, from the open intervals, $(0,6)$, $(6,12)$ and $(0,12)$, which do not. And then we ask to which of these different intervals are numerical measures to be ascribed, and whatever answer we give, we are led either to ignore or else to double-count some limit element. If we are to stay in line with ordinary practice, we have to reckon that $[0,6]$, $(0,6)$, and indeed, $[0,6)$ and $(0,6]$, all measure the same; but if they are all to have the same measure, we must ascribe to $[0]$, $[6]$ and $[12]$, and to many other entities, measure zero, and must deem to be the same entities which although "almost everywhere" the same, differ in respect of quite a large number of points or other limit elements. Extensive magnitudes need, besides the extra-logical equivalence relation that picks out equal lengths, equal angles, or equal durations, at different places, in different directions, or at different dates, a further quasi-logical, perhaps topological, relation that assimilates co-extensive extensions differing only in respect of limit elements.

It follows that in a sense limit elements have no magnitude. Points have no length, lines no area, surfaces no volume. Of course, this does not preclude lines having length or surfaces area, but that is a different sort of magnitude. So far as the extensive magnitude under consideration is concerned, limit elements are to be assigned zero magnitude. Intuitively it seems quite acceptable, besides being forced on us by the logic of our theory of measurement. But it gives rise to problems.

11.6 Zeno

If limit elements have no magnitude, and if, as appears often to be the case once infinite operations are admitted, limit elements are the only ultimate constituents of extensive magnitudes, then it is difficult to see how extensive magnitudes can have any magnitude either. It is not a new problem. Zeno found it very difficult to see how an extension, such as a line or surface or volume, that did have magnitude could be made up of entities, such as points, that did not. If we bisect a line one inch long an infinite number of times, we shall end up with a point. So points, it seems, are all that lines are made up of. But points have no length. So, however many points there may be in a line, their total length must be zero, since nought times anything is nought.[12]

The problem can be resolved by appeal to Cantor's distinction between denumerable and non-denumerable infinities. A denumerable infinity, $\aleph_o$, can be regarded as being itself a limit, the limit of all the natural numbers, each one of which is finite. Since, for any finite number n,

$$n \times 0 = 0,$$

it is right to argue that for any finite number n the magnitude of n items, each having no magnitude, is itself zero, and so the limit, as n tends to infinity is zero too:

$$\sum_{n \to \infty} (n \times 0) = 0.$$

But non-denumerable infinities cannot be regarded as limits of the natural numbers. Although the first half of Zeno's argument stands, and infinite divisibility leads in the limit to points of zero magnitude, we can no longer maintain that their sum must be defined as

$$\sum_{n \to \infty} (n \times 0),$$

but are free to maintain without paradox that it is incommensurably greater, and thus could well be a non-infinitesimal quantity.

It is tempting to think that there being a non-denumerable infinity of instants is not only a necessary but a sufficient condition of their constituting a non-infinitesimal interval; but this is not so. When we refine our intuitions about magnitudes into Lebesgue Measure Theory, we find that there can be sets of non-denumerably many points to which no measure can be assigned. Cantor's discontinuum is one example. Another illuminating one, due to Vitali,[13] proves the existence of an unmeasurable set provided

---

[12] Aristotle, *Physics*, VI, 9, $239^b - 240^a$.

[13] Here adapted from H.L. Royden, *Real Analysis*, New York, 1968, pp.52-53, 63-64. I am indebted to my colleague, Dr. D.J.A. Welsh, for drawing my attention to this result. See also D. van Dalen, H.C. Doets and H. de Swart, *Sets: Naive, Axiomatic and Applied*, Oxford, 1978, ch.III, §5, Th.5.3, p.269; Tarski's decomposition of a sphere into two equal spheres illustrates the same point.

(1) the measure of each interval is its length,

(2) measure is countably additive, and

(3) measure is translation-invariant.

Intuitively it is easier if we consider not an interval of a straight line but the circumference of a circle, for which, then, (3) yields that the measure of any subset of the circumference should be invariant under rotation round the centre of the circle. We construct, as it were, a Paul Jones dance. First we thin out the circumference by forming a partition, where two points are members of the same equivalence class if they differ, along the circumference, by a rational number, and then, by the Axiom of Choice, take just one member from each equivalence class. This yields a set, still uncountably infinite, but smaller—infinitely smaller, so to speak— than the original class. It has many gaps in it. We then rotate this ring. We consider all the cases where it has been rotated by $r_i/2\pi$ radians, where r_i is the ith rational number in some standard enumeration. It is easy to show that any two such rotations will yield sets with no member in common, and hence that every point on the circumference will be in one and only one of the sets. If we have countable additivity (condition (2)) the measure of the whole circumference will be the sum of the countably infinite set of Paul Jones sets generated by rotation of the original one through $r_i/2\pi$ radians for each i. If we have translation invariance (condition (3)) we have each Paul Jones set having the same measure. And if we have condition (1), we must assign to the whole circumference some finite measure, namely unity, its length. But these three conditions are inconsistent. If any Paul Jones set has zero measure, the measure of each of the others must be zero too, by translation invariance, and so the total of them all must be zero too by countable additivity, contrary to condition (1); and if any Paul Jones set has a non-zero measure, the same measure must be assigned to each of the others, and the total of them all must be infinite, again contrary to condition (1). Either way we have a contradiction. Essentially what we have done is to divide an interval by $\aleph_0$, a countable infinity, and then multiply it again by the same number, and thus reproduce Zeno's paradox.

This result seems surprising to us, reared on set-theoretical approaches to measure theory. We should understand it as indicating the limitations of that approach, and as showing that something more is needed if a set is to have a finite positive measure than that it should contain a non-denumerable infinity of members: non-denumerability is a necessary condition of escaping from Zeno's paradox, but not a sufficient one; certain properties of order are required too—an interval must contain not only a non-denumerable infinity of instants but must be so arranged as to constitute the order-type of the continuum. We should, therefore, for this reason as well as that adduced in §11.2—that measures need to be assigned by some method accessible to others, and not by the *fiat* of an individual mathematician—be wary of taking over measure theory from the mathematicians as an elucidation of our basic concepts of extension and magnitude. Measurable sets are not just sets, and even if we start with measurable sets, we can easily be led by set-theoretical operations into non-measurable ones.

Even when what we are assigning numbers to are abstract entities subject to Boolean operations, as when we assign probabilities to propositions, propositional functions, propensities, or predicates, we should not assume that those abstract entities are best understood as sets, or think exclusively in terms of additive set theory. Although set theory provides a paradigm example of a Boolean lattice, it is not the only one, and propositions, propositional functions, propensities, and predicates, are equally Boolean and no less respectable, and it is better to leave set theory out of it, and work out directly what the calculus of probabilities must be from the need to marry the Boolean algebra of propositions, or propositional functions, or predicates, with the arithmetical algebra of the real numbers. Whereas with lengths, durations, angles and weights, the addition rule depended on there being physical conditions under which extensive magnitudes were together, and together formed one connected whole, with probabilities we depend on entirely conceptual arguments for adding, or multiplying, or complementing them.[14] Subjective approaches, in terms of beliefs and expected utilities, are subject to similar constraints of rationality, and yield similar results. We may need to go further. The propensities we ascribe to ψ-functions in quantum mechanics

---

[14] See further, J.R.Lucas, *The Concept of Probability*, Oxford, 1970, esp. ch.3. See earlier, R.T.Cox, *The Algebra of Probable Inference*, Baltimore, 1961, and I.J.Good, *Probability and the Weighing of Evidence*, London, 1950, Appendix II. See further, C.Howson and P.Urbach, *Scientific Reasoning*, 2nd ed., Chicago, 1993, pp.89-96.

are not Boolean, and we may need some new concept of probability that maps a non-Boolean algebra into the real interval [0,1].

Set theory is inherently discrete and sharp, and although some mathematicians have sought to develop "fuzzy set theory", it sounds perilously close to self-contradiction. Probabilities, like many other magnitudes, are often approximate and not sharp. On the basis of a large number of trials, I can say that the probability is probably approximately equal to the frequency, but that is all. The fact that no matter how large the sample is, the possibility of an extraordinary coincidence can never be absolutely ruled out, has bothered many theoreticians who have identified truth with probability 1 and falsehood with probability 0. A more blurred picture, with truth being the neighbourhood of 1, and falsehood being the neighbourhood of 0, accords better with actual practice, and is truer to the logic of assigning measure to magnitude. We accept as true a hypothesis whose probability is, in a succession of trials, tending towards 1, and reject as false a hypothesis whose probability is, in a succession of trials, tending towards 0: construed in terms of set theory, the dominant feature is that these probabilities never actually reach 1 or 0; viewed as the initial segment of an abstractive class, the identification with truth or falsity seems quite natural.

Although a useful tool of analysis for resolving problems that arise in the course of integration and elsewhere, measure theory, as currently practised by mathematicians, does not give us an adequate account of what is involved in assigning numbers to portions or extensions, which cannot be characterized in terms of cardinality alone, but must invoke also some concept of order that lies outside the confines of pure set theory.

11.7 Measures and Numbers

Now that we have buttressed the principle that the measure of the whole is the sum of the measures of the parts, we can develop the numerical theory of measurement. It is essentially a theory of proportions or ratios. We take some magnitude as a unit. Since we have some, extra-logical equivalence relation, we can pick out other extensions that are equivalent to the unit, and in particular can arrange to have two or more of them together forming an unseparated whole. We can thus not only add magnitudes generally, but form multiples of the standard unit. We can likewise divide

it equally, and thus determine, within some degree of approxima-
tion, a rational number corresponding to the ratio between a given
magnitude and the unit. For practical purposes that is enough.
Eudoxus went further, and gave a criterion for one ratio of magnitudes being equal to another ratio of magnitudes even when the
magnitudes were incommensurable, and not exactly represented by
any rational number. We can thus conceptually accommodate the
ratio of the diagonal to the side of a square, or of the circumference to the diameter of a circle, and, going beyond the limitations
of practicality, assign to magnitudes not merely rational numbers
but real numbers as well.

Usually the choice of unit is arbitrary, but the zero is fixed, since
the limits are assigned zero size. Thus distance, length, breadth,
area, volume, and duration have a natural minimum to which a
zero quantity must be assigned. With other sorts of magnitude it
is less clear. Probabilities are necessarily non-negative. Mass is
non-negative, but not necessarily so: negative weight makes perfectly good sense, and negative electric charge is accepted as fundamental. The zero of potential energy seems quite arbitrary, and
that of temperature depends on advanced thermodynamic theory
rather than anything to do with the theory of measurement or our
ordinary understanding of hot and cold.

The natural zero of extensive magnitudes constitutes another
root of 0. Nought as a natural number was a quotity, defined in
terms of the negative existential quotifier, and 0 was characterized symbolically by Peano's axioms, and could be characterized
further in terms of recursive definitions of addition and multiplication. Once we have grounded addition and multiplication, we
can generalise the concept of a group to a field—a group with two
interlocking operations, + and ×—and characterize 0 as the identity element for + and as the "universal" element for ×.[15] And
if a field is ordered and complete, then it is isomorphic with the
real numbers.[16] By itself, however, this characterization is formal
and empty. We can fill it out, as Eudoxus, Dedekind and Cantor
did, by defining real numbers in terms of rationals, so that the real
number 0 is defined ultimately in terms of the natural number 0.
But now we see how we can also characterize the number 0 as a

[15] See above, §4.4.

[16] See above, §9.7.

mereological minimum, like Pythagoras' points, which had neither parts nor magnitude.[17] We can name this mereological minimum quantity 'zero' to distinguish it from the quotity nought.

Smallest Numbers

Zero is the measure of the minimal limit,
the lowest proportion, the lowest ratio,
the least non-negative real number.

Nought is the cardinal number of the null class.

0 is the abstract number that has no predecessor.

O is the identity element for addition.

O is the universal element for multiplication.

It might at first seem a contradiction in terms to speak of a mereological minimum. Mereology is serial and dense, and has no minima and no next. The answer lies in the addition rule, which is essential if we are to have a genuine scale, and not merely an ordered set of degrees. To apply the fundamental principle that for extensive magnitudes the whole is the sum of its parts, we need a criterion of extensive magnitudes together forming a whole. It cannot be that they overlap, for then we should be double-counting the overlapping regions. It must be that they share a common boundary. But then again we should be in danger of double-counting, or else failing to take account of boundaries, unless we have a principle that boundaries, and limit elements generally, have measure zero. Although there are no minimal portions, measuring has to take cognizance of limits, to all of which it must assign a unique minimum measure—zero.

In some cases a natural unit is given too: the most obvious example is angle, and hence time; a more *recherché* but equally fundamental one is the velocity of light. In each case we identify the unit by extra-logical considerations. We take 2π radians to be the true unit because of a symmetry property peculiar to trigonometric

---

[17] See above, §2.5.

functions, and this, though far from contingent, is a feature of trigonometry, not the theory of measurement itself. It is only from the standpoint of the Special Theory of Relativity that the velocity of light seems to be the natural unit. And although in both of these cases there is good reason for adopting the natural unit, we can adopt some other unit and work with that; we can measure angles in degrees and speeds in knots. So far as the theory of measurement is concerned, the choice of unit is fundamentally arbitrary.

The arbitrariness of the unit is a typical feature of the measurement of magnitudes. In a way it reflects the independent nature of the addition rule. In the elementary arithmetic of the natural numbers addition can be defined recursively in terms of the successor function, and the unit for multitudes is thus defined ultimately in terms of *next after*: with magnitudes, by contrast, there is no such fundamental definition; any two extensive magnitudes that are together can be considered as a single one, with the measure of the sum being the sum of the measures of the parts. We do not learn what adding is generally by learning first what it is to add one, and no particular unit is presupposed by addition.

There are thus three choices involved in measuring magnitudes, as opposed to only two in counting multitudes. We have to specify the item—this pat of butter—and the magnitude in issue—'How much does it weigh?' or 'How much does it cost?'—and also the unit—ounces or grams: pounds or dollars—before we have specified our question completely; in order to count we need only the sort of individuals to be counted—people or books—and the relevant gathering or group—in this room, or in the Bodleian Library.

A comparison with quantum mechanics is illuminating. For a quantum measurement, we need first to specify the system, whose state is described by the ψ-function. We need secondly to choose what sort of measurement to make, that is, what magnitude— energy, momentum, spin—we are interested in, described, somewhat misleadingly, as an "observable", for example, H representing energy. As a result of the measuring process, represented in quantum mechanics by the operator associated with the observable, for example, $\hat{H}$, the ψ-function collapses into an *eigen*-function, with an *eigen*-value, which is expressed as a certain numerical value in, say, electron volts, where, again, it is our choice to express our measurement in electron volts rather than ergs or joules or megawatt-hours.

	Multitude	**Magnitude**
Question	How many?	How much?
	Quot?	*Quantum?*
asked of	group or gathering	portion or extension
(examples)	men in the room	pat of butter
	cards in skat	field
need to say	(i) individuals (ii) group	(i) item (ii) magnitude (area/weight/cost) (iii) unit (acre/oz/gr/£/$)
generic answer	quotity	quantity
expressed by	cardinal (*i.e.* natural) number	ratio to unit rational or real number
specific answer	15	7.8 acres/4oz/£2/$3

Table 11.7.1

Chapter 12
Down With Set Theory

12.1   Theory of Multitudes

Set Theory occupies a crucial position in mathematics. The whole of mathematics, it is often maintained, can be "reduced" to set theory. But it is also the most problematic part of mathematics. It is the only branch of mathematics in which contradictions have been found. It has been axiomatized in a number of different ways to avoid inconsistency, but we are none too confident that the axiomatizations are indeed consistent, and are divided as to their several merits. New axioms have been proposed for set theory, not all consistent with one another, and we are unclear how to evaluate them, or what their status really is.

Set theory suffers from the ambitions of its friends. The Logicists hoped to reduce the whole of mathematics to set theory, regarding it as part of logic, with sets being the successors of Frege's difficult concept of *Umfang*, usually translated 'extension',[1] was construed as meaning 'set', and cardinal numbers were construed by the Logicists as sets of equinumerous sets. After Russell showed naive set theory to be inconsistent, the axiomatized versions had a much weaker claim to be accounted part of logic. Most of modern set theory is better described as transfinite arithmetic. And whereas Frege's programme of defining the natural numbers 0, 1,

---

[1]   See above, §4.6. The translation is unfortunate, as the word 'extension' suggests the possibility of shared boundaries, as in the previous two chapters.

2, *etc.* in purely logical terms would have been a great achievement, to define 0, 1, 2, *etc.* by means of transfinite arithmetic does
not seem a great step forward. Similarly, set theory *can* be used
to represent other parts of mathematics. Every monadic predicate
can be represented by suitable subsets, and relations, and hence
also functions, can be represented by Cartesian products of suitable subsets; but once again, this is no great catch. Although every
relational structure has a model in set theory, all the work is in determining *which* subsets are needed in the model. Often the model
will have to exclude some subsets—if it is serial, it must exclude
the empty set and the universal set.[2] We cannot rely on set theory alone to establish truths about orderings or other structures;
although it may be useful on occasion in furnishing helpful models. It is not the perfect paradigm of all orderings or all relational
structures.

Transfinite arithmetic is a fascinating subject. If we construe
sets as Cantorian counters whose sole function is to have cardinal
powers, or to be arranged in ordinal sequences, we have an interesting, and possibly respectable, Theory of Multitudes—indeed
a Theory of Mega-Multitudes—analogous to the Theory of Magnitudes discussed in previous chapters. Whereas the entities to which
we could ascribe magnitudes were dense, or even continuous, the
entities to which we could ascribe multitudes are discrete, with an
ordering, therefore, that is non-serial, and perhaps, per-very-haps,
with a single maximum and minimum. IF it has a single maximum and minimum, it is a lattice, as described in Chapter Nine,
which exerts pressure on our theory of multitudes to conform to the
paradigm. Without that pressure, we should naturally incline to
a tree-like structure, with minimal atoms rather than a minimum
null set. Axiomatic Set Theories recognise this by postulating an
Axiom of Foundation (or Axiom of Regularity) securing the existence of ultimate indivisible *ur*-elements.[3] Under pressure from the
paradigm, the lime-tree structure of magnitudes has been turned

---

[2] R.R. Stoll, *Sets, Logic and Axiomatic Theories*, San Francisco, 1961, ch.1,
p.52.

[3] Though P. Aczel, "Non-Well-Founded Sets", CSLI Lecture Notes, No.14,
1988, Stanford, Ca, USA, has developed a set theory with an Anti-Found-
ation Axiom, which is consistent with Zermelo's and Fraenkel's other
axioms.

into a Boolean lattice, in which any two sets can be conjoined or
disjoined, with a null set as minimum, and an indication towards a
universal set as maximum. The idealized Boolean lattice of §9.11
mirrors our thinking with adjectives. We consider all the entities
of an appropriate sort, that possess some property, and then either
reach a global conclusion or concentrate on a particular one. If we
take all the rational numbers whose square is less than 2, we conclude that the set is bounded, but if we take any individual one,
we conclude that it is not the greatest member of the set. The
square root of 2 is not a rational number, but can be introduced
as a *set* of rational numbers. Such reasoning is unobjectionable,
constrained as it is in our ordinary use of set theory by a background understanding of the logic of adjectives, which are always
relativised to some suitable universe of discourse. It is very convenient, and for that reason often worth putting up with the null
set and the suggestion of a universal set, which in practice is relativised to a suitable universe of discourse. Set theory from this
point of view is a structure we have insisted on completing so as to
ensure that Boolean operations can always go through, somewhat
as complex numbers are a structure we have made complete so that
algebraic operations can always go through.

Sources of Set Theory

1. Failed Fregean *Umfangen*
2. Cantorian Counters
3. Lattice Paradigm
4. Arguments with Adjectives

It is very convenient. But it exacts a conceptual price, when
generalised from particular contexts to principles of universal application. The null set seems to many too insubstantial to exist,
while the universal set is altogether too much to stomach. The
unbridled use of Boolean operations can take us outside the range
of intelligibility. Boolean meetings are usually all right—the intersection of the set of human beings with the set of mammals living
in the British Isles is unproblematic—but only specially suited sets
can be joined together—men and women can, but not men and
irrational numbers; in this there is an analogue with the restricted
conditions under which extensive magnitudes could constitute a

single unseparated whole. Nor are Boolean complements always acceptable—the set of non-black things is a questionable subset of non-ravens. In our ordinary thinking we distinguish nouns from adjectives, and while we are fairly willing to be pushed towards a Boolean logic for propositions and for predicates, standing in for adjectives, we have legitimate scruples about the use and composition of nouns.

Being subject to diverse intellectual pressures, we have not been able to frame a coherent concept of a set; textbooks on set theory find it embarrassingly difficult to explain to the reader what the object of study is. It is not surprising that the naive theory of sets turned out to be inconsistent, and current controversies about which further axioms should be adopted may in part be attempts to articulate different concepts of what a set really is.

12.2 Russell's Paradox

Russell proved naive set theory inconsistent. He constructed a paradoxical set—the set of all sets that are not members of themselves—and asked whether it was a member of itself or not. Whichever answer was given, a self-contradiction ensued. It followed that set theory as then practised, was inconsistent.

Most sets are not members of themselves. If asked whether $x \in x$, we should say No. It is only of extraordinary entities that we are disposed to say that they in any way include themselves: perhaps the catalogue of a library features in itself as one of the books in the library, and in set theory it would be reasonable to suppose that there was a set of all sets, which would then have itself as a member. Such sets Russell called "extraordinary sets", and for them it would be the case that $x \in x$ whereas for the ordinary sets it would be the case that $\neg(x \in x)$, or $(x \notin x)$ for short. We thus have characterized a property, of *being ordinary*, which most sets possess, though some do not. Formally we say $\phi(x)$ iff $x \notin x$, where ϕ stands for *is ordinary* We then consider the set of all ordinary sets. This set, which we call z, is defined by the condition,

$$(Ax)(x \in z) \leftrightarrow \phi(x).$$

Is this set ordinary or extraordinary? If it is ordinary, it is not a member of itself, and so, not being a member of itself, possesses the property ϕ; but in that case it is a member of z, the set of all ordinary sets, that is the sets possessing the property ϕ, and so is extraordinary, contrary to our supposition. If, on the other hand, it is an extraordinary set, then, being a member of itself, it possesses the property ϕ, and so is an ordinary set, again contrary to supposition. Either way we are led to inconsistency: if it is ordinary, then it is extraordinary; if it is extraordinary, then it is ordinary. Formally, if $\phi(z)$, then $(z \notin z)$ by definition of ϕ, and so $\neg\phi(z)$, since z is the set of all those sets that possess ϕ: but if $\neg\phi(z)$, then $\neg(z \notin z)$, again by definition of ϕ, which is to say $(z \in z)$ and so $\phi(z)$, since z is the set of all those sets that possess ϕ. In brief, if $\phi(z)$, then $\neg\phi(z)$, and if $\neg\phi(z)$, then $\phi(z)$: that is,

$$\phi(z) \leftrightarrow \neg\phi(z),$$

which is a straight inconsistency.

12.3 Responses to Paradox

Russell concluded that not all apparently meaningful predicates really were meaningful—in particular the predicate 'being a member of oneself', and hence also the predicate 'not being a member of oneself'. The reason for this lay in the Theory of Types, which required that $\in$, the epsilon of set-membership, could only stand between two terms where the latter was one type higher than the former. If that is so, then $(x \in x)$ and $(x \notin x)$ are ill-formed, and the expression $\{x | x \notin x\}$ is ill-formed, and does not refer to anything at all, any more than the phrase 'the has square sturdily us cannot' does. Russell's Theory of Types turned out to need further ramification, and to be quite impossible to work with. In *Principia Mathematica* the Axiom of Reducibility was postulated, without any further justification, to undo some of the damage that its restrictions imposed on mathematical argument.

    The Theory of Types can be defended. Russell's paradox was in some way self-referential. A set that has itself as a member needs to refer to itself in any listing of its members, but until it has itself been fully specified, the listing is not complete. It is like trying to pull oneself up by one's bootstraps. Or, in computer terms, a self-referential class cannot be properly defined, because the definition will get one into a loop from which there is no escape. Russell's "Vicious Circle" principle has intuitive plausibility if we adopt a nominalist or constructivist attitude to mathematical entities.[4] But it has not been generally accepted as providing a

---

[4] See further below, §15.3.

satisfactory response to Russell's paradox. For one thing, it seems to exclude too much. More fundamentally, Gödel's theorem and its cluster of corollaries show that any simple ban on self-reference can be evaded, and that the trouble, if it is trouble, lies deeper. And so, although Quine's New Foundations can be seen as a successor to Russell's own response to his paradox, formalised versions of the Theory of Types have not found favour with mathematicians.

From a philosophical point of view, however, it would be quite acceptable to impose some restriction on the predicates to which the Axiom of Comprehension could be applied. There might be a deep ontological fact about the Platonist world of mathematical entities—a true report brought back by a voyager who had travelled in Cantor's paradise. Some universals exist: they can be characterized by means of a suitable predicate, and the set of all those things that possess the property in question can be referred to by the equivalent referring phrase. A Platonist can accept a modified Axiom of Comprehension, but owes us an account of the Platonic forms, and how we are to tell those that genuinely exist from unreal ones described by implausible characterizations cooked up by clever logicians.

The Axiom of Comprehension can also be defended on nominalist grounds. "A law (program) is more basic than a graph."[5] An argument then suggests itself to show that programs are more select than mere extensional graphs. For there are only a denumerable infinity, $\aleph_0$, of programs that can be specified, and a nondenumerable number of graphs, that is to say, sets determined only by their members, which accords with the Platonist claim that there are some restrictions on what should count as a real universal. But we need to be cautious; we have already availed ourselves of the fact that there are more qualities than we can specify, in using second-order logic to quotify over predicates in order to exclude the unwanted intruders into the realm of natural numbers. Although not every set is a universal, there are more things in the Platonic heaven than can be described in first-order philosophy.

In the absence of a satisfactory theory of predicate types,[6]

---

[5] D. van Dalen, H.C. Doets, H. de Swart, *Sets: Naive, Axiomatic and Applied*, Oxford, 1978, p.x. M.Hallett, *Cantorian Set Theory and Limitations of Size*, Oxford, 1984, §1.3, pp.32-40.

[6] See further, §13.6.

mathematicians have sought to avoid the paradoxes by amending
the Axiom of Comprehension, so that it applies only to already existing sets instead of generating fresh ones *de novo*. It becomes the
Axiom of Subsets.[7] Given any set, it enables us to pick out a subset
of those elements of the original set that have some specified prop-
erty: if y is a set, and F a predicate, then $\{x | x \in y \wedge F(x)\}$ is a
set too, but it does not pick out any particular set of elements
having that property from the whole universe of discourse. Given
the set of ravens, we can pick out the set of those ravens that are
black, and equally the set of those ravens that are not black: but
we cannot just pick out the set of black ravens from all existent
entities. We must start with some definite set—the set of ravens,
or the set of birds, or the set of animals, or even the set of material
objects—from which to pick out some subset characterized by the
property in question: but we are not entitled to talk of the set of
all those elements that possess the property in question, unless it
is taken to be a subset of an antecedently specified set.

The most common version of set theory in use by mathematicians today is Zermelo–Fraenkel set theory, usually known as ZF.
Besides the Axiom of Subsets, it has the Pair Set Axiom and the
Power Set Axiom. The former entitles us to form the set of just
two elements—$\{x, y\}$—the latter to form the set of all the subsets
of any given set. Also, given a set of sets, we can form the union
of them all, that is to say the set that contains all the elements of
each. These all enable us to form sets, but only if we are given some
to begin with. Zermelo–Fraenkel set theory has two axioms to give
an initial stock of sets. The Null Set Axiom specifies that the null
set shall be a set, and the Axiom of Infinity stipulates the existence
of a set with a denumerable infinity of elements.[8] If we think of
the Axiom of Subsets, the Pair Set Axiom and the Union Axiom
as rules of inference, entitling us to draw inferences from already
established well-formed formulae, then the Null Set Axiom and the
Axiom of Infinity correspond to the axioms of a logistic system,
giving us the initial well-formed formulae from which others can
be inferred.[9]

---

[7] Also known as the "Axiom of Replacement".

[8] It is this axiom that justifies the charge that set theory is really transfinite
arithmetic.

[9] We can dispense with the Null Set Axiom, by using the Axiom of Subsets

Axioms for Zermelo–Fraenkel Set Theory
1 Extensionality
2 Subsets
3 Pair Set
4 Power Set
5 Union Set
6 Null Set
7 Axiom of Infinity
8 Axiom of Foundation
9 Axiom of Choice (AC)
10 Simple/General Continuum Hypothesis (CH, GCH)

These axioms differ from those for naive set theory in that the Axiom
of Subsets replaces the Axiom of Comprehension.

The analogy with a logistic system shows Zermelo–Fraenkel set
theory in a constructivist light. Sets are not discovered, but generated. We are sparing with them, and avoid the paradoxes by
playing safe, being unwilling to admit any sets that subsequently
cause trouble. If we have played sufficiently safe, we shall never find
ourselves in trouble, though we may find ourselves not allowed to
use arguments which seem inherently plausible. Zermelo–Fraenkel
set theory is—perhaps—safe, but at the cost of being rather restrictive.

One way in which Zermelo–Fraenkel set theory is uncomfortably
restrictive is in its inability to represent innocuous well-formed formulae of predicate logic. It may be acceptable to be disallowed from
talking about black ravens until some suitable set—ravens, birds,
or animals—has been established, but it is awkward not being able
to say that ravens are black—$r \subseteq b$—until we have established the
existence of a set of black things. To remedy this, von Neumann distinguished sets from classes, and allowed classes to be introduced
by the Axiom of Comprehension, and to have members (so that
terms for classes could stand to the right of the $\in$ of class membership), but retained Zermelo's restriction on the formation of sets,

with a self-contradictory specification: but at this stage transparency is
more important than economy, and it is a peculiar feature of set theory,
differentiating it from Mereology, that the null set is a set.

which alone could be members of sets (so that only terms referring to sets could stand to the left of the ∈ of class membership). Only sets can be *members of* anything, but classes, however formed, can *have members*. We can compare the distinction between sets and classes with that between nouns (substantives) and adjectives; and say in brief, that the full theory, known as von Neumann–Bernays–Gödel set theory, which can be seen as a half-way house between Russell's generous Axiom of Comprehension and the restrictive rules for sets allowed by Zermelo and Fraenkel, is a theory of nouns and adjectives, whereas Zermelo–Fraenkel set theory is a theory of nouns only: von Neumann–Bernays–Gödel set theory can represent 'Socrates is human', whereas Zermelo–Fraenkel can express only 'Socrates is a man'.

From the philosophical point of view, we can see great merits in von Neumann–Bernays–Gödel set theory. It allows us to distinguish substantives from adjectives, and develop their different logics separately, thus undoing the damage that predicate calculus has done to our understanding, with its virtual suppression of individual variables.[10] But still there are difficulties. The word 'class' is a substantive: it invites us, in spite of the explicit prohibition, to wonder about the class of all classes, and the class of those classes that are not members of themselves. From the mathematical point of view, we find in Zermelo–Fraenkel set theory all that we require for doing transfinite arithmetic. There are many problems still, but the substantial entities best suited for ascribing cardinal or ordinal numbers to are substantival sets.

12.4 Formal Approaches

The response to the paradoxes had been to formalise. Formalisation, as always, enables us to scrutinise arguments more closely, and see where a fallacy may have entered in. But once set theory was formalised, it was natural to consider it from a purely formal point of view. Zermelo–Fraenkel set theory can be formulated in first-order logic as a straightforward axiomatic theory in which there is one additional binary relation, ∈, and a number of special axioms. ∈ is always taken to be irreflexive, and so asymmetric; Russell takes it to be intransitive, which is necessary if we are to follow Peano, and insist upon the distinction between membership and

---

[10] See above, §4.3.

Axiomatic Set Theory arose as a response to Russell's Paradox.

Three Families (in order of popularity):

1. Zermelo–Fraenkel
   a works only with sets (nouns)
   b has Axiom of Subsets
2. von Neumann–Bernays–Gödel
   a works with sets (nouns) and classes (adjectives)
   b has Axiom of Comprehension for classes
   c has Axiom of Subsets for sets
3. Russell and Quine (New Foundations)
   a works with sets (nouns or adjectives)
   b has Axiom of Comprehension
   c has stringent restrictions on predicates

---

set-inclusion; so that $x \in y$ and $\{x\} \subset y$ are altogether different. Gödel takes $\in$ to be transitive, which, if not very intuitive, is simple and useful, neatly fitting the lattice paradigm, and justifying the Axiom of Union. In either case we can consider Zermelo–Fraenkel set theory as a formal first-order system, just like formal geometry or Peano Arithmetic, and ask the same questions about it, as we do about them:

1. Is ZF consistent?
2. Is ZF provably consistent?
3. Is ZF complete?

We can further ask, in the light of some additional axioms that have been proposed:

4. Does $ZF \vdash$ Axiom of Choice?
5. Does $ZF \vdash \neg$Axiom of Choice?
6. Does $ZF \vdash$ (General) Continuum Hypothesis?
7. Does $ZF \vdash \neg$ (General) Continuum Hypothesis? *etc.*

The answer to all the questions, except—we hope[11]—the first, is NO.[12]

---

[11] Quine's original formulation of his New Foundations was shown to be inconsistent, though that inconsistency was remedied by Wang.

[12] For a full account, see A.J.Dodd, *Consistency Proofs in Set Theory*, Oxford, 1984.

We know from Gödel's second theorem that we cannot prove Zermelo-Frankel set theory consistent within either Zermelo-Frankel set theory itself or Peano Arithmetic[13]—though we might be able to prove it in some other way. But provided it is consistent, further axioms can be added without thereby making it inconsistent. Gödel proved that the Axiom of Choice (often abbreviated as AC), and the Continuum Hypothesis (often abbreviated as CH), were consistent with the other axioms of Zermelo–Fraenkel set theory, and Cohen proved that they were independent of them. We can also ask whether they are independent of each other, and whether the same holds good if we replace CH by GCH, the General Continuum Hypothesis. That is:

8. Does $ZF, AC \vdash CH$?
9. Does $ZF, CH \vdash AC$?
10. Does $ZF, GCH \vdash AC$?
11. Does $ZF, GCH \vdash CH$?
12. Does $ZF, AC, CH \vdash GCH$?

Many of the answers, which are mostly negative, will emerge in subsequent discussion. For the present, the fact that some proposed axioms, such as the Axiom of Choice, are independent of the others shows that the others are not syntactically complete.

Since the Axiom of Choice and the Continuum Hypotheses are independent of Zermelo–Fraenkel set theory, it is often suggested that there are different set theories just as there are different geometries. Perhaps $\{ZF \cup AC \cup GCH\}$ is like Euclidean Geometry, and $\{ZF \cup \neg AC \cup \neg GCH\}$ is like a non-Euclidean Geometry. But apart from significant disanalogies, to which Gödel has drawn attention,[14] set theory is not just a formal system, any more than geometry or arithmetic is; it has conceptual links with other branches of mathematics, which constrains the range of formally possible interpretations.

These semantic questions are more difficult to handle: we are not clear what the intended model of Zermelo–Fraenkel set theory is, nor how its axioms are to be evaluated, and what considerations should incline us to accept or reject them. The latter will be discussed in §12.6-§12.9; but first there is an apparent paradox, that in whatever way we formalise set theory, some models are

---

[13] See above, §8.9.

[14] See below, §15.5.

clearly not intended ones, like the non-standard interpretations of
Peano's Axioms in first-order logic.[15]   It is a consequence of the
Löwenheim–Skolem Theorem.

12.5   The Skolem Paradox

The Löwenheim–Skolem Theorem constitutes, together with the
Compactness Theorem and the Completeness Theorem, a cluster
of theorems characterizing first-order logic.   It states that every
first-order theory that has an infinite model has a denumerably
infinite model.[16]   This is particularly embarrassing for Zermelo–
Fraenkel set theory (or any other axiomatic set theory formalised
in first-order logic), since it is possible to prove the existence of
a non-denumerably infinite set as a consequence of the Power Set
Axiom and the Axiom of Infinity.[17]   It seems paradoxical that there
should be a denumerably infinite model of a theory in which we can
prove the existence of non-denumerable sets: but what the Skolem
paradox, as it is called, really shows, is, once again, the inade-
quacy of first-order logic.[18]   We are able to construct a denumerable model of Zermelo–Fraenkel set theory because in first-order
logic we cannot quotify over predicates but only use them as free
variables, replacing them by any one of the available predicates,
of which there are only a denumerable number.   Many conceivable sets, therefore, are beyond our means of referring to them,
and escape our notice, and the Power Set Axiom shows not that

---

[15]   See above, §6.3.

[16]   T.Skolem, "Some remarks on Axiomatized Set Theory", tr. and reprinted
in Jean van Heijenoort, ed., *From Frege to Gödel*, Cambridge, Mass, 1987,
pp.290-301.

[17]   See further Jean van Heijenoort, ed., *From Frege to Gödel*, Cambridge,
Mass, 1987, pp.205-6. See also, Geoffrey Hunter, *Metalogic*, London, 1971,
§48-§49, esp.pp.207f., D.C.Makison, *Topics in Modern Algebra*, London,
1973, ch.3, §2, pp.54-60; J.Myhill, "On the Ontological Significance of
the Löwenheim–Skolem Theorem", in Irving M. Copi and James A. Gould,
Contemporary Readings in Logical Theory, New York, 1967. See further,
A.George, "Skolem and the Philosophical Significance of the Löwenheim–
Skolem Theorem: A case study for the Philosophical Significance of Mathematical Results", *History and Philosophy of Logic*, **6**, 1985, pp.75-89.
There are many other discussions of the Skolem paradox.

[18]   See below, §13.5, §13.7.

the power set absolutely cannot be put in a one–one correlation with the members of the original set, but that it cannot be so correlated by any relation *within the model*. The model that the Löwenheim–Skolem Theorem proves to exist is a non-standard one, lacking certain essential features of the intended model, much as non-standard models of Peano's Axioms lack certain essential features of the natural numbers. In each case first-order logic proves an inadequate means of capturing all that we wanted to express. As with Peano Arithmetic, it is the fact that first-order logic has been cut down to size, so that it shall be completely axiomatizable, that is its undoing when it seeks to encapsulate all that the theory is intended to cover. The general philosophical moral is the same: our understanding of mathematics goes beyond the formal speci-fication of concepts and formal rules for drawing inferences about them.[19] So far as set theory by itself is concerned, rather than take a formalist approach to it, we should consider it in relation to the rest of mathematics, and in particular in the context of how we *use* set-theoretical *arguments* in mathematical discourse.

12.6   The Axiom of Choice

The Axiom of Choice can be expressed in many ways. It tells you that you can pick one member out of each of an infinite set of sets. Or, equivalently, that there is a choice function from sets into members of those sets. Or again, that every set can be well-ordered. Whitehead and Russell postulated it, under the name "Multiplicative Axiom" as one of those they needed for the devel-opment of the logicist foundations of mathematics. In the form of Zorn's Lemma it was used to legitimise an "And so on" type of argument somewhat similar to that castigated by Dedekind in his letter to Keferstein.[20] There are many other versions of the Axiom of Choice, and it is difficult to prove them all equivalent.[21]

---

[19]   Compare J.Myhill, "On the Ontological Significance of the Löwenheim–Skolem Theorem", in Irving M. Copi and James A. Gould, *Contemporary Readings in Logical Theory*, New York, 1967, p.50, "The second philosoph-ical lesson of the Löwenheim–Skolem is that the formal communication of mathematics presupposes an informal community of understanding".

[20]   See above, §5.3.

[21]   See H. and J. Rubin, *Equivalents to the Axiom of Choice*, North Holland, 1963.

For a long time it was taken for granted that a mathematician could pick one member out of each of an infinite set of sets. It was only when set theory was being formalised in the face of the paradoxes, that it was realised that a distinct principle of selection

---

Thought

The Löwenheim–Skolem Theorem should encourage us to hope that

$$ZF, AC \not\models$$

(*i.e.* there is a model of ZF together with AC)

For there is a denumerable model of ZF. Let us enumerate it. Then every subset of elements in the model will have a "least" element. So in order to choose one element out of an infinite lot of sets, adopt the rule of always choosing the least element. But this is too easy. We cannot be sure that "sets" according to the definition of ZF will be represented by sets in the model— after all it is a non-standard model.

Instead, let us use the recursive way in which ZF introduces sets. For some model of ZF we can define "constructible sets" recursively, and hence ordinally. For any set, x, choose the "least" constructible y that is a member of x.

So $ZF, AC \not\models$

---

was being invoked. The question was formulated then as whether the *Axiom* of Choice was *true*, rather than whether the *Principle* of Infinite Arbitrary Choice was *legitimate*. If we restrict the concept of truth to formal provability, we know the answer. The Axiom of Choice is independent of the other axioms of ZF. Gödel proved that the Axiom of Choice was consistent with the rest of Zermelo–Fraenkel set theory; and Cohen proved that its negation was likewise consistent. In each case the consistency proof was a relative one, by producing a model of either $ZF \cup AC$ or $ZF \cup \neg AC$ within ZF, so that if either $ZF \cup AC$ or $ZF \cup \neg AC$ were inconsistent, the proof of inconsistency could be reproduced in just ZF. Gödel uses "constructible sets", Cohen the technique of "forcing", to produce within ZF models that satisfy also either the Axiom of Choice or its negation. The working in both cases is very heavy, but the underlying principle is, once again, an exercise of shut-eye. Instead of seeing all the sets that Zermelo–Fraenkel set theory is intended to characterize, the logician sites himself in the set-theoretical universe and half shuts his eyes so that he can see only a select subset of all the conceivable sets.[22] Much as in the case of the Löwenheim-Skolem theorem, where the limitations of first-order logic make invisible the correlations that demonstrate the non-denumerability of the real numbers, so by positioning himself carefully enough, and closing his eyes sufficiently tightly, the only sets the logician can see are ones that satisfy AC (or $\neg AC$). A lot of work is needed to assure him that the AC-ness (or $\neg AC$-ness) he observes at first will be preserved as new sets come into view through the operation of the axioms of ZF that generate new sets from old.

These negative results leave open the question of the status of the Axiom of Choice. Some mathematicians have doubted it. They do so on three different grounds. Constructivists dislike it (unless the universe can be restricted to constructible sets), because it asserts the existence of a set without having any means of specifying the members of that set. We cannot program a computer to operate the Axiom of Choice. What use then is it to say simply that there *is* a set? The answer is that existence licenses talk about what exists, and if I am told of a non-null set, I can pick on one of its members without loss of generality, and argue about that one. It is true that a computer cannot do this, but this is because a computer cannot make arbitrary choices at all, not because it cannot make infinitely many. If we articulate new principles of mathematical reasoning, we are stepping back from practical computer arithmetic, and engaging mathematicians, not computers, in argument about what is in principle possible. Whereas computers operate from behind a veil of ignorance, and only do what they are programmed to do, mathematicians empathize, and sharing a common rationality and a common desire to know the truth, can envisage themselves making all the choices that need to be made, without having to be told how.

In addition to constructivist scruples, there was also a general queasiness felt by mathematicians about set theory: they suffered

---

[22] For an illuminating account, see J.N.Crossley and others, *What Is Mathematical Logic*, Oxford, 1972, ch.5, pp.70-77.

from guilty fears that Cantor's paradise was too much fun, and felt they ought to sacrifice some of their favourite principles of mathematical inference, as an expiation for having entered forbidden territory, and aspired to knowledge that was too wonderful for them. By itself this generalised feeling of guilt would not have picked out the Axiom of Choice as particularly meet to be sacrificed, but the Axiom of Choice seemed, thirdly, to lead to certain paradoxes in the way of non-measurable sets and Hausdorff's paradox; though, once again, it is not clear that it is the Axiom of Choice that is to blame: provided we distinguish the magnitudes that we can measure from the multitudes that set theory is about, we can discern other ways out of these difficulties.[23]

Some mathematicians have in consequence rejected the axiom, and tried to make no use of it. But although some results could still be obtained, albeit more tediously, many others could not; and hence, it was argued on the other side, the axiom must be accepted as true, because mathematics would be "mutilated" without it. That argument, by itself, cannot be conclusive, though it carries some weight, and is strengthened by the consideration that the Axiom of Choice enables many results to be proved easily that can be proved, but only with much greater difficulty, without it, and more generally the axiom systematizes and illuminates much of transfinite arithmetic. Stronger still is the fact that it had long been taken for granted, and was used, at first without question, indeed, almost unwittingly, in the course of mathematical argument, and only formulated as an axiom when mathematicians were trying to be scrupulously self-conscious about the arguments they were using.[24]

Gödel at one time held that we might be guided to adopt the Axiom of Choice as true by a Platonist insight analogous to the sense perception which verifies hypotheses about the world of nature.[25]

---

[23] See above, §11.1, §11.7.

[24] Penelope Maddy, *Realism in Mathematics*, Oxford, 1990, ch.4, §2, pp.114-123, gives an intelligible and concise account.

[25] "What Is Cantor's Continuum Problem", in Paul Benacerraf and Hilary Putnam, eds., *The Philosophy of Mathematics*, 2nd ed., Cambridge, 1983, pp.483-484; but in an earlier version (reprinted in Kurt Gödel, *Collected Works*, ii, Oxford, 1990, pp.184-185) he thought that "Cantor's conjecture will turn out to be wrong". See, more fully, G.H.Moore's "Introductory

We might also be led to adopt some further axiom from which the Axiom of Choice could be derived as a theorem. Indeed, one such axiom, $V = L$ has been proposed. If the whole universe, V, could be identified with just the constructible sets, L, then all sets would be well-ordered by their order of construction, so that we could select a well-ordered set containing just one member from each of an infinite set of sets. That could be justified on constructivist grounds, but few set theorists want to cut the universe down to size so drastically, and seek other, less formal justifications. The Axiom of Choice stemmed naturally from the "God's-eye" view of Cantor:[26] God could survey every one of an infinite set of sets, and choose one member out of each of them, and they would, by His election, constitute a genuine set. Even without Cantor's theology the extensional view of sets suggests that in spite of our being unable to specify a choice function, the set that it would have specified should nonetheless exist.

These arguments are persuasive to many, but not conclusive, and raise questions of existence we have not yet been able to resolve. As with Peano's Fifth Postulate, it is helpful to consider the sort of inference it seeks to legitimise. In its traditional form it extends an entirely unobjectionable principle of finite choice to infinity, much as Peano's Fifth Postulate legitimises argument by recursion and thus extends *Sorites* Arithmetic to Peano Arithmetic. Although neither is entailed by the axioms of the unextended theory, each is strongly suggested by them, and can be given a similar dialectical justification. We cannot program a computer to make all those choices, but we can envisage the choices being made, and leaving aside the details as irrelevant, pick up the thread of the argument after they have been made and go on from there. If the disputant objects, we challenge him to say which of the choices was impossible, and since each of the sets was non-empty, there is no sticking point on which he can take his stand. Nor can *he* make out that only finite choices are legitimate, because 'finite' is not a concept that can be expressed in first-order logic.[27] But if he refuses to concede the principle of infinite choice, he cannot be made to. We may think his position defective, much as ω-inconsistent ones

Note to 1947 and 1964", *op.cit.* p.159.

[26]   See below, §13.9.

[27]   See above, §7.7, §7.9.

are, but he cannot be forced to concede on pain of inconsistency, only persuaded by the reasonableness of argument.

The dialectical elucidation of the Axiom of Choice parallels a similarly dialectical account of the Axiom of Determinacy, an alternative axiom that has been proposed in recent years. The Axiom of Determinacy is inconsistent with the Axiom of Choice. If we are persuaded by the arguments of the previous paragraph to extrapolate from finite to infinite choice, we must abandon the Axiom of Determinacy forthwith. It represents a different development of set theory whose chief interest is that it is the most explicitly games-theoretical axiom in current mathematics—much more so than the Axiom of Choice, which although it can, and as I maintain should, be viewed as rules for a dialogue between two parties, who are interacting with each other, and both seeking mathematical understanding, is more usually viewed either as an optional extra to a formal system, or as a dubious claim to existential truth.

12.7 The Continuum Hypotheses

Cantor's diagonal argument shows that the real numbers cannot be put in a one–one correlation with the natural numbers.[28] We can also see that the cardinal number of the set of real numbers cannot be greater than $2^{\aleph_0}$; for each real number can be expressed as a binary decimal:

$$\ldots b_n \ldots b_3 b_2 b_1 . a_1 a_2 a_3 \ldots a_n \ldots$$

(in ordinary practice we leave out initial 0s). Each of these is of order-type $^*\omega + \omega$, but can be re-arranged to be of order-type ω thus:

$$a_1 b_1 a_2 b_2 a_3 b_3 \ldots a_n b_n \ldots$$

and there are only $2^{\aleph_0}$ such entries (but there will some double-counting of numbers on account of recurring decimals). Cantor spent many years trying to prove that the cardinal number of the continuum was exactly equal to $2^{\aleph_0}$, but without success. The Simple Continuum Hypothesis postulates that there is no set with cardinality greater than that of the natural numbers and less than that of the power set of the natural numbers, from which it would follow that the cardinality of the continuum is exactly that of the power set of the natural numbers. The General Continuum Hypothesis postulates that for any $\aleph$ (aleph) there is no transfinite

---

[28] See above, §7.2.

cardinal between it and the cardinal number of its power set; that is, for any α, $2^{\aleph_\alpha} = \aleph_{\alpha+1}$. Hence the set of $\aleph$s thus defined, $\aleph_0, \aleph_1, \ldots \aleph_n, \aleph_{n+1} \ldots$, leaves nothing out: or, to put it more paradoxically, the General Continuum Hypothesis has as a consequence that the transfinite cardinals do *not* form a continuum, or even a dense ordering, but only a discrete one (though this might well be the case even if the General Continuum Hypothesis were not true).

The Simple and the General Continuum Hypotheses are consistent with, but independent of, Zermelo–Fraenkel set theory (provided Zermelo–Fraenkel set theory is itself consistent). The proofs are similar to those for the Axiom of Choice. But although formally they are in the same case as it is, they feel different. They are negative existential propositions, rather than rules of inference. One is inclined to feel that there is a fact of the matter—a geographical feature of Cantor's paradise—which one day a voyager will discover and report back to us. It is simply a defect of the Zermelo–Fraenkel formalisation of set theory that although it enables us to ask the question 'How many points are there in a continuum?', it cannot provide an answer.

Gödel thought further axioms might suggest themselves that would decide the matter. Indeed, the formal provability results are not so negative as before. Although in Zermelo–Fraenkel set theory the Simple Continuum Hypothesis is consistent with, but independent of, the Axiom of Choice, the General Continuum Hypothesis implies it. That is:

although	9.	$ZF, CH \nvdash AC$,
nevertheless	10.	$ZF, GCH \vdash AC$, and,
obviously,	11.	$ZF, GCH \vdash CH$.

But the General Continuum Hypothesis is, of course, equally in question. Like the Axiom of Choice, it can be derived from $V = L$. Alternatively, instead of cutting the universe down to size, some have sought to inflate it, by postulating a Very Large cardinal, but it is not clear whether it will result in there being more cardinal numbers, so that there will be some between $\aleph_\alpha$ and $2^{\aleph_\alpha}$, or in expanding $\aleph_\alpha$ so that it is only one step below $2^{\aleph_\alpha}$.

12.8 Axioms and Existence

The axioms of formalised set theory are taken existentially, as making true statements about abstract entities, rather than operationally, as licensing certain moves in a mathematical exercise.

The Axiom of Choice asserts the existence of a set containing just one member from each of an infinite family of sets. Platonist questions arise, as they do over the status of universals, about bare multitudes that could conceivably be counted, but without other features, abstract entities stripped of all characteristics save that of being members of other sets or having other sets as members of themselves. In particular, there are problems of impredicativity. If sets exist independently of the human mind, there is no difficulty in characterizing a set in terms that presuppose it: if, however, sets are merely the constructs of the human mind, then we must take great care, in constructing a characterization of a set, not to presuppose that the set has already been constructed. As with Intuitionism, questions of existence cannot be separated from questions about validity.[29]

The existential implications of the Axiom of Comprehension are the most troublesome. There are two reasons. The first is that it posits the existence of some substantial entity on the strength of there being a predicate, or a quality that could conceivably be characterized by a predicate. The second is a failure to grasp a further difference in the logic of nouns naming substantial entities.

In general our rules for forming new nouns are more stringent than those for forming new adjectives; while predicates are moderately Boolean, capable of being negated, conjoined and disjoined without too much discomfort, individual terms and variables are more resistant to Boolean operations. Just as I cannot talk of non-men, although I can describe entities as being non-human, so I cannot disjoin and talk of men-or-white-things, *etc.* (even though I can *con*join further specifications to an individual variable, and talk of white men, black men, or old men). A useful analogy, as regards negation, is with recursively enumerable sets.[30] Recursively enumerable sets have some principle of generation, which gives them a sort of unity, and enables us to answer the question "How many?". We can enumerate all the theorems of first-order

---

[29] See above, ch.7, §7.5.

[30] See §8.8.

logic, and say that there are $\aleph_0$ of them, but we cannot speak so comprehensively of the non-theorems. They do not have a positive unifying characteristic, but only negatively lack one. It is only when we embed them in some larger set—the well-formed formulae of first-order logic—that we can pick out the ones that lack the property of theoremhood, and say how many there are. Of course, sets are not confined to recursively enumerable sets. But recursive enumerability is a useful illustration of a property of collections that is not preserved under complementation. Sometimes two sets are complementary—men and women both have characteristic features specific to their kind—and the complements of recursive sets are themselves recursive; but just as recursiveness cannot be taken for granted, so we cannot assume that the complement of a set will be a set, unless the complementation is relativised to some universe of discourse that does have some unifying principle that comprehends it as a coherent whole.

We should be similarly chary of disjoining sets. The Pair Set Axiom is ontologically embarrassing. It enables us to lump together any two things we care to specify, and, if iterated, to produce finite sets of quite disparate elements. Outside mathematics we are wary of unnatural zeugma. Dogs form a natural kind, and irrational numbers, we are readily persuaded, do, but not their union, $\{dogs\} \cup \{irrational\ numbers\}$, even though it could be specified as $\{x|x\ is\ a\ dog\ and/or\ x\ is\ an\ irrational\ number\}$. Much as separated parts do not form one coherent whole, so disparate sets cannot be disjoined to form one *bona fide* entity.

The mismatch between the more-or-less Boolean logic of adjectives and the decidedly non-Boolean logic of nouns underlies the traditional problem of the substantial unity over the adjectivally characterized many. But there is a further problem arising from the many being composed of individual units, each being an entity— some sort of substance. The units need to be individuated so as to be countable. We need to specify whether it is cards, court cards or suits we are counting, if we are to say how many there are in a game of skat. But we do not need to be able to count individuated entities in much of our abstract talk. The quality of mercy is not strained, we say, and understand what is meant, even though we have no idea of its cardinality. I can talk about all the colours in the spectrum, and say that most mammals cannot see them, without being able to count them, or discriminate between them as one merges into another. Sets need principles both of comprehension and individuation, as shown by the two senses of "Now we are six" discussed in Chapter Four.[31] In the one case—"Now we are six years old, we are too old to cry"—the force of our all being six is given dialectically by a simple challenge: you can pick on any case you like—say Stephanie—and I claim she will turn out to be six. In the other case it is not enough to be able to argue in each instance you choose to raise: I have to have the whole collection in issue if I am to maintain that we, being six, can play ring o' ring of roses together. In the case of the natural numbers it was not enough to be ready to show of any natural number you cared to instance that it could be reached in a finite number of steps from 0. We needed to show that the axioms of Peano Arithmetic were, in second-order logic, monomorphic, so that when we spoke of them, we were speaking precisely, and not just waving a hand over an indeterminate crowd of entities that might, for all we knew, include Julius Caesar. Sets are what we can ask "How many?" of, and therefore cannot afford to be indeterminate.

It is, as we saw in §3 of this chapter, the merit of von Neumann–Bernays–Gödel set theory that it attempts to accommodate the difference, allowing Comprehension for classes, but only Subsets for sets. Much of mathematics can be done with classes—particularly equivalence classes—where we want to talk about all the ordered pairs of natural numbers whose cross-products are the same,[32] or all the positive rational numbers whose square is less than 2, without wanting to count them or assign a cardinal power to them. But von Neumann–Bernays–Gödel set theory has its difficulties. The logical geography of the concept *class* is still unclear. And logic of adjectives, though more Boolean than that of substantives, is not as sharp as we would wish. Most thinkers have put it down to size; they have reckoned that some classes are too big to behave properly. But the problem lies not so much in large size as in an inherent indeterminateness in the force of the word 'all'. The universal quotifier, (A), is like the necessity operator, $\Box$; and necessity is allied to inference.[33] But inference, we have seen, cannot be completely formalised. However fully we formalise a particular

---

[31] §4.3.

[32] See above, §3.7.

[33] See above, §7.11, and below §15.3, §15.4.

system which is strong enough for arithmetic, there are further inferences not covered by our formalisation, but indisputably valid. Inference in mathematics is fuzzy-edged. And this fuzziness carries over to necessity and the universal quotifier. When we talk about all classes, we wave our hands over we know not exactly what. Challenged to say of any particular instance whether it was covered by our "handsweep", we may be able to answer, but we do not have an antecedent specification we could have given in advance—or rather if we had given one in advance, we should then have found it inadequate.

12.9 The Axiom of Extensionality

The Axiom of Extensionality plays a key role in set theory. It reflects the concern of mathematicians to put forward a coherent account of multitudes, but points in a different direction from the Axiom of Comprehension, and from one point of view it has nominalist overtones, implying that a set just *is* its members. It goes with the Axiom of Choice and Pair Set Axiom, allowing a set to have an infinite number of members, all arbitrarily chosen, with no common characteristic to bind them together, and seeing no difficulty in two entirely disparate sets being joined together in unnatural union. Difficulties disappear if we can invoke the aid of theology. Cantor was deeply religious, and much influenced by St Augustine. He conceived set theory, as an account of the transfinite, from a God's-eye point of view. God can see each of the members of a set individually, all in one glance of the infinite mind. Cantor was thus able to be a nominalist as regards universals in their own right, relying on the organizing power of the omniscient Deity to gather together the diverse members of a set into one coherent entity.[34] Although often taken in our own time to be committed to platonic realism, set theory in its origins was much more a version of theological nominalism, and still retains a nominalist tinge. Frege talked of the Extension of a Concept in order to direct attention away from the intension, the meaning, and towards the bare relation of multiplicity that held between objects and concepts. The

---

[34] See M.Hallett, *Cantorian Set Theory and Limitations of Size*, Oxford, 1984, pp.35-37. Hallett complains that the Augustinian principle that the infinite is made finite to God, is no help to atheists, and provides them with no explanation for the "oneness of sets", which remains a mystery in the absence of some intensional principle.

Axiom of Extensionality abstracts from all adventitious features of
universals or classes that might interest or distract the philosopher
(important though these may be for identifying the set), and concentrates attention on the bare countable[35] bones, entities about
which we can ask "How many?".[36]

As we saw in Chapter Nine,[37] the Axiom of Extensionality
should be compared with the Identity of Indiscernibles. The Identity of Indiscernibles lays down that[38]

$$a = b \quad \text{iff} \quad (AX)(a \in X \leftrightarrow b \in X)$$

whereas the Axiom of Extensionality lays down that

$$a = b \quad \text{iff} \quad (Ax)(x \in a \leftrightarrow x \in b)$$

Both are Relational Equivalences: as we have seen, granted any
relation,[39] we can always define an equivalence, although in general, converse relations do not define the same equivalence class,
as, for example, spouse and sibling. The Identity of Indiscernibles
is true of Secondary Substances, *e.g.* elements in the Periodic Table, but for Primary Substances we allow that there can be more
than one specimen of a species, qualitatively identical though numerically distinct, with temporal and spatial differences acting as
non-qualitative differentiating conditions.

We can thus contrast the effect of the two principles:

Identity of Indiscernibles   Every Specimen is a Species
Axiom of Extensionality   Every Aggregate is a Genus.

The Identity of Indiscernibles cannot hold of primary substances,
or we should foreclose the possibility of change. If something is to

---

[35] The word 'countable' here does not carry the sense of finite-or-denumerable,
but indicates only that we can begin to count a set—even an "uncountable"
one.

[36] See further below, §16.3.

[37] §9.11.

[38] Actually, it is enough to say
$$a = b \quad \text{iff} \quad (AX)(a \in X \rightarrow b \in X).$$
We have capital Xs, because some predicates may define classes that are
not sets.

[39] Here qualities are included as one-place relations.

change, there must be some respect in which it is different, although
in all essential respects it remains the same, so as to be the same *it*.
And if one thing can at different times differ in this non-essential
respect, it is logically possible that at the same time there should
be two things the same in all essential respects, but differing in this
non-essential respect. That is to say, it is logically possible that
there should be two things which are qualitatively identical but
nevertheless two, not one. The possibility of change implies two
categories which though not necessarily possessing all the features
of our concepts of time and space, possess some of the fundamental
ones, and are, so to speak, proto-time and proto-space. To insist
on the Identity of Indiscernibles is thus to restrict one's discourse
to one in which there is no possibility of change, and no occasion
for the application of temporal and spatial concepts. This accords
with Plato's stipulation about the proper object of mathematical
contemplation, but has important modal implications which should
not be overlooked.

The Axiom of Extensionality has a similar conceptual context.
In ordinary discourse we can envisage two aggregates being co-
extensive without being the same. It may be the case that all
man-eating tigers are tigers which had unhappy childhoods and
that all tigers which had unhappy childhoods are man-eating tigers,
but we should hesitate to say that the two were identical. The two
aggregates differ in "intension"—they are specified differently by
terms having a different meaning. There could be a tiger that
had an unhappy childhood, but overcame its warping effect, and
did not take up man-eating: and there could be a tiger that had a
happy childhood brought up by excellent parents who gave it every
advantage a tiger could have, and yet took up man-eating just for
the hell of it. Although two descriptions may, as it happens, refer to
the same entities, they would, were circumstances different, differ
in their *Bedeutung* as well as their *Sinn*, and so are different from
a logical point of view.

The difference is most obvious when we contrast a finite set
specified individually by name with a co-extensive one characterized by an "open" description. I may be talking about John's
girl-friends, who, so I maintain, are all blue-eyed blonds. You instance Sheila, who is raven-haired and has brown eyes. I deny that
Sheila is one of John's girl-friends. I may be wrong about this, but
I am not contradicting myself, whereas if we specify the aggregate

by name—Sally, Sue, Shirley, Sandra, Sheila and Samantha—it is
a contradiction to make out that Sheila is not a member of this
aggregate. Again and again in non-mathematical argument we distinguish "open" aggregates, which although they may in fact have
only a finite number of particular members are specified in some
general way, from "closed" ones specified by name which could not
have any other members than those they have. In Professor Hare's
treatment of moral philosophy it is a characteristic feature of moral
judgements that they can be "universalised", and held to be applicable to open and not just closed aggregates. Similarly, sound
inductive arguments can be characterized in terms of "projectible"
properties, but not in terms containing some particularising reference, as in the definitions of 'grue' and 'bleen'. If we adopt the
Axiom of Extensionality we are excluding such distinctions and
the possibilities they imply from our consideration. We are dealing only with aggregates that logically could not contain any other
members than those they actually contain. In the simpler parts
of mathematics this is certainly so: the set of even prime numbers
could not contain any other members than are contained in the
singleton set $\{2\}$. But since deductivism is false, and not all mathematics can be reduced to deductive inferences from tautologous
premises, the modal collapse enforced by the Axiom of Extensionality is questionable.

If different (*i.e.* non-synonymous) descriptions can refer to the
same set, two consequences follow: in the first place, sets are some
sort of substance, not pure predicate-qualities: and secondly, sets
cannot be purely intensional, as programs are. To this extent set
theory takes an anti-nominalist stance. Conversely, if a set is not
just simply its members, we can talk about it without having, either
actually or in principle, itemised all its members. It is then legitimate, which otherwise it would not be, to talk about sets defined
in terms of totalities encompassing themselves, which we need to
do in using a Dedekind cut, for instance, to prove the Fundamental
Theorem of Analysis. Most mathematicians find this unexceptionable, because they take a realist view of sets, and believe they can
be referred to without being completely specified. They hold, *pace*
Leibniz, that we can sometimes say something about something
without saying everything about it. Certainly, we do not need to
be totally specific to talk about a person, or a material object,
or even a tune. With these, the degree of specificity required for

successful reference depends upon the context and what we want
to say about the thing referred to: if we only want to argue from
general features, we do not need to specify exactly. It seems reasonable to think the same of sets, but that is to accord them some
substantial status over and above that given them by the Axiom
of Extensionality.[40]

The existential thrust of Zermelo–Fraenkel set theory can be
seen as the converse of its being abstracted from particular rea-
sonings. In particular applications we can dispense with the Pair
Set Axiom, the Union Set Axiom, the Axiom of Infinity, as we can
argue for the sets we need in the particular case. When we are arguing generally we need some existential assurance to license further
discourse. We cannot talk about things if they do not exist,[41] and
whereas in particular arguments we establish the existence of the
thing we are talking about in the course of argument, we cannot
be sure of always doing this at higher levels of generality.

12.10 Conclusion

The formal approach to set theory yields a number of interesting
formal results, which are tabulated below as answers to the questions raised in §12.4.

1.	Is ZF consistent?	DON'T KNOW
2.	Is ZF provably consistent?	NO
3.	Is ZF complete?	NO
4.	Does $ZF \vdash AC$?	NO
5.	Does $ZF \vdash \neg AC$?	NO
6.	Does $ZF \vdash (G)CH$?	NO
7.	Does $ZF \vdash \neg(G)CH$?	NO
8.	Does $ZF, AC \vdash CH$?	NO
9.	Does $ZF, CH \vdash AC$?	NO
10.	Does $ZF, GCH \vdash AC$?	YES
11.	Does $ZF, GCH \vdash CH$?	Yes, of course
12.	Does $ZF, AC, CH \vdash GCH$?	NO
13.	Does $ZF, V = L \vdash CH$?	YES
14.	Does $ZF, V = L \vdash AC$?	YES

Of these results, Gödel proved (5) & (7):
$$ZF, AC \nvdash; \quad ZF, CH \nvdash; \quad ZF, GCH \nvdash .$$

---

[40] See further below, §15.3.

[41] See above, §7.5, and below, §15.1.

Cohen proved (4) & (6):

$$ZF, \neg AC \not\vdash; \quad \neg ZF, CH \not\vdash; \quad \neg ZF, GCH \not\vdash \text{ (forcing)}.$$

All these results (except in one paradoxical sense the first[42]) are on the assumption that ZF is in fact consistent.

These results are predominantly negative, and offer no guidance about which principles to adopt. Indeed, the Skolem paradox implies that the theory cannot adequately characterize its subject.

Set-theoretical thinking is pervasive throughout mathematics, but has been occluded by the use of sets as objects of thought. The Logicists claim it as part of logic, though not recognised as such until the middle of the nineteenth century. Various patterns of argument then emerged and were accepted as valid, without anyone's realising what was being assumed; the Axiom of Choice, in particular, was often unwittingly invoked, and was only gradually distinguished as a separate principle, and perhaps in need of further justification. Further justification can be offered in terms of a dialogue between two rational truth-seekers, but the inferential approach requires a much fuller account of mathematical inference than has been thus far forthcoming.

The theory is worse than the practice. Mathematicians apply set theory quite sensibly, neither invoking the Axiom of Comprehension to define a set of sets that-are-not-members-of-themselves, nor using the Pair Set Axiom to join Julius Caesar with a natural number. Set theory in practice is more sensibly applied than set theory in theory. Nearly always some universe of discourse is covertly presupposed, within which the Pair Set Axiom, the Power Set Axiom, and the Union Set Axiom, are unobjectionable. If only we could learn to preach what we practise!

After the discovery of the paradoxes, it became less plausible to claim set theory as merely logic: whereas the simple Comprehension Principle which was expressed by Frege's Axiom V was simple and intuitive, the axiomatization developed to exclude the paradoxes was finicky and unintuitive, much more like a special mathematical theory than simple logic. Instead of being concerned with patterns of argument, modern set theory is concerned with sets as objects of thought. Sets are abstract entities stripped of all characteristics save that of being members of other sets or having other sets as members of themselves. They are bare multitudes that

---

[42] See above, §8.9.

could conceivably be counted, but without other features. Since finite counting is rather dull and best left to computers, the focus of interest in set theory is on infinite sets, and what goes under the name of set theory is not a simple Boolean manipulation of simple multitudes, but better described as transfinite arithmetic.

The logicist programme of reducing the whole of mathematics to set theory takes on a new light. It no longer seems to effect a reduction to logic: indeed, it is not much of any sort of reduction to define the small natural numbers in terms of transfinite arithmetic. Admittedly, models are useful, and the general availability of set-theoretic models is very useful. Set theory is a tool, often a valuable one; but it no longer offers a fundamental insight into the real nature of mathematics.

We may state our conclusions, rather summarily, in the table below:

Conclusions

1. Set Theory should be a Theory of Multitudes, $\pi\lambda\acute{\eta}\theta\eta$ (*plethe*), in contrast to Measure Theory, which is about magnitudes, $\mu\epsilon\gamma\acute{\epsilon}\theta\eta$ (*megethe*). In the former we can always ask How many?, in the latter How much? Unfortunately, Set Theory has been a cuckoo in the mathematical nest, and has tried to oust, or at least take over, all other branches of mathematics. It is not up to it.

2. Because Set Theory took on too much, it tripped over the paradoxes, and has been reeling ever since. Set-theorists are more concerned with not being able to say anything wrong than with being able to say many things right.

3. Set Theory should be seen as an articulation of some principles of mathematical reasoning, much as P5 should be seen not so much as an axiom, postulating truth, but as a rule of inference, legitimating argument by recursion. We first argue set-theoretically in the course of doing other bits of mathematics, and then reflect on our modes of argument and abstract general principles of reasoning.

4. Set Theory is often a polite name for Transfinite Arithmetic. Closer attention to the Trades Description Act would be advantageous.

Chapter 13
Chastened Logicism?

13.1 Logicism

The logicist programme is generally reckoned to have failed. Frege had hoped to found arithmetic on logic, but the intuitive theory of sets—the successors to his *Umfänge*—turned out to be inconsistent,[1] and when we abandoned intuitive set theory, and replaced it by some axiomatized version, it lost its innocent simplicity, and no longer seemed like logic. But once we distinguish transfinite arithmetic, which is much more a mathematical theory than an articulation of logical principles, from arguing with adjectives, which has a good claim to be just logic, the fundamental objection to the logicist programme is removed.

There remain other objections. Frege's own system was inconsistent because of his

Axiom V $(\mathrm{A}F)(\mathrm{A}G)((\{\hat{x} : Fx\} = \{\hat{x} : Gx\}) \leftrightarrow (\mathrm{A}x)(Fx \leftrightarrow Gx))$.

But George Boolos and Crispin Wright have re-examined Frege's original argument to see what can be salvaged, and have shown that Axiom V was not really needed.[2] There is room for argument

---

[1] See above, §12.2.

[2] G.Boolos, "The Consistency of Frege's *Foundations of Arithmetic*", in Judith Jarvis Thompson, ed., *On Being and Saying: Essays for Richard Cartwright*, Cambridge, Mass., 1987, pp.3-30; reprinted in W.D.Hart, ed., *The Philosophy of Mathematics*, Oxford, 1996, pp.185-202. Crispin

whether their alternative to Frege's Axiom V is a purely logical principle, but it is no longer a foregone conclusion that it is not.

Whitehead and Russell were trying to establish a Strong Logicist thesis, which claimed:[3]

1. The *concepts* of mathematics can be derived from logical concepts through explicit definitions. (compare constructivism)
2. The *theorems* of mathematics can be derived from logical axioms through purely logical deductions.

They succeeded in defining natural numbers and proving Peano's Postulates. But in order to do this, they needed axiomatic set theory, including the Axiom of Infinity and the Axiom of Choice, and a highly artificial and implausible Axiom of Reducibility to undo the damage done by their Theory of Types. In spite of great achievements, they had not carried through the Strong Logicist programme to a successful conclusion, and it became apparent that it was something they could not do. But it was only the Strong Logicist programme that had failed. We need to distinguish that from a chastened logicism, which, though less ambitious and less sharply defined, expresses important truths about mathematics.

Set theory was required, in the opinion of many of those who thought about the foundations of mathematics, in order to avoid recourse to second-order logic. Frege and Dedekind had availed themselves of second-order logic to generalise over concepts and over chains, and did not regard this as weakening their claim to be Logicists, but by the middle of the Twentieth Century it was widely held, largely at the behest of Quine, that logic, properly so called, should be restricted to "first-order logic", that is the logic of the sentential functors, $\neg$, $\rightarrow$, $\wedge$, $\vee$, *etc.*, together with identity and the existential and universal quotifiers restricted to quotifying only over individuals, and not anything else, such as qualities or quotities themselves. We need to consider what should be counted as logic, as well as the sense that should be given to the claim that mathematics is grounded in logic.

Wright, *Frege's Conception of Numbers as Objects*, Aberdeen, 1983. In using his formulations of Hume's principle and Frege's Axiom V, I have transposed into my logical symbolism.

[3] Rudolf Carnap, "The Logicist Foundations of Mathematics", *Erkenntnis*, 1931; translated and reprinted in Paul Benacerraf and Hilary Putnam, eds., *The Philosophy of Mathematics*, 2nd ed., Cambridge, 1983, p.41.

13.2 What Is Logic?

In ordinary discourse the word 'logic' is used in a variety of senses, often taking its colour from what it is being contrasted with. Feminists are infuriated when men say that women are emotional rather than logical, and scientists talk of the logic of an experiment as opposed to the actual observations made. Historians often account for a statesman's actions in terms of the logic of the situation, as opposed to some personal predilection of his or the fortuitous result of happenstance. Philosophers used to talk of inductive logic at the same time as maintaining that logic was purely deductive. In these and many other contrasts, although the exact sense of the word 'logic' varies, the force of the contrast is the same: logic is topic-neutral, something that does not vary with personalities, empirical data, or the chance concatenation of events. It is, in the terminology of the Schoolmen, the "Universal Ordinary" studying patterns of inference that are not peculiar to any particular subject, but are common to all. It abstracts from particular instances, and considers only the general form.

But our concept of logic is under strain. Set against the drive for universality is the requirement of cogency. Hence the demand that logical arguments be so incontrovertible that it would be inconsistent to refuse to concede the conclusion, having admitted the premises. Logical arguments, on this showing, will be those that must be accepted, on pain of making oneself incommunicable with. They are valid, simply in virtue of the meaning of words, and without meaning there can be no communication. Granted that we want to be understood, there is maximal cogency in such inferences.

Nevertheless, it is unsatisfactory to characterize logic in terms of inconsistency alone. For one thing, there are many arguments valid in virtue of the meaning-rules of natural language, which it would be inconsistent to controvert, but which do not properly belong to the realm of logic: 'he is an uncle: so he is not an only child', 'today is Monday, so tomorrow is Tuesday' are maximally incontrovertible, but not general in their application. And, as we have seen, inconsistency is not the only sanction. A sceptic can deny an old-fashioned inductive argument if he wants, without being inconsistent or making himself unintelligible; rather, he denies himself all possibility of knowledge of general truths or of those not yet experienced, if he will not ever generalise or extrapolate from what he already knows to what he would like to know.

Faced with these difficulties in characterizing logic, philosophers can formalise, replacing non-deductive inferences by suitably stipulated axioms. Deductive inference, represented formally by the single turnstile, $\vdash$, then becomes a matter of abiding by the rules laid down, and the sanction for those who break the rules is simply that they are not playing the game.

This formal characterization of logic is attractive; we could reasonably hope to program a computer to act according to explicit rules concerned solely with the **syntax** of strings of symbols. But we still have to decide which symbols to have. Bureaucrats are very fond of acronyms, and use strings of letters rather than meaningful words, but it does make their discourse logical. Only rather few symbols deserve to be accounted logical symbols.

If we adopt the semantic approach, and seek to distil logic from various fields of discourse, as what is common to all valid argumentation, we reach a similar problem. We can form an idea of a "logical constant"[4] as that which is the same in all patterns of argument, but there is a suspicion of arbitrariness in deciding what exactly is a logical constant, and what not; is 'is identical with' a logical constant?

13.3　Boolean Plus

When we argue, we draw inferences because we disagree. If we did not disagree, we should not argue at all. As it is, being autonomous beings, we are capable of having our own ideas, each seeing things differently from others, so that when I give vent to my views, you need not accept them. You can say No, and I can say No to your No, thereby reasserting my original contention.[5]

But we do not merely contradict each other. We give reasons. Each appeals to considerations the other is likely to concede, and draws inferences from them to support his side of the dispute. I put forward a proposition, and from it infer the truth of another proposition: p **therefore** q, which we might symbolize as

$$p \ \Vdash q,$$

---

[4] The terms 'logical constant' and 'connective' are used indiscriminately by logicians. I shall use 'logical constant' in semantic contexts, 'connective' in syntactic ones, and 'functor' to cover both.

[5] See above, §7.5.

to avoid favouring either the syntactic ⊢ or the semantic ⊨. We do not just draw inferences, however; we may need to discuss them, in which case we may, as in the Deduction Theorem, consider the equivalent implication, arguing about the truth of the proposition $p \rightarrow q$, rather than the validity of the inference

$$p \Vdash q.$$

Equally, we may reverse the order of argument, and contend that q **because** p.[6]

Once we have some concept of negation and implication, we can define the other sentential connectives. Although ¬ renders the meaning of 'not' moderately well, → is significantly different from 'if . . , then . . ', as also ∧ (or &) from 'and', while 'or' in ordinary English is ambiguous between the inclusive and exclusive sense, only the former being expressed by ∨. Nevertheless, they constitute a "regimented" version of the connectives used in ordinary language, and provide the logical constants for a topic-neutral formal logic.

The familiar sentential connectives are not the only ones. There are sixteen possible truth tables for binary connectives linking two variables, each of which can take either of two values, TRUE or FALSE. We often add ↔ (or ≡), for 'if and only if', and sometimes ⊤ for TRUE, and ⊥ for FALSE. The latter can be used as a primitive instead of ¬. (Indeed, instead of having one of these together with → (or ∧, or ∨), we can define both negation and all the binary sentential connectives in terms of just one, | or ↓, non-conjunction or non-disjunction; but this is somewhat artificial.) Whatever primitives we choose, we have a Boolean Algebra, B_2, for propositional calculus, which goes a long way towards articulating the formal structure of argument in every field of discourse.

But propositional calculus is not the whole of logic. We often modify propositions. We can outline possibilities, or recognise necessities, or consider counter-factual conditionals. We can engage in fiction and tell stories, or consider obligations, or distinguish the conjectural from the well-established. We can hope, expect, fear, warn, promise or threaten about things to come, and can remember, ponder, relate, or explain, the past. All these activities

---

[6] See Gilbert Ryle, "If, So, Because", in M.Black, ed., *Philosophical Analysis*, Ithaca, N.Y., 1950.

have some propositional content—we can say what the content of our hopes, wishes, judgements or romances is, and pick out entailments and inconsistencies among them—but cannot be represented in terms of propositions alone.

Grammatically, modification of a proposition is often expressed in English by the use of an auxiliary verb, and in inflected languages by a change of mood or tense. But whatever the shift of tense or mood, and whether it is expressed by an auxiliary verb or some more complicated locution, such as 'it is possible that ...' or 'it was going to be the case that ...', the modified proposition stands in some relation to the original one, and is still something that can be agreed with or disagreed with, accepted or rejected, shared or repudiated. It is reasonable to regard the modified proposition as still being itself a proposition, and therefore to see the various modifiers as *unary operators*, or *unary functors*, which operate each on a single proposition to yield a single proposition.

The unary operator may stand for any one of a wide variety of modal or tense auxiliary verbs, or adverbs, or propositional phrases. It is not to be assumed in advance that every modal operator in ordinary speech can be expressed adequately in modal logic: but it is a useful exercise to see how far we can go in considering the formal possibilities enriching propositional calculus by a simple basic unary operator, and the constraints on the rules of inference and axioms it is reasonable to recognise. Having added to propositional calculus a unary operator, which we may symbolize as $\Box$, with the same formation rules as $\neg$, we need to consider possible rules of inference and axioms governing the use of $\Box$. There is a wide range of possibilities. But there are constraints: we must not have too many rules, or our operator will be degenerate, definable in terms of the ordinary sentential connectives, and our logic will be nothing more than ordinary propositional calculus; if we have too few, however, our operator will lose all contact with the connectives of ordinary logic, and our modified discourse will no longer be a logic at all. If we are to give sustained attention to a mode of discourse, words must have their ordinary meanings, and analytic propositions must hold as well within the modalised discourse as outside it; and therefore, as far as propositional calculus is concerned, tautologies must remain tautologies when modified. Since every tautology is a theorem of propositional calculus, and *vice versa*, we stipulate

If Γ is a theorem, so is $\Box\,\Gamma$,

    i.e., If $\vdash \Gamma$ then $\vdash \Box\,\Gamma$.

This rule of inference is characteristic of all modal logics (logics with an additional unary modifying operator), and is known as the Rule of Necessitation.

The Rule of Necessitation ensures that logical theorems remain logical theorems when modalised, but does not by itself suffice to legitimise standard inferences in modalised discourse: it enables us to introduce $\vdash$ into a mode of discourse, but not to use it to make inferences within it. If we are to carry ordinary inferences over into modalised discourse we need the further rule

    If $\Gamma \vdash \Delta$, then $\Box\,\Gamma \vdash \Box\,\Delta$.[7]

But in accordance with the tendency of modern logic to replace inferences by implications, the question whether modalised inferences are real inferences, that is whether $\Box\,(\Gamma \rightarrow \Delta), \Box\,\Gamma \;\vdash \Box\,\Delta$, becomes the question whether a modalised implication $\Box\,(\Gamma \rightarrow \Delta)$ yields a straightforward implication between the modalised parts of it, $\Box\,\Gamma$ and $\Box\,\Delta$. We therefore lay down as an essential axiom for modal logic

    G $\Box\,(\Gamma \rightarrow \Delta) \rightarrow (\Box\,\Gamma \rightarrow \Box\,\Delta)$.

The axiom G entitles us to infer $\Box\,\Delta$ from $\Box\,(\Gamma \rightarrow \Delta)$ and $\Box\,\Gamma$ in two steps of *Modus Ponens*.

The Rule of Necessitation together with the Axiom G ensures that modalised discourse is **"inferentially transparent"**. Essentially what we require is that we should be able to make the same inferences within modalised discourse as in unmodalised discourse. If there is a good argument about kicking the ball—e.g. that in order to kick it, one must approach it, or that if one kicks it, the result will be that it moves—the same argument should hold within the context of obligatory kicking, alleged kicking, future kicking, or past kicking. Else modal discourse becomes inferentially opaque.

If modal discourse is to avoid logical chaos, it must be subject to the Rule of Necessitation and Axiom G, which together constitute the standard minimum system of modal logic: these, in effect, govern its interrelationships with $\vdash$ and $\rightarrow$. In order to place it as fully as possible in the context of propositional calculus, we need also to consider its interrelationship with $\neg$. As a first try, we might think that it would "commute" with negation, *i.e.*

---

[7] Aristotle, *Prior Analytics*, I, 15, 34^{a}22 − 24.

$$\vdash \Box \neg p \leftrightarrow \neg \Box p,$$

but in that case the modal operator would become vacuous, so far as propositional calculus was concerned.

The non-theorem $\Box \neg p \leftrightarrow \neg \Box p$ consists of two conjuncts, $\Box \neg p \rightarrow \neg \Box p$ and $\neg \Box p \rightarrow \Box \neg p$. While we cannot have both, we can, and should hope to, have one; else our modal operator $\Box$ will have so little to do with the ordinary logical constants that there will scarce be a logic worth talking about. Although we could choose either, and the decision is, as we shall shortly see, in some sense arbitrary, we shall choose the former conjunct, $\Box \neg p \rightarrow \neg \Box p$. The reason is that we naturally want to secure a certain "modal consistency" for our operator. Consistency requires that no well-formed formula of the form $p \wedge \neg p$ can be a theorem. We naturally go further—though it *is* further—and lay down that not only is $p \wedge \neg p$ not a theorem, but that the negation of $p \wedge \neg p$ is a theorem, that is,

$$\vdash \neg (p \wedge \neg p).$$

This is a theorem of ordinary propositional calculus. In considering the relation between $\Box$ and $\neg$, we may reasonably look for a comparable stipulation, *viz.* $\vdash \neg(\Box p \wedge \Box \neg p)$, which is equivalent to

$$\vdash \Box \neg p \rightarrow \neg \Box p,$$

the former of the two conjuncts. This in turn is equivalent to

$$\vdash \Box p \rightarrow \neg \Box \neg p,$$

or, writing $\Diamond$ for $\neg \Box \neg$,

$$\vdash \Box p \rightarrow \Diamond p,$$

which is a characteristic thesis of modal logic, known as the axiom D.

Almost all interesting systems of modal logic have D as an axiom. It yields four out of the six possible interconnexions between $\Box$ and $\wedge$, $\vee$ and $\neg$, and we cannot add either of the others on pain of modal degeneracy. We can therefore argue for it as giving us as much, in the way of interconnexion between the modal operator $\Box$ and the connectives $\wedge$, $\vee$ and $\neg$ of propositional calculus, as we can hope to have. These rules for $\Box$ make it the **most highly structured non-trivial operator relative to the Boolean operators**.

There is a parallel with topology. Topology can be seen as an enrichment of the Boolean algebra of sets. We can, as we saw in Chapter Ten,[8] axiomatize topology in terms of a unary operator, the interior operator, which is a function from sets into sets, just as $\Box$ is a function from propositions into propositions; and then we find a close parallel between the axioms of topology and those of a particular modal logic, **S4**. The fact that in standard expositions of topology we pick out a family of sets—the open sets—which are distinguished by certain infinitistic properties suggests an approach to modal logic in which the often-remarked parallel between necessity and the universal quotifier, itself often regarded as an infinite conjunction (and between possibility and the existential quotifier, regarded as an infinite disjunction) is probed further.

13.4 Iterated Modalities

Although the system that contains D goes as far as possible in relating the modal operator with the sentential connectives of propositional calculus, it leaves other questions unanswered. It tells us nothing of the relation between modalised and unmodalised discourse, nor of any relations between iterated modal operators, which may be all of essentially the same sort, but may also be differentiated from one another. Axioms giving rules for such relations can be laid down, giving rise to different logics, according to what rules are adopted. The Aristotelian axiom T, $\vdash \Box p \rightarrow p$, 'what must be, is', specifies a relation between modalised and unmodalised discourse, and holds in most modal logics, though not in those concerned with ethics and what we ought to do: the axioms 4 and 5, which are typical of the systems **S4** and **S5**, specify relations between iterated modal operators of the same type; the axiom B, which is typical of the system **B**, does both; and the quotifiers can be usefully viewed as modal operators differentiated from one another by virtue of the variables they bind.

These different modal logics are intricate, and hard to make sense of, if we consider them only from a syntactical point of view. Kripke provided a semantics in terms of "possible worlds" which casts light on each of them, and their relations with one another. He considered each unmodalised logic as having its universe of discourse in a "possible world" that might, or might not, be related to

----

[8] §10.2.

other possible worlds by an "accessibility relation". The semantic definition of $\Box$ was given by the stipulation that $\Box p$ should be true in a possible world if and only if p was true in every possible world accessible from it. It is moderately easy to see, then, that where the accessibility relation is reflexive, if $\Box p$ is true, p must be true also, so that T holds in that modal logic. It further follows that T holds only in such cases. Similarly, the axiom 4, characteristic of **S4**, which lays down that $\vdash \Box p \rightarrow \Box\Box p$, will hold if and only if the accessibility relation is transitive. It is more tricky to assure oneself that the "Brouwerian" system **B** which has as its axiom B, $\Diamond\Box p \rightarrow p$, is associated with a symmetric accessibility relation, and that **S5** is associated with an equivalence accessibility relation, but once these points are taken, we understand why it is that the system obtained by adding B to **S4** turns out to be **S5**.

The accessibility relation of **S4** is transitive, but not symmetric.[9] Relations that are not symmetric have converses that are different. For each modal logic which does not have B as an axiom or theorem, there will be another modal logic with the converse accessibility relation. We could use an "inverse" modal operator, $\Box^{-1}$, but that usage has not been adopted. Prior's Tense Logic is the most interesting logic based on an asymmetric accessibility relation. Instead of $\Box$, and $\Box^{-1}$, he has H for 'it has always been the case that', and G for 'it is always going to be the case that'; likewise he has P for 'it was at sometime the case that', and F for 'it will at sometime be the case that', instead of $\Diamond$, and $\Diamond^{-1}$.[10]

Tense logic helps us to expand our conception of possible worlds. Normally we think of only a limited number of them, sharply separated. But the accessibility relation could give rise to a dense, or even a continuous, order, with infinitely many possible worlds, nestled close together. Indeed, if we contemplate the many-worlds interpretation of quantum mechanics, with the world bifurcating as each probability collapses into one certainty or another, there are

---

[9] **S4** is normally taken to have T as one of its axioms, in which case the accessibility relation will be antisymmetric, giving rise to a quasi-ordering (see §9.7): but T is not a thesis of Prior's tense logics, and there the accessibility relation is irreflexive, and gives rise to a strict ordering.

[10] For fuller and illuminating discussion of Kripke semantics, see Brian F. Chellas, *Modal Logic*, Cambridge, 1980, esp. chs. 1 and 3; and G.E.Hughes and M.J.Cresswell, *Introduction to Modal Logic*, London, 1968, ch.4.

$2^{(2^{\aleph_0})}$ possible worlds already. Even if we are reluctant to multiply universes to that extent, we can express in modal terms the requirement that the accessibility relation be not only transitive, but dense. In Prior's terminology the former is secured by stipulating that $FFp \rightarrow Fp$ and the latter by stipulating that $Fp \rightarrow FFp$, or in standard modal terms $\vdash \Box p \rightarrow \Box\Box p$ secures transitivity of the accessibility relation, and $\vdash \Box\Box p \rightarrow \Box p$ secures density of the accessibility relation. Somewhat surprisingly, we can even secure continuity. Prior cites an axiom of Cocchiarella's which we would write, using his operators, $(Gp \rightarrow HG(Gp \rightarrow PGp)) \rightarrow HGp$[11] or, in modal terms,

$$\vdash (\Box p \rightarrow \Box^{-1}(\Box p \rightarrow \Diamond^{-1}\Box p)) \rightarrow \Box^{-1}\Box p.$$

We can also characterize the global structure of accessibility relations in modal terms. **S4** has a transitive accessibility relation; **S4.2** has a transitive accessibility relation with a lattice structure; **S4.3** has a linear transitive accessibility relation. Tense logic is unlike most modal logics in which T (that is, $\Box p \rightarrow p$) holds, since it needs not to assimilate the present to either the future or the past. D follows from T, and is unremarkable in those systems. But if we have D without T, then the accessibility relation is not reflexive (or T would hold) and the effect of D is to require that it be serial. If a relation is serial, it has no maximum, but it does not follow that it has no minimum: the successor relation, for example, will always yield a greater natural number, but does not rule out there being a least. We see then that D may hold without its mirror image, $\Box^{-1}p \rightarrow \Diamond^{-1}p$, holding. Prior is thus able to express in his tense logic the *separate* possibilities of there being a beginning and an end to time.

Thus far the iterated modalities have all been of the same basic type. But, clearly, there could be more than one type. Often they will be entirely independent of one another. 'I know that' and 'It is reported in *The Times* that' do not mesh for non-*Times* readers. The only cases that will give rise to a logic developed from what we already have, is when the distinct operators are not all acting globally on well-formed formulae of propositional calculus,

---

[11] A.N. Prior, *Past, Present and Future*, Oxford, 1967, p.72. Cited above, §9.7.

but selectively, some on one, and some on other, parts of a well-formed formula with Boolean sentential connectives. We shall need to flag the operators and those terms they operate on. Instead of bare $\Box$ and $\Diamond$, we shall distinguish them by subscripts, $\Box_x$ and $\Diamond_y$, *etc.*, and shall need then to indicate the scope of their operation, and thus ultimately to assign subscripts to those primitive terms susceptible to their modalising influence. Thus the general form of such a well-formed formula will be something like

$$\Box_x(\Diamond_y p_x \rightarrow (q_{x,y} \wedge r)),$$

where p is susceptible only to $\Box_x$, q is susceptible to $\Box_x$ and to $\Diamond_y$, and r is susceptible to neither.

At this stage it becomes obvious that what we are doing is to re-invent the quotifiers: $\Box_x$ is the universal quotifer, standardly expressed by $(\forall x)$ and in this book by $(\mathrm{A}x)$; $\Diamond_y$ is the existential quotifer, standardly expressed by $(\exists y)$ and in this book by $(\vee y)$. Similarly we could write $p(x)$, $q(x,y)$, r, but actually write $F(x)$, $G(x,y)$, or, saving brackets, Fx, Gxy. The rule of necessitation becomes the rule of generalisation:

$$\text{If} \vdash \Gamma \text{ then } \vdash (\mathrm{A}x)\Gamma$$

The axiom G becomes

$$(\mathrm{A}x)(Fx \rightarrow Gx) \rightarrow ((\mathrm{A}x)Fx \rightarrow (\mathrm{A}x)Gx).$$

The thesis D, $(\mathrm{A}x)Fx \rightarrow (\vee x)Fx$ holds in all non-empty universes, and follows from the equivalent, postulated in most systems, of T, $(\mathrm{A}x)Fx \rightarrow Fx$ (or, in some systems, $(\mathrm{A}x)Fx \rightarrow Fa$, where a is an individual name).

Besides the well-known cases where we have quotifiers binding different variables, we can consider modal predicate calculus where a modal operator interacts with a quotifier. It is fairly easy to prove

$$\vdash \Box(\mathrm{A}x)Fx \rightarrow (\mathrm{A}x)\Box Fx,$$

but the converse implication,

$$(\mathrm{A}x)\Box Fx \rightarrow \Box(\mathrm{A}x)Fx,$$

known as the Barcan formula, is not a thesis of the predicate version of **T** nor of **S4** (though it is of mainline predicate versions of **S5**).[12] The universal quotifier thus differs from simple conjunction, since

$$\vdash (\Box p \wedge \Box q) \rightarrow \Box(p \wedge q),$$

---

[12] See, G.E.Hughes and M.J.Cresswell, *An Introduction to Modal Logic*, London, 1968, pp.142-144 and 178-182.

which is again reminiscent of the characterization of topology in terms of open sets, where any finite intersection of open sets is itself open, but an infinite intersection of open sets may not be open itself.[13]

We may choose not to admit polyadic predicates, $q(x, y)$, or $G(x, y)$, and to confine our extension of logic to monadic predicates, $p(x)$, or $F(x)$, alone. In that case we have the monadic predicate calculus, which, like propositional calculus, is (two-way) *decidable*. Given any well-formed formula, we can tell in a finite number of steps, whether *or not* it is a theorem. Monadic predicate calculus, however, is extremely restricted, and it is natural to extend logic to include polyadic predicate calculus (generally known as predicate calculus *simpliciter*), which allows two-place predicates (and more-than-two-place predicates) expressing relations. If two-place predicates are allowed, we are allowing the logic of relations[14] as part of logic, and can define one two-place predicate with the properties of the Successor, and hence formulate Peano's postulates, and wonder whether the implication from Peano's postulates to the Gödelian sentence is a theorem or not, and hence conclude that the polyadic predicate calculus is not two-way decidable,[15] though nonetheless generally accepted as part of logic.

We thus see how modal logic and quotificational logic are natural developments from a Boolean system we are led to adopt by the importance of inference and negation. The logic of relations plays a crucial role in displaying the interconnexions between different modal logics. It would be difficult on this showing to draw any profound distinctions, or claim that some, but not others, of these studies were to be properly accorded the title of "logic".

Quine disagrees. He urges us to confine the term to first-order logic, that is to say, first-order predicate calculus with identity, on the grounds that only first-order logical theories display "Law and Order", and he regards modal logic as belonging with witchcraft and superstition.[16] Quine's exclusion of modal and tense logic seems irrational, but there are arguments for insisting that quotification should be only over individual, and not over predicate,

---

[13] See above, §10.2.

[14] See above, ch.9.

[15] See above, §8.8.

[16] W.V.Quine, *Word and Object*, Cambridge, Mass., 1960, p.242.

variables. Predicates are ontologically more suspect than individuals, and have a different logic. More immediately, second-order logic lacks the **completeness** that first-order logic has, and is liable to give rise to paradox and inconsistency.

13.5 Completeness

Whereas first-order logic is complete, second-order logic is not.[17] Many well-formed formulae can be formulated in it which are independent of the axioms but which are valid, that is, true under all natural interpretations.

It is often seen as a great merit of first-order logic that it is complete, and thus reconciles the syntactic and semantic approaches,[18] so that we need not worry about distinguishing them, so long as we stick to first-order logic, and can use $\vdash$ and $\models$ more or less interchangeably. On the syntactic approach we define the sentential connectives, $\wedge$, $\vee$, $\neg$, $\rightarrow$, corresponding to regimented versions of our familiar 'and', 'or', 'not', 'if', by their inference patterns; on the semantic approach we define the analogous logical constants by truth-tables. It is moderately easy thus far to see that every syntactic entailment is valid semantically:

$$\text{If}\quad P \vdash Q \quad\text{then}\quad P \models Q,$$

and *vice versa*

$$\text{If}\quad P \models Q \quad\text{then}\quad P \vdash Q.$$

In particular, analytic propositions are tautologies, and *vice versa*:

$$\text{If}\quad \vdash Q \quad\text{then}\quad \models Q,$$

and

$$\text{If}\quad \models Q \quad\text{then}\quad \vdash Q,$$

---

[17] Gödel proved the completeness of first-order logic, using, it should be noted, infinitistic methods (cf. §15.7): Henkin proved *a* completeness theorem for second-order logic, which depends on admitting, besides the primary interpretations, some further secondary ones: but the secondary interpretations are unnatural, and not at all what we should expect on the normal semantic approach. See further below, §15.9.

[18] See above, §3.5.

In virtue of the former we say that the propositional calculus is **sound**, and in virtue of the latter we say that the propositional calculus is **complete**.[19]

If we add the quotifiers, (Ax) and (Vx), we have to be careful in specifying their inference-patterns, and especially, what exactly should count as models. Provided we quotify only over individual variables, we can establish both soundness and completeness, and this still holds good if we extend the simple first-order predicate calculus, by adding, with appropriate rules, the further two-place predicate, $=$, representing identity. That is to say, if P, Q are any well-formed formulae of first-order logic,

$$\text{If} \quad P \vdash Q \quad \text{then} \quad P \models Q,$$

and

$$\text{If} \quad P \models Q \quad \text{then} \quad P \vdash Q;$$

or, more succinctly,

$$\vdash Q \quad \text{if and only if} \quad \models Q.$$

The completeness of first-order logic not only reconciles the syntactic and semantic approaches, but, more sophisticatedly, is seen as a token of the adequacy of our axiomatization: it shows that we have captured in our syntactic notion of theoremhood the desirable semantic property of being true under every interpretation. From this it follows that, since syntactic proof-procedures can be "mechanized", a computer could be programmed to churn out every theorem, and thus, thanks to the completeness theorem, every valid well-formed formula of first-order logic. First-order logic is thus "computer-friendly", whereas second-order logic is not, since there is no corresponding way of producing every one of its valid well-formed formulae. In first-order logic we have a positive (although not a negative[20]) test for any particular well-formed formula's being true under all interpretations. It is very tedious, but in the long run it will work: we simply program a computer to produce every theorem in a systematic way, and check whether or not it is identical with the well-formed formula in question; if it

[19] See above, §3.5.

[20] See above, §8.8.

is, then that well-formed formula is valid, is true under all interpretations; if it is not, the computer grinds on and produces the
next theorem. In second-order logic we cannot do this. Although
we can still program a computer to generate every *theorem* in a
systematic way, so that if a well-formed formula *is* a theorem, it
will turn up sooner or later in the list the computer spews out,
not every valid well-formed formula is a theorem.[21] That is, there
are some well-formed formulae which are true under all natural
interpretations, and so reasonable candidates for being accounted
logical truths, but are not theorems according to the axioms and
rules of inference of the system, and so could not be discovered or
identified by any computer search.

Most logicians have regarded this as a defect of second-order
logic. But the argument is two-edged, and can be seen as showing not the adequacy of the axiomatization, but the limits of the
formalisation. First-order logic is complete, but only in the way
eunuchs are. Eunuchs are able to do everything they want to do,
but cannot want to do what other men want to do. First-order
logic can prove every well-formed formula that is expressible in
first-order logic and is true under all interpretations, but cannot
express many propositions that other logics can. It secures complete success in its ability to prove propositions by cutting down
its ability to formulate them. We cannot say things in first-order
logic we might naturally want to say—for example that a set of
well-formed formulae is satisfiable in any finite domain, or that
an ordering is well-ordered, and so with its expressive ability thus
truncated, it is not surprising that it can prove those relatively few
well-formed formulae it can formulate.

The incompleteness of second-order logic can thus be regarded
in another light, showing it to be more juicy than first-order logic,
and thus capable of grounding more substantial truths. Certainly,
in second-order logic we sometimes seem to be led to propound
further truths, such as the Axiom of Choice, or various versions of
the Axiom of Infinity, which were not in any sense already implicit
in the axioms, but suggest themselves as being additional axioms.[22]

---

[21] George S. Boolos and Richard C. Jeffrey, *Computability and Logic*, Cambridge, 2nd ed., 1980, ch.16.

[22] Alonzo Church, *Introduction to Mathematical Logic*, Princeton, 1956, ch.V,
§54, p.315.

13.6 Paradox

It is not only completeness that has told in favour of first-order logic. Consistency is in issue as well. Second-order logic is suspected of inconsistency. It is thought to be equivalent to set theory—to quotify over qualities is very like quotifying over sets—and it is possible to reproduce the "heterological paradox" in unbridled second-order logic: for if we can **both** quotify over predicates **and** allow predicate variables to occupy the same positions as individual variables, then we can consider those predicates that are self-applicable—those for which it is true that $F(F)$—and those that are not—those for which it is true that $\neg F(F)$—and define the latter as a predicate of predicates, that is define

$$H(F) \quad \text{iff} \quad \neg F(F);$$

We then ask whether the predicate H, thus defined, is, or is not, predicable of itself. Either answer leads to a contradiction: if $H(H)$ then $\neg H(H)$; if $\neg H(H)$, then the defining condition is satisfied, and so it is true that $H(H)$.

The argument stinks. Expressed in the unfamiliar terminology of sets, we may be led to accept the definition of extraordinary sets which are members of themselves,[23] but the concept of a "heterological property" of not being self-applicable is hard to take. Nor does the formalism of the predicate calculus encourage us to stifle our objections. Predicate variables are different from individual variables, and any definition involving $F(F)$ is manifestly ill-formed. We may quotify over qualities, but that does not make them the same as individual substances. Sometimes, no doubt, we can refer to particular qualities and talk about them, but that is not to say that they are exactly the same as the individuals that are normally talked about as possessing them.

The standard formalisations of predicate calculus are crude. They draw only one distinction, that between individual terms and predicate terms, and blur all other distinctions. Moreover, the individual variables are down-graded to doing hardly any logical work, being little more than glorified logical blanks,[24] like the x in $\int F(x)\,\mathrm{d}x$. All the work is done by the predicates, and, except for

[23] See above, §12.2.

[24] See W.V. Quine, *Methods of Logic*, Harvard, 1951, §12.

sometimes requiring that the universe of discourse be non-empty, no consideration is given to range or the logical shape of the individual variable. A logic that permits us to contrapose 'all ravens are black' into 'all non-black things are non-ravens' is not a logic that is sensitive to type-distinctions. We need, as we have seen,[25] to take individual variables seriously. We need to register in our formalism the fact that not only are predicate variables ineligible to occupy the positions reserved for individual variables, but often one individual variable cannot occupy the place of another. It makes perfectly good sense to ask whether the square of a cricket pitch is green, but not whether the square of 22 is. Ryle pointed out that there were many "category distinctions" in our conceptual scheme as expressed in ordinary language,[26] and that many philosophical errors arose from neglecting them, but the distinctions are more fluid and difficult to discern than he made out. In some senses, geographical and institutional, the University of Oxford is of a different type from the Oxford Colleges, but in other respects they are on the same footing—I am perfectly happy to accept cheques from both. Instead of an absolute, possibly ontological distinction between one categorial type and another, there are many different distinctions depending on context, which any formal system will find it difficult to register.

Equally with predicates there are many type distinctions we observe in our ordinary thought: '   is green' can be predicated of cricket squares, '   is generous' cannot. When we quotify over predicates, there is an implicit restriction of the range of quotification to predicates of the appropriate type. If we say someone has all the properties of Napoleon, we do not consider whether he might be a perfect square, and on discovering that Napoleon was not a perfect square conclude that neither is the person we are talking about: being a perfect square is a property that Napoleon neither possesses nor does not possess. Unclarity on this score does not greatly matter so long as we are considering only the positive predicates, since if we were mistakenly to ask the improper question

---

[25] §4.3, §12.3 and §12.8.

[26] Gilbert Ryle, "Categories", *Proceedings of the Aristotelian Society*, **49**, 1938-9; reprinted in *Logic and Language*, Series II, ed. A.G.N.Flew, Oxford, 1953, pp.65-81; and Gilbert Ryle, *The Concept of Mind*, London, 1949, pp.16-18.

whether or not Napoleon possessed the property of being a perfect square, we should return a negative answer and not ascribe perfect squaredom to the man we were talking about. But once we are dealing with negation, and consider someone who does not have all the properties of Napoleon, we may be tempted to ascribe to him non-perfect-squaredom and our troubles begin. Individual terms have a different logic, less liable to lead us astray. Whereas predicates, like propositions, can be negated and disjoined, it makes no sense except in some wider, specified context, to talk of a non-man, or a man-or-irrational-number.

We make use of type distinctions in our ordinary thinking and speaking, but characteristically articulate them when some particular inference is in question instead of seeking to lay down general rules in advance. The formation rules we already have are enough to rule out 'heterological' as ill-formed. No formal system is likely to be sensitive to all the nuances of ordinary language, and rule out every sort of nonsense, but that, although a barrier to the complete formalisation of logic, is not a conclusive objection to every quotification over qualities or quotities. We are right to be as reluctant to allow a predicate's either being or not being applicable to itself, as we are to a set's either being or not being a member of itself, but we have to confess that we have not yet formulated an adequate formal theory of predicates. This is in line with the general incompletely formalisable nature of second-order logic, but it is a confession, not a boast.

13.7 Second-order Logic

Second-order logic differs from first-order logic in a number of other important ways:[27] they are listed, together with those already discussed, in the table on the next page.

Although the differences are real, they hardly justify excluding second-order logic from being part of logic. For one thing, many of the differences, though alleged to favour first-order logic, actually tell the other way; and, anyway, there is no compelling argument for picking on those differences as decisive, in comparison with others,

---

[27] See G. Boolos and R. Jeffrey, *Computability and Logic*, 2nd ed., Cambridge, 1980, ch.18. See also C.D. Parsons, "Objects and Logic", *Monist*, **65**, 1982, pp.498-505; and J.B. Moss review in *British Journal for the Philosophy of Science*, **36**, 1985, pp. 437-455.

not held to be decisive, and in the face of continuing similarities between second-order logic and other systems accepted without question.

	First-order Logic	Second-order Logic
1.	Complete *i.e.* $\models A \Longrightarrow\ \vdash A$	Only *Henkin*-complete We cannot secure that if A is true under all *principal* interpretations, then $\vdash A$
2.	So if $\models A$ then we can, given enough time, prove $\models A$	No effective positive test for validity
3.	Compact	Not compact
4.	Löwenheim-Skolem theorem holds	Löwenheim-Skolem theorem does not hold
5.	Peano Arithmetic not monomorphic	Peano Arithmetic monomorphic
6.	Some well-formed formulae true, but not provable	All arithmetical truths prov- able from Peano's postulates

The first two of the differences listed in the table have already been shown to be really to the advantage of second-order logic.[28] Compactness—the feature that a set of well-formed formulae is consistent provided every finite subset is—has, like completeness, been taken as a virtue. It goes with first-order logic's being finitely axiomatizable, and such that a computer can be programmed to do it. First-order logic is, essentially, a finitistic calculus, in which, therefore, every valid well-formed formula that can be expressed in its formalism can be proved in a finite number of steps. But compactness is really a demerit. It trades on the finiteness of a proof-

---

[28] In §13.5.

sequence, and is counter-intuitive, leading once again to there being non-standard models of arithmetic, though by a different route
from that of Gödel's theorem.[29] Its finitistic features are purchased
at the price of our never being able to specify completely what we
are talking about (4 & 5). The Löwenheim–Skolem theorem is
really a liability rather than an asset, showing, as it does, that
in first-order theories we cannot in general specify our models, or
even their cardinality.[30] We have already explored the awkward-
ness of Peano's postulates not being monomorphic in first-order
logic, and Gödel's incompleteness theorem is a notorious embarrassment. Even the concept of identity cannot be defined in ordinary first-order predicate calculus, but has to be characterized by
extra *ad hoc* axioms. Second-order predicate calculus, by contrast,
is able to define identity without special extra axioms, and is able
to specify exactly what we are talking about.

Second-order logic thus seems a natural further development of
logic from its Boolean core. It is hard to justify our jibbing at this
particular step. If it is the incompleteness of second-order logic that
debars it from being a proper logic, should not the undecidability
of first-order logic tell equally against that? Once we go beyond
propositional calculus, we are led to modal logics with iterated
modalities, and to quotificational logic with intertwined quotifiers,
and the logic of relations. Though the next step *is* a further step,
with considerable further implications, it is one we should take. If
we have free predicate variables, it would be unreasonable not to be
able to quotify over them; otherwise, we should be in the position
of being able to specify that a universe of discourse was infinite,
but not that it was finite.

There are trade-offs. First-order logic is finitely axiomatizable,
but cannot express finitude: second-order logic can express finitude, but is not finitely axiomatizable, and our axiomatization is
always liable to turn out to be incomplete and inadequate for our
purposes. If we formalise second-order logic incautiously and ill-
advisedly, we run into paradox and inconsistency, whereas first-
order logic has simple formation rules which secure us against any
danger of meaninglessness—but at the cost of often being unable
to express our meaning at all.

[29]   See above, §6.3.

[30]   See above, §12.5.

If second-order logic is admitted as being part of logic, important consequences follow. The fact that it is not complete means that there are well-formed formulae which are true under all reasonable interpretations, but cannot be proved from the axioms by means of the rules of inference. Truth, once again, outruns formal provability.[31] And, more important for our present purpose, cannot be explicated in terms of analyticity.

13.8 Analytic and *A Priori* Truth

Many philosophers have found it difficult to give an account of mathematical truth, because they have taken it for granted that mathematical truth must be either analytic or synthetic, and if synthetic empirical, and if analytic empty. Since it is difficult to take the Protagorean view that it is empirical, they have been forced to the view that the whole of mathematics is a vast set of tautologies.[32] Traditional Logicism supports that view. If all mathematical truths are, ultimately, truths of first-order logic, then they are theorems, and anyone who denies them is guilty of inconsistency. But once we give up the identification of logic with first-order logic, we are no longer impelled to downgrade mathematical truth to mere tautology.

Whereas first-order logic is axiomatizable and complete, and it can be reasonably maintained that its theorems are analytic, second-order logic is not completely axiomatizable, and seems to generate truths which are not mere reformulation of the original axioms. They are not analytic. They do not just tell us what was in the original axioms and rules of inference of second-order logic. The Axiom of Choice cannot even be formulated in first-order logic. It has some similarity to Peano's fifth postulate—and Poincaré argued that mathematics was not analytic just because it employed argument by recursion.[33] The reasoning which impels us to generalise from *Sorites* Arithmetic to Peano Arithmetic, impels us also to accept the Axiom of Choice as true. If so, it is in some

[31] See above, §8.11.

[32] See, for example, A.J.Ayer, *Language, Truth and Logic*, London, 1936, ch.4; or Bertrand Russell, *History of Western Philosophy*, London, 1946, p.860, pbk., London, 1991, p.786: mathematical knowledge is all of the same nature as the "great truth" that there are three feet in a yard.

[33] See above, §6.5.

sense synthetic—it is not a deductive consequence of our explicit axioms of set theory—but it is not *a posteriori* in Kant's sense. The Continuum Hypothesis is in the same case, and arguably the axioms of infinity. The axioms of geometry, again, are not analytic, and though the Riemannian geometry of the General Theory may be adopted *a posteriori* on the basis of empirical evidence, the arguments adduced in Chapter Two were altogether different. So, too, are the arguments for extending the natural numbers to the integers, and the integers to the rationals, the rationals to the reals, and the reals to the complex numbers. Such truths, if they are truths, and if we do know them, are known not on the strength of sense experience, and are in that sense known *a priori*. They are, as regards their logical status, synthetic propositions, and, as regards their epistemological status, known *a priori*, if known at all. How such synthetic *a priori* propositions are possible remains an open question, but once we launch out from the restricted compass of first-order logic, it is a question we not only have to face, but can hope to answer.

Non-Analytic Propositions

1. Peano's Fifth Postulate—it was on account of its employing argument by recursion that Poincaré argued that mathematics was not analytic. (See above, ch.6, §6.5.)
2. Various versions of the Axiom of Infinity.
3. The Axiom of Choice.
4. The Continuum Hypotheses, together with various other, more *recherché* axioms suggested for set theory.
5. The axiomatic extension of the natural numbers to include the negative integers, the rational numbers, the reals, and complex numbers.
6. The axioms of different geometries.

The justification of these is not uniform. It involves in part a reassessment of traditional ideas of what it is to know something, and in part a closer examination of the interpretations, principal or secondary, under which valid well-formed formulae come out as true.

Chapter 14
Mathematical Knowledge

14.1 Synthetic *A Priori?*

If mathematical knowledge is synthetic *a priori*, we owe an account of how it is possible. Some deny that. In her most recent book,[1] Professor Maddy argues that though extrinsic justifications of the axioms of set theory may be sought and found, they are not essential. Set theory is a going concern, and is quite all right as it is. The argument from use is weighty, in mathematics as in ordinary language, but, *pace* Wittgenstein and his followers, it is not conclusive. A mathematical practice could have to be abandoned, not only on account of an internal inconsistency, but because it presupposed propositions which were, on grounds quite external to mathematics, untenable. The very fact that many American philosophers of mathematics feel obliged to find an accommodation between mathematics and their naturalist metaphysics, witnesses to their not being totally disconnected.

Empiricists deny the possiblity of *a priori* knowledge absolutely, and seek to accommodate it in other ways. Professor Kitcher gives a causal account of a docile schoolgirl who believes that what her teachers tell her is warrantedly true.[2] As an explanation of how some people acquire mathematical abilities, it has much truth; the multiplication tables often are learned by rote. But we are seeking

---

[1] Penelope Maddy, *Naturalism in Mathematics*, Oxford, 1996.

[2] Philip Kitcher, *The Nature of Mathematical Knowledge*, New York, 1983, pp.91ff.

a justification, not a psychological explanation—even in the best-run schools some naughty boys ask why six sixes are thirty six, and are not prepared to accept the teacher's say-so as an adequate reason for believing it to be true. A hard-line empiricist may refer vaguely to the experience of previous generations, and encourage us to accept mathematics as the hard-won wisdom of the many and the wise, but once we have felt the force of Plato's *Meno* argument, we shall seek a more compelling account of cogency.

Fundamentally we feel the force of reason, and we cannot give a full formal account of reason. Unless we secure absolute validity at the price of absolute vacuity, we shall reach an end of arguing, where no more can be said, and we can only hope that the desire to know, and the ability to reason, will enable the person we are arguing with to abandon opinions held because they were his in favour of judgements held because they are true. But though that is the ultimate stage, there are many partial prescriptions and formalisations, which may enable him to see the error of his previous ways, and enable us also to detect flaws in our presentations, and see the whole issue in a more rational light.

The requirements of rationality afford adequate justification for adopting the Principle of Recursive Reasoning, Argument by Iterated Choice, and for there being infinite possibilities, and hence for various axioms of infinity; but there is an alternative view of the axioms, connected with meaning rather than rationality, which is also relevant to the completeness theorems. The axioms of different geometries are often seen as implicitly defining different concepts of point and line. The axiomatic extension of the natural numbers to include the negative integers, the rational numbers, the reals and complex numbers, can be viewed as articulating further our concept of number, as can the Axiom of Choice and other axioms of set theory, our concept of a set. This offers a different view of the valid but unprovable well-formed formulae of second-order logic. For there is *a* completeness theorem, due to Henkin.[3] But it involves secondary (*i.e.* non-principal) interpretations on unnatural models. If we extend the number of models taken into consideration, we reduce the number of well-formed formulae which will be true in all of them. Hence, if we admit weird models of second-order

---

[3] See Alonzo Church, *Introduction to Mathematical Logic*, Princeton, 1956, Metatheorem **546, p.314, and generally ch.5, §54, pp.307-315.

propositions, we have fewer well-formed formulae that are true in all of them, and it is easier for them all to be provable. The range of admissible models is thus of crucial importance in determining what shall count as a logical truth. With regard to models of Peano Arithmetic in first-order logic we were able to say which was the standard one and which were non-standard ones even though the difference could not be formulated in first-order terms. When we embed one theory in another, we restrict the range of available models. Some, non-Desarguian, models of projective plane geometry are not models of three-dimensional projective geometry. In rejecting non-Desarguian models of projective plane geometry we are discerning the shape of the models we had in mind when we sought axioms for projective plane geometry. But this is not a matter of arbitrary choice. Just as do have an idea of the intended model of the natural numbers, and reject non-standard ones, even if they satisfy a first-order specification of Peano's axioms, so the wider concept of *number*, of *dimensional space*, and—arguably—of *set*, are not constitutively defined by their definitions, but have a life of their own. On the strength of intuitions about what are the naturally intended models, I restrict the range of standard interpretations, and thus have a wider range of well-formed formulae that are true in all of them.

Second-order propositions on this showing *are* true in virtue of meanings, but not just the meanings of the terms involved, and thus not analytic in any derogatory sense. Rather, meanings in mathematics are not as fixed as the Formalists suppose, and may develop in a rationally coherent direction, much as they do in ordinary language. Meaning, in particular, is tied up with inference patterns, and hence with the validity of inferences.[4] Thus the Gödelian extensibility of valid inference beyond any pre-assigned formal limits, is paralleled by an extensibility of meanings in a way not licensed by antecedent rules, but rational none the less.

---

[4] See above, §3.3.

14.2 Not Seeing But Doing

Mathematical knowledge is very largely knowledge how to do things, rather than knowledge that such and such is the case. We learn how to do long division, solve quadratic equations and differential equations, how to do vectors and tensors and Fourier analysis. We differentiate and integrate and solve, and the whole theory of groups is naturally expressed in terms of transformations we carry out, rather than theorems we contemplate. In spite of the scorn poured by Plato and Aristotle on the operational language used by geometers,[5] group-theoretical considerations constituted a good argument in favour of Euclidean geometry; and we (and Euclid[6]) still talk of squaring and extracting square roots, and believe that in order to get hold of a concept and grasp what it really comes to, we need to have much practice in manipulating it. It is in our hands as well as our eyes that we humans excel. Besides the many visual metaphors we have for intelligent activity, we have some from the hands: ὑπολαμβάνω (*hupolambano*) 'grasp', 'comprehend'. The usage is not just a regrettable *façon de parler*, but an aspect of arguing which cannot be eliminated altogether, however much we formalise it. This was one reason why Formalism failed. It could not entirely eliminate *know-how* in favour of *know-that*, and required mathematicians to be able to exercise a minimal skill in recognising when a rule of inference applied, and on occasion a much more *recherché* one in assuring themselves that a particular formal system could be interpreted so as to apply to a particular model.[7]

Sometimes, admittedly, we can replace *know-how* by *know-that*, and advantageously so, when we want to formalise arguments in order the better to scrutinise them. Nevertheless, the real import of some axioms, such as Peano's Fifth Postulate or the Axiom of Choice, is more clearly discerned if they are seen as rules of inference, rather than assertions of recondite fact.[8] Moreover, Gödel's theorem shows that however far we go in articulating our inferences as instances of some specified rule of inference, there will

---

[5] See above, §2.7.

[6] See above, §2.2.

[7] See above, §3.6, and below, §14.3, §14.4.

[8] See above, §6.5, and §13.6.

still be further inferences, evidently valid, not covered by the specified rules.[9] Drawing valid inferences is a mathematical activity that cannot be fully formalised, and must be accounted one of the things a mathematician does, rather than truths he sees.

Once we see the mathematician as an active operator who does things he knows how to do rather than a passive percipient of eternal truths, mathematical knowledge appears much less puzzling.[10] Whereas claims to know that something is the case invite questions "How do you know?", which we are hard put to answer, claims to know how to do something are vindicated by actually doing it. Moreover, I know not only how to do things, but what I shall do,[11] and what I can do. As a doer I have freedom of choice. Choice not only gives sense to the quotifiers, allowing you to choose the worst case for my thesis, or me the best case, but offers us a way into the modal concepts of possibility, impossibility and necessity.

But mathematics is not just a collection of personal skills, and personal choices. The canons of success are interpersonal. We need to consider not just what I can do, but what in principle might be done; we have to move from "the actual operations of human agents" to "the ideal operations performed by ideal agents".[12] Kitcher claims, in imitation of Mill, that "arithmetic is a permanent possibility of manipulation",[13] or, more formally, that mathematics is "the constructive output of an ideal agent" (though, somewhat nervously, disclaiming any actual belief in God).[14] The God's-hand view is illuminating. St Augustine and Cantor were able to accept the actual infinite because God could actually survey it. Divine omnipotence is the right modality for the mathematician's 'can'. In our sublunary world we can aspire towards it by means of quotifiers and more human modal operators. Although poor mortal that I am, I cannot count all the natural numbers, it remains the case that, given any particular number, I can go on to the next; and if I could not, someone else could. I can not only report on

[9] See above, §8.11.

[10] See C.Ormell, *The Peircean Applicability of Mathematics*, London, 1997.

[11] See above, §1.5.

[12] P.Kitcher, *Mathematical Knowledge*, New York, 1983, p.117.

[13] p.108.

[14] ch.6 generally, esp. pp.108-122 and n.18.

my own actual abilities, but consider what someone might be able to do in hypothetical circumstances, and what it would be like if what could be done were done. We thus have epistemic access to a wide range of impersonal possibilities, which we can suppose to be actual. The puzzling feature of mathematical modality,

Ab Posse valet consequentia Esse,

begins to look less inexplicable, as also its corollary, that what is, is necessarily so.[15] Considerations of omnipotence are illuminating, but not to be presumed upon. Mathematicians, like political theorists, tend to be "egotheists", each seeing himself as God, and not having to take seriously the imperfections of himself and his fellow men.[16] My drawing an inference is not a guarantee of its being valid. Mathematical claims are contestable, and may be challenged and vindicated.

14.3 Pattern Recognition

The argument of the two previous sections shows that mathematical knowledge depends crucially on the correct discernment of patterns. The experience of mathematicians bears this out. Although we break down proofs into a number of steps, we do not comprehend them as that. To understand a proof we need to see it as a whole. It is a common experience to follow each individual step of a proof, but not to be able to see what it all adds up to, not to be able to grasp it as a whole. Often, after having worked at the details for a long time, comprehension comes suddenly in a flash, and the different bits fall into place, and it all comes together.[17] When that happens, we are moderately sure that we do understand the proof, and could reproduce it if necessary on another occasion, whereas until then we had not got hold of it, and though we might mug it up and memorise it for an examination, we did not really have it in our minds, and could not claim really to know it.

---

[15] See above, §1.6, §7.10, and below, §15.6.

[16] See above, §11.2.

[17] M.D.Resnik, "Mathematical Knowledge and Pattern-Cognition", *Canadian Journal of Philosophy*, **5**, 1975, p.32, reports how for many years he had studied Bernstein's theorem, and could reproduce the proof in teaching it to others, but it was only on reading Cohen's presentation that he really understood it, with all the disparate pieces falling into place. See also his *Mathematics as a Science of Patterns*, Oxford, 1997, esp. ch.11.

This experience is widespread, but in recent years has been discounted in our thinking about the epistemology of mathematics. In part this has been due to the teaching of Wittgenstein, who ridiculed the probative value of the "got it" experience. He argued that by itself an experience of having got it, was of no consequence: the proof of the pudding was in the eating; if a schoolboy could reproduce a proof in an exam, he would get full marks, irrespective of whether he had had the "got-it" experience, and if he could not reproduce it, he would get no marks, no matter how strongly he had felt that he had got it. Wittgenstein's argument is cogent against someone who maintains that first-personal experience is by itself conclusive evidence of mastery of some technique. But that is not what is claimed. If, as is generally observed to be the case, the "got-it" experience is regularly associated with a subsequent ability to produce and deploy the proof on demand, it gives a reliable indication of the nature of that ability. It shows that the ability is not a collection of disparate competences to take separate steps, but an integrated ability to take each step in the context of the others as part of a complete manoeuvre focused on an over-all goal. Many abilities are of this sort—swinging a golf-club so as to propel a golf ball to the next hole, for example—and there are various indications of this being so. In the case of an intellectual ability like that of understanding a mathematical proof, most of those indications are bound to be first-personal reports of introspective experience. But to discount those out of hand is behaviourist prejudice, and simply precludes our ever having an informed understanding of what it is to understand.

Much of mathematics is concerned with discovering and communicating intelligible *Gestälten* which will make proofs surveyable, and enable the mathematician to discern the outline of the wood, without being distracted and confused by irrelevant detail of the trees. Granted the decimal notation, we can see at once that

$$7034174 + 6594321 = 13628495.$$

The decimal notation has a dual aspect: it not only provides in a mechanical way a numeral for each natural number, but is also a polynomial in '10', so that we can reduce the otherwise unsurveyable calculation to a small number of much more manageable ones.[18] In a similar way, Goodstein's theorem, which at first sight

[18] I owe this illuminating point to Mark Steiner, *Mathematical Knowledge,*

seems highly counter-intuitive, becomes obviously true, once we replace finite numbers by transfinite ones.[19] We seek new ways of looking at problems, so as to be able to get a grip on them, and twist them round to clear all obstruction to their solution. The theory of groups, Galois theory, the exponential and trigonometrical series, give us new looks, enabling us to focus on the point at issue, and understand clearly and distinctly what the question is, and what its answer must be.

Philosophers of mathematics in recent years have had problems with pattern recognition. They feel that Platonic "seeing" is a metaphor, not an account. Nevertheless, we often do recognise patterns. We recognise faces, voices, tunes, smells and tastes. Beethoven's Fifth Symphony is a pattern. I can recognise instances of it, and in recognising particular instances recognise in them the generic type. We characteristically use visual metaphors, but it is not only visual patterns that we recognise, and it is useful therefore to stress non-visual instances of pattern recognition, and to think of the theory of groups as being exemplified in campanology, or in turning round a sheet of paper, or in the manipulations of a solid object. Besides tunes and voices, we can also recognise the style of composers, and more generally literary style. Sometimes even it is possible to recognise a mathematician's style of argument. Style is peculiarly elusive and highly personal, and the fact that we can often recognise the style of a particular person is reason for thinking that personality is something real. A Platonist is quite entitled to ground his claim that mathematics is real on our being able to recognise a pair, a triplet, a foursome, as instances of two, three, or four; to see squares as being square, and to talk about the square and its diagonal.

Just as a large part of learning ornithology or radiography is the development of the ability to form and recognise the relevant patterns, so in mathematics a large part of the skill lies in being able to do the same, and handle them with dexterity when needed.

Cornell University Press, Ithaca, NY, 1975, ch.1, pp.43-45. See above, §7.8, §7.9.

---

[19] For a simple account, see Roger Penrose, "On Understanding Understanding", *International Studies in the Philosophy of Science*, vol.11, no.1, March, 1997, pp.11-15. Like Penrose, I owe the example to Dan Isaacson, Fellow of Wolfson College, Oxford.

Admittedly, it remains unclear exactly what this ability is. It could be that recognition really was re-cognition, as Plato argues in the *Meno*; or that we have an innate ability, as Chomsky holds with regard to linguistic patterns, to select in accordance with certain principles of classification rather than acquiring it entirely from experience. But it is just a fact of human intellectual powers that what we talk about, and communicate as reports of what we have perceived, goes beyond the stimuli operating on our sense organs. Those who, for extraneous metaphysical reasons, would deny to mathematicians the ability to discern patterns, should, in all consistency, disclaim the ability generally, and in particular disallow the Formalist's ability to recognise a formal inference pattern, and the sceptical philosopher's ability to use linguistic patterns to express his doubts.

Nevertheless, caution is needed. It is dangerously easy to make use of some perceptual metaphor. Although when we perceive, we characteristically construe our perceptual stimuli in terms of some pattern, we can also recognise one pattern within the framework of another, as when we see the diagonal of a square as the side of a larger square. The difference is crucial, and reveals itself in the logic of mathematical discourse. Suppose Hardy or Gödel or Cohen told me that they had perceived the falsity of the Continuum Hypothesis. They try and point it out (de-monstrate) it to me. I fail to see. Could I just accept their word for it? Only in a necessarily provisional way. Although I can take it on trust that Fermat's Last Theorem has been proved by Wiles,[20] the trust is not in his veracity, but that he will be vindicated by independent assessments of his proof. Mathematics is quite different from history or geography, where we can achieve knowledge only if we are willing to take it second-hand from authorities who were in the right place at the right time to observe.

More plausibly I attribute my failure not to my not being in the right situation, but my perceptual incapacity. Perhaps I suffer from "continuum blindness", analogous to colour blindness. Suppose that a minority—but only a minority—of competent mathematicians report that following the demonstration, they, too, can see it to be true. Would we accept this, and say that the others were, like me perceptually defective? Or would we credit the

<hr>

[20] See above, §7.4.

minority with a special power of perceptual discrimination, in the way that a minority of human beings can taste phenyl-thio-urea?[21] No. Mathematical knowledge not only does not depend on the authority of the observer, but does not respect the authority of the wise in the way that literary critics, jurisconsults, historians and other scholars should. Although on occasion we will accept the say-so of a mathematical colleague that some proposition is proved, or some purported proof valid, we could not be content to leave it there. We want more—that any competent mathematician *who tries*, should be able to make out the pattern, and validate the proof, for himself. There must be an *independent* criterion of competence. Mathematics is different from histology. In histology it is almost, if not quite, a test of competence to be able to see, with the aid of a microscope, bodies in the cell. The tests of mathematical ability, however, are more various, and mathematical discernment is not tied to any particular sense, and is permeable to argument. It would not be enough if there were a stable minority of mathematicians who could discern the truth of the Continuum Hypothesis and could communicate about it among themselves. The mathematical community is necessarily in principle an open community, enshrining the principle that there is open access to mathematical truth, open to all committed truth-seekers.

We are left with a paradox. The claim of mathematics to offer open access to all comers is belied by the fact that only rather clever people can do mathematics well. The paradox is resolved when we see mathematics not as a monologue, but as a dialogue, in which the cleverness of the mathematician is balanced by the unselective choice of respondent, and the cogency of mathematical argument is shown by his being forced to concede the inferences the mathematician wishes to draw.

14.4 Lakatos

The history of mathematics is much messier than we are supposed to suppose. Most important theorems were false when first enunciated. It is only gradually, as counter-examples are discovered and guarded against, that definitions are tightened up, and the

---

[21] Jonathan Bennett, "Substance, Reality and Primary Qualities", *American Philosophical Quarterly*, **2**, 1956, pp.1-17, esp.pp.9-10; reprinted in C.B.Martin and D.B.Armstrong, eds., *Locke and Berkeley*, London, 1969; see also his *Locke, Berkeley, Hume: Central Themes*, Oxford, 1971, p.95.

theorems properly proved. A great mathematician has a deep insight, and puts forward a proof or a concept, which wins general acceptance. Later doubts arise. Sometimes the argument itself is suspect—some series has been summed to infinity illegitimately, or some denominator has gone to zero. At other times the method of proof applied elsewhere leads to contradictions,[22] or a counter-example emerges.[23] The proof is re-examined, and some hole noticed—an extra condition tacitly assumed, or some possibility overlooked. Often it is a simple matter to tighten up the definitions, or to add some extra conditions narrowing the range of the theorem's applicability. Sometimes there are two competing concepts—*e.g.* Leibniz' and Weierstrass' concepts of the continuum—which are refined and distinguished only as something that is true of the one is not proved to the satisfaction of those who are working with the other. The concepts are then distinguished, and we have a simple bifurcation of topic, as some mathematicians work with the one, and others with the other.

Two important, but contrasting, morals are to be drawn. The first is that the process of mathematical discovery is dialectical. It is not, as we commonly assume, a steady incremental process as theorem is added to theorem, and the stock of mathematical truth is monotonically increased, but a zigzag movement, in which claims are made, but sometimes countered, and needing to be withdrawn, at least temporarily, until objections can be met, and difficulties overcome. Over the course of history, the typical connective of mathematical argument has not been uniformly 'therefore' but often 'but'. But this is not the only moral. The other is that though controversies have raged, they have usually been settled in the end, and settled positively. Theorems have been disputed, narrowed, emended, but very few have been found fatally flawed. Temporary withdrawals there have been, but very little ground has been permanently lost. The proofs may have seemed defective to later critics, but the truths have nearly always been vindicated.

Mathematicians tend to despise the history of their subject. Like scientists, they do not read the works of their predecessors, but prefer modern textbooks. They reckon that the history of the

---

[22] As Cantor's proof of the Power Set theorem became Russell's proof of his paradox.

[23] As happens time and again in the argument of ch.10, §§10.3-10.8.

subject is irrelevant to its content; and that the heuristic process of discovery and the logic of justification are totally distinct. That view has been controverted, most notably by Professor Lakatos.[24] Lakatos maintains that the two cannot be sharply separated, and that we *can* learn the logic of justification from considering the history of discovery, in much the same way as Kuhn does in the philosophy of science. Lakatos' favourite example is Euler's theorem that in a simple polyhedron V, the number of vertices, added to F, the number of faces, is two more than E, the number of edges. In symbols: $V + F = E + 2$

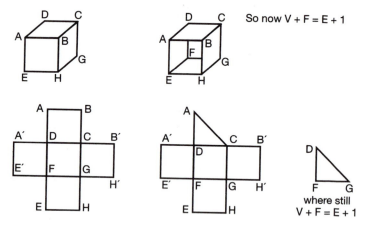

Figure 14.4.1 Euler's proof that $V + F = E + 2$, by removing one face ($ABHE$) cutting open the polyhedron (which increase the number of edged and vertices equally), laying the sides out flat, triangulating them, and removing them one triangle at a time.

He discusses this at great length, producing large numbers of apparent counter-examples, which can be ruled out only by various "exception-barring" clauses. After a very full discussion he pro-

[24] Imre Lakatos, *Proofs and Refutations*, Cambridge, 1976; and *Mathematics, Science and Epistemology*, Cambridge, 1978. See also Philip Kitcher, "Mathematical Rigor—Who Needs It?", *Noûs*, **15** 1981, pp.469-493, esp. p.482; and his *Mathematical Knowledge*, New York, 1983, chs.7-10; and M.D.Resnik, "Mathematical Knowledge and Pattern-Recognition", *Canadian Journal of Philosophy*, **5**, 1975, pp.25-39, esp. p.33.

duces a definitive proof in terms of "k-polytopes".[25] A k-polytope is a k-dimensional figure: a polyhedron is a 3-polytope; its faces are 2-polytopes; their edges are 1-polytopes; and their vertices are 0-polytopes. He defines k-chains, boundaries, closed k-chains, and circuits, in terms of which he can also characterize what it is for a 3-polytope to be simple. A k-chain is the sum of k-polytopes; the boundary of a k-polytope is the sum (*modulo* 2) of the $(k-1)$-polytopes which belong to it; a k-chain is a closed k-chain iff its boundary is zero; a closed k-chain is called a k-circuit; a k-circuit bounds iff it is the boundary of a $(k+1)$-chain; a polyhedron is simply connected iff all its 2-circuits and all its 1-circuits bound; a surface is simply connected iff all its 0-circuits bound.

Granted these definitions, the theorem becomes:

All polyhedra, all of whose circuits bound, are Eulerian. And all polyhedra in which circuits and boundary circuits coincide, are Eulerian.

k-chains can be viewed as N_k-dimensional vector-spaces over the field of residue classes *modulo* 2. We can thus view the theorem as one about vector-spaces:

If the circuit-spaces and boundary circuit spaces coincide, the number of dimensions of 0-chain space minus the number of dimensions of 1-chain space plus the number of dimensions of 2-chain space equals 2.

In that form it can be proved, with a certain amount of tedious algebra.

The sceptical reader may ask "How much has been achieved? Do not the definitions mirror the original proof, so that all we are really saying is that for those polyhedra for which Euler's theorem holds Euler's theorem holds?". Lakatos admits that all the work is in assuring oneself that the definitions really capture the concepts originally invoked. There is much claim and counter-claim in determining exactly what the definition of the concept should be. Once we have specified the concept exactly, the rest of the proof goes through easily.

The emphasis is on concepts. The proof is like a spanner. The first attempts at proof are like spanners which do not exactly fit, and so do not really turn the nut. As we try to engage them, they

[25] pp.109-116.

slip, and we then try to tighten the adjustable spanner, or find a fixed spanner, so as to obtain a closer fit.[26] But if we tighten it up too much, it will not go on at all, and many trials may be needed before we find one that is snug without being too tight.

We develop our grasp of concepts in the same way as we articulate proofs. Again, it is a dialectical process, with initial definitions being criticized and faulted, and new ones refined to obviate objection. The infinitesimals of Newton and Leibniz were open to the objections of Berkeley:[27] Weierstrass circumvented those objections by giving an ε-δ account in terms of a universal and an existential quotifier. Robinson met them head-on, by using the fact that Peano's axioms are not monomorphic to produce a model containing weird numbers greater than infinity, whose reciprocals had just the property, of being neither finite nor zero, that infinitesimals had been required to have. Dirac's delta function was similarly introduced originally with a thoroughly unsatisfactory definition, which only later was tidied up and made rigorous.

It is natural to see these successive approximations to the "true" concept in issue as exercises in Platonic or Aristotelian definition. We have at first only a vague idea of what we are after, but by arguing about it, and trying to see what its implications are, we come to focus on it more closely, and discern more exactly what really is at stake.[28] We are being led back to epistemological Platonism again. We are being asked to recognise patterns. We have to see with the eye of the mind that a certain theorem about linear vector spaces is

---

[26] To deal with the coincident hands of a clock, discussed in §3.6, we need an 11-sided spanner, not, as we first thought, a 12-sided one.

[27] George Berkeley, *The Principles of Human Knowledge*, Dublin, 1710, §§130ff., and *The Analyst*, London and Dublin, 1734; reprinted in A.A.Luce and T.E.Jessop, eds., *The Works of George Berkeley, Bishop of Cloyne*, London, 1951, iv, 62-102.

[28] Lakatos himself draws a different conclusion, and adopts a quasi-empirical view of mathematics, largely on the grounds that the axiomatic approach is inadequate, and in order to parallel Popper's philosophy of science. But the quasi-empirical account is inadequate too, and gives no account of the coerciveness of mathematical proof. See Zheng Yuxin, "From the Logic of Mathematical Discovery to the Methodology of Scientific Research Programmes", *British Journal for the Philosophy of Science*, **41**, 1990, pp. 377-399, esp. §§1.2, 1.3.

isomorphic with Euler's original theorem about polyhedra, in much the same way as we have to be able to tell that an uninterpreted calculus studied by the formalist applies to a particular model, or that the theory of groups applies to bells pealing, or to rotations and reflections of a dihedron, or to twists of a Rubik's cube.[29] These are not great feats of pattern-recognition, like that called for by Hardy when he gazes at the distant range of mountains,[30] but they are instances of pattern-recognition nonetheless, and holistic, in that if we overlook some detail, some crucial exception or some instance of double-counting, we may be misled into accepting a fallacious proof, just as many mathematicians overlooked some crucial feature of what it was to be a polyhedron when they sought to prove Euler's theorem.

14.5 Cogency and Dialogue

Mathematical proofs must be cogent. Although their holistic aspect is important, they are not like moral or political arguments, or those that arise in disputed matters of literary criticism. They are not cumulative, and we cannot end by striking a balance between two sides of the case, both of them weighty. Nor can we agree to differ: any difference of opinion must be pursued until resolved. If there is any doubt whether the instance in question actually fits the pattern proposed, or a particular inference is valid, or any other objection, we must go into it, and settle it. Mathematical arguments are not mathematical arguments at all, unless they are effectively incontrovertible. Once we have understood a valid proof, we must recognise that the conclusion has to be true, and as we urge it on another, we are pressuring him to concede, however much he would like to resist, that we have made out our case beyond all question.

We secure incontrovertibility by *fiat*. Arguments are both expanded and contracted. They are filled out to make them deductively valid, and narrowed in scope, so as not to apply in controvertible cases. We lay out a proof so that all controvertible points must be granted in advance. If any detail is doubted, we specify it in the *data*. If any assumption can be contested, we articulate it as an axiom. Thus the Axiom of Choice was gradually recognised to be questionable, and so was stated as an explicit axiom,

---

[29] See above, §3.6, §14.3.

[30] See above, §1.5.

which must be postulated if certain inferences were to be allowed. We seek total explicitness in order to block every hole, and leave the respondent with no option except either to concede, or else discontinue the dialogue. Where we cannot cast an argument in incontrovertible form, we discontinue the dialogue, deeming it not to be a mathematical argument at all. Indeed, some philosophers would deny that controvertible arguments are valid arguments at all. For the most part, however, we are willing to recognise inductive arguments, historical arguments and moral arguments, as arguments, but reckon the questions they address to be outside the purview of mathematics.

Plato sought to secure that there *could* be no gainsaying a mathematical argument by having all mathematical arguments deductive.[31] In his development of the idea of dialectic, he came to think of the respondent as utterly bloody-minded, who would not be persuaded by anything less than the fear of inconsistency, since the one sanction capable of coercing every recalcitrant reasoner into conceding the validity of each step was self-contradiction. Modern mathematicians, likewise, have construed the respondent as a moron, who can follow algorithmic procedures, but not exercise any understanding on his own. An argument was not really cogent unless it worked even on morons and sceptics.

But that ideal of absolute cogency, which could compel the assent of even the most recalcitrant respondent, has proved unattainable. Even the most extreme Formalist has to be willing to recognise some patterns of inference, and is susceptible to informal arguments at the meta level leading to hitherto unformalised Gödelian arguments.[32] Though it accords with the conventions of contemporary mathematical discourse that you should treat me as a fool, I do not like being treated as too much of a fool: it gets boring, if you go on proving to me every time that $2 + 2 = 4$. We cut corners. We have to. Not only is time limited, and patience, but our ability to digest fool-talk is limited too. A fully formalised proof is incomprehensible. I cannot see the wood for the trees. I am not a computer, and cannot remember very quickly, or do lots of trivial operations in a nanosecond. Perhaps I think laterally, perhaps in parallel, certainly holistically, and need to be able to see where I am going

---

[31] §1.7, §1.8.

[32] See above, §§3.3, 3.6, 8.11, 14.2.

and to keep track of the thread of the argument. So we moderate our fool-talk, and only itemise the steps that might reasonably be doubted. It is also unnecessary to assume that sure-fire sanctions are needed every time to force my consent. Mathematicians not only lack the patience, but also are free from the limitations, of morons. They are not Thrasymacheanly bloody-minded sceptics; they share a common concern to know the truth, and therefore are willing to make assumptions for the sake of argument, and concede hopeless cases before being actually check-mated in an actual contradiction.

The argument of Chapter Three[33] that instead of the intelligent and cooperative young men of Plato's preference, opponents must be assumed to be stupid and obstinate, was too extreme. Deductive argument, which must be allowed on pain of inconsistency, is *not* the paradigm, but, rather, a limiting case, where dialogue collapses into monologue, since the claim of anyone who disputes it contradicts itself, and so is, to all intents and purposes, unsayable. Mathematicians, though critical, are not complete sceptics; our hypothetical respondent should be fashioned in their image, not that of the utterly disagreeable fool, contesting every step until driven into inconsistency. There are many cases where I can count on his agreement, not because he must want to be understood, but because he is a rational truth-seeker, who will not niggle needlessly.

14.6 On Behalf of the Fool

Fools provide the foil for cogency. It is they who enable the mathematician to distinguish his insights from those of the metaphysician, the moralist, or the poet. But they are not, we have seen, absolutely moronic and totally bloody-minded; nor are they just victims waiting to be compelled by cogent argument to concede the truth of theorems; they are essential collaborators, who will not niggle needlessly. But they are critical collaborators, and will, on occasion, not accept some line of argument, and fail to feel the force of some sanction. Different fools feel the force of different sanctions, acknowledge the cogency of different types of argument, and generate different philosophies of mathematics. Intelligence and willingness to cooperate are not the same. One man can be rational but unreasonable, another reasonable but not very clever.

[33] In §3.3.

The Intuitionists assume a high standard of mathematical ability in the respondent, but no willingness to make moves for the sake of argument. Classical mathematicians impute to their hypothetical respondents much less ability to recognise a proof when they see one, but a great readiness to play the game in order to discover truth rather than simply to win. By engaging whole-heartedly in the dialogue, responding to challenges and being willing to risk refutation, they enable the possibilities of the dialogue to be exploited more fully, giving rise to further cogent patterns of argument. They thus make available arguments by *reductio ad absurdum*, which the Intuitionists are bound, by reason of their unreasonableness, to forgo.

Intuitionist fools, though unreasonable, claim to be very clever, and always able to recognise a valid proof when they see one. If we were all agreed about what was a proof, we should not need to have any characterization of proofs, and could simply say that we recognised a proof when we saw one. The options then open to us would be either Intuitionism or Epistemological Platonism. We could be Intuitionists if we were inclined to be idealists (in the old, metaphysical sense), and consider things as they appeared to us rather than attach any sense to them as they were in themselves. Intuitionism is the mathematical analogue to phenomenalism. If, however, we were inclined to be realists generally, we should be Platonists, and regard our ability to recognise proofs as a quasi-visual ability—the exercise of the eye of the mind—by means of which we apprehended the real pattern of the universe.

On the score of intellectual ability Intuitionism and Epistemological Platonism lie at one extreme and Formalism and Finitism at the other. Intuitionists and Epistemological Platonists assume that we all share a complete common rationality, and that there is really no doubt as to what constitutes a mathematical argument, and we just recognise valid proofs in the same way as we just know what the natural numbers are. Formalists assume no common rationality beyond the minimum needed for communication, and this itself spelled out in explicit rules. As we assume less and less rationality and willingness to cooperate, we are naturally driven to deductive argument, which must be acknowledged as cogent if communication is to be possible and if we are to play the Formalists' game at all. Formalists, however, are prepared to respond to challenges, survey end-games as a whole, and reach meta-mathematical conclusions on the basis of what they can see to be possible, whereas Finitists are not prepared to make any moves on their own account, and will not concede defeat until an inconsistency is actually reached. Only *Sorites* Arithmetic is available to them, whereas Peano Arithmetic is available to those of wider vision, which leads them to avoid not merely inconsistency but ω-inconsistency as well.

Dialectical argument, with challenges as well as straightforward proofs, is essential if we are to extend cogent argument to the transfinite. In order that a proof should be incontrovertible it was required to be finite, so that we could demonstrate its validity in a finite number of steps.[34] Otherwise, it seemed, we should be left in the air, never being able to clinch the argument. If anyone disputed its validity, we needed to be able to take him through it, bit by bit, and leave him unable to gainsay any of the steps. But in a dialogue, if anyone disputes its validity, we can challenge him to show where it is wrong, and examine whatever inference he says is invalid, and rub his nose in the fact that it is not. We can, further, justify a claim about an infinite number of instances, by challenging the disputant to cite a single counter-instance, confident that if he did so, we could show him wrong. This strategy makes use of the fact that every descending sequence of ordinals is finite, enabling us, in a context of challenge and response, to work backwards, and pinpoint any fallacy or unreasonable doubt, if there is either, and otherwise concede the cogency of the claim across the whole infinite field. Instead of having to go on for ever, waving our hand implausibly over an infinite number of instances, we can get our teeth into a definite, finite case, and chew through it to incontrovertible refutation. A "dialectical" justification of the Principle of Recursive Reasoning enables us to overcome the inherent finitude of incontrovertibility, and shows that it is an admissible form of argument, though not one for which a justification could be extracted from a recalcitrant reasoner by appeal to the Law of Non-contradiction alone. The Principle of Infinite Arbitrary Choice can be defended in somewhat the same way. If a sceptic questions our making an infinite number of choices, we ask him where the line is to be drawn between legitimate finite choices and illegitimate infinite ones. We do not in this case, as we do when justifying the Principle of Recursive Reasoning, have already to hand a knock-down refutation of whatever answer he may give; but we can put the sceptic on the

---

[34] See above, §3.3.

defensive, having to defend a distinction which he needs to draw, and for which he has no obvious justification.

Although fools can be distinguished, they are not always distinct. I am not a single fool of utter stupidity, but a whole host of fools, of different degrees of foolishness on different occasions. Sometimes I am quite intelligent, and can take many small steps in my stride, so that the mathematician, by integrating a number of small steps into one block, and dealing with only a few such blocks, secures the surveyability of the proof, but always with the proviso that if I am dubious about any particular point, he can address me in my new-found stupidity, and argue that particular point until I am satisfied. Furthermore, whichever of my foolish selves the mathematician chooses to address on a particular occasion, he has to address in the knowledge that there are other fools around, who may interject objections if his inferences are not, by their standards, cogent. I may not be Thrasymachus myself, but he is listening to our conversation, ready to interrupt, if he thinks I am being too soft, and agreeing too readily to the claims the mathematician is putting forward.

Fools perform further useful functions. They force us to distinguish our various rules of inference, and separate what can be established only with their aid, from what can be proved by other means. They also may be themselves forced to articulate their doubts, and thereby belie their dubiousness. The Finitists cannot say what 'finite' means without the aid of second-order logic, itself deeply infinitistic. Boundaries are difficult to draw without being able to overstep them. An intelligent and helpful fool will stumble when a new sort of inferential leap is asked of him, but in the dialogue in which he articulates his difficulty, bridges may emerge that will enable the mathematician to lead him across to new fields of enquiry. As the Formalist explains his ideal of a formal system, he engages in informal reasoning about it, and thus is led to see the cogency of Gödel's argument, and so to realise that no complete and exhaustive formal characterization of a mathematical proof is possible.[35]

The fool is neither an utter fool, nor possessed of an immediate intuitive grasp of all mathematical truths, but occupies some mid-

---

[35] See above, §8.11; see also John Myhill, "Some Remarks on the Notion of Proof", *Journal of Philosophy*, LVII, 1969, pp.461-471.

dling position, which itself is under tension, since on the one hand there are always further proofs, of a type not previously envisaged, which he can be brought to acknowledge as cogent, while on the other there is always a certain pressure towards greater articulateness, so as to make the proof accessible to those with a smaller basis of shared insights. The questions the fool asks are real questions that the mathematican needs to answer: but the very fact that he asks them—the terms in which he phrases them—shows that they are not the unanswerable questions of the sceptic, but ones that can be answered from the conceptual resources involved in the very asking of them.

14.7   Hilbert

The account of mathematical knowledge thus far given has failed to quiet the doubts of some philosophers, or set at rest the fears felt by some mathematicians that philosophers were going to destroy the intellectual respectability of their subject. Some philosophers respond by avoiding the challenge of trying to account for mathematical knowledge, and make out that mathematics is not true at all, but only a useful pretend. "Mythological platonism", however, is implausible: we do not put maths books on the fiction shelves. Hilbert can be seen as a mathematician who tried to keep mathematics for mathematicians, safe from philosophical niggles about knowledge and truth.

Hilbert put forward his programme in the shadow of the paradoxes, and sought also to ward off Intuitionist attacks.[36] Radical in his methods, he was conservative in his interests, and hoped to combine the security of austere Formalism with the richness of the new fields of study. He came from geometry. In Euclidean geometry we do not always have it that two lines intersect in a point; they do unless they are parallel, but if they are parallel they have no point of intersection. This is awkward, and in homogeneous geometry we introduce points at infinity, and a line at infinity, which is "where" parallel lines meet. The introduction of points at infinity is a safe extension of Euclidean geometry to obtain greater uniformity; it does no harm, and makes arguments easier to articulate. But can we be sure that it does no harm? Not every extension of an axiomatic system is harmless. If I extend a system by a new

---

[36] See further above, §§12.2, 12.3, 7.4-7.7.

symbol *tonk* with the rules of inference that it follows from $A \lor B$ and yields $A \land B$, we shall have made our system inconsistent.[37] We need to make sure our new system is consistent, that is, that our extension is a *consistent* extension of the original system. If only we could show transfinite set theory to be consistent, it would be freed from suspicion of paradox and lurking inconsistency. Once we have a consistency proof for homogeneous geometry, we can continue to operate it with a clear conscience that in the process of making geometry smoother, easier to work with, it has not exposed the whole enterprise to self-contradiction.[38]

But doubts could still arise. Although the cardinal sin of inconsistency was out of the question, other inferences might have been legitimised that, though not disastrous, were none the less invalid. To forestall any such imputation, Hilbert required that the new system not only be consistent, but, so far as it overlapped with the old system, it should introduce nothing new; clearly the system of homogeneous geometry will have some new well-formed formulae, namely those containing the new terms, 'point at infinity' and 'line at infinity', and some of these may be theorems of the new system: but if there are no well-formed formulae that can be expressed solely in terms of the old system that are theorems of the new system but not the old, then the new system is a "conservative" extension of the old. In that case it is *very* safe. It does not involve us in anything new, but merely puts the old in simpler and more uniform form. It would be hard to cavil at such an extension. It is, one might suggest, a mere notational device. Any substantial objection to the extended system must be an objection to the old, and if the old is above suspicion, then the new must be also.

Hilbert hoped to treat the arithmetical infinite like the geometrical points at infinity. Instead of *Sorites* Arithmetic, in which I take 515 steps to prove $F(257)$ from $F(0)$ and $F(n) \rightarrow F(n')$, I apply P5 to prove $(Ax)F(x)$ and then use Universal Instantiation, in three lines. Peano Arithmetic does not prove anything more about the natural numbers than *Sorites* Arithmetic does, but it does it much more neatly. In the ordinary arithmetic of

[37] See A.N.Prior, "The runabout inference ticket", *Analysis*, **21**, 1960, pp. 39-39; reprinted in P.F.Strawson, ed., *Philosophical Logic*, Oxford, 1967, pp.129-131.

[38] Michael Detlefsen, *Hilbert's Program*, Dordrecht, 1986, p.8.

the whole numbers, we have the symbols $0, 1, 2, 3, 4, 5, 6, \ldots N \ldots$ to which we should like to add the symbol ∞ so as to have $0, 1, 2, 3, 4, 5, 6, \ldots N \ldots \infty$. The extra symbol is just a notational addition which enables us to express concisely operations like Σ_1^∞, which can be explained in terms of only finite numbers, but are much more perspicuously written with the aid of the symbol for infinity. If we can formalise our rules for the use of ∞ and can show that these rules constitute a consistent extension of the axioms for the arithmetic of just the finite numbers, then it is safe to extend our arithmetic of the finite numbers to include ∞ as well.

Part of Hilbert's programme is, then, to formalise systems and show them to be consistent. Instead of considering homogeneous geometry or infinite number theory as being *about* anything, we consider these systems only syntactically, simply as formal systems, without any interpretation in mind. Such formal investigations may reveal that they are syntactically consistent. If so, no inconsistency can arise from using them. But what is their status? Are they only, as the hard-line Formalists aver, games played with meaningless signs on paper? No: for they are conservative extensions of systems assumed to be all right; they therefore have an intended and standard interpretation for all except the "ideal" elements. Except for the points and line at infinity, the symbols of formal homogeneous geometry can be interpreted in the same way as in ordinary Euclidean geometry, that is as points and lines and circles, *etc.* So they are all right. Even if a philosopher has some doubts about interpretation, they are in no worse way than they were before the introduction of ideal elements. As for the points and line at infinity themselves, they are "carried" by the rest of the interpretation. It is much the same as with the account of theoretical entities in physical theories given by the Logical Positivists. They held that only sense-data really existed, but that it was all right to talk about atoms, electrons, and protons, because theories expressed in terms of them could yield predictions that were subject to empirical test: although they did not really exist, yet it was useful to talk about them as if they did; they were fictional entities, but useful ones in as much as they played a part in discourse which did yield statements about what really did exist. For Hilbert finite calculations with natural numbers have the same basic status that sense-data had for the Logical Positivists. They are "contentful", *inhältlich*: they confer reality on the whole system that is, in part, interpreted in terms of them. The symbol ∞ is carried by the finite natural numbers that keep company with it, and are themselves contentful.

We can now see the shape of Hilbert's programme. Hilbert combines caution with generosity. He is cautious in that he will not accept any form of reasoning just because it has been used by mathematicians or yields delightful results, but insists that any system be scrutinised and not accepted until it has been certified as safe from inconsistency and unwarranted innovation. In this he is as stringent as Descartes was in rejecting current modes of thought until they had been re-assessed. But he is much more relaxed than Descartes in the stringency of the test applied. Descartes would not admit any inference if it was logically possible for it to be gainsaid: only if it was self-contradictory to contradict the conclusion, having conceded the premises, was an inference sound, so that if it were not contradictory to deny that I had a body, having allowed that I did exist, then I could not be said necessarily to have a body. Hilbert is much more relaxed. I can extend a system, so as to legitimise new inferences, in any way I please, so long as I know I shall not thereby run into inconsistency, and shall not say anything new about old-timers. He achieves this freedom of manoeuvre by severing the semantic links between the ideal elements and any supposed referents: 'points at infinity' do not refer to any points on, or just beyond, the Euclidean plane; ∞ is not another number lurking over the horizon of the natural numbers. These terms have no reference at all. They are just symbols, whose only significance derives from the extended systems in which they play a part, which extended systems do have a meaning because of the reference of other-than-ideal elements. Hilbert allows us to re-enter Cantor's paradise, but only on the strict understanding that it is a fairy tale, which has verisimilitude, because sometimes it mentions real people, and says demonstrably true things about them, but is not to be taken literally *tout court.*

Much of Hilbert's programme, therefore, was concerned with providing consistency proofs. On this score he was puritan, rather than liberal. Only finitary reasoning was to be employed in establishing the consistency of some system. Although once the consistency of a system employing infinity was established, infinity could be used with a clear conscience, the consistency proof itself must be finitary. Only so would absolute security (*Sicherheit*) be secured. But is there absolute security? We can agree that some inferences are less open to doubt than others, and that in the face of the paradoxes we do well to justify those inferences that have been impugned by means of others less open to objection. But the assumption that there is some class of inferences which are absolutely above suspicion has not been made out. Hilbert assumes that "finitary" inferences are, but it is not clear exactly what these inferences are. We cannot define 'finite' in first-order logic. Only if we already have the concept of infinity can we specify what the inferences are that do not rely on it. There is not a clear finitary definition of the finitary inferences that are alleged to constitute the class of absolutely safe inferences. We cannot in finitary terms know when we are finitarily safe.

In any case it is not true that in practice long chains of finitary inferences are safe. We are much more likely to make an error in a long calculation involving only finitary inferences than in a short one using the principle of mathematical induction. Maybe this is not what Hilbert had in mind, but it is enough to cast doubt on the concept of security as a clear and adequate guide to the inferences a mathematician can take for granted in seeking to justify others. Instead of an absolute class of real, safe calculations, in terms of which all others ought to be justified if they can, we have a gradation of inferences, some of which are more open to question than others, but none evidently suspect and none guaranteed to be above all suspicion.[39]

It is generally reckoned that Gödel's second theorem put paid to Hilbert's programme, but some philosophers contend that, far from constituting a threat to Hilbert's programme, Gödel's theorems are a protective shield, which protect it from diagonalized embarrassment and refutation.[40] Much turns on how Hilbert's programme

[39] For other discussions of Hilbert's programme see: M.Giaquinto, "Hilbert's Philosophy of Mathematics", *British Journal for the Philosophy of Science*, **34**, 1983, pp.119-132; Michael Detlefsen, *Hilbert's Program*, Dordrecht, 1986; G.Kreisel, "Hilbert's Programme", in Paul Benacerraf and Hilary Putnam, eds. *The Philosophy of Mathematics*, 2nd ed., Cambridge, 1983, pp.207-238; P.Kitcher, "Hilbert's Epistemology", *Philosophy of Science*, **43**, 1976, pp.99-115.

[40] Judson C. Webb, *Mechanism, Mentalism and Metamathematics*, Dordrecht, 1980; and Michael Detlefsen, *Hilbert's Program*, Dordrecht, 1986.

is construed. He was himself a classical mathematician, trying to shore up classical mathematics against sceptical attacks by availing himself of unimpugnable methods of argument, but sensitive to other arguments too. From that standpoint Gödel's theorems are damaging. A classical mathematician can feel their force, and be rationally persuaded that absolute *Sicherheit* is unattainable. But the conclusion that absolute *Sicherheit* is unattainable may itself be unattainable by "safe" methods. A sufficiently determined sceptic may be able to go on not seeing that his sceptical position is untenable.

Hilbert was too extreme. His meta-mathematics was too austere, his ontology too relaxed. Consistency proofs give us confidence to embark on new fields of mathematics without fear of disaster, but do not need to be finitary; nor need the new field be merely a conservative extension of the old, provided we are ready to justify any new inferences not already available in the old. But questions about ideal elements are not to be ruled out of court. We are not, *pace* the Logical Positivists, precluded from asking questions about electrons, quarks, and electromagnetic waves, even though the sense-experience on which our physical theories are based is very different. It may be that ∞ is "carried" by the finite numbers, but questions can be asked all the same. If we moderate the rigour of Hilbert's programme, we can accommodate the successive extensions of mathematical theories in the "bed theory of truth".

14.8 The Bed Theory of Truth

In Chapter Two we proved Desargues' theorem for three dimensions, though in two-dimensional projective geometry it cannot be proved and has to taken as an additional axiom. But we are quite sure that it should be taken as an axiom. For one thing, non-Desarguian geometry is, we are told, very messy. But even more important, we think two-dimensional geometry ought to be embeddable in three- and more-dimensional geometry. We generalise. Wherever possible, we see a mathematical proposition, theory, or example, as a special case of something more general with a wider range of applications. We embed theories in larger theories. These theories are often, *pace* Hilbert, not conservative. Propositions which can be expressed in the terminology of the more limited theory turn out to be theorems of the larger theory, though not of the more limited one. We cannot, therefore defend the larger theory as being just a convenience, which enables us to prove in three lines what could be proved otherwise in 515 lines. It proves more. Also embedment goes in a different direction from that of the classical logicist programme. There we justify axioms by showing them to be theorems of a *more basic* theory: here the theory is *more general*.

Often the two directions are intertwined. In the classical logicist programme real numbers are defined as sets of rationals, rationals as equivalence classes of positive rationals, and positive rationals as equivalence classes of natural numbers.[41] But the point of the construction is not to produce complicated collocations of natural numbers, but to *extend* the concept of number to other sorts of number—rational numbers, negative numbers, real numbers, complex numbers. Although the details of the extension are different in each case, and the conceptual commitments different also, the strategy is the same, and should be compared with the extension of two-dimensional to three-dimensional projective geometry. In the case of geometry, there is a natural generalisation from two to three, and from three to any finite number, and from any finite number to a denumerably infinite number, of dimensions. In the case of numbers there is no parameter, such as dimension number, which invites extension, but rather some ideal of completeness[42] that leads us to extend the concept of number in order to be able always to carry out some operation which hitherto could not be carried out uniformly in every case. It is good to be able to divide a dozen apples among two, three, four, or six people, but what if we are a party of five? Instead of just saying "Five into twelve won't go", or "Five into twelve goes twice with remainder two", it is often better to say that five into twelve is 12/5, and to be able to express this as $2\frac{2}{5}$: equally, if I owe the bank money, instead of their owing me, it is possible to indicate the fact by writing it in red, or typing 'o/d' after the figures in my bank statement; but the use of the minus sign is simpler and easier. It is a more sophisticated requirement that there should always be a square root, not only of perfect squares, like four, nine, sixteen, *etc.*, but of two,

---

[41] See above, §3.7.

[42] Used here in a different sense from those of the formal logicians, as in §3.4, §15.5.

three, five, *etc.*; and even more sophisticated that there should be square roots of negative numbers, so that every quadratic, indeed every analytic, equation should have a root. None the less, these requirements are made, and can be met if we extend numbers in suitable ways. And hence we are led not merely to rational and negative numbers, as expounded in §3.7, but to real numbers and complex numbers as well.

But it is not good enough just to require, and then to assume that entities exist meeting our requirements. Bertrand Russell, in a famous phrase, said that the method of postulating entities had all the advantages of theft over honest toil.[43] The jibe strikes home. Once we abandon a hard-line formalist position, we cannot expect to be able simply to lay down by *fiat* what entities there are, and say, as it were, "*Volo, ergo est*". Were complex numbers invented or discovered? In either case we owe an account, ultimately of their title to exist, and immediately of how we know that complex number theory is true.

Complex numbers are often defined as ordered pairs of real numbers, with fresh definitions of addition, multiplication, and their inverses. The rules for addition and subtraction are straightforward: the operations on complex numbers are symbolized by large circled signs, which are then defined in terms of ordinary operations on real numbers thus:

$$(a, b) \oplus (c, d) = (a + c, b + d)$$

$$(a, b) \ominus (c, d) = (a - c, b - d)$$

The rule for multiplication is more complicated as regards the second pair of each ordered couple:

$$(a, b) \otimes (c, d) = ((a \times c) - (b \times d), (a \times d) + (b \times c))$$

The rule for division is very complicated, but need not be considered here.

Granted these rules, it follows that in the special case where $b = 0$ and $d = 0$,

$$(a, 0) \oplus (c, 0) = (a + c, 0 + 0) = (a + c, 0)$$

---

[43] Bertrand Russell, *An Introduction to Mathematical Philosophy*, London, 1919, ch. VII, p.71.

$$(a, 0) \ominus (c, 0) = (a - c, 0 - 0) = (a - c, 0)$$

and

$$(a, 0) \otimes (c, 0) = ((a \times c) - (0 \times 0), (a \times 0) + (0 \times c))$$
$$= (a \times c, 0)$$

So if we translate

$$(a, 0) \longmapsto a$$
$$\oplus \longmapsto +$$
$$\ominus \longmapsto -$$
$$\otimes \longmapsto \times$$

we have our familiar real number theory back again. Though we have extended the real numbers, so that now every polynomial equation has a root, we have not really lost anything, because by considering just those complex numbers in which the "imaginary part", that is the second of the ordered pair, is zero, we have an exact replica of the real numbers.

There are thus *two* relations between the newly defined complex numbers and the old real numbers: the theory of complex numbers is a special part of the theory of real numbers; and there is a special part of the theory of complex numbers which is isomorphic to the theory of real numbers. On the standard logicist account the latter relation is just a happy accident. When we are talking about complex numbers, we are really talking about ordered pairs of real numbers with rather a funny multiplication rule, and it just so happens that complex numbers of the form $(a, 0)$ turn out to behave just like real numbers a. But it was no accident. We wanted complex numbers to be an extension of real numbers, and so needed there to be a special part of the theory of complex numbers that was isomorphic to the theory of real numbers. We do not think that $(a, 0)$ is rather like a—we think that it *is* a, only now embedded in a more extended universe, so that we can attach sense to $\sqrt{-1}$, and can say that every number has a square root. The standard account involves us in a lot of double talk, in which we have not only the natural number 1, but the rational number $\frac{1}{1}$, the integer $1 - 0$, the real number that is the Least Upper Bound of all the proper fractions, and the complex number $(1, 0)$, with only a similarity, not complete identity, between them. But it is not just typographical economy that discourages us from distinguishing between them on all occasions of their use; it is also, and more importantly, the sense of an underlying identity of concept in all cases, in spite of the occasionally relevant differences. We do not think that the complex number $(1, 0)$ is really an ordered pair of two least upper bounds of sets of equivalence classes of ordered pairs of equivalence classes of ordered pairs of natural numbers. Such a construction is toilsome, and is not what we want or are prepared to work with.

The virtue of such a construction is, rather, that it proves that the theory of complex numbers is consistent provided the theory of real numbers is. Exactly the same arguments apply as with non-Euclidean geometries.[44] So we have not just postulated entities regardless: we have at least met the first requirement of consistency. Moreover, in virtue of there being a special part of the theory of complex numbers which is isomorphic to the theory of real numbers the theory of complex numbers can claim to be a genuine *extension* of the theory of real numbers. In constructing a model with ordered pairs of real numbers, we are not just playing about with models, but are carefully creating a bed in which real number theory can be seen as being embedded. The complex operations, $\oplus$, $\ominus$ and $\otimes$, are seen as complex versions of the corresponding $+$, , and $\times$, because when restricted to complex numbers whose imaginary part is zero they are exactly analogous. Hence we are justified as fully as anyone could reasonably demand in our use of similar symbols to express those operations, and in considering the operations on complex numbers to be essentially the same as those on real numbers, while being, when not restricted to complex numbers that lack an imaginary component, complete in the sense that every number, even the analogues of negative real numbers, has a square root, and every polynomial equation has a root. If pressed on the score of consistency or existence, we rely on the complex numbers being modelled within the real numbers, and claim that if the real numbers are consistent then so are the complex numbers, and that if the real numbers exist, then so do ordered pairs of them. If pressed on the use of the same terms for operations on complex numbers as for operations on real numbers we point out the exact analogue between real numbers and the restricted part of complex numbers in which the imaginary component is zero; and completeness follows from the special properties of the model

---

[44] See above, §2.3.

we have made, and justifies us in adopting complex numbers not merely as an extension of real numbers but as one in which certain basic operations can be carried out uniformly and invariably, instead of only under certain conditions.

Greater uniformity has been the criterion in the successive extensions of the concept, and corresponding theory, of number, and has provided the justification of its rules and axioms. We are justifying axioms not by deducing them from some more basic ones, nor by some inductive argument, but by some search for greater generality, in which we generalise not from observation and sense-experience, as in genuine inductive arguments, but in the goals we set ourselves and the *desiderata* we lay down for a mathematical theory. We seek more and more general theories; and if a proposition which cannot be proved in one theory, and has to be postulated as an axiom in that theory, can none the less be proved in another, more general, theory in which the first theory can be embedded, we accept that fact as a good reason for having it as an axiom in the smaller theory.

The bed theory of truth is super-Hilbertian. Like Hilbert, it is formalist, replete with all the rigour that Formalism offers, but not just a free-floating game, because it is *inhältlich*, anchored in the fundamental logic of quotifiers, modal operators and transitive relations. But the bed theory of truth goes beyond Hilbert, and makes stronger claims. It is not confined to conservative extensions of theories, but embraces non-conservative extensions too, in which the proposition in question can be proved only in the extended theory and not in the smaller one. And it claims not merely availability as an optional formal exercise, but truth, because we are led to them by our desire for greater generality in application, or search for greater uniformity in operation.

14.9 Mathematical Knowledge

Mathematical knowledge is *a priori*. Plato's argument against Protagoras holds. Mathematical knowledge is not about the world of sensible experience, but about the way we think—the way we have to think, if our thought is to be more than the fleeting consciousness of a subjective self. Mathematical knowledge is knowledge of the way concepts are connected, and is constrained not by experience of the external world, but by our own self-knowledge as agents, reflecting on what we do, and what we can envisage our being able to do in other circumstances, and by necessities of communication and cooperation with other truth-seekers.

Concepts, in being connected with one another, form patterns, and mathematicians recognise these patterns, and point them out to other mathematicians. But pattern-recognition is *not* a form of perception, the patterns being exemplified as much in the way we do things and in the structure of our thinking, as in what we perceive by our senses. It is the force of reason, not factual observation, that compels consent. Although sometimes we accept proofs second-hand, we do not have to, whereas in history and geography, if we were not in the right place at the right time, we have to accept other men's word for how things were. Rather than observe how things happen to be, and what patterns they fit into, the mathematician discerns patterns in themselves and the necessary connexions between them. But although he needs to be a man of discernment, his discerning is not authoritative, as that of a historian or literary critic sometimes is. Mommsen's judgement is to be respected because it is Mommsen's. But we do not believe Fermat's Last Theorem on Fermat's say-so: only if there is a proof, open in principle to any mathematical enquirer, is Fermat's Last Theorem proved. Though we may sometimes accept some mathematics second-hand, it is necessarily the case that we do not necessarily have to. In mathematics, as in the natural sciences, there are no privileged authorities; only, whereas in the natural sciences, universality is secured by experimental observation, which is in principle open to anyone, universal access is secured in mathematics by arguments that cannot be gainsaid by anyone concerned to know the truth.

The requirement that mathematical proof be universally accessible, leads to modified Formalism. We formalise mathematical arguments, though not fully, in order that they shall be effectively incontrovertible. Many of the inferences are deductive inferences which can be formalised in first-order logic, and which effectively reduce the argument to a monologue. But not all are. Some arguments involve quotification over monadic or polyadic predicate variables, expressing qualities or relations, which can only be formulated in second-order logic; some arguments obtain their purchase through a dialogue, sometimes requiring the respondent to move to a meta-level, and view the course of argument as a whole, and reason about it informally. Implicit in our adopting formal systems and use of symbols in accordance with formal rules are the Rules of Substitution and of Generalisation; but implicit in our reasoning about formal systems informally at the meta-level is the principle that reason transcends rules, and cannot be adequately explicated in terms of rule-following alone. We often formalise for good reason, but ought always to acknowledge that formal argument does not exhaust the whole range of rationality. When we formalise, we project into monologous form arguments that are essentially dialectical: and sometimes if we want to understand the rationale of an axiom or principle monologously expressed, we need to go back to the underlying dialogue, where the parties, being rational, can each see the other's point of view, and thus, for instance, recognise the necessity imposed on his choices by the other's possibilities of choosing.

Formal approaches require axioms, but cannot adequately account for them. Mathematicians often cite beauty, harmony and depth as reasons for accepting an axiomatic theory as true. These are good reasons, but we need to be more specific. In Chapter Two a variety of different considerations were adduced in favour of the axioms of Euclidean geometry. The Pythagorean rule was simpler than the corresponding distance rule for non-Euclidean geometries. Euclidean geometry was more non-committal than any other, and therefore better suited to constituting the arena on which various physical theories were compared, and not itself predisposed towards one of the physical theories in issue. There were group-theoretical considerations for preferring the Euclidean group, under which Euclidean geometry is invariant, to any group characteristic of some other geometry. The successive extensions of the concept and theory of number from the natural numbers to the complex numbers was driven by ideals of uniformity and generality. In set theory Platonist and nominalist views about the existence of universals bear on our adopting or rejecting other axioms, and Bolzano and others have adduced further *a priori* arguments in favour of the Axiom of Infinity.

These are cogent considerations; comparable ones operate in the natural sciences. Some thinkers have sought to justify the axioms used in mathematical theories on an analogy with the physical sciences where the axioms are reckoned to be true on account of their consequences being found to agree with observation. Gödel explicitly makes the comparison in the passage quoted in Chapter One,[45] But the analogy is broken-backed. Mathematical intuition is not some sixth sense, and if it were it would not explain the relevance of mathematics to the empirical world observed by our ordinary means of perception.[46] Physical theories in fact are accepted as true not solely because they have been verified empirically, but on grounds of "logicality and harmony"[47] and Field holds:

> ...it is then plausible to argue that considerations other than applications to the physical world, for example, considerations of simplicity and coherence within mathematics, are grounds for accepting some proposed mathematics axioms as true and rejecting others as false.[48]

Gödel argues more fully:

> Secondly, however, even disregarding the intrinsic necessity of some new axiom, and even in case it has no intrinsic necessity at all, a probable decision about its truth is possible also in another way, namely, inductively verifying its "success". Success here means fruitfulness in consequences, in particular in "verifiable" consequences, i.e., consequences demonstrable without the new axiom, whose proofs with the help of the new axiom, however, are considerably sim-

---

[45] §1.5.

[46] The most careful and sympathetic exegesis of Gödel's views is given by P.Maddy in *Realism in Mathematics*, Oxford, 1990, and especially in her *Naturalism in Mathematics*, Oxford, 1996. H.Wang, *A Logical Journey*, Cambridge, Mass., 1996, reports many further discussions with Gödel.

[47] R.C.Tolman, *Relativity, Thermodynamics and Cosmology*, Oxford, 1950, §29, p.53.

[48] H.Field, *Science without Numbers*, Princeton, 1980, p.4; quoted by Maddy, in her *Realism in Mathematics*, Oxford, 1990, p.159.

pler and easier to discover, and make it possible to contract into one proof many different proofs. The axioms for the system of real numbers, rejected by the intuitionists, have in this sense been verified to some extent, owing to the fact that analytical number theory frequently allows one to prove number-theoretic theorems which, in a more cumbersome way, can subsequently be verified by elementary methods. A much higher degree of verification than that, however, is conceivable. There might exist axioms so abundant in their verifiable consequences, shedding so much light upon a whole field, and yielding such powerful methods for solving problems (and even solving them constructively, as far as that is possible) that, no matter whether or not they are intrinsically necessary, they would have to be established in the same sense as any well-established physical theory.[49]

But once again an important point is being obscured by a false analogy with physical science. We can adduce considerations of simplicity and coherence both for and against various axioms about the size of the set-theoretical universe and the existence of large cardinals. The Axiom of Choice can be held to be actually *true* on the grounds that with it we can prove numerical and other propositions which can be shown to be true without it, though with much greater difficulty.

We can understand Gödel in the light of the two previous sections. He is going beyond Hilbert. He claims a much more full-blooded truth, and, moreover, the extended theory does not have to be conservative. Provided some consequences of an additional axiom are provable without it, and none are false or implausible, we may accept the axiom as true. In the case of the natural sciences, however, the observations on which inductive arguments are based have empirical content, and confer content—though possibly of a markedly different kind—on the generalisations and theories they support. If, like Hilbert, we regarded propositions about the natural numbers as *inhaltlich*, we could then use them to confer content on more *recherché* realms of discourse. But that, *pace*

---

[49] K.Gödel, "What is Cantor's Continuum Problem?", Paul Benacerraf and Hilary Putnam, eds. *The Philosophy of Mathematics*, 2nd edn., Cambridge, 1983, p.477; reprinted in *The Collected Works of Kurt Gödel*, ii, ed. S.Feferman, Oxford, 1990, p.261.

Kronecker, needs to be argued for. It can. The natural numbers can be grounded in the quotifiers, themselves logical constants essential if communication is to take place between intelligent beings. Equally essential are the transitive relations, giving rise to concepts of similarity and equality on the one hand, and to various sorts of order on the other. Not only the inferences, but the content of mathematics is based on the necessities of communication and cooperation among truth-seekers. This is the most important insight of Logicism.

Mathematics has developed from that foundation through a series of more-or-less formal systems having greater and greater generality, coherence and uniformity. If Logicism gives guidance about the foundations of mathematics, our architectonic view of its structure emphasizes the importance of pattern-recognition. And this partial re-instatement of epistemological Platonism raises once again the ontological question, whether the patterns discerned by the mathematician really exist.

Chapter 15
Realism Revisited

15.1 Existence and Reality

In Chapter One we saw that Plato was led to his realist position by reason of the fact that mathematical truth was known *a priori* and by the inability of Empiricism to accommodate that fact. But platonic realism gave an unsatisfactory account of mathematical knowledge, and was objected to on account of its ontological commitments. It seems to fill the universe with unwelcome extra entities, which economical metaphysicians would prefer not to have to find house room for. But the question "If not platonic realism, then what?" has not been satisfactorily answered. We need to reconsider realism, and whether mathematical entities really exist; or, more precisely, in just what senses they can be said to exist.

Existence is not only a profession of ontological commitment. It is also, as we saw in Chapter Seven,[1] a counter in argumentative discourse. To exist is to be talkable about. It licenses discussion by warding off the conversation stopper "But there is no such thing".[2] Its force, therefore, often depends on context, and the objection anticipated. The extreme case—*e.g.* the greatest prime number—is where the referring expression is a contradiction in terms. Against such an objection, bare consistency is enough. In first-order logic the Completeness Theorem establishes that any consistent set of

---

[1] §7.5.

[2] See above, §7.5 and §12.9.

well-formed formulae has a model, and consistency proofs for non-Euclidean geometry, non-Desarguian geometry and non-standard models of Peano's axioms are all we need for us to be able to talk about them with a clear conscience. But it is only in few cases that bare consistency suffices.[3] Non-standard models of Peano's axioms do not rate high ontologically, lacking even ω-consistency. Fictions, too, can be talked about, and shadows, but though discourse about them is allowed to be intelligible, it is not taken seriously—it is not for real.

The word 'real' makes for misunderstanding. In part it is a chameleon word, taking its colour from its context; but it also retains a core of meaning from its etymological origin, which exercises a pervasive pressure on our intimations of reality. Like the word 'good', it takes its colour from its context: the reality of real butter is quite different from the reality of a real gentleman, in each case taking its sense from what it is being contrasted with. 'Unreal' wears the trousers, as Austin used to say.[4] The logic of opposition comes into our understanding of realism. The content of mathematical realism is largely constituted by its not being various alternatives that have been canvassed and found wanting.

> If Not Formalism, Intuitionism,
> Finitism, or something,
> then What?
>
> perhaps Realism after all.

But the word 'real' is not just defined by its opposites. There is an etymological element too. It comes from the mediaeval Latin *realis*, itself derived from *res*, a thing, and still carries many connotations of thinglikeness. The defence of mathematical realism, therefore, needs to be conducted on two fronts. On one it is a campaign of "defeating the defeaters": on the other it is an exercise of

---

[3] See G.M.Hunter, "Is Consistency Enough for Existence in Mathematics", *Analysis*, **48**, January 1988, pp.3-5.

[4] J.L.Austin, *Sense and Sensibilia*, ed. G.J.Warnock, Oxford, 1963, ch. VII, p.70. Compare, Aristotle's elucidation of the meaning of the word 'just' in *Nicomachean Ethics*, V,1,8; 1129a31ff.

disentangling different themes, determining to what extent mathematical entities are thinglike, and how this should bear on their ontological status.

Plato legitimated talk about abstract entities.[5] In this sense numbers exist. We can talk about them: they reach the minimal level of existence, and so are entities in Resnik's terminology.[6] But objections can be raised on metaphysical grounds to according them any greater ontological status. Some Formalists see themselves as radicals, who will not admit to the fabric of the universe abstract, non-material entities. They do not want to be committed to saying that numbers exist, and so are attracted by accounts of mathematics which portray it as being not about abstract entities but merely about the figures we draw on blackboards. Ontological Formalism goes with a nominalist position as regards universals, and often some form of behaviourism as regards mental entities. But in spite of heroic efforts to squeeze mathematics into a Procrustean, non-numerical bed, the results are unconvincing.[7] If one were a nominalist or behaviourist, one might persevere, but there are many implausibilities in either system, quite apart from their inability to account for mathematics. After all, what we write on blackboards, are not just collocations of chalk particles, but symbols, having significance for human beings by reason of their being used in accordance with rules.

Materialists believe that things are the only things to exist, and therefore deny existence to mathematical entities. They could be right. But their own speech belies their professions of existential unbelief. Nineteenth-century materialists believed the world was made up of hard massy atoms of just 92 basic types, and in their explanations attached great importance to these 92 types, which were organized in the Periodic Table. Their twentieth-century followers, who explain the origin of species, and all human behaviour,

---

[5] §1.4.

[6] M.D.Resnik, *Mathematics as a Science of Patterns*, Oxford, 1997, p.247n.

[7] The most convincing attempt is by H.Field, *Science without Numbers: a Defense of Nominalism*, Princeton, 1980. The best critique is by J.P.Burgess and G.Rosen, *A Subject with No Object*, Oxford, 1997. See also S.Schapiro, "Mathematics and Reality", *Philosophy of Science*, **50**, 1983, pp.523-548; S.Schapiro, "Conservativeness and Incompleteness", *Journal of Philosophy*, **80**, 1983, pp.521-531.

in terms of evolution, are equally committed to the importance of species and kinds, especially biochemical substances, such as DNA, in their explanation. Physicalists reduce everything to physical terms, and say "It is all in the Schrödinger equation", which could again conceivably be true, but sits ill with a denial of existence to Hilbert space.

Quine starts from a position of scientific naturalism, and argues against those natural scientists who maintain that since no scientific instruments can observe mathematical entities, mathematical entities do not exist. Against them he deploys an *argumentum ad homines* that since science can be done only with the aid of mathematics, and mathematics can be done only with the aid of set theory, sets must be allowed to exist, as the *sine qua non* of scientific reasoning. Much recent work in America has been dotting the *i*s and crossing the *t*s of subsequent debate. It is reasonable to hold that natural science is substantially true, less so to suppose that it alone is. Mathematics is presupposed not only by natural science, but by all our thinking. Reductive accounts of mathematics, which seek to explain away mathematical discourse as being merely a fiction, or a *façon de parler*, need to discharge a heavy burden of proof before we should take them seriously.

Intuitionism, in spite of its other difficulties,[8] is cheap ontologically. It demands no commitment to abstract or supersensible entities. Intuitionists need only believe that human beings have minds, and some of them sometimes do mathematics. Such tenets are difficult to deny, but do not by themselves account for the phenomena. Mathematicians do not just talk about their states of mind, in the way that psychiatric patients sometimes do: the fact that I think I have a proof does not show that I do have one: Hobbes thought he had a proof that $\pi = 3\frac{1}{8}$. My experiences of opining I have a proof are corrigible, and the object of the exercise is the truth we arrive at, not the means of getting there.

Other ontologies have been canvassed. Often they seem open to obvious objection. If a metaphysical system that ruled out mathematical realism were supported by good arguments, it would be reasonable to try and squeeze mathematics into the preferred metaphysical mould, but it is a big IF, and would take us far beyond the confines of this book. Instead, at the cost of ignoring much

---

[8] See above, §7.4-§7.7.

Procrustean work that has been attempted, especially in North America, I shall turn to the different strands of thinglikeness that go to make up our notion of reality.

Reality is objective. It is independent of my subjective choice and state of mind, and exists in its own right, without regard to my wanting it or knowing it. If I do not like it, that is my problem, not its. I must accept it willy-nilly. It follows that numbers, like ordinary things, exist independently of our minds and wills, and can therefore be referred to in an objective way, but do not depend on being referred to for their existence. They exist independently of our constructions, so that there is no objection in principle to impredicative definitions.

Mathematical realists also hold that mathematical truths are objectively true, irrespective of whether we know or believe them. Knowledge should track truth, rather than being constitutive of it. We may not know whether there is an even number that is not the sum of two primes, but that is quite irrelevant to the question of whether there is such a number or not. If numbers are self-subsistent objects, then either there is such a number, or there is not. The mathematical realist is committed to the Law of the Excluded Middle, and the Principle of Bivalence, in these standard cases.

At this point, however, disanalogies between mathematical objects and material objects begin to reveal themselves. Mathematical objects are not completely determinate, in the way material objects are taken to be. Moreover, though they are independent of us, they are not independent of one another. They lack the "aseity" that traditionally has been ascribed to the most real forms of reality. Our realism, therefore, must be a modified one.

15.2 Self-Subsistent Objects

Numerals can be nouns. As a grammatical fact it is indisputable, but we may wonder whether they meet the logical requirements for really denoting something objective. Frege argued that they did. The natural numbers were "self-subsistent objects" (*selbständige Gegenstände*); numerals when used as nouns clearly referred to definite objects because there were workable criteria of identity and difference; we can tell that 'six of one' and 'half a dozen of the other' refer to the same number in each case, because when used

as quotifiers they are equinumerous. Hume's principle[9] furnishes
an adequate criterion of identity:

$$\mathcal{N}^= \qquad \mathcal{N}x : Fx = \mathcal{N}x : Gx \leftrightarrow (\mathrm{V}R)(Fx \vdash\dashv_R Gx)$$

the Number of fs equals the Number of gs if and only if
there is a one-one relation R correlating the fs with the gs.

Essentially, an equivalence relation is being cited to justify abstracting from the many instances equivalent to one another in
some respect to that respect as an abstract entity. It is often done.
Frege's own example of direction remains convincing:

$$\mathcal{D}^{\|} \qquad \mathcal{D}(a) = \mathcal{D}(b) \leftrightarrow (a \parallel b)$$

the Direction of a is the same as the Direction of b if and
only if a is parallel to b.

Mathematicians regularly use equivalence classes to introduce and
define new entities. In §3.7 we abstracted the fraction $\frac{1}{2}$ from the
equivalence class of ordered couples $\{\{1;2\},\{2;4\},\{3;6\},\dots\}$,

$$\mathcal{F}^- \qquad \mathcal{F}(\frac{a}{b}) = \mathcal{F}(\frac{c}{d}) \leftrightarrow (a \times d = b \times c).$$

Similarly with integers the mathematician does not just talk about
differences airily, but can show the respondent how to tell which
difference is which. We identify directions, fractions and integers
by means of equivalence classes, and just as we can show that 50%
is the same as $\frac{1}{2}$, we can use the principle $\mathcal{N}^=$ to convince Ernie and
Johnny that they are referring to the same natural number, and
that their difference is no more profound than if one was talking of
'six of one' and the other of 'half a dozen of the other'.

Hume's principle is less general than Axiom V, and looks more
ad hoc. Frege wanted a formal rule, itself an evident logical truth,
and thought he had found it in his Axiom V, postulating for every
predicate F a set (as we should say) $\{\hat{x} : Fx\}$. It was tempting, but
unnecessary, impossible and disastrous. It was tempting, because
sets are essentially countable.[10] But it was unnecessary. We can

---

[9] David Hume, *Treatise on Human Nature*, Bk.I, Part iii, Sect.1, in Selby-
Bigge's ed., Oxford, 1888, p.71.

[10] As in §12.9, the word 'countable' does not carry here the sense of finite-
or-denumerable, but indicates only that we can begin to count a set—even
an "uncountable" one.

abstract from parallels without having any firm idea of how many different classes of parallel lines there are, just as we can talk of the colours of the rainbow, on the strength of what they have in common, in spite of not being able to distinguish between them sharply enough to be able to count them. Equivalence classes are not always sets. We cannot *identify* natural numbers *with* any actual equivalence class, because the equivalence class changes, as particular n-membered sets come into, or go out of, existence, whereas the natural number n does not. At one time the class of all three-membered sets did not have the set of my children as a member; at a later stage it did; at a later stage still, it did not. But three is immune to the changes and chances of family size. Maddy takes this as a decisive objection to identifying natural numbers with such actual classes of actual sets;[11] but that is not an objection to identifying them *by means of* equivalence classes, as that which all the equivalence classes have in common. In §11.3 equivalence relations identified different types of magnitude, establishing what things are the same as regards weight, duration, length, or angle. Multitude is in the same case as magnitude. If we are willing to allow that weights and lengths exist, we should be willing to allow that numbers do so too.

Equinumerosity has further significance when viewed in a purely mathematical context. It is a minimal isomorphism.[12] It is constituted by a one-one mapping of individuals, whereas isomorphisms generally require that the one-one mapping should also map certain predicates, relations and functions into corresponding ones, $< X; Q_1, Q_2, Q_3, \ldots; R_1, R_2, R_3, \ldots; f_1, f_2, f_3, \ldots >$ into $< X'; Q_1', Q_2', Q_3', \ldots; R_1', R_2', R_3', \ldots; f_1', f_2', f_3', \ldots >$.[13] Isomorphism expresses similarity of structure. Structures that are isomorphic with one another have the same pattern. Granted some isomorphism, indicating some similarity of structure, we can abstract, and consider the pattern common to all the instances.

We need to be careful. The words 'structure', 'pattern', 'model', have an ambiguity built into them, that puzzled Plato, and still confuses modern thinkers. Plato was puzzled by the "third man",

---

[11] Penelope Maddy, *Realism in Mathematics*, Oxford, 1990, ch.3, §3, "Frege numbers", pp.100-102.

[12] See above, §4.6, and §9.3.

[13] See above, §9.3.

but the problem is better formulated now in terms of the Periodic Table. At the time of the Big Bang enormous numbers of atoms were created, with the same atomic number, the same atomic weight, the same number of electrons, and so the same chemical properties. Each atom of protonium, as we may call *pukka* hydrogen, to distinguish it from deuterium and tritium, has all these properties in common with every other atom of protonium, which properties we assign to the first place in the Periodic Table, revealing protonium's resemblance to the alkali metals on the one hand, and to the halogens on the other. As we begin to understand quantum mechanics, we see how quantum mechanics allows just one possibility for protonium, and how, at the Big Bang, individual protonium atoms had to be modelled on this one prototype. Individual protonium atoms are seen both as *instantiations* of a set of defining properties, and as copies of an ideal type, which they therefore *resemble*. But if the prototype resembles other protonium atoms, we then look for some further set of properties which it, along with the others, shares. An infinite regress is easily set up, and only with difficulty avoided, as patterns are thought of both as what is common to different instances, and as what they are all modelled on. Frege's Axiom V led to inconsistency because, being formulated formally, it was not able to distinguish sharply enough qualities possessed by many instances from qualities referred to by a uniquely referring expression. It seems that we cannot have a formal abstraction rule.[14] The question whether particular instances of abstraction are permissible depends on the particular equivalence relation, and sometimes on its range. The relation of *being parallel to* is valid locally on the surface of the earth, but not globally; schoolboy riddles about the colour of bears, and Stephen Hawking's analogy with the beginning of time, depend on its breakdown at the North Pole. Perhaps the relation of equinumerosity fails to apply when we are dealing with the class of all sets—what other collection could it be equinumerous with?—in which case the transfinite cardinal number of such a class would be ill defined, much as the direction North at the North Pole is. Abstracting is limited by a number of common-sense restrictions which have not been fully formulated, but can be articulated in particular cases to

[14] Compare M.D.Resnik, *Mathematics as a Science of Patterns*, Oxford, 1997, ch.12, esp. pp.258-259.

exclude unreasonable entities, such as sets that are not members of themselves, or the property of heterologicality.

These considerations are enough to vindicate Frege's logical claim that the natural numbers are self-subsistent objects, which can be firmly referred to, identified and discussed. The entities of mathematics, though abstract, are respectable objects of tough discourse, in which loose talk is effectively criticized and weeded out. Metaphysical objections may still be made, but the very fact of there being many different instances of the same pattern counts in favour of its objective reality. In other realms of discourse where we can refer to things under different names or descriptions, we have a strong tendency to take, as the object referred to, that which is most invariant, the underlying common feature, factoring out the differences of nomenclature, expression, or description.[15] A metaphysician may, nonetheless, wish to eschew all talk of abstract entities, but then must abjure the Periodic Table, the spectrum, and almost the whole of interesting discourse.

15.3　Meaning and Impredicativity

Impredicative constructions are those in which an entity is defined in terms of some totality that includes the entity itself.[16] If a catalogue in a library lists every book in the library, it must include itself. If the barber is the man who shaves every man in the village, then we are implicitly referring to him in our description of him.

Impredicativity has been under suspicion in mathematics, but is

---

[15] Compare in sense perception "Phenomenal Regression to the Real Object"; see Thomas Reid, *Essays on the Intellectual Powers of Man*, Essay II, ch.xix *ad fin.*; pp.265-266 in 1783 ed., p. 325 in *Collected Works*, Edinburgh, 1853; R.H.Thouless, *British Journal of Psychology*, **21** & **22**, 1931; J.J.Gibson, *The Perception of the Visual Field*, Cambridge, Mass., 1930, pp.167-172; O.L.Zangwill, *Introduction to Modern Psychology*, London, 1950, pp.30-34; R.S.Woodworth, *Experimental Psychology*, London, 1963, pp.486-487.

[16] Hao Wang, *From Mathematics to Philosophy*, London, 1974, p.77; or Kurt Gödel, "Russell's Mathematical Logic", reprinted in P.Benacerraf and H.Putnam, *Philosophy of Mathematics: Selected Readings*, 2nd ed., Cambridge, 1983, p.455, n.13, <an impredicative definition is one which defines an object> "α by reference to a totality to which α itself (and perhaps also things definable only in terms of α) belong".

difficult to avoid. If impredicative definitions are illicit, mathematics would be maimed. Cantor's diagonal argument, showing that there are more real numbers than natural numbers, would be ruled out. The Bolzano–Weierstrass theorem depends crucially on the acceptance of impredicative definitions, given only by the Cantor–Dedekind account of real numbers.[17] Mathematicians, therefore, have gone on using impredicative definitions, but with a bad conscience; and when sceptics tell them they ought not to, they half agree, and feel ashamed.

Part of the suspicion arises from the paradoxes in set theory. If we were to rule out impredicative definitions we should exclude the rogue sets that give rise to Russell's paradox.[18] It is better, some thin-skinned mathematicians feel, to enter the kingdom of truth without the Bolzano–Weierstrass theorem, than with it to be consigned to the Sheol of inconsistency. But the remedy not only cuts out too much, but fails to exclude the cancer of self-reference. Once we have infinity, we can code a formal system into itself, and diagonalize to produce Gödelian sentences with paradoxical consequences.

Impredicativity can also be argued against on nominalist and constructivist grounds. If we are trying to give an account of mathematics from first principles, impredicative definitions seem to involve us in a vicious circle. We very much want to be able to take Dedekind cuts of real numbers. Each of these defines a particular real number in terms of two sets which between them include

---

[17] Paul Bernays, "On Platonism in Mathematics", reprinted in Paul Benacerraf and Hilary Putnam, *Philosophy of Mathematics: Selected Readings*, 2nd ed., Cambridge, 1983, p.260; Hao Wang, *From Mathematics to Philosophy*, London, 1974, pp.123-124; Michael Hallett, *Cantorian Set Theory and Limitation of Size*, Oxford, 1984, p.30.

[18] See above, §12.2, §12.3. See also A.N. Whitehead and B.A.W. Russell, *Principia Mathematica*, Cambridge, 1910, I, 37. R. Carnap, "The Logicist Foundations of Mathematics", English translation in P.Benacerraf and H.Putnam, *Philosophy of Mathematics: Selected Readings*, 2nd ed., Cambridge, 1983, pp.41-52, esp. §III, pp.46-49. (Ramsey differed: see F.P.Ramsey, "The Foundations of Mathematics", *Proceedings of the London Mathematical Society*, Ser.2, Vol.25, Part 5, 1925, pp.338-384, esp. §III; reprinted in F.P.Ramsey, *The Foundations of Mathematics*, ed. R.B. Braithwaite, London, 1931, pp.1-61, esp. pp.32-49.

all the real numbers. It is alleged that this is objectionable, since we mention all the real numbers in constructing a Dedekind cut. But we do so only in general terms, and do not need to particularise each of them individually, and certainly not the particular one that the Dedekind cut will identify. There is no problem about impredicative definitions if sets, and other mathematical entities, exist independently of our creating or constructing them, and the purpose of definition is simply to identify, not to constitute, the entity under discussion. The set of all real numbers whose square is not less than 2 does indeed include $\sqrt{2}$, which it also identifies as its greatest lower bound, but we knew what it was to be a real number without needing to be able to say what this particular real number was.

But the Axiom of Extensionality, it may be objected, precludes this. If sets consist solely and exclusively of their members, there is nothing to catch hold of until each and every member has been adequately specified. This, it is held, is a simple consequence of taking the Axiom of Extensionality seriously. But the Axiom of Extensionality offers a criterion of identity of sets, not a criterion for *identifying* them. It tells us when from the standpoint of set theory two sets are to be regarded as being one and the same set, but it does not tell us how sets are to be identified.[19] And it is clear that it could not, if infinite sets are to be admitted at all. An infinite set cannot be specified by listing its members, and a non-denumerably infinite set cannot be specified by spelling out a program which could in principle list all its members. If I start talking to you about the set of all real numbers, I do not have to pretend that, granted sufficient patience on your part, I could specify them individually. It is enough that you should be able to tell of any putative real number whether it was one or not. Were that not so, we could not have any concept of a real number, for there are uncountably many of them, and only a denumerably infinite number of possible characterizations of particular real numbers.

The issue is one of reference. If mathematics is just a game, mathematical entities owe their existence entirely to our construction of them, and have no existence apart from our say-so. And then, unless our specification is complete—in the way the rules of chess are—it will fail to refer to anything definite. But mathemat-

---

[19] See above, §12.9.

ics is not just a game, played in accordance with arbitrary rules laid down by *fiat*, subject only to the constraints of consistency. It is a dialogue carried on between seekers after truth, who share objectives beyond the bare one of being able to communicate, and the shared openness towards truth makes them sensitive to pressures which guide them towards a common identification of incompletely specified objects.

This is pre-eminently true in the case of the natural numbers. Even though in first-order logic there are non-standard models of the axioms of Peano Arithmetic, I know which model you are intending to characterize by the axioms of Peano Arithmetic because I know the sort of thing you are likely to be trying to talk about. In particular, I can understand your wanting to refer to the *smallest* model, that is to say the intersection of *all* sets that contain the number 0 and are hereditary under the successor relation. I can understand this wide-ranging sense of the word 'all' without your needing to be able to offer a finite conjunction or an infinite enumeration of them all. I can do this because I am not a mere moron responding to your programming, able only to follow "effective" procedures, but an intelligent being with a mind of my own, who can think for myself, and in particular project myself into your position, and see from your point of view what you are driving at. I can therefore understand a free-ranging sense of 'all', and not only a tightly specified one, and hence have available not just the resources of first-order logic, but those of second-order logic. I can quotify over predicates, and qualities, and sets, and thus give monomorphic characterizations of the natural numbers.

We feel that we know what the natural numbers are: Peano's axioms are a pretty good characterization of them, but not a complete one, that would lead a computer to the precise model we had in mind. They are a gesture in the direction of what we want to talk about enough to indicate the topic of discussion, even though our specification may be inadequate to tie it down precisely. We might then be led to say that our understanding of the natural numbers stems from direct acquaintance, and not from any axiomatic account; but the perceptual metaphor would be misunderstood. Our knowledge of the natural numbers is direct knowledge: but it is direct by intention, not by some form of sense perception.

The incomplete characterization of the natural numbers by Peano Arithmetic not only tells against the adequacy of any axiomatic or constructivist approach generally, but constitutes a particular example of a mathematical entity referred to by a description which is good enough but essentially incomplete.

The claim that meanings have a life of their own is dangerous. The word 'all' is fuzzy-edged. In the case of the real numbers it was sharp enough, but in the case of the cardinal numbers it is not. For at each stage there we shift our stand, and having asked "how many cardinals thus far?", construe the answer as yet another cardinal number, which could be encompassed by a new 'all'. Each 'all' is perfectly all right in its own way, but none of them is a final 'all', capable of being applied to 'cardinal number' without further specification. It needs detailed scrutiny to determine whether or not the totality in issue is well defined or not. And once again, it seems, no adequate formal rules can be promulgated.[20]

Dummett agrees. He argues that there is an inherent vagueness even in the concept of the totality of natural numbers, because there is no possibility of closure either in regard to what counts as a proof of a proposition concerning all natural numbers or in regard to the definable properties of natural numbers.[21] If our mathematical concepts are deeply indeterminate, it puts in question the argument from the incompleteness of second-order logic in §13.5. For there is *a* completeness theorem, due to Henkin.[22] But it involves secondary (*i.e.* non-principal) interpretations and unnatural models. If we extend the number of models taken into consideration, we reduce the number of well-formed formulae which will be true in all of them. Hence, if we admit weird models of second-order propositions, we have fewer well-formed formulae that are true in all of them, and it is easier for them all to be provable. The range

---

[20] Alexander George, "The Imprecision of Impredicativity", *Mind*, **96**, 1987, pp.514-518, argues further that the very concepts of predicativity and impredicativity are inherently vague, not only in content but in application. See also Charles Parsons, "The Impredicativity of Induction", in L.Cauman, I.Levi, C.Parsons, and R.Schwarz, eds., *How Many Questions?*, 1983, pp.132-153, esp. p.135.

[21] M.A.E.Dummett, "The Philosophical Significance of Gödel's Theorem", reprinted in *Truth and Other Enigmas*, London, 1978, discussed by Mary Tiles, *Mathematics and the Image of Reason*, London, 1991, pp.150-151.

[22] See Alonzo Church, *Introduction to Mathematical Logic*, Princeton, 1956, Metatheorem **546, p.314, and generally ch.5, §54, pp.307-315.

of admissible models is thus of crucial importance in determining
what shall count as a logical truth.

But the situation is not hopeless. We can secure determinacy
up to a point by formalising, and we can know which models we
intend to mean. With regard to models of Peano Arithmetic in
first-order logic we were able to say which was the standard one
and which were non-standard ones even though the difference could
not be formulated in first-order terms. When we embed one theory in another, we restrict the range of available models. Some,
non-Desarguian, models of projective plane geometry are not models of three-dimensional projective geometry. In rejecting non-
Desarguian models of projective plane geometry we are discerning
the shape of the models we had in mind when we sought axioms for
projective plane geometry. In the same way if we can prove propositions about the theory of numbers only by analytic means,[23] we are
unpacking more about what we have in mind when we talk about
the natural numbers, namely that they should be embeddable in
the reals.

But this is not a matter of arbitrary choice. We do have an
idea of the intended model of the natural numbers, and reject
non-standard ones, even if they satisfy a first-order specification of
Peano's axioms. Concepts like *number, dimensional space*, and—
arguably—*set*, have a life of their own. They are not constitutively
defined by their definitions, which act more as "cues" we then in-
terpret, as it were stereoscopically, in much the same way as we do
in sense perception[24] and in the many uses of metaphor in poetry
and in ordinary discourse. I come to know what natural numbers
are from learning to count and to tell how many items there are in
some collection, but then extrapolate in a rational, non-arbitrary
way, and am able to distinguish them from non-isomorphic models
of Peano Arithmetic as well as embedding them in the reals. On
the strength of intuitions about what are the naturally intended
models, I restrict the range of standard interpretations, and thus
have a wider range of well-formed formulae that are true in all of
them.

Second-order propositions on this showing *are* true in virtue of
meanings, but not just the meanings of the terms involved, and

[23] See, *e.g.*, passage from Gödel quoted in §14.9.

[24] See above, §16.2.

thus not analytic in any derogatory sense. Rather, meanings in mathematics are not as fixed as the Formalists suppose, and may develop in a rationally coherent direction, much as they do in ordinary language. Meaning, in particular, is tied up with inference patterns, and hence with the validity of inferences.[25] Thus the Gödelian extensibility of valid inference beyond any pre-assigned formal limits, is paralleled by an extensibility of meanings in a way not licensed by antecedent rules, but rational none the less.

15.4 Bivalence and Determinacy

Truth is a perpetual possibility of being wrong. I can claim truth, but not lay hold of it. It outruns provability, and always may elude my grasp, and turn out to be other than I thought.[26] Claiming that a proposition is true does not, in general, preclude its being controverted by someone else without his thereby showing himself inconsistent. In claiming truth, therefore, I have to sit loose to proving it, and lay myself open to being challenged and controverted. I have to acknowledge that I may be wrong, and allow you to maintain that I actually am. If I foreclose that possibility absolutely, I abandon my claim to be telling the truth, and am merely opinionating, or optating, or postulating, or just exercising my vocal chords. It is because truth is *not* constituted by my say-so but is thought of as independent of me, something I aspire to, but may not succeed in actually attaining, that the Intuitionist critique of classical logic fails. Truth is not what I assert but what my assertions ought to express. The meaning of what I say is constituted not by their assertability conditions alone but by the truth conditions I would like them to satisfy. These conditions are not completely sewn up in much the same way as mathematical objects are not completely characterized. In both cases the incompleteness is permissible because of the objectivity of the whole enterprise, and tolerable because of the shared rationality of those who undertake it. In asking you to suppose that Goldbach's Conjecture is either true or false, I do not have to spell out exactly some proof that it is true or that it is false, because you seek after truth too, and have enough commitment to truth to have some idea of what it would be like for either Goldbach's Conjecture or its negation to

---

[25] See above, §3.3.

[26] See above, §8.11.

be proved true. Hence the Principle of Bivalence and the various versions of the Law of the Excluded Middle are acceptable.

They are also mandatory if we are serious in wanting to know the truth. Granted a high degree of commitment on both our parts we dance very close together as we dance the dialectical dance, and are very ready to assume something for the sake of argument, if only to be shown that it must be wrong, in which case its contradictory must be right. *Tertium non datur* arises from the close community of interest of those who share a great concern to know what the truth is. More generally, the critique of classical logic by the Intuitionists, like the critique of impredicative definitions by the Constructivists, is based on a supposed subjectivity of mathematical discourse, which can be refuted not only, as they suppose, by making mathematics out to be about an external, though non-material, world, but by acknowledging a universal, and hence inter-subjective, validity in mathematical arguments when carried out between rational beings.

Nevertheless, the Principle of Bivalence does not always apply to mathematical entities. Is the Euler line 3 inches long? It is not that we do not know: rather, it is that the question, although apparently well-formed, is not about a unique particular which could be either 3 inches long or some other length. Although we can talk about the triangle, and say many true things about it, we cannot say whether it is scalene, isosceles, right-angled, or equilateral, nor how big it is. The sort of entity we are talking about is characterized by the questions that may be properly asked and answered about it. Abstract entities are thus unlike material objects in not being fully determinate. We never can say, in Euclidean geometry, how large a triangle is: it is part of the constitutive aim of geometry, in spite of its etymology, that it should be unconcerned with actual linear measures, dealing only with the shapes of things, independent of sizes. In much the same way we can say that the average Englishman has 2.8 children, and that he has British nationality, but not whether his wife is called Mary. Again, most future events are likewise lacking in a definite truth-value as of now—it is not as of now true that I shall scratch my nose at 12 noon on Christmas day next year, or that you will make a proposal of marriage then, nor as of now false that I shall or that you will.[27]

---

[27] Aristotle, *De Interpretatione*, ch.9, 18^{a}28ff.; J.R.Lucas, *The Future*.

Traditionally it has counted against the substantial reality of abstract objects that they lack complete determinateness. Although we may talk of them, they are just logical fictions, like the average Englishman, or insubstantial possibilities, like the as yet undecided future. They are not ultimate particulars in the way that material objects, and sometimes minds or persons, are often taken to be, and hence are not really real. Einstein regarded determinacy as a mark of reality—it was the gravamen of his EPR critique of quantum mechanics that it failed to accord to quantum systems the determinacy that reality required. But now that the prospect of completing quantum mechanics as Einstein wanted is vanishingly small, we are having to picture reality no longer as made up of atoms, quintessential things, each one possessing all the physical properties there are, but as altogether more indeterminate; and abstract entities can no longer be criticized for not possessing a determinacy that is not possessed by the ultimate elements of physical reality themselves.

15.5 Competing Truths

One argument for Realism is that it explains unanimity. The reason why wise men agree that there is a moon, is that the moon exists. And so, *per contra*, irresoluble disagreement argues against there being some fact of the matter to which the opinion of competent thinkers should converge. In the present age anti-realists cite the existence of different set theories as a refutation of realism.[28] They argue that if there were a truth of the matter ascertainable by the eye of the mind, we should know which set theory was the right one, and would accept that, rejecting alternatives as nonstandard. Similarly in an earlier age the fact that there were non-Euclidean geometries was seen as undermining the objectivity of human knowledge.

But the rivalry between different set theories cuts both ways. It may be, in part, due to a confusion of concepts, with different axioms articulating different concepts of what a set really is, but the fact that we can ask the question which one of them is right tells in favour of Realism. It shows that at least we understand these theories realistically, as making statements which are either true or

---

[28] S.F.Barker, "Realism as a Philosophy of Mathematics", in J.J.Buloff, ed., *Foundations of Mathematics*, Berlin, 1969, pp.1-9.

false. It seems a real question whether the Continuum Hypothesis is true or not. Cantor thought it was true: Gödel that it was false; and Cohen reckoned that in the end we should all agree that it was *obviously* false.[29] They all believed that there was a fact of the matter which the axioms of set theory ought to express, and were inadequate or false if they failed to bring out the right answer to the question. It is open for the sceptic to maintain robustly that Cantor, Gödel, Cohen and other workers in the fields were all in error in supposing there was an answer to their questions: equally, it is open for the Realist to decline to opine that great men should so much misunderstand what they were doing as to think it was a meaningful enquiry when in fact it was meaningless.

In any case, the anti-realist account does not give the whole picture. In the first place, the analogy with geometry is weak. Gödel points out that whereas both the Fifth Postulate and its negation have models in the geometry which lacks either axiom, there is no comparable model of set theory to which the negation of some disputed axiom has been added. Such an extended set theory yields no new theorems about integers, whereas new theorems about integers (verifiable in individual instances) can be derived from set theory to which has been added the disputed axiom itself.[30] In any case, geometry is not just a formal system, but is linked to other disciplines, which constrain the choice of those geometries we actually want to use;[31] and set theory similarly is not just an account of some universe of abstract entities, but a codification of methods of argument, and not every way of arguing is equally good.

We draw back from accepting that there just are different set theories, and we can take our pick. Instead, we cast around for some way of deciding between them; certainly it seems entirely natural to ask whether any given axiomatization of set theory is the right one, and in particular to ask whether the Axiom of Choice, or the Continuum Hypothesis, or the General Continuum Hypothesis,

---

[29] P.J.Cohen, *Set Theory and the Continuum Hypothesis*, New York, 1966, p.151.

[30] Kurt Gödel, "What is Cantor's Continuum Problem?", P.Benacerraf and H.Putnam, *Philosophy of Mathematics: Selected Readings*, 2nd ed., Cambridge, 1983, pp.482-483; reprinted in S.Feferman *et al.*, *Kurt Gödel: Collected Works*, II, New York, 1990, pp.266-267.

[31] See above, §2.6-§2.8.

should be adopted. If that question be allowed, it would appear that there is a truth of the matter over and above any axiomatization of set theory.

As set theory has been axiomatized, successive axioms have commended themselves to mathematicians, as being true, though not derivable from the axioms already propounded. There is a fair measure of agreement about most of these axioms, which has tended to grow with the passage of time. There is thus some consensus on the truth of these axioms which is not due to formal proof. It is not just a matter of *fiat*; mathematicians are disinclined to say that they are simply choosing to play one game rather than another. Although there have been different schools of mathematics in different places at different times, mathematicians cannot agree to differ about the validity of a mathematical argument in the way musicians could agree that their preferences were a matter of taste. If there is disagreement, at least one party is wrong, and ought to change their views in order to bring them into conformity with the truth. Although, like other human beings, reluctant to admit themselves to be wrong, mathematicians in principle hold themselves ready to change their mind about the truth of any particular axiom, should good reason be given. Their postulating these axioms is corrigible, and has already resulted in a large measure of agreement. In the cases where there is still much disagreement about the axioms, it is reasonable to expect that in due course a consensus will emerge among mathematicians as to which is the correct one. That is to say, we expect there to be, and actively seek, some convergence in our acceptance of axioms.

These three features, Corrigibility, Convergence and Consensus, are characteristic of objectivity, and lead us to reckon that in our thought about mathematical objects we are being guided to agreement on their properties, which is not due to our sharing a common proof-procedure, since in these cases there is no formal proof, and must therefore be due to each one of us apprehending their properties for himself. Thus Gödel argues:

> For someone who considers mathematical objects to exist independently of our constructions and of our having an intuition of them individually, and who requires only that the general mathematical concepts must be sufficiently clear for us to be able to recognize their soundness and the truth of the axioms concerning them, there exists, I believe, a satis-

factory foundation of Cantor's set theory in its whole original extent and meaning, namely, axiomatics of set theory
interpreted in the way sketched below.[32]

In the fullness of time we may come to have rational grounds for
accepting, or for rejecting, the Continuum Hypothesis, the General
Continuum Hypothesis, the Axiom of Choice, and other disputed
axioms of set theory.[33] Unless we can be sure that there is no way
in which we could be led rationally to accept or reject disputed
axioms, the fact that there are alternative set theories does not tell
against there being an objective question which of them should be
regarded as being canonical.

15.6 Contingency and Structure

Mathematical objects are less thing-like than material objects not
only in not being fully determinate, but in not being independent
of one another. It is a mark of reality to be independent of us, and a
traditional attribute of ultimate reality was that it should be complete in itself and independent of every other thing—"aseity", as it
was sometimes termed. But mathematical entities do not enjoy a
lonely self-sufficiency. Benacerraf was right to criticize logicist definitions of cardinal numbers on this score. Each cardinal number
seemed to stand alone, independently of all the others:[34] the seven
stars in the sky were quite separate from the six proud walkers,
whereas we should want to insist that it was essential to being seven
that it came next after six, and in identifying twelve as the number
of the Apostles, we are also committing ourselves to the implication
that if one falls out then eleven will be the number that went to
heaven.[35] The structure is as important as the individual numbers
in themselves. It was a weakness of the cardinal approach that it
played down the importance of the relations between them,[36] but

---

[32] Kurt Gödel, "What is Cantor's Continuum Problem?", p.474/p.258; see
also pp.484-485/pp.268-269.

[33] Penelope Maddy, *Realism in Mathematics*, Oxford, 1990, ch.4, pp.107-149,
gives an illuminating account of the arguments for and against various
proposed axioms in set theory.

[34] See Figure 4.7.1 in §4.7.

[35] See above, §.4.2.

[36] See §4.7.

Benacerraf goes too far the other way when he claims "for arithmetical purposes the properties of numbers which do not stem from the relations they bear to one another in virtue of being arranged in a progression are of no consequence whatsoever".[37] The natural numbers, we saw,[38] are not just a structure, a progression of order-type ω, but are also quotities, anchored by nought's being the number for when there are no things; the first natural number, 0, is tied to the universal negative quotifier $(A\ )\neg$, (or the negative existential quotifier $\neg(V\ )$). So, too, although there is much we can say about the structure of transitive relations in a general way, we need also to consider particular equivalence relations and particular ordering relations.

These *caveats* notwithstanding, structuralism expresses an important truth. Mathematical entities are not self-subsistent in the way material objects are. Although mathematical entities can be referred to uniquely in a variety of ways, and to that extent at least are independent of us and like material objects, which also can be referred to uniquely in a variety of ways, and are independent of us, they are not independent of one another. Venus would still be Venus, even if it were knocked out of orbit by an asteroid, and was no longer the Evening Star; but twelve could not cease to come after eleven and before thirteen, or cease to have 144 as its square. I can move the chairs around, re-arrange my books, and sadly resign myself to the fact that when the tree in the Quad is finally felled, the Quad will still exist: but I cannot alter the geography of the world of forms. No earthquake could alter the distant range of mountains that Hardy was pointing out to Littlewood,[39] or make

---

[37] Paul Benacerraf "What Numbers Could Not Be", in Paul Benacerraf and Hilary Putnam, eds., *The Philosophy of Mathematics*, 2nd ed., Cambridge, 1983, p.291. See also M.Resnik, "Mathematical Knowledge and Pattern Cognition", *Canadian Journal of Philosophy*, **5**, 1975, pp.25-39; "Mathematics as a Science of Patterns: Ontology and Reference", *Nous*, **15**, 1981, pp.529-550; "Mathematics as a Science of Patterns: Epistemology", *Nous*, **16**, 1982, pp.95-105; *Mathematics as a Science of Patterns*, Oxford, 1997; S.Shapiro, "Mathematics and Reality", *Philosophy of Science*, **50**, 1983, pp.525-548; "Structure and Ontology", *Philosophical Topics*, 1989, **17**, No.2, pp.145-171. *Philosophy of Mathematics*, Oxford, 1997.

[38] §5.2.

[39] §1.5.

it the case that 1729 was not the sum of two cubes.

The structural rigidity of mathematics gives further insight into its modal features. Mathematical truth is modal in two different ways: it is inescapable, and it could not be other than it is. It is the inescapability of mathematical truth that has engaged the attention of most philosophers, and it has been one of the chief arguments of this book that it should not be construed solely as the deductive necessity we must conform to on pain of inconsistency, but should be construed with respect to a range of sanctions that might move rational truth-seekers to concede the cogency of an argument. But the non-contingency is equally important. It is what gives pattern-recognition epistemological clout. Literary critics perceive patterns, but with them it is a matter of simple recognition, and if another literary critic does not recognise it, there is no more to be said. With mathematics there is. The patterns are interlocked in such a way that a mathematician who does not recognise one pattern is committed to denying other patterns that he cannot fail to recognise. It is this feature that gives mathematics its feeling of solid reality. It is not simply that from where I sit I see a pattern staring at me in the way that sometimes I suddenly see a face jumping out of a chaotic configuration on a page; but in addition I realise that if I were to view it from your position, I should still be able to make out the face, given suitable guidance, on account of the other shapes you already acknowledge. You already acknowledge this-and-this curve, and so must concede that it could be part of an eye, and that-and-that one part of an ear similarly. Failure to see the whole is not just failure to see the whole, but failure also to follow through lines of argument already acknowledged to be cogent. And because it does not just depend on my being able by myself to form the necessary *Gestalt*, but is something that another mathematician must see, even from his point of view, there is a binocular solidity about mathematical truth which convinces us of its objective reality.

Mathematical truth, then, is modal not just because it is inescapable, but because it is unalterable. It could not be other than it is. It could not be the case that 257 was not a prime number. The primeness of 257 is tied in with its other features, and those of its predecessors and successors. The patterns descried by the mathematician interlock. No one part can be altered without altering other, and indeed all the other, parts, and hence each has to be exactly what it is, because of being part of a connected and totally interrelated whole. In other disciplines there is some element of happenstance: things could have been different; but they are not, and we just have to learn how they are, and accept that as a given fact. In mathematics, by contrast, there are no given contingent facts. For mathematical propositions it cannot be the case that $p \wedge \Diamond \neg p$, or, to put it another way,

in mathematical discourse $p, \Diamond \neg p \vdash$.

This in turn yields

$$p \vdash \Box \, p,$$

or, alternatively, if we substitute $\neg p$ for p, and use the Law of Double Negation,

$$\Diamond p \vdash p,$$

the principle *Ab posse valet consequentia esse*[40] which, as we have seen, is peculiar to mathematics, and expresses its "modal flatness".[41]

The non-contingency of mathematics arises from the nature of mathematical objects—ἐνδέχεσθαι γὰρ ἢ εἶναι οὐδὲν διαφέρει ἐν τοῖς αἰδίοις (*endechesthai gar e einai ouden diapherei en tois aidiois*)[42]—and explains the peculiarities of mathematical knowledge, and the attractions of the deductivist approach. Mathematical objects are patterns, mostly patterns of patterns, though sometimes patterns of quotities or of transitive relations. Since they are constituted by their connexions, the Identity of Indiscernibles applies to them, foreclosing any possibility of change,[43] or any possibility of witnesses being needed to report how things happened actually to be. Instead, if a mathematician refuses to concede the truth of a mathematical proposition, we point out how it is interrelated with other mathematical propositions which, we hope, he will acknowledge to be true. Essentially, we are searching round for patterns he will recognise, and on the basis of them pointing out the new

---

[40] As this is the converse of axiom T, we might call it T^{-1}.

[41] See above §1.6, §12.9, §14.2.

[42] Aristotle, *Physics* III, 4, 203^{b}30, With timeless entities to be possible is no different from to be.

[43] See above, §12.9.

pattern we want him to recognise also. But pattern-recognition is itself difficult to talk about, and we naturally articulate it in terms of assumptions or hypotheses we are taking for granted, and therefore asking him to grant. The right use of language, which lies at the basis of deductive argument, is very largely a matter of recognising patterns and using the right word to describe them. So, if mathematical truth is about the interrelation of patterns, mathematical argument will be in terms of the right use of language to describe patterns, and the implications of that language, and hence of deductive inference. It will be natural to follow Plato, and construe mathematical argument as being entirely deductive, and adopt a purely axiomatic approach to mathematics. For the most part the axiomatic approach will serve us well. It is only when we are considering the foundations of mathematics generally that the status of the axioms comes into question, and we want to be able to ground them rather than merely postulate them, and it is only on the margins, when we are considering some extension of an axiomatic system to encompass a wider or deeper range of truth that we are sensitive to pressures that cannot be expressed in terms of bare consistency alone. Our modality then is widened, and, while conceding the consistency of, say, non-Desarguian 2-dimensional projective geometry, deny it serious ontological status. Mathematical modality, and hence also mathematical existence, is constrained not only by the need to communicate, but by the shared ideals of seeking truth, beauty and generality.

15.7 Coherence and Depth

Mathematicians often feel that they are up against some solid reality not just because it is independent of their wills, but because it manifests surprising interconnexions, which were never intended by those who devised the formalism. In our first fumbling formulations of mathematical truth, we seem to be touching the tip of an iceberg, which later reveals surprising cross-links like Euler's equation

$$e^{i\pi} = -1,$$

or the expression of the Golden Mean by the continued fraction:

$$\frac{1}{2}\cos 36° = \cfrac{1}{1 + \cfrac{1}{1 + \cfrac{1}{1 + \cfrac{1}{\cdots}}}}.$$

The Realist senses that there is an underlying structure which integrates diverse relations together, and reveals them as parts of one coherent whole.[44] Hardy is able to make out the distant peak because it is the culmination of a ridge, possibly below the horizon or obscured by clouds, that connects it with other peaks more clearly seen. Gödel repeatedly argues for the real existence of mathematical entities because they integrate different aspects of mathematics in something of the same way as material objects can be argued for on the score of their integrating the many different manifestations of those material objects in sense experience.

> It seems to me that the assumption of such objects is quite as legitimate as the assumption of physical bodies and there is quite as much reason to believe in their physical existence. They are in the same sense necessary to obtain a satisfactory system of mathematics as physical bodies are necessary for a satisfactory theory of our sense perceptions, and in both cases it is impossible to interpret the propositions one wants to assert about these entities as propositions about the "data" ...[45]

This is a telling argument. Often we argue from appearances to an underlying reality because we thereby give a more unified account, and bring diverse phenomena under one schema of explanation. We argue not only from sense experience to the existence of material objects,[46] but from overt behaviour to minds and from observed results of experiments to the laws of nature they exemplify.

Some of these inferences could be described as "inferences to the best explanation", but really we are dealing with a wider category, in which we seek to integrate and unify as well as to explain. Such

---

[44] These two examples are due to Mark Steiner, "Mathematical Explanation", *Philosophical Studies*, **34**, 1978, pp.135-151, and "Mathematical Realism", *Noûs*, **17**, 1983, pp.363-385, and to Michael D. Resnik and David Kushner, "Explanation, Independence and Realism in Mathematics", *British Journal for the Philosophy of Science*, **38**, 1978, pp.141-158.

[45] Kurt Gödel, "Russell's Mathematical Logic", and "What is Cantor's Continuum Problem?", P.Benacerraf and H.Putnam, *Philosophy of Mathematics: Selected Readings*, 2nd ed., Cambridge, 1983, pp.456-457; reprinted in S.Feferman *et al.*, *Kurt Gödel: Collected Works*, II, New York, 1990, pp.128-129, see also p.484/pp.268-269.

[46] See above, §16.1, n.14.

inferences are not deductive. We cannot convict the phenomenalist, the behaviourist, or the instrumentalist, of inconsistency, however unreasonable their positions may seem, but the mathematical Realist is entitled to claim a right to draw similar inferences, and not be deterred by the fact that they are not deductive ones that must be conceded on pain of inconsistency.

Depth is also important. It is a term of high praise when spoken by mathematicians of a proof. Deep theorems are ones that bring together results from diverse fields, enabling them all to be seen as part of the same underlying pattern. The metaphor makes perfect sense on a realist construal of mathematics, but carries no meaning for the Formalist, the Finitist, the Constructivist, or Intuitionist. Unless an alternative account is offered of there being a deep, architectonic structure nobody had ever anticipated, a rational philosopher should acknowledge the existence of some sort of mathematical reality.

15.8 Laws of the Laws of Nature

The arguments adduced to counter scepticism about the substantial reality of mathematical entities often take the form of showing that other realities are equally open to attack. In consequence, mathematical reality is often assimilated to physical reality, and the truths of mathematics to the truths of physics, all the more so in recent years, when the sharp distinction between analytic and synthetic has been queried. Quine holds that in the face of unfavourable empirical evidence, there is always a choice as to which proposition should be given up, so that no proposition is indubitably analytic. But that conclusion goes further than his argument warrants. It is true that the distinction is not always as sharp as was made out. We refine definitions, particularly in science, to take account of new knowledge: whales have become mammals; it is no longer analytically true that the atomic weight of oxygen is 16, or of hydrogen 1.008. But it does not follow that every proposition is up for grabs in the face of empirical evidence. Two raindrops can merge, one bit of chocolate can be broken into two, two rabbits left together become twenty: but we do not say that $1 + 1 = 1$ or $1 = 1 + 1$ or $1 + 1 = 20$. Rather, we say that drops of rain are not articulate, pieces of chocolate are not individuals, but can be divided, and rabbits are very fecund. Instead of modifying our arithmetic, we deny its applicability. Although mathematics can be applied to the external world, we are not merely talking about the ordinary external world. As Frege said:

> The laws of number . . are not really applicable to external things: they are not laws of nature. What they do apply to are judgements about things in the external world: they are the laws of the laws of nature. They assert not connexions between phenomena, but connexions between judgements: and among judgements are included the laws of nature.[47]

But if mathematical truths are no longer regarded as analytic, whose truth is secured solely by the meaning of the terms involved, we may be tempted to follow Kant and account for their truth as projections of our schematic requirements onto the world around us. We organize our temporal experience into a single linear sequence, our spatial experience into a three-dimensional Euclidean framework, and construe successive events as causally determined, in order to make sense of what is going on. And so too, on a new Kantian account, we stipulate not just geometry but mathematics generally, in order to have an adequate framework for dealing with phenomena.

There is much to be said for this approach. The account given of geometry in Chapter Two emphasizes pragmatic considerations and the requirements of intellectual utility and flexibility; and the dialectical approach suggests that some inferences are guided by the shared purposes of our dialogue, rather than being read out of the phenomena. From this, it is sometimes argued that mathematical truths are merely stipulations we lay down for reasons of social psychology, painted on the world in the same way as, according to Mackie, our moral values are the projections of our prejudices; and then Intuitionism would be the appropriate philosophy of mathematics. But the argument does not hold. It may well be that we characterize events in terms of cause and effect, in order to make sense of experience, but it does not follow that causality is merely in the mind's eye, or that there is no necessity in nature. The most general features of our understanding of nature—the non-cyclic one-dimensionality of time, the three-dimensionality of space, the continuity of space and time, the Lorentzian structure of spacetime—can be argued for *a priori*, without their being made

---

[47] G.Frege, *The Foundations of Arithmetic*, tr. J.L.Austin, Oxford, 1950, §87, p.99e.

thereby to be mere predilections we happen to have and insist on fitting experience into. Laws of the laws of nature, like the laws of nature themselves, are discovered and formulated by human minds; but are not just human artefacts, since they are subject to various constraints, which are rational constraints, not psychological predilections. The formulations are fallible, and are open to correction in the light of further reasoning. Reason is a mark of reality. To the extent that the laws of the laws of nature are reasonable, they are real. And they can be reasonable without having to be analytic.

If some mathematical truths are not analytic, we may ask whether they could have been otherwise, and, without contradicting ourselves, try to imagine a world in which they do not hold or have no application. If we were fish, and lived in an aqueous world in which there were not sharp boundaries, Should we be able to distinguish one individual from another? should we have any groups of individuals to apply quotifiers to? Or, again, if our experience wers purely olfactory, would mathematical concepts be inapplicable? Perhaps. Or, again, perhaps not. Any conscious ratiocinating being must have some concept of himself distinct from everything else, and any communicating being must have some concept of an individual he is communicating with that is different from himself. Persons are monads, necessarily different from one another, since each has a mind of his own, and is capable of making it up for himself differently from everybody else.[48] The necessary uniqueness of the individual person provides a basis for the application of quotifiers, and for developing the concept of quotities. Furthermore, if two communicating individuals are to be able to be talking about the same thing, although sometimes talking about different things, their universe of discourse must be integrated into one, though containing different things. There must be some principles of togetherness, as well as some differentiation. Something like the relational logic of Chapters Nine and Ten, will be needed, in order to accommodate the difference of degrees, involving the more and the less, the difference of kinds, involving definite boundaries, and the ascription of numbers to the objects of perception.

Many mathematical truths are grounded in central parts of our conceptual structure, which could not, realistically, be dispensed

---

[48] See J.R.Lucas, "A Mind of One's Own", *Philosophy*, **68**, 1993, pp.457-471.

with. They are conceptual truths, neither empty analytic tautologies, nor empirical truths liable to empirical refutation.

15.9 Chastened Isms

The view of mathematics that has emerged can best be described as "Chastened Logicism". It is both wider and shallower than traditional Logicism. It is wider in having a much wider concept of logic. Although we can see some austerely attractive features in first-order logic, we need to quotify over predicate, as well as individual, variables, and to be concerned with relations and modal operators. Mathematics is not just the science of numbers, based ultimately on the quotifiers, but studies also function, structure, isomorphism, equivalences and order, all based on relations, and different types of necessity, occurring in proof theory and argued about by Intuitionists.

Mathematics is not

(1) Empirical
(2) Just a Game
(3) A Mental Construction
(4) A Quasi-seeing of a Super Geography

     but is a rational activity.

Chastened Logicism is also shallower. It does not claim that the concepts of mathematics can be defined explicitly in terms of logical concepts alone, nor that the theorems of mathematics can be deduced from logical axioms alone,[49] but only that the concepts and theorems of mathematics can be *grounded* in logic. Grounding is a much weaker notion. Some of the primitive notions of mathematics can be explicated in purely logical terms, and under simple conditions truths about them can be established as theorems of logic. In first-order logic we can express the proposition that there are two and only two universities which have two and only two proctors, and what it is to be an equivalence or an ordering relation, and we can prove simple truths, for example that one and one makes two, or that no ordering relation can be an equivalence relation. But we introduce new concepts by extrapolation and generalisation, not just by explicit definition, and we argue for new axioms and rules of

---

[49] As in §14.1.

inference not just by showing that it would be self-contradictory to deny them, but that it would be unreasonable in a variety of other ways. Quotifiers are logical concepts, and once we have defined the numerical quotifiers, it is tempting to generalise, and see the quotities as having the structure of the ordinals, with order-type ω. But neither first-order logic nor second-order logic has the means for defining quotities, or for quotifying over them. And, thanks to Gödel's theorems, we do not now expect there to be any formal logical system that can accommodate all the constructions and proofs we intuitively find significant and valid. We cannot obtain the absolute security the Formalists fought for. Worse, our intuitions are not only not formally fool-proof, but have in fact proved fallacious on a number of occasions. In generalising, particularly in standing back and taking into account, meta-theoretically, our own theoretical activities, we skirt the edge of inconsistency, and cannot be sure that a Cantorian fate does not await us. Mathematical thinking is poised between ambition and failure. Where it differs from other, equally fallible, intellectual enterprises, is in being much more self-critical, much more insistent in putting every argument through a destruction test, rejecting all those that could be gainsaid with any show of reason.

It may be objected that Chastened Logicism is too indeterminate to be of much interest. It makes much less definite claims than Strong Logicism. Instead of explicitly defining 7 by giving a definition that can always replace it, we merely introduce it, first in familiar concepts, then abstractly. We start by learning the meaning of the word 'seven' in contexts such as 'There are seven stars in the sky' and learn to rephrase this as '7 is the number of stars in the sky', and similarly '7 is the number of days in the week', and '7 is the number of those who went against Thebes'. Abstracting from these contexts, we identify the number 7 as what is common to all these instances, and establish certain fundamental truths about it—that it follows 6, and is followed by 8—as theorems of logic by proving the relevant theses about numerical quotifiers. We recognise the pattern, abstract its salient features, characterize those, and go on to a formal structure, of which the numerical quotifiers are a model. What was wrong with Frege's approach was not his grounding mathematics in logic, but his seeking extreme formal rigour. The way he formalised his logic proved inconsistent, but that was a fault of his formalisation, not of his logic. Second-order logic *is* consistent. Where it falls down—on Frege's *desideratum*—

is that it is not fully formalisable, *i.e.* recursively axiomatizable. This may be regretted. If we cannot formalise fully, we cannot be absolutely fool-proof. At the end of his life, in a letter to Ludwig Darmstaedter, Frege asked "How do we get from these concepts <the numerical quotifiers> to the numbers of arithmetic in a way that cannot be faulted?",[50] and the answer is that we can get from the numerical quotifiers to the numbers of arithmetic, because we are doing it, and children are learning how to do it, but not in a way that cannot be faulted, because that degree of infallibility is not available to mere mortals.

Logicism cannot give explicit definitions; it cannot reduce all mathematical theorems to theorems of logic; there is an element of hand-waving, which may conceal serious sloppiness. But it is of value none the less. It answers the question "What are we talking about?", and gives guidelines for assessing claims to mathematical truth. It locates mathematics in the area of logic. Mathematical concepts are like logical concepts. Numbers come out of the same drawer as quotifiers and logical constants, not sense-data or material objects or inferiority complexes. Like logic, mathematics is—in a sense—topic-neutral, and can have all sorts of different applications; hence, in part, the difficulty of saying what it is about.[51]

An analogy with moral philosophy is illuminating. The elucidation of value judgements in terms of imperatives is like Strong Logicism. It cannot be carried through: there are too many value judgements which resist translation into simple imperatives. But the imperative theory is right in locating value judgements in the realm of guides to action. Value judgements which never, either themselves or others they were linked with, could give us guidance on what to do in some situation, would not be value judgements at all. Value judgements get their purchase because some value judgements, in some situations, under some conditions, are tantamount to imperatives in as much as they tell us what to do. Similarly mathematics, although not reducible to logic, gains its

---

[50] H.Hermes, F.Kambartel and F.Kaulbach, eds., *Frege's Posthumous Writings*, Chicago, 1979, p.253; quoted by H.T.Hodes, *Journal of Philosophy*, **89**, 1984, pp.133-134.

[51] Like the House of Peers in Gilbert and Sullivan's *Iolanthe*, it does
"nothing in particular,
and does it jolly well".

purchase, and connects with the rest of discourse, because some mathematical statements, in some situations, under some conditions, are tantamount to statements expressible in terms of logic alone. The meaning of mathematics is anchored in the meaning of 'none'—perhaps it was an intimation of this that made Plato attach such significance to τὸ μὴ ὄν (*to me on*)—and 'same as' and 'more than'. Mathematical concepts are developed by generalisation and extrapolation, but in disciplined ways: the Bed Theory of Truth requires a double constraint, that the extended theory can be modelled within the original theory, and the original theory within the extended theory, in the latter case with the original structure fully reproduced. Mathematical arguments often are deductive derivations, expressible in formal logic, and where they are not, mathematicians on occasion put them into deductive form, citing any additional principles needed as explicit premises. These additional principles, though not stemming from the requirement of bare communicability, are justified by reference to other dialectical constraints of reasonableness, or as extrapolations of principles already accepted. But these justifications are not copper-bottomed: there is something creative about mathematical reasoning that goes beyond any formal account in terms of antecedently specified rules of inference, or the need to avoid inconsistency, important though these are.[52]

Merits of Logicism

Logicism Explains

1. mathematical knowledge not based on observation;
2. emphasis on proof and need for incontrovertibility;
3. generality and many applications of mathematics;
4. difficulty in specifying the objects of mathematics.

Realism is still the best word to describe what most mathematicians believe in, as best securing the objectivity of mathematics; but it, too, is chastened, needing to shed many of the misleadingly

---

[52] For a fuller discussion of Logicism, see Mark Steiner, *Mathematical Knowledge*, Cornell University Press, Ithaca, NY, 1975, ch.1; Ian Hacking, "Where Does Mathematics Come From?", in his review of Philip Kitcher's *The Nature of Mathematical Knowledge* in *New York Review of Books*, February, 1984, pp.36–38.

material connotations of reality. Mathematical Realism expresses
the claims that:

1. We can talk about mathematical entities: there is no need to
   explain them away or give a reductive analysis of them.
2. We can refer to mathematical entities without completely characterizing them, and therefore can quotify over them impredicatively in process of defining them.
3. Mathematical entities have properties independently of our
   knowing what they are, and so are subject to the Law of the
   Excluded Middle and the Principle of Bivalence.
4. We discover mathematics rather than invent it.
5. Mathematics is significant and relevant. Mathematics describes
   the necessary relations between patterns. The application problem for mathematics is no different from the application problem for scientific or everyday concepts.
6. Mathematics is profound, showing deep coherences between areas apparently quite diverse.
7. There is open access to mathematical truth. Anybody, even
   an uneducated slave-boy, can follow a mathematical argument,
   and acknowledge its force. You do not have to be well situated,
   either socially or geographically, to do mathematics.

These merits, however, are purchased at some ontological cost: the
underlying reason why most philosophers are unhappy with mathematical Realism is that it seems to over-populate the universe
with objects. We now see, however, that the Realism we ought
to espouse is more concerned with objectivity than objects—at
least objects of the objectionable sort. It is a Realism whose non-
subjectivity is based on rationality rather than opaque thinginess.
The reason why mathematical truth is hard and ineluctable is not
that it is a quasi-material object, which stands in the way of my
getting past it, and blocks my efforts whatever I do, but that as
I come more and more to understand what is at stake, I see that
I should be acting unreasonably to deny its truth. Mathematical
reality is not Out There but In Here.

Because mathematical truth depends on reason, it is intersub-
jective. I can choose what things I like or am going to do, but it is
not up to me to choose what is true. My truth claims are always
corrigible. More than that, our truth claims are always corrigible:
it always makes sense to say that we have all got it wrong, and that
the moons of Jupiter really do exist, or that there is an even num-

ber not the sum of two primes. But, though it makes sense, it is often a provable error to maintain it, and it would be unreasonable to continue in error once it is pointed out. Although our concept of proof is not as rigid or unambiguous as is commonly supposed, and it may take some time to develop a satisfactory proof of a well-known theorem, mathematical disputes tend to be resolved, and a high degree of consensus tends to emerge in time. In this, mathematics is in much better case than most of the humane disciplines. Mathematical opinion is strongly convergent. And since what it converges to is not constituted by its convergence, it is reasonable to suppose that it is something objectively true, and our coming to believe that it is true is because we are reasonable men.

The rationality of mathematics explains its objectivity, its ineluctability, and its coherence and depth. The aspect of Realism that is most difficult to accept is its seeming to suggest that mathematical objects are disposed in contingent relations to one another, which could well have been different, and are not of any importance in themselves. What we are in fact concerned with are not a disparate set of entities each on its own, but *patterns*, whose structure is an essential part of their being what they are, and whose interrelations with one another could not have been different. It is, so to speak, a *model*, a canonical model, for second-order logic. The existential claim is strong enough to license our talking about the model, and quotifying over properties and relations. We cannot axiomatize completely any theory that will bring out as theorems all and only those well-formed formulae that are true in that model, but we can be led by various considerations to conclude that certain well-formed formulae which are not theorems of the axiomatization we have thus far formulated are nonetheless true.

We end up, therefore, with a chastened Realism—a rational Realism sustaining a chastened Logicism—based on second- rather than first-order logic, and hence not completely axiomatizable, not analytic, and grounded in ordinary concepts and the patterns of inference they exemplify.[53]

---

[53] See further Mark Steiner, "Mathematical Explanation", *Philosophical Studies*, **34**, 1978, pp.135-151; Mark Steiner, "Mathematical Realism", *Noûs*, **17**, 1983, pp.363-385; and Michael D. Resnik and David Kushner, "Explanation, Independence and Realism in Mathematics", *British Journal for the Philosophy of Science*, **38**, 1978. pp.141-158.

Envoi

Much has not been achieved. The nature of being and the foundations of knowledge have not been properly discussed, nor have any assured conclusions been commended. What has been offered is very much an exercise in "philosophy of" rather than in "pure foundational philosophy". I have started from mathematics as a going concern, something we are familiar with, and which we generally accept as a valid form of knowledge, and have tried to work back from mainstream mathematics to its sources, which I have located in the foothills of logic. But I have not attempted to give a fully worked out account of logic itself, as Frege was led to do. Nor have I done justice to the question of the ontological status of mathematical entities. It may be that I should be more full-bloodedly a Platonist. Some of my best mathematical friends are Platonists, and I am far from saying that they are wrong, or that from a metaphysical point of view the fact of mathematical knowledge does not tell against various reductionist philosophies, such as materialism, and forces us to acknowledge the existence of substantial entities other than material objects or the microphysical atoms and baryons of natural science.

These are genuine questions which I pass over here not because they are unimportant but because they lie outside the scope of this work. Such knowledge is high and we cannot easily or quickly attain unto it. I have aimed lower, in order to be able to make some progress in a shorter compass of time, if only as a preliminary step towards tackling more difficult questions in due course. If we work backwards from mathematics as it is currently understood, we shall have some idea of what an all-embracing theory of being or of knowledge will have to accommodate when we come to try to articulate one. It may be then that we shall find that some of the starting points that we have worked back to in this book are quite unsatisfactory from a wider point of view, and that we could never reach them from a pure foundational standpoint, and so could not go by means of them to arrive at any true mathematical knowledge. In that case we should have to ground our mathematical knowledge differently, or else abandon it altogether and assign it to the scrap heap of the history of ideas along with astrology and phrenology. But such a conclusion would *pro tanto* count against the metaphysical system which required it. It is not a serious possibility that we should be required by reason to junk any substantial part of mathematics. The only serious possibility is that a more all-embracing view of what exists or the justification of knowledge will lead us to assess differently the positions we have worked back to in this book, and to try to ground mathematics in some other, securer ground. To that extent the conclusions of this work are, and always must remain, provisional and tentative. Foundations always can be shaken by some deep philosophical earth-change, and need subsequent underpinning or replacement. But if we change the simile from architecture to arboriculture, and consider not the foundations but the roots of mathematical knowledge, it is reasonable to claim that these are the roots, and that, in the climate of opinion in past centuries and within the general field of mathematical enquiry, mathematics has grown, and is likely to go on growing, from these roots.

Summaries

I hope that this book will be read by students, many of whom will have to write papers of their own. I therefore give the heads of argument they need to consider. It is not just kindness on my part. Philosophy is not simply a set of doctrines that can be learned, but an activity, a thinking through problems, trying to clarify the issues, groping towards solutions, feeling the force of objections, and finally coming up with the least bad answer available. Although answers are important, and the ones in this book the best that I can think of, they make sense only in the context of the questions being asked. Each reader needs to ask them afresh, and in articulating his own answers, will formulate them differently from what is offered here. But if these notes help towards informed disagreement, I shall be well content.

Numbers
(Chapters Four, Five, Six and Eleven)

Need to distinguish different sorts of numbers:

whole numbers, fractions, negative numbers, real numbers, complex numbers, transfinite numbers, vectors.

Usually quaternions and tensors are not reckoned to be numbers, nor $\{\top, \bot\}$. But it is not clear why.

Three Approaches: Cardinal, Ordinal, Abstract.

1. Cardinal: Answers to question 'How many?'; None, One, Two, Three, ...
2. Ordinal: Place in a list; First, Second, Third, ...
3. Abstract: Symbols defined by formal rules;
   $0, 1, 2, 3, \ldots, 10, 11, \ldots,$
   $20, \ldots 1024, \ldots, 1,000,000,000,000,000 \ldots$
   $10^{10^{10}} \ldots \ldots$

I Cardinal Approach

The Cardinal Approach sees

a) the Natural Numbers as answers to question 'How many?', so must be of a logical shape to fit into quotifiers

b) the Natural Numbers as able to stand on their own and be talked about, so are self-subsistent objects which do not have to be defined only contextually

Chief exponents: Frege, Russell

Merits

1. Locates mathematics on conceptual map

2. Explicates numerical quotifiers in first-order logic

3. Can explicate numbers in terms of set theory

Demerits

3a) Set theory inconsistent or complicated

3b) Which Sets? (§4.7)

3c) Requires counting at meta-level

4. Fails ordinally (§4.7, p.113)

II Ordinal Approach

Chief exponents: Dedekind, Cantor, [Peano], Kronecker

Merits

1. Gives systematic account

2. Explicates 'and so on'

3. Offers definitions of (Dedekind)-infinite and -finite

4. Adequate for all reasonable arithmetic

Demerits

1. Fails to distinguish Counting Numbers from other progressions of order-type ω: 101,102,103,...

2. Fails Cardinally

3. Dedekind uses set (*system*) theory: Peano needs second-order logic, or else fails to characterize the natural numbers monomorphically (§6.3)

III Abstract Approach

Chief Exponents: Peano, all modern treatments

Merits

1. Axiomatic

2. Clear and intuitive

3. Focuses attention on Fifth Postulate (Principle of Recursive Reasoning)

Demerits

1. Does not give explicit definition of 'natural number', 'nought', or 'successor'

2. Fails to characterize the natural numbers monomorphically (§6.3) in first-order logic

Schools

Note: Separating the philosophy of mathematics into separate schools is artificial. The different schools of thought distinguished below interpenetrate one another, and most thinkers adopt elements from several different tendencies of thought. I do. And at the end I offer my own verdict, to enable the reader to know where I stand, and where he disagrees with me.

I Empiricism
(§1.1-§1.3, §2.4, §14.1)

Chief exponents: Protagoras, Mill, Gillies, Kitcher

Chief critics: Plato, Frege

Brief reading: J.S.Mill, *A System of Logic*, London, 1843, Book II, chs. 5 & 6, Book III, ch.24

Criticized: G.Frege, *The Foundations of Arithmetic*, 1884, tr. J.L.Austin, Oxford, 1950, §7

Further reading: D.A. Gillies, *Frege, Dedekind, and Peano on the Foundations of Arithmetic*, Assen, 1982, chs. 3 & 4. C.G.Hempel. "Geometry and Physical Science", *American Mathematical Monthly*, **52**, 1945; reprinted in H.Feigl and Wilfrid Sellars, *Readings in Philosophical Analysis*, New York, 1949, pp.238-249. Philip Kitcher, *The Nature of Mathematical Knowledge*, New York, 1983.

II Platonism
(Chapters One and Fifteen)

Chief exponents: Plato, Gödel, Hardy, most working mathematicians.

Chief critics: Plato, Intuitionists, Formalists, North American Naturalists, most modern philosophers

Need to distinguish Ontological Platonism (Do mathematical objects really exist?) from Epistemological Platonism (Do we see the truth of mathematics with the "eye of the mind"?)

Brief reading: Roger Penrose, *The Emperor's New Mind*, Oxford, 1989, pp.112-116; or, with more consideration of mathematical implications, P.Bernays, "Sur la Platonisme dans les mathématiques", *L'Enseignment Mathématique*, **34**, 1935, pp.52-69; tr. in Paul Benacerraf and Hilary Putnam, eds. *The Philosophy of Mathematics*, 2nd ed., Cambridge, 1983, pp.258-271.

Criticized by S.F.Barker, "Realism as a Philosophy of Mathematics", in J.J.Buloff, ed., *Foundations of Mathematics*, Berlin, 1969, pp.1-9.

Demerits: Ontologically extravagant, Epistemologically *simpliste*, Unsatisfactory account of necessity.

III Formalism
(Chapter Three, §14.7)

Chief exponents: Hilbert, von Neumann, most modern mathematicians in their actual practice.

Chief critics: Plato, Frege, Poincaré

Brief reading: J. von Neumann, "The Formalist Foundations of Mathematics, tr. from *Erkenntnis*, 1931, in Paul Benacerraf and Hilary Putnam, eds. *The Philosophy of Mathematics*, 2nd ed., Cambridge, 1983, pp.61-65; reprinted in A.H.Taub, *John von Neumann Collected Works*, New York, 1961, vol.2.

Need to distinguish different varieties of Formalism:

1. ontological formalism
2. method of formalisation
3. epistemological formalism
4. study of formal systems

Arguments in Favour:

1. Anti-metaphysical: nominalism, reductionism, instrumentalism, nothing-buttery

2. Accounts for Cogency

3. Quest for Certainty

4. Logical Geography of Scotland (§3.5)

5. Different axiomatizations of geometry and set theory

6. Enables us to abstract and see general patterns:

   a) Projective Geometry: Duality

   b) Theory of Groups

   c) Topology and **S4**

7. Analogy with Logical Positivist view of Science [Hilbert]

Arguments Against:

1. Vacuous

2. Fails to account for truth of mathematics

3. Fails to account for depth/significance of mathematical theorems

4. Circular—assumes at the meta-level what it proves at the object level; [Poincaré]

5. Non-monomorphism of First-order Peano Arithmetic

6. Gödel's Theorem

7. Application Problem

IV Logicism
(§3.7, Chapters Four, Five, Six and Thirteen, §15.8, §15.9)

Chief exponents: Plato, Frege, Russell, Whitehead, Carnap, Bostock

Chief critics: Quine, Benacerraf and most modern philosophers of mathematics

Brief reading: Rudolf Carnap, "Logicist Foundations of Mathematics", tr. from *Erkenntnis*, 1931, in Paul Benacerraf and Hilary Putnam, eds. *The Philosophy of Mathematics*, 2nd ed., Cambridge, 1983, pp.41-52.

Need to distinguish Strong Logicism from weaker varieties

Merits

Logicism Explains:

1. mathematical knowledge not based on observation
2. emphasis on proof and need for incontrovertibility
3. generality and many applications of mathematics
4. difficulty in specifying the objects of mathematics

Difficulties of Logicism:

No clear idea of what logic is. Does it include set theory? Is it just first-order logic? Are logical inferences just those in accordance with a formal rule of Inference?

V Intuitionism
(§7.4-§7.7)

Chief exponents: Brower, Beth, Heyting, Dummett, Bishop. Ignored or silently dismissed by most working mathemticians.

Reading: M.A.E. Dummett, "The Philosophical Basis of Inuitionistic Logic", in H.E. Rose and J.C. Shepherdson, eds., *Proceedings of the Logic Colloquium, Bristol*, 1973, North-Holland, pp.5-40; reprinted in Paul Benacerraf and Hilary Putnam, eds., *The Philosophy of Mathematics*, 2nd ed., Cambridge, 1983, pp.97-129. or M.A.E. Dummett, *Elements of Intuitionism*, Oxford, 1977, ch.1, pp.9-31.

Merits:

1. Cheap ontologically; no need to postulate abstract entities. Mathematics exists in the mind of mathematicians
2. Welcome emphasis on the communal aspect of mathematical thought

Demerits:

1. Fails to distinguish proof from what is proved

   1.1 Can understand theorem without understanding proof

   1.2 Different proofs of same theorem

2. Implausible rejection of arguments by Dilemma and by *Reductio ad Absurdum*

3. Elimination Rules as important as Introduction Rules

4. Vague boundary of what is effectively computable: Is effective Procedure any more intelligible to a non-Intuitionist than a platonist concept of truth conditions is to an Intuitionist? [Alexander George, "The Conveyability of Intuitionism", *Journal of Philosophical Logic*, **17**, 1988, pp.133-156.]

Verdict

The Epistemological Platonists were right to see the *a priori* nature of mathematical knowledge, but failed to account for its compellingness; they also were right to stress the importance of pattern recognition, but wrong to think we invariably all agreed about what patterns there are. The Intuitionists were right to hold that mathematical proofs are something special and *sui generis*, but, like the Platonists, wrong to think we all agreed about them without further explication of their universal and coercive character which we have to acknowledge even in the face of initial disagreement. The Formalists were right to see the importance of casting proofs into incontrovertible form, and therefore expressed as step-by-step derivations, but wrong to think it was simply a matter of following out formal derivations from axioms merely postulated. The Logicists were right to ground the concepts of mathematics in logic, and to seek to justify axioms by appeal to logical considerations, but the traditional Logicists were wrong in seeking explicit definitions, in justifying axioms only by deducing them as analytic theorems in first-order logic, and in confining logic to monologous argument alone.

Index

Note: references are to sections, except where chapters or pages are indicated. The more important references are printed bold, and are listed first when no previous entry might help to elucidate the term.